# THE TRIBULATION CHURCH

# THE TRIBULATION CHURCH

Louis Moesta

**WordFire Press**
Colorado Springs, Colorado

THE TRIBULATION CHURCH © 2012 Louis Moesta

Originally published by WordFire Press as
THE CRUCIBLE AND THE CROWN
© 1999 Louis Moesta
Revised 2012

WordFire Press

All rights reserved. No part of this book may be reproduced or transmitted in any form or by any means, including photocopying, recording or by any information storage and retrieval system, without the express written permission of the copyright holder, except where permitted by law.

Scripture quotations, unless otherwise noted, are from the Revised Standard Version of the Bible, copyright © 1946, 1952, 1971 by the Division of Christian Education of the National Council of the Churches of Christ in the USA. Used by permission.

Published by
WordFire Press, an imprint of
WordFire Inc
PO Box 1840
Monument CO 80132

ISBN: 978-1-61475-046-8

WordFire Press Trade Paperback Edition: June 2012
Printed in the USA

**www.wordfire.com**

# Contents

Acknowledgments ................................................................... i
Introduction ....................................................................... iii
Dedication ......................................................................... vii
1. The Last Trump and the First Resurrection ........................... 1
2. The Church ................................................................... 20
3. The Church and the Tribulation ......................................... 42
4. Tribulation .................................................................... 70
5. The Millennium and Its Population .................................... 100
6. Imminence .................................................................. 141
7. The Wrath of God ......................................................... 184
8. Dispensationalism and the Times of the Gentiles ................. 204
9. Prophecy (Fulfilled and Unfulfilled) .................................. 228
10. The Old Testament Feasts ............................................. 247
11. The Unities ................................................................. 287
12. The Great Commission .................................................. 318
13. The Blessed Hope: The Resurrection-Rapture .................... 362
    Afterword .................................................................. 405
    About the Author ......................................................... 407

# Acknowledgments

I owe a debt of gratitude to a number of people for helping to make this book a reality. My earliest indebtedness is to Wm. Sanford LaSor of Fuller Seminary. He had the faith in me to make me a teaching fellow in Greek and Hebrew. But beyond that, if ever I had a mentor, it was he. He engaged me in assisting him in developing his Greek syllabus. Under his guidance, I learned the challenges and rewards of research, and without those tools, this work would not have emerged as it is today. I am grateful to many for encouraging me to write this work.

A special word of thanks is due my family, who patiently put up with my refrain over the years: "I have to work on the book." Special gratitude is due to my dear wife, Louise, who willingly sacrificed her own time to the demands of "the book."

Years ago, my dearest childhood friend, Audrey Hicks, was the first to put writing spurs in my side when she issued a challenge to me to use the abilities God had given me. A prized friend, Bill Ashe, cheered me on in my efforts and encouraged me to complete the task. Don Hagner, from Fuller Seminary, graciously read the manuscript and gave me assurance that I was on target. Missionary friends, Jim and Renata Bultema, who stayed at our house, discussed issues with me and helped me search for a title.

During the first half of 1989, I became very ill and feared that I might not live to complete this project. God was gracious and restored me to health. I rejoice that I was able to finish the course He laid out for me.

Thank you, one and all!

# INTRODUCTION

I have found it quite a challenge to write a book that I have often felt shouldn't have to be written. Almost all the books written on the return of Christ in the last decade or two have focused on the assumption that Christ will rapture the Church first, and then the tribulation will begin. In my youth and in the early days of my conversion, this was the position I took. I had teethed on the Scofield Bible. I had a passion for prophecy—particularly those areas of prophecy that dealt with the last days and the return of Christ. It was comforting to have the prophetic word explained to me and clarified by a series of footnotes and comments in that Bible. And it was easy for Scofield to do, since he was steeped in dispensational dye.

I went on to train at a Bible institute, where the teaching generally conformed to the teaching of Scofield and the dispensational preachers I had heard—both in my own church and in others with which I was associated. But it was dispensationalism itself that brought this unity. Indeed, as a young believer, I was strongly urged not to attend any meetings that were not "fundamental." I, therefore, assumed that there was but one reasonable teaching regarding eschatology—Christ would come before the tribulation to rapture His Church. It was only later, after studying the Scriptures for myself, that the doubts arose, then grew, and finally could no longer be ignored. The Lord took me on a long and sometimes grueling odyssey, which finally brought me to the conviction that the Church will see the hard days of the tribulation before it revels in the glories of transformation.

After I reached this conclusion, I found more and more Scripture that affirmed it. I decided not to read the few works that supported my new position, because I did not want to be influenced by other postribulation writers, but by Scripture alone. I also focused on the major works that were being written in support of my former pretribulation position, in order to interact with them on the basis of Scripture and logic.

Although I have read from Dwight Pentecost's Things to Come and some works by Theodore Epp, John Wesley White, and Charles Ryrie, I have concentrated on two men in particular who seem to represent the pretribulation position strongly on two key levels. John F. Walvoord stands out as a key theological and scholarly spokesman for the position. His book, The Blessed Hope and the Tribulation, is a conscientious and thorough study of this position. The other representative author is Hal Lindsey, who has become the expert detail man and the popularizer of the system. I have carefully studied Lindsey's The Late Great Planet Earth, The 1980's: Countdown to Armageddon, The Terminal Generation, The Promise, There's a New World Coming, and The Rapture.

But I am convinced that the position and teaching of these writers regarding the timing of the rapture is in error. It is not my purpose to launch an attack against them, or others who hold their views, but rather to demonstrate the errors in their teaching. When I state a position of the pretribulationists in the book, I will be stating it clearly as it appears in their writings. Almost without exception, the position has been expressed either in Walvoord's book or in one of the works I have listed by Lindsey.

Walvoord, in the introduction to his book, contrasts works written from a pretribulation point of view with those written from a posttribulation perspective. He feels that the posttribulationists tend to attack the viewpoints of the pretribulationists, whereas the pretribulationists set their reasons down in an orderly arrangement and defend against attacks from the other side.

This may be true, for the most part, but one must analyze the reasons for it. Posttribulation writers probably assumed that the posttribulation teaching was the most accepted position among Bible scholars before the innovation (and that quite recently) of the teaching of pretribulationism. It was also probably assumed by posttribulation writers that pretribulationism was simply another error of interpretation that would be exposed, so that posttribulationism would continue to stand as the traditional position.

Perhaps it is time, as Walvoord suggests, for someone to step forward and present the posttribulation position again, as part and parcel of the entire fabric of Scripture and of the plan or program of God. It is my purpose, as a major part of this work, to show the logical unity of the posttribulation position with the totality of God's purposes in Scripture. Just as Walvoord and others have documented their disagreements with the posttribulation position, so must I examine the errors in their system.

They point out that although pretribulationists sponsor many prophetic conferences, posttribulationists have hardly any. While this may be true, there has been an awakened interest in recent days in such meetings. In September of 1989, Omega Ministries sponsored the End-Times Prophecy Conference in Anaheim, California. This may represent a significant beginning for us in such endeavors. I have more than once pondered the paradox that those who see that certain events will happen before the rapture do not set up seminars to discuss the signs of the times, while those who believe that nothing must happen before the rapture spend so much time talking about the things that will happen after they are gone!

## Dedication

*To the world's true heroes.
To those who through the ages have lived with
blood, sweat, and tears, who have plumbed the depths
of the crucible and counted not their lives dear.*

*To God's precious martyrs,
of whom the world was not worthy,
this book is dedicated.*

# 1

## THE LAST TRUMP AND THE FIRST RESURRECTION

*The Last and the First*
*Lord, spur the day of final trumpet sound*
*When saints both dead and quick in bliss unite,*
*In primal resurrected bodies found,*
*To hail the Morning Star; dismiss the night.*

### THE LAST TRUMP

Trumpets played an important role in the life of the Hebrews.

Trumpets were used for assembly, for battle, or for festive rejoicing. In the New Testament, little is said about trumpets. Some of what is said is for background information, for a point of illustration, or for a simple comparison. For example, the Lord may tell His followers not to be like the Pharisees, who sound the trumpet before them to call attention to themselves and their works. Or Paul might encourage his readers to communicate the things of the Lord clearly so they might not be like a trumpet giving out an uncertain sound. Or John might say that he heard a voice that sounded like a trumpet. We will only deal with those passages that describe a summons by the Lord for believers or that otherwise relate to the end times.

But such passages are few. The book of Revelation describes seven trumpets that are sounded between the opening of the seven seals and the pouring out of the seven bowls (Rev. 8:2, 7–8, 10, 12; 9:1, 13; 11:15). They introduce signs or plagues sent upon the earth by the Lord. Three other passages picture a single trumpet that will sound in the end times and summon believers together to meet the Lord. This trumpet will catch up dead and living saints to meet the Lord (1 Thess. 4:16–17). It will sound at the end of the tribulation to gather His elect together (Matt. 24:29–31). It is called the last trumpet, which will raise up the dead believers and transform the living ones (1 Cor. 15:51–52). Thayer's Greek-English Lexicon of the New Testament refers to "the last trumpet" as "the trumpet after which no other will sound."

The Corinthians passage says that at the last trumpet, the dead believers will be raised and the living believers will be changed. If pretribulationism is to be believed, what of the trumpets of Revelation 8–11 sounding after the last trumpet? One cannot have a last trumpet and then introduce seven more new trumpets. And Jesus tells us that after the tribulation, the angels will be sent "with a loud trumpet call" to "gather his elect" (Matt. 24:29–31). Is this still another trumpet after the last trumpet? If so, for what purpose?

The Matthew passage says that the elect will be gathered "from the four winds, from one end of heaven to the other" (v. 31). The corollary passage in Mark states that the gathering will be "from the four winds, from the ends of the earth to the ends of heaven" (13:24–27). The four winds mentioned in both Matthew 24 and Mark 13 come from the four quarters of heaven, but their province or area of influence is the earth. This was so even in the Old Testament where Jeremiah says, "I will bring upon Elam the four winds from the four quarters of heaven; and I will scatter them to all those winds, and there shall be no nation to which those driven out of Elam shall not come" (49:36). Here the origin and destination end up being equal counterparts. The four winds come from their source and drive Elam to their opposites or counterparts (that is, the north wind drives Elam to the south wind) so that Elam was scattered everywhere on earth. Indeed, in Revelation 7:1 they are called "the four winds of the earth." In addition, the Mark passage adds that this gathering will be "from the ends of the earth." It is obvious, then, that after the tribulation, the trumpet will sound and people will be gathered by it from every part of the earth.

In Revelation 20, when "the souls of those who had been beheaded for their testimony to Jesus ... and had not worshipped the beast ... came to life," it is called "the first resurrection" (4–6). The other, or second, resurrection is shown in verses 11–15 when "the sea gave up the dead in it, Death and Hades gave up the dead in them."

In 1 Corinthians 15, that great resurrection chapter, the order of resurrections is given in verses 21–24: "For as in Adam all die, so also in Christ shall all be made alive. But each in his own order: Christ the first fruits" (the initiating resurrection on which all others depend), "then at his coming those who belong to Christ" (the first resurrection—see Rev. 20:4–6; 1 Cor. 15:51–52; 1 Thess. 4:13–18; and Matt. 24:29–31). "Then comes the end, when he delivers up the kingdom to God the Father after destroying every rule and every authority and power" (the general resurrection or second resurrection of Revelation 20:21–24).

There is no warrant for breaking up the first resurrection of Revelation 20:4–6, the resurrection Paul calls "at his coming those who belong to Christ" (1 Cor. 15:23), into two or more parts—a rapture and a subsequent resurrection or two (martyred tribulation saints, and perhaps, Old Testament saints) when Christ touches the earth. Although Revelation 20:4–6 makes no mention of the pretribulation sleeping believers, it does not mean they are not included at this time. It would be just as logical to assume that we do not have access to the Father and forgiveness of sins at the same time in our redemption since these two aspects of salvation are mentioned in different Scriptures. Indeed, all of the Scriptures referring to the resurrection of believers represent a single or unified resurrection event. Also, in speaking of Christ's return, Paul refers to "the coming of the Lord Jesus with all his saints" (1 Thess. 3:13).

What of the calling of the elect "from one end of heaven to the other"? Certainly it is not the recalling of Israel back to the land. Israel is on earth, not in heaven. Besides, if the rapture had occurred seven years earlier, the Lord would have contradicted Himself by telling us that we would be raptured at the last trump, if another trump sounds here seven years later. What it obviously should not mean is a raptured group from seven years earlier now called to join the slain brethren from the tribulation. There are two major considerations against this idea. First, "the elect" used as a noun everywhere else in the New Testament means believers in Christ. There would need to be some clearly compelling evidence to cause us to depart from its natural meaning here. It puts too great a strain on logic to suppose that they were gathered in the rapture seven years earlier and then are gathered here again at the end of the tribulation. Second, there can only be one last trumpet. To divide this into two phases as the first resurrection has been divided into multiple phases by the pretribulationists is demanding too much of the plain meaning of the word last. As Thayer states, the last trumpet is clearly "the trumpet after which no other will sound." To make a penultimate (or next to last) trumpet sound and then an ultimate (or final) trumpet sound, and then to have those two sounds separated by seven years, and to call both sounds together one last trumpet forces the concept of "last" beyond reasonable limits. We can speak of the last days, but here we speak in the singular of the last trumpet.

There are at least three possible interpretations of this calling. First, it might simply be a parallelism meaning "worldwide," as does "the four winds." In the Mark 13:27 passage, however, it is described as a gathering "from the ends of the earth to the ends of heaven," which is a more fitting contrast. This leaves a second and third possibility.

The second possibility might simply mean the calling of any living believers who are not actually on the earth or even in its atmosphere. Although, at first blush, this might seem either simplistic at best, or inventive at worst, let us bear in mind that His second advent is back to a modern technological world, as His first was to a simple one. How do we, today, explain the concept of a worldwide viewing of that event—"and every eye shall see Him"—if not on the basis of technological triumphs of communication? When I attended Moody Bible Institute in 1946, before any man or manmade object had been flung into space, I marveled at a verse in Deuteronomy when I discovered its possible implications, and I wrote in the flyleaf of my Bible: "concerning possibility of space travel before His return, see Deuteronomy 30:4." This verse reads, "If your outcasts are in the uttermost parts of heaven, from there the Lord your God will gather you, and from there he will fetch you." People have already gone into space. The United States even had its own plans for a permanent space station within a few years, and plans were being discussed for a moon colony as well.

The third possibility is that the spirits of believers who have fallen asleep in Jesus are here in view. In 2 Corinthians 5:1–8, Paul established several things about the body/spirit relationship of the believer. For us to be "away from the body" is to be "at home with the Lord." The highest desire Paul had was to be alive at the Lord's return and "be further clothed, so that what is mortal may be swallowed up by life." He also knew, however, that if death were to come, he would be "at home with the Lord." But he recognized that such a condition represented a sort of holding pattern. Even though we ultimately have the glorified body, "a building from God, a house not made with hands, eternal in the heavens," we do not gain possession of it at death. Indeed, he speaks of death as being "unclothed" or being "found naked." This is a partial explanation for the restive spirits of the saints under God's altar at the breaking of the fifth seal described in Revelation 6. True, they had a desire to be vindicated, but note that the Lord did not reply, "Be content. You are with me." Rather, He gave them a temporary covering for their "unclothed" condition: "a white robe." But their spirits are in heaven. Even their eternal house is in heaven. Paul says that "at the last trumpet ... the dead will be raised imperishable" (1 Cor. 15:52) and that at "the sound of the trumpet of God ... the dead in Christ will rise first" (1 Thess. 4:16). If the spirits of the believers are in heaven and if their new bodies are in heaven (perhaps an entirely different part of heaven), and if they are to be "raised" from earth, the logical sequence would appear to be the calling of their spirits (and their new bodies) to the spot where their old bodies lie, there to be gloriously resurrected in those new spiritual bodies.

Although this would explain the gathering "from the ends

... of heaven," it would only partially explain the gathering "from the ends of the earth" (Mark 13:27). The gathering in respect to "the ends of heaven" involves the spirit and new body of the saints (the eternal "house not made with hands eternal in the heavens") possibly brought to a resurrection spot on earth. But there must be a more complete meaning of the gathering "from the ends of the earth." Certainly the transformation of the living bodies of believers scattered throughout the whole earth who also need to be gathered during the resurrection/rapture would fulfill this sort of a complete gathering "from the ends of the earth." Thus, we have the gathering of those who sleep in Christ (those in heaven) and those who live in Christ (those on earth) to come together in this joint or unified meeting.

## The First Resurrection

The passage that introduces the term "the first resurrection" is found in Revelation 20:4–6: "Then I saw thrones, and seated on them were those to whom judgment was committed. Also I saw the souls of those who had been beheaded for their testimony to Jesus and for the word of God, and who had not worshipped the beast or its image and had not received its mark on their foreheads or their hands. They came to life, and reigned with Christ a thousand years. The rest of the dead did not come to life until the thousand years were ended. This is the first resurrection. Blessed and holy is he who shares in the first resurrection! Over such the second death has no power, but they shall be priests of God and of Christ, and they shall reign with him a thousand years."

There is much information given to us in the passage. We have a resurrection at the end of the tribulation. It is called the first resurrection. It includes the Christian martyrs of the tribulation. It also includes those Christians who lived through the tribulation and did not receive the mark of the beast. In addition, there are others included who do not belong to either of those groups, but who also "share" in that resurrection. We could logically conclude that they were all former believers not listed in the other two groups. All these shall escape the power of the second death, and they shall reign with Christ for a thousand years.

What appears so clear from this text, however, is doubted by the pretribulation school. They raise objections to the meaning rendered above. Their objections fall into two basic categories: (1) the meaning of the word first, and (2) the idea that this resurrection comes after Christ's actual coming to earth and only includes the Christian martyrs of the tribulation. Let us consider the merits of these objections in order.

**What Does "First" Mean?**

Pretribulationists do not give the traditional meaning of "first" to the word "first" that is found in this text. They contend that it is not to be understood as the number one resurrection, since that distinction belongs to the resurrection of Christ. Together with Christ's resurrection, they also see another resurrection coming before this one, which would further distinguish it from the number one resurrection. That earlier resurrection, they point out, is found in Matthew 27:52–53, which records that at the time of Christ's crucifixion tombs "were opened, and many bodies of the saints who had fallen asleep were raised, and coming out of the tombs after his resurrection they went into the holy city and appeared to many." As a result of the fact that Christ and these saints had previously been raised, pretribulationists say that what is called here "the first resurrection" is not the number one resurrection, but is first only in the sense that it comes before the last resurrection described later in Revelation 20.

The argument that "first" does not mean first brings to mind a line from "The Miracle Worker." Kate has been suggesting to Keller that another doctor might be able to help Helen. Keller rises and declares emphatically, "Katie, he can't." His son, James, then responds facetiously, "Father stands up, that makes it a fact" ("The Miracle Worker," Act I, Scene 2).

It is curious that no pretribulationist has difficulty in accepting the plain and literal meaning of "first" when it occurs eight times earlier in the book of Revelation. The Lord speaks of Himself as "the first and the last" (1:17 and 2:8). The church in Ephesus had left the love that she "had at first" or her "first love" (2:4). John hears again "the first voice" he had heard in Revelation 4:1. We are introduced to "the first living creature" in 4:7. "The first angel" blows his trumpet in 8:7. The second beast "exercises all the authority of the first" in 13:12. In 16:2, "the first angel" pours his bowl upon the earth. Apparently the literal meaning of "first" is not suspect in any of these verses. The word also occurs after 20:5–6. In 21:1, we are told of the passing away of "the first heaven and the first earth." In describing the jewels adorning the twelve foundations of the New Jerusalem, John tells us that "the first was jasper" (20:19). Finally, the Lord repeats His identity: "the first and the last" (22:13). Once again there would seem to be no difficulty in accepting "first" as literal. In all of the verses cited nothing precedes the "first" one mentioned. This is the character or distinctiveness of the word. It has not changed that character in 20:5–6.

To say that Christ's was "the first" and the "number one" resurrection is to misunderstand Christ's place in the scheme of the resurrection. His resurrection was so distinct, so different, as to put it in a separate category.

To begin with, He stood in contrast to those who would later be resurrected. He was the God-man; we, mere men. He was the ransom; we, the ransomed. His resurrection was the validation of His ransom being accepted; ours, the consequence of His because we belong to Him. This is why Paul, in speaking of the resurrection order does not call Him the first in a series, but the "first fruits" of that resurrection (1 Cor. 15:20). The first fruits in the Old Testament was not the harvest, and, in essence, did not belong to the harvest itself, but was a harbinger or promise of the actual harvest. Because it existed, there would be a harvest. Christ is the template. He is the archetype. As the prototype model, He is not part of the production that follows, though He is the pattern for it.

Thus, what follows in 1 Corinthians 15 is an actual double order of the resurrection: (1) "those that are Christ's at his coming," and (2) "the end" when He delivers up the kingdom. This corresponds logically to (1) "the first resurrection" of Revelation 20:4–6, and (2) the earth and the sea giving up their dead after the millennium, described later in that same chapter.

To argue that Jesus was the first resurrection at all, one must distinguish between two different kinds of resurrection. There were resurrections before His. There were resurrections in the Old Testament. There were people in the New Testament (such as Lazarus) who were raised by Jesus Himself. But all of these were temporal resurrections—they would all die again. Christ's was the first eternal resurrection in a glorified body. Romans 6:9 states that "Christ being raised from the dead will never die again; death no longer has dominion over him." It was this kind of resurrection that distinguished it from all previous resurrections. What, then, do we say of those saints who came out of their graves in Matthew 27:52–53? Were they part of the phenomenon of Christ's resurrection? That is, did they rise in eternal bodies, so that they were partakers of that glory? There is nothing to suggest that they shared a glorified resurrection, and there is much to suggest that they merely came forth from their graves in revitalized mortal bodies.

If they had been raised in glorified bodies at the time of Christ's resurrection, then they would have been part of the first fruits of the resurrection together with Christ. Not only would this detract from the uniqueness of that resurrection, but it would have also eroded some of the glory that was His alone at that time, rather than enhancing it. He stood alone, and His resurrection would guarantee future resurrections.

Furthermore, in passages that argue for the resurrection (specifically 1 Corinthians 15), no hint is given of any resurrection but Christ's. Paul marshals the witnesses of His resurrected body, but not a word is said of any other resurrected bodies. Surely, if theirs had also been glorified resurrections, Paul could also point to them and their resurrections as proof of his argument: "There is a resurrection and we can point to Christ and His fellow resurrectees, and we can also point to the many witnesses of these resurrections." But it is Christ and His resurrection alone that is used as proof. When Paul lists the order of resurrection, he says, "Christ the first fruits," not "Christ and those who came out of the grave at His resurrection the first fruits" (1 Cor. 15:23). Not only is there silence here, but we can also find no reference in any other New Testament passage to these resurrected bodies. They are never found accompanying Jesus. In His resurrected body, Jesus was, in a sense, a fish out of water. He did not belong to this earthly scene. His was a glorified body with amazing abilities unrestricted by earthly laws of physics—it was a body suited for heaven.

If those who came forth from the grave were also in glorified bodies, where did they go? What did they do? What happened to them? They had no place on earth in glorified bodies. But if they were recently deceased "saints," they had homes and families to return to, and it is not surprising that we should hear no more about them from that point on—just as we heard no more about others who had been raised during Christ's ministry. They went home to family and friends and eventually died again.

One of the most telling arguments against the idea of glorified bodies for them (as sharing in kind in Christ's resurrection) is the fact that they do not appear at the ascension. If they are also glorified at His resurrection, they should also share in His ascension. They cannot wander the earth as freaks of nature. They belong in heaven. But they are not found before the ascension, at the ascension, or on earth after the ascension.

So, Christ's resurrection is listed first in categories of the resurrection, but as the first fruits. He is the source of what will follow. Any resurrection that follows is a resurrection of what had been a mortal human being. And there are two resurrections that do follow: the first resurrection, described in 1 Corinthians 15, 1 Thessalonians 4, and Revelation 20; and the second resurrection, pictured in 1 Corinthians 15 and Revelation 20. The "first resurrection" is the first resurrection.

## When Does the *First* Resurrection Occur?

The second claim of the pretribulationists regarding those who are part of the "first resurrection" in the Revelation 20:4-6 passage is that it takes place after Christ arrives on earth and that it only includes the Christian martyrs of the tribulation period.

But there is no clear support for this assumption, that this resurrection occurs after Christ's arrival on earth. A close study of the Greek text points to exactly the opposite conclusion—namely, that this resurrection took place before the scene viewed by John in verse 4. John begins with the use of a perfect participle: they "had been beheaded." Then he follows with verbs in the aorist tense, meaning that these things had happened in a time before the present moment (that is, connected with the past) but that they carried on the force of the perfect tense already used to set the timeframe in place. The Revised Standard Version even carries on the perfect in its translation: "who had not worshipped the beast or its image and had not received its mark on their foreheads or their hands." The very next phrase is couched in that same aorist tense, "They came to life." Then comes the phrase, "and reigned with Christ a thousand years." Based on what preceded the statement, it is impossible to say they came to life in the very timeframe in which John initially views this scene of them reigning with Christ. One could just as easily have said, "They had come to life, and they reigned with Christ a thousand years." It is as if one were to say, "My family and I had been to London earlier, and I went to Buckingham Palace and saw the changing of the guard. We flew to America and lived there for ten years." Our flight is part of the same past with our London experiences, but it is the focal point for a new beginning. Thus, the "living again" is part of the same past as the refusal to "worship" the beast and to "receive" its mark, but it is the focal point for a new beginning in the millennial kingdom.

A more critical problem is involved in the idea that the resurrection relates only to the martyred dead who had refused to worship the world ruler immediately preceding this time and who consequently died for their faith. A careful exegesis of the original text indicates that most of our translations today are misleading about the identity of one particular group in the verse. Using the RSV as an example, following the description of "the souls of those who had been beheaded for their testimony to Jesus and for the word of God," the text reads: "and who had not worshipped the beast or its image and had not received its mark on their foreheads or their hands." This would suggest one group of believers here—the tribulation martyrs who would not give allegiance to the beast. Other translations like the King James Version, The Living Bible, The New International Version, Good News for Modern Man, and The New Testament in Modern English (J. B. Phillips) respectively, use similar expressions: and which, and who, They, They, and those who. These translations give the same impression. The difficulty lies in the fact that they translate a particular Greek word as if it were a definite relative pronoun: "who." There are Greek devices to express a definite relative pronoun idea. None of them are used at this point, however. What is used is the Greek word οιτινης (masculine), which is the plural form of the indefinite relative pronoun "whoever" or "everyone who." Just as striking and convincing is the fact that this relative pronoun differs in gender from "the souls ψυκας (feminine) of them who had been beheaded." As a feminine word, its relative should agree with it. To mean the same group, the word should be αιτινης, but instead it is the masculine form indicating another group.

This is not just the isolated opinion of an individual. It is accurate meaning and sound exegesis. Both Bauer, Arndt and Gingrich's A Greek-English Lexicon of the New Testament and Thayer's A Greek-English Lexicon of the New Testament list as the primary, generic, or generalized meaning of the word (οιτινης) as "whoever" or "everyone who" and both put the usage in Revelation 20:4 under that meaning. Furthermore, two single volume commentaries, The New Bible Commentary by Davidson, Stubbs and Kevan and Commentary on the Whole Bible by Jamieson, Fausset and Brown recognize this translation, which results in the description of two separate groups: the martyred saints of the tribulation on the one hand, and the living saints of the tribulation on the other. Thus the phrasing should read: "Also I saw the souls of those who had been beheaded for their testimony to Jesus and for the word of God, and everyone who had not worshiped the beast or its image and had not received its mark on their foreheads or their hands." For even clearer understanding, we could paraphrase it: "Also I saw the souls of those who had died by beheading during the tribulation for their testimony to Jesus and for the word of God, and I also saw everyone else who had not worshiped the beast or its image and not received its mark on their foreheads or their hands and had outlived the tribulation."

What does this mean? It means that two separate groups are involved in a common experience. Who are these groups? They are the beheaded tribulation saints who died for their faith during that tribulation, and they are also all the other tribulation saints who survived that tribulation period, but did not worship the beast or receive its mark. What is their common experience? If we were dealing only with dead saints and their experience in "the first resurrection," we would expect the Greek word εγειρω to be used, for this is the common word used for raising bodies from the dead. But if we are dealing with a group of dead believers and a group of living believers, a word would have to be used that could fit both the raising of the dead, on the one hand, and the changing or transforming of the living mortal bodies, on the other. This is exactly what John does. There is no exact Greek word that has such a meaning. In fact, when Paul speaks of the phenomenon in 1 Corinthians 15:51, even though he says "we shall be changed," he elaborates in the next verse by stating that "the dead will be raised ... and we shall be changed," probably to point out the great differences in the change of the two groups. In speaking of that joint change, John uses a word in the aorist tense that literally means, "They lived." The King James Version translated it literally that way. Others struggled with the translation, coming up with various "renewal" ideas: "they had come to life," "they came to life again," "they lived again," and so on. The concept of "living" was as good a concept as any. It cannot be pressed to mean that they began to live spiritually, since they did that the moment they had believed in Christ. That the dead lived obviously meant they were resurrected. That the living lived meant that they lived a new and different kind of life—one that Paul defined as immortal and incorruptible.

What, then, do we have here? We have nothing less than the raising of dead believers and the transforming of living believers, as Paul describes in 1 Corinthians 15:51–52. How does this fit in with the pretribulationist claim that there is no textual indication in the passage that the resurrection involves anyone beyond the martyred tribulation saints, such as the Church as a whole?

When we study any subject in Scripture that is treated in two or more passages, we need to apply what could be called the law of collation or the law of synthesis to get the complete and balanced teaching on that subject. By placing the elements of the subject next to each other, we can see the varied facets complementing each other in a satisfying and fulfilling mosaic. We cannot understand the subject without this unifying element, and we cannot take one of the parts under examination without an awareness that it remains only a part of that whole. We dare not ignore the other pieces and their implications in arriving at conclusions about the subject itself.

This can be illustrated by an example from the Old Testament and by two examples from the New Testament. In the book of Numbers, twelve spies were sent into Canaan to spy out the land. Because ten of them insisted that they couldn't do what God asked (only Joshua and Caleb suggested obeying God), the Lord would not permit Israel to enter the land. In a speech to Moses, God said, "none of the men who have seen my glory ... shall see the land ... But my servant Caleb, because he has ... followed me fully, I will bring into the land" (14:20–25). Later, in a speech to Moses and Aaron together, the Lord said "not one shall come into the land where I swore that I would make you dwell, except Caleb the son of Jephunneh and Joshua the son of Nun" (14:26–35). If we were we to stop with the speech to Moses alone, we would conclude that Joshua was not permitted to enter the land. Taking the two passages together, we know they both would go into the land.

In the New Testament there are many different passages about prayer, but some people have built entire doctrines on the subject based on a single verse about prayer. Some might claim on the basis of Luke 11:10 that one simply needs to ask and God will answer his prayer. Another might go back to verse 8 and claim that continual asking is the answer. Others assert that it all depends on faith because that's what the Bible says in Matthew 21:22. If one has enough faith, God must answer. Because of the charge by Jesus to ask in His name (John 14:13), still others use the phrase "in Jesus name" as a magic wand. If you use the formula words, God will definitely answer. There are those who believe that it is all a matter of pure living, because the Savior tells His disciples that they could ask for anything they wanted and receive it, if they would abide in Him and His words would abide in them (John 15:7). First John 3:22 states that keeping His commandments and doing what pleases Him causes us to receive from Him whatever we ask. Then there is a school of thought that proposes that we simply discover what God's will is in a certain area and pray for that. We cannot fail to receive our request, since 1 John 5:14–15 tells us that this is a sure road to success. According to the law of collation, however, we only get the full and balanced teaching of prayer by comparing Scripture with Scripture, laying the pieces side by side and combining the elements into a unified whole.

We see a similar pattern in passages that deal with the great commission. In Matthew 28:18 the charge is given to "make disciples ... baptizing them ... teaching them." In Luke 24:47 a different concept is stressed. Some content of the message is given. There was to be the preaching of "repentance and forgiveness of sins," and the program was to begin in Jerusalem. In Acts 1:8 the Jerusalem beginning is repeated, but then the order of advancing the program is marked out: to the whole of "Judea" followed by "Samaria" and then the very "end of the earth." To say that the great commission was simply preaching the message of repentance and forgiveness of sin as if that were the sum and substance of the mission, without considering discipling and the order of propagation, would be a mistake and only a partial statement of what the mission was all about.

How does the law of collation apply to the teaching of resurrection/rapture? At the "coming" of the Lord, there are at least eight things that occur at the resurrection/rapture itself and at least six other things that accompany that event. At the resurrection/rapture the following things happen rapidly:

1. The last trumpet sounds (1 Cor. 15:52; 1 Thess. 4:16).
2. A cry of command is heard (1 Thess. 4:16).
3. The archangel's call rings out (1 Thess. 4:16).
4. Dead Christians rise (1 Cor. 15:52; 1 Thess. 4:16).
5. Living Christians are changed (1 Cor. 15:42, 52).
6. These are caught up ("raptured") together (1 Thess. 4:17).
7. They are "gathered together" (2 Thess. 2:1).
8. They shall meet the Lord (John 14:3; 1 Thess. 4:17; 2 Thess. 2:1).

Then there are at least six things that accompany the resurrection/rapture at His coming:
1. The judgment seat of Christ (2 Cor. 5:10; Luke 14:14)
2. The marriage supper of the Lamb (Rev. 19:7, 9)
3. His coming with all His saints (1 Thess. 3:13)
4. His judgment of the nations (Matt. 25:31–46)
5. His sitting upon His throne (Matt. 25:31)
6. Christians reigning with Him (Rev. 5:10; 20:4; Matt. 19:28)

Let us return to the eight happenings of the resurrection/rapture. First, let us consider the four passages of Scripture from which these eight things have been gathered. According to the pretribulation school, the three principle "rapture" passages are 1 Corinthians 15:51–52, 1 Thessalonians 4:13–18, and John 14:3. In addition, they classify 2 Thessalonians 2:1 as a verse that deals with the rapture. By limiting ourselves only to these passages, we have seen eight things happening. But none of the passages contains all eight. 1 Thessalonians 4 contains six of the eight and is, therefore, the most comprehensive statement. It is the only passage where we hear of the archangel's call and the cry of command. More important, it is the only passage that mentions the "rapturing" of the Church. Yet, pretribulationists classify the other three passages as "rapture" passages. And rightly so, for they are properly applying the law of collation. 1 Corinthians 15 contains three of the eight elements, including the concept of living believers being "changed" or transformed. But it is significant that out of the four passages it is the only one that contains this truth. Because of the law of collation, however, we rightfully assume that this truth belongs in the other three passages even though it is not expressly mentioned in them. 2 Thessalonians 2:1 contains only two ideas: "gathering" and meeting the Lord, and, yet, we are right in assuming that all the other six elements belong there. John 14:3 has only the one element of meeting the Lord. But we are right in maintaining that it is a "rapture" passage that carries with it the weight of all of the other seven elements even if they are not explicitly stated.

What do we learn from this? Unless the context makes it clear that we are dealing with a nonresurrection/rapture theme (such as the cry of command for Lazarus to come forth, the Revelation trumpets of judgment, or the gathering of people to hear Jesus preach), we learn that where a resurrection/rapture theme is found we might expect to find the other elements implied. That is precisely what we have seen in Revelation 20:4. In the two tribulation groups that "lived again," we saw the resurrection of those who died in Christ and the "changing" or transformation of those who were alive and remained until the coming of the Lord. Thus, we expect that all the other elements were also present at that time.

In John 11:25–26, we find an unexpected passage in which we have both the resurrection of believers who have died and the imparting of life to those who are alive. When Martha mentioned the resurrection at the last day, Christ said that He is that resurrection. But in the context of that last-day resurrection, He stated that He also is the life. The resurrection obviously relates to what He says next: "he who believes in me, though he die, yet shall he live." The death is literal (a physical death) and the "shall live" is literal (and physical). "I am the life" would relate to the next statement and it would be consistent to view that statement as literal (and physical) also. Thus, it should be rendered: "whoever lives (physically) and believes in me shall never die (physically)." This is the transformation half of the resurrection/rapture and corresponds to the "I am the life" statement. It is implied that Lazarus would be in this resurrection. But this resurrection was the one Martha mentioned as taking place "at the last day," which would place it at the end of the last days, or at the end of the tribulation. This also corresponds with what John said about the two groups in Revelation 20:4.

In Matthew 24:29–31, we see an event that takes place after the great tribulation. In this event two of the eight happenings, or elements, of the resurrection/rapture are stated and a third is probably implied. The Lord sends out his angels (we could assume that the archangel of 1 Thessalonians 4:16 is included since it does not say that only some of the angels were sent out). There is a "loud trumpet call" and we must assume that it is the last trumpet since it sounds at the end of the tribulation period (which produced the seven trumpets of judgment). Furthermore, His angels "gather" His elect. This is a rarely used word in the New Testament and is the same word that is used in 2 Thessalonians 2:1, which describes Christians being "gathered together" to meet Him at the rapture. A gathering together of the elect as He is coming in the clouds could hardly present a clearer picture of the rapture. And it occurs at the end of the tribulation.

We have seen the law of collation in respect to the rapture as it applies to Revelation 20:4; John 11:25–26; and Matthew 24:29–31. Is there any other passage in Revelation where it might be in view? There is a verse where clearly one of these happenings, or elements, takes place at the end of the tribulation, and probably a second is seen as well. In 18:4, John states that he hears a voice from heaven. Since it is another voice, we can look to the voice just before it and see that it was the voice of an angel. This indicates that the second voice was also the voice of an angel. To suggest that it could be the archangel's voice is not unreasonable. It is fascinating that the word for "voice" used here is also used in the New Testament to mean the sound of a musical instrument, a call, or a cry. Thus, it could include all the reverberations of 1 Thessalonians 4:16 (the cry of command, the archangel's call, and the sound of the trumpet). What is certain is that whatever the voice is, there is definitely a "cry of command." John heard the words, "Come out of her, my people." When Lazarus was called forth from death, it is this very word that is used to indicate what he did in response to the resurrection command. Some pretribulationists have tried to find a rapture in Revelation 4:1, where John is told to "Come up hither." In order to do this, however, they have to spiritualize John to make him a type of God's people. Here, one does not have to spiritualize anything. The Lord is clearly speaking to His own. He says (either directly or through His archangel), "Come out of her, my people." As we read the descriptions of Babylon (out of which His people are called), it is evident that it is more than just a place or location. It is also the materialistic world system. It is thus fitting that the Church should be called out of her before her final judgment begins.

Therefore, when we see the resurrection in Revelation 20 producing raised dead believers and changed living believers who go on to reign with Christ, it is enough to tell us that we are dealing with the resurrection/rapture. Then when we hear God's call for His people to leave Babylon (in chapter 18), we can recognize the relationship within His mosaic.

*The last trump and the first resurrection:*
*from Him—the First and the Last.*

# 2

# THE CHURCH

## Church History

*The dawning Church awaits the heav'nly dove.*
*He comes in birthing power; gifts supplies;*
*Dispatches envoys of Messiah's love.*
*They teach, they strive, they, conq'ring, die, they rise.*

The Church of Jesus Christ is the most powerful organization on earth. His Church is the storehouse of God's multiplied wisdom.

The Church is the mystery of Christ. The reason that the Church of Christ is so powerful is because Christ Himself supplied it with that power. When Christ spoke to Peter of the establishing of the Church, He said, "I tell you, you are Peter, and on this rock I will build my church, and the powers of death [or the gates of Hades] shall not prevail against it" (Matt. 16:18). There is no other organization ever founded by religion or society that rests in this power. Death or Hades can conquer them all. The Church of Christ incipient becomes the Church triumphant.

His Church is the storehouse of God's multiplied wisdom because God chose it for that purpose from eternity past. It is through the Church "that ... the manifold wisdom of God might now be made known to the principalities and powers in the heavenly places ... according to the eternal purpose which he has realized in Christ Jesus our Lord" (Eph. 3:10–11). It was not princes and kings He chose for this honor. It was not the angelic hosts. It was not even the archangel. It was the Church. And it will demonstrate His wisdom to the angelic powers.

The Church is the mystery of Christ. But God revealed to Paul and his fellow apostles and prophets what that mystery is: "how the Gentiles are fellow heirs, members of the same body, and partakers of the promise in Christ Jesus through the gospel" (Eph. 3:6). This was the amazing mystery that none of the older prophets knew, that God would take believing Jews and bring this message of peace to the Gentiles, then meld believing Gentiles together with the former household of God and make of them both one new man in Christ.

The Greek word for church is εκκλησια, meaning "assembly," and, for the most part in the New Testament, it means "church" as God's redeemed assembly. It comes from a base word that means "call out" or "call forth." The Church is the assembly that God called forth from the world to be His people. There are a few scattered instances in the New Testament where the term refers to the Old Testament assembly or congregation or to a simple gathering of people for a meeting, such as a public forum. In almost all other cases, it refers to the Christian Church. Most of the references are applied to local or individual churches. There are a few passages (about two dozen) where the term refers to the universal Church or the Church as a combined body.

Nine of the twenty-three clear references are found in Ephesians, another four in 1 Corinthians, and three more in Acts, for a total of sixteen. So there are only seven other references to the Church universal in the rest of the New Testament Scriptures. This makes it a rare reference apart from those three books.

This does not mean that the idea is rare, only that the term itself is rare. The concept of the assembly that God called forth from the world to be His people comes to us on page after page of the Word. Searching for New Testament terms that are the equivalent of the Church has proved to be one of the most challenging and rewarding studies I have ever undertaken. It was like finding a costly and many faceted jewel that sparkles with its own brilliance the more it is turned. I have discovered thirty other terms, each with its own peculiar flavor and relationship. The list is by no means exhaustive, but it is instructive and enlightening. The study has the potential to be developed into a separate book, but for the sake of the present study, I will only touch briefly on most of these terms.

There will be some equivalent terms that occur in only one passage or in only one verse of Scripture. At other times, as in the case of church, saint, kingdom, disciples, brethren, or children, there are a number of occurrences and I have chosen only some of the more representative ones. In some cases a term will be used exclusively of the Church (e.g., saints), or will sometimes represent the Church, or will refer to something else in addition, as in the case of brethren or children. The reader will find great profit in being well armed with an exhaustive concordance and pursuing these terms as they occur in the New Testament.

Almost all of the terms that follow lend themselves to a natural threefold division. There is a corporate, or all-inclusive term that is the equivalent of "Church." Almost always there can also be found a term to indicate one individual within the corporate group. Finally, there is also usually a term used showing the relationship that the Lord has to this particular group or to these individuals. A classic and easily understood example of such a division would be as follows: a corporate term for church is the "flock," an individual member of that flock is a "sheep," and the relationship of the Lord to those sheep is that of the "shepherd" or the "Good Shepherd."

The thirty-one terms, including the word church itself, can be divided into three major categories: the Positional-Transformational, the Architectural, and the Relational. Under each of these categories, the Scriptures reveal a many faceted gem which is His Church.

## Positional-Transformational Terms

### Calling Terms

**1. Corporate:** the Church—"on this rock I will build my church, and the powers of death shall not prevail against it" (Matt. 16:18). **Individual:** Saint—"all the churches of the saints" (1 Cor. 14:33). **Lord's Relationship:** God, who calls—"To the church of God which is at Corinth, to those sanctified in Christ Jesus, called to be saints" (1 Cor. 1:2); the Lord, who adds—"And the Lord added to their number day by day those who were being saved" (Acts 2:47); and the Spirit, who sanctifies—"sanctified by the Spirit" (1 Pet. 1:2).

Though the words are in no way related in stems either in English or in Greek (εκκλησια/αγιος), they are related in concept. The church represents the "called out" people of God. A saint is one who has been sanctified or dedicated to God. That which is sanctified has been set aside or made suitable for ritual purposes. In addition, we have just seen from 1 Corinthians that God has called members of the Church to be saints, just as He has called out the Church to be His people. We can also see that the churches are churches of the saints. Thus a local church need be no larger than two or three saints. As Christ said in Matthew 18:20: "where two or three are gathered in my name, there am I in the midst of them."

**2. Corporate:** the Elect—"Who shall bring any charge against God's elect?" (Rom. 8:33). **Individual:** the Elect—"The children of your elect sister greet you" (2 John 13). **Lord's Relationship:** God, the Father—"chosen (elect) by God the Father" (1 Pet. 1:1–2).

"Elect" or "chosen" means to choose out. It shares the selection process with the terms Church and saint. The one selected is separated from the group from which he came. Thus the Lord chooses out someone (elects him or her), sets him apart from the group (makes him a saint) and places him in the Church (or assembly of saints). He has been called out of the former group into a new group.

The equivalent of "Church" (or "saints") and "elect" can be seen by comparing 1 Corinthians 14:33 ("the churches of the saints") with Colossians 3:12 ("Put on then, as God's chosen ones, holy and beloved, compassion ... patience"). The term "chosen ones" in the Colossians verse is the same word as "elect" (indeed, the King James Version translates it "the elect of God"), and the word holy is the same as "saints." This word, in turn, is the same word used in the Corinthians verse. A good translation of the Colossians verse would be, "Put on then, as God's elect, saints and beloved ones ..." So the Corinthians verse says that the Church = the saints and the Colossians verse says that the saints = the elect. Thus, the elect are the Church.

**Redemptive Terms**

**1. Corporate:** Saved—"For by grace you have been saved through faith" (Eph. 2:8). **Individual:** Saved—"what must I do to be saved?" (Acts 16:30). **Lord's Relationship:** Savior—"our great God and Savior Jesus Christ" (Titus 2:13); and Deliverer—"and so all Israel will be saved; as it is written, 'The Deliverer will come from Zion' " (Rom. 11:26).

The Church is the company of the saved. In his address to the elders of Ephesus, Paul told them "to care for the church of God which he obtained with the blood of his own Son" (Acts 20:28). We were the lost sheep, the lost coin, and the lost son, but He found us and saved us from our lost estate.

**2. Corporate and Individual:** Blood freed—"Jesus Christ ... who loves us and has freed us from our sins by his blood" (Rev. 1:5); Blood washed—"These are they who have come out of the great tribulation; they have washed their robes and made them white in the blood of the Lamb" (Rev. 7:14); Blood cleansed—"the blood of Jesus his Son cleanses us from all sin" (1 John 1:7); Blood redeemed—"In him we have redemption through his blood" (Eph. 1:7); Blood ransomed—"you were ransomed ... with the precious blood of Christ" (1 Pet. 1:18–19); and Blood obtained—"the church of God which he obtained with the blood of his own Son" (Acts 20:28). **Lord's Relationship:** Lamb of God—"Behold the Lamb of God, who takes away the sin of the world!" (John 1:29).

The Church of God is that group that has been transformed by the transaction whereby Christ's blood is given for man and man is made acceptable to God: "the church of God which he obtained with the blood of his own Son" (Acts 20:28). This transformation has many faces to present to us—washing, freeing, cleansing, redeeming, and ransoming—but each face presents the beauty of sacrifice and love.

**Glorious Terms**

1. **Corporate:** Lights—"you shine as lights in the world" (Phil. 2:15); and Children of light—"walk as children of light" (Eph. 5:8). **Individual:** Light—"You are the light of the world" (Matt. 5:14); and Child (inferred) of light (also Eph. 5:8). **Lord's Relationship:** Light of the world—"The true light that enlightens every man was coming into the world" (John 1:9).

There is perhaps no figure that draws a sharper contrast between God and Satan, good and evil, life and death, and salvation and condemnation than the figure of light and darkness. The apostle Paul tells us that "the Father, who has qualified us to share in the inheritance of the saints in light ... has delivered us from the dominion of darkness and transferred us to the kingdom of his beloved Son" (Col. 1:12–13). This Son "is the head of the body, the church" (Col. 1:18). Not only can we see on this basis that those in the light are part of the Church, but we are also part of that group called "the saints in light" (v. 12). The saints and the Church are one and the same thing. Furthermore, we are "transformed into the kingdom of his beloved Son." To be in the kingdom is to have been born again, according to John 3:3. We, then, as lights, are the Church and are "in Christ," that is, in Him who is the Light of the world.

2. **Corporate:** Conquerors, and **Individual (inferred):** Conqueror—"in all these things we are more than conquerors through him who loved us" (Rom. 8:37). **Lord's Relationship:** the Lord who loved us (same verse) and King of kings and Lord of lords—"On his robe and on his thigh he has a name inscribed, King of kings and Lord of lords" (Rev. 19:16).

In an amazing array of promises, the Lord Christ pledges great blessings to those who conquer in each of the seven churches in Revelation 2 and 3. If these churches are a picture of the churches down through the ages and of our modern day churches, then these promises tell us that the one who conquers is in the Church universal. To the one who conquers in the church at Ephesus, "I will grant to eat of the tree of life"; to the one in Smyrna, he "shall not be hurt by the second death"; in Pergamum, "I will give some of the hidden manna" to him; in Thyatira, "I will give him power over the nations"; in Sardis, "he ... shall be clad ... in white garments"; in Philadelphia, "I will make him a pillar in the temple of my God ... and I will write on him the name of my God, and the name of the city of my God, the new Jerusalem ... and his own new name"; and in Laodicea, "I will grant him to sit with me on my throne, as I myself conquered and sat down with my Father on his throne." The very language used in these promises to the conquerors is the language of privileges that belong to the Church.

### Architectural Terms

### Building Terms

**1. Corporate:** House and Stones—"and like living stones be yourself built into a spiritual house" (1 Pet. 2:5). **Individual (inferred):** Stone (same verse). **Lord's Relationship:** Cornerstone—"I am laying in Zion a stone, a cornerstone chosen and precious ... the very stone which the builders rejected has become the head of the corner" (1 Pet. 2:6–7).

In the very first mention of the Church, Christ said He was going to build His Church (Matt. 16:18). This makes any kind of structure in the New Testament that He is said to build or be part of a very special building, and, more important, it makes it the Church itself. The importance of this particular building in 1 Peter is that it is not a lifeless or passive thing, but it is a living and spiritual house.

**2. Corporate:** Temple—"Do you not know that you (plural) are God's temple and that God's Spirit dwells in you?" (1 Cor. 3:16). **Individual:** Temple—"Do you not know that your body (singular) is a temple of the Holy Spirit within you, which you have from God?" (1 Cor. 6:19). **Lord's Relationship:** Spirit (same verse).

This carries the figure of the living house a step further and shows us a major function of the living building. Perhaps no image illustrates more clearly the sanctity and dedication of the Church than that of the temple. It is filled with God's Spirit and it calls forth worship of God and service to Him.

**City Terms**

**1. Corporate:** City of God—"You are the light of the world. A city set on a hill cannot be hid" (Matt. 5:14); "For he looked forward to the city which has foundations, whose builder and maker is God" (Heb. 11:10); and "But you have come to Mount Zion and to the city of the living God, the heavenly Jerusalem" (Heb. 12:22). **Individual:** Fellow citizen—"These all died in faith, not having received what was promised, but having seen it and greeted it from afar, and having acknowledged that they were strangers and exiles on the earth. For people who speak thus make it clear that they are seeking a homeland" (Heb. 11:13–14); and "So then you are no longer strangers and sojourners, but you are fellow citizens with the saints" (Eph. 2:19). **Lord's Relationship:** Builder/God—"the city ... whose builder and maker is God" (Heb. 11:10).

As the spiritual house was living, so is the city, for it is "the city of the living God." This city is also equal to our light (Matt. 5:14) and corresponds to the "saints in light" (Col. 1:12). This shows that we are dealing with yet another term that means the Church. The significance of this city in relationship to the Church will bloom even further in the next example.

**2. Corporate:** New Jerusalem—"And I saw the holy city, new Jerusalem, coming down out of heaven from God, prepared as a bride adorned for her husband; ... Then came one of the seven angels who had the seven bowls full of the seven last plagues, and spoke to me, saying, 'Come, I will show you the Bride, the wife of the Lamb.' And in the Spirit he carried me away to a great, high mountain, and showed me the holy city Jerusalem coming down out of heaven from God" (Rev. 21:2, 9–10); and "the city of the living God, the heavenly Jerusalem" (Heb. 12:22). **Individual:** Israel's tribes/twelve apostles—"It had a great, high wall, with twelve gates, and at the gates twelve angels, and on the gates the names of the twelve tribes of the sons of Israel were inscribed ... And the wall of the city had twelve foundations, and on them the twelve names of the twelve apostles of the Lamb" (Rev. 21:12–14). **Lord's Relationship:** Temple/Lord/Lamb—"And I saw no temple in the city, for its temple is the Lord God the Almighty and the Lamb" (Rev. 21:22).

It has doubtless become clear that the city of God (used as the previous term) is none other than the New Jerusalem. Indeed, it is called "the heavenly city" and "the city which has foundations" (Heb. 12:22; 11:10). We see in the Revelation passage what those foundations are. Then we see that it is also called "the wife of the Lamb." In Ephesians 5:21–33, Paul uses an extended simile of a man's marital relationship to his wife. In verse 32 he states that this relationship "refers to Christ and the church." Thus, we can easily equate the New Jerusalem to the wife of the Lamb, or the wife of Christ, which in turn is the Church. Therefore, the New Jerusalem is the Church.

Paul uses another figure in Galatians to show the same truth. He says that the law (Mount Sinai) is "the present Jerusalem," but that "the Jerusalem above is free, and she is our mother" (4:21–31). If the New Jerusalem, "the Jerusalem above," is our mother (the mother of believers) she represents, again, the Church. Finally, when Jesus told His disciples that He was preparing a place for them in His Father's house, what would that house be, if not the New Jerusalem? (See John 14:3.)

## RELATIONAL TERMS

### Name Terms

1. **Corporate:** Nazarenes, and **Individual (inferred):**

Nazarene—"For we have found this man a pestilent fellow, an agitator among all the Jews throughout the world, and a ringleader of the sect of the Nazarenes" (Acts 24:5). **Lord's Relationship:** Nazarene—"And he went and dwelt in a city called Nazareth, that what was spoken by the prophets might be fulfilled, 'He shall be called a Nazarene' " (Matt. 2:23).

By extension we can logically conclude that what Tertullus called the "sect of the Nazarenes" was nothing else but the Church, or, more exactly, the Christian churches that Paul founded and nurtured, since the rest of Acts and the epistles of Paul tell us that that was his only vocation following his conversion.

**2. Corporate:** Christians—"For a whole year they met with the church, and taught a large company of people; and in Antioch the disciples were for the first time called Christians" (Acts 11:26). **Individual:** Christian—"yet if one suffers as a Christian, let him not be ashamed, but under that name let him glorify God" (1 Pet. 4:16). **Lord's Relationship:** Christ—"Simon Peter replied, 'You are the Christ, the Son of the living God' " (Matt. 16:16).

The very name shows the relationship His followers had to Christ and it indicates that they were His people. The Gentiles gave the name to believers, and it was very similar to a term that developed in the 20th century: "Jesus people." Since this term was related to the believers in the church at Antioch, it is natural to see that it means "one who belongs to the Church of Christ."

### Subordinate Terms

Addressing marital relationships in Ephesians 5, Paul says: "As the church is subject to Christ, so let wives also be subject in everything to their husbands" (v. 24). A number of relationships follow, which cast Christians as those who are subject to or subordinated to Christ. By their very nature, then, they show that they are the Church. In many cases, however, there are additional accounts in Scripture that indicate even further instances of their direct definition as the Church.

**1. Corporate:** Believers—"And more than ever believers

were added to the Lord" (Acts 5:14). **Individual (inferred):** Believer—"But to all who received him, who believed in his name, he gave power to become children of God" (John 1:12). **Lord's Relationship:** Son of God—"You are the Christ, the Son of the living God" (Matt. 16:16); Son of Man—"But that you may know that the Son of man has authority on earth to forgive sins" (Matt. 9:6); and Truth—"Jesus said to him, 'I am ... the truth' " (John 14:6).

Belief is at the heart of a saving relationship to God. Not only do we have the truth that we are saved "by grace" and "through faith" (Eph. 2:8), but we are also told that the new birth comes through believing (John 1:12). Immediately following the birthday of the Church, "all who believed were together and had all things in common" (Acts 2:44). It is obvious, therefore, that the Church was comprised of "believers."

**2. Corporate :** Servants—"But thanks be to God, that you who were once slaves of sin ... have become slaves of righteousness" (Rom. 6:17–18). **Individual:** Servant—"His master said to him, 'Well done, good and faithful servant; you have been faithful over a little, I will set you over much; enter into the joy of your master.' "/"And the Lord's servant must not be quarrelsome but kindly to every one, an apt teacher, forbearing" (Matt. 25:21; 2 Tim 2:24). **Lord's Relationship:** God—"But now ... you ... have become slaves of God" (Rom. 6:22); and Master—"A disciple is not above his teacher, nor a servant above his master" (Matt. 10:24).

At the very heart of the concept of subjection or subordination is the word servant or slave. And yet, on the day of Pentecost, when Peter stood up to explain the birth of the Church through the coming of the Spirit to the people assembled in Jerusalem, he said that it was a fulfillment of a prophecy of Joel, who said that God had declared: "in the last days ... I will pour out my Spirit" not on kings and princes, not on prophets and priests, but "on my menservants and my maidservants" (Acts 2:17–18). So it was that the Church that had just been born consisted mainly of God's "servants."

**3. Corporate:** Followers—"the sheep hear his voice ... and the sheep follow him" (John 10:3–4). **Individual:** Follower—"If any man would come after me, let him deny himself and take up his cross and follow me" (Matt. 16:24). **Lord's Relationship:** the Way—"Jesus said to him, 'I am the way' " (John 14:6).

Acts 8:3 reports that "Saul was ravaging the church." In the process of doing this, he headed for Damascus "so that if he found any belonging to the Way, men or women, he might bring them bound to Jerusalem" (9:3). Those who followed Christ were said to belong to the Way, and this makes them the Church, since it was that group that Saul was ravaging.

**4. Corporate:** Disciples—"By this all men will know that you are my disciples, if you have love for one another" (John 13:35). **Individual:** Disciple—"A disciple is not above his teacher" (Matt. 10:24). **Lord's Relationship:** Teacher and Lord—"You call me Teacher and Lord; and you are right, for so I am" (John 13:13).

A disciple was one who had a deepened sense of dedication. He believed, but he wanted to know more. He was a follower, but he had a sharpened sense of commitment. He wanted to study to become like his teacher. He was, in the noblest sense, an apprentice. Those who followed Christ thus in His ministry and those who, after His death and resurrection, stood for and spread their faith were disciples. They were the core of the Church and its ministry. As "Saul was ravaging the church," he was "breathing threats and murder against the disciples of the Lord" (Acts 8:3; 9:1). But after his conversion, he was with Barnabas in Antioch and "for a whole year they met with the church ... and in Antioch the disciples were for the first time called Christians" (Acts 11:26). So, both before and after Saul's conversion, it was acknowledged that the disciples were the Church.

**5. Corporate:** Kingdom—"To him who loves us and has freed us from our sins by his blood and made us a kingdom" and "unless one is born anew, he cannot see the kingdom of God" (Rev. 1:5–6; John 3:3). **Individual:** Heir—"Has not God chosen those who are poor in the world to be rich in faith and heirs of the kingdom which he has promised to those who love him?" (James 2:5). **Lord's Relationship:** King—"the Lamb will conquer them, for he is Lord of lords and King of kings" (Rev. 17:14).

The one figure that is used more than any other in the New Testament to designate the Church is that of the kingdom of God or its equivalent, the kingdom of heaven. Jesus said, "Unless one is born anew, he cannot see the kingdom of God" (John 3:3). The new birth is essential for entry into the kingdom of God, which is the Church universal. The same is true of the term "kingdom of heaven." When Jesus responded to Peter's confession of faith that He was the Son of the living God, He said, "on this rock I will build my church ... I will give you the keys of the kingdom of heaven" (Matt. 16:16). That is to say, "The Church I will build is the kingdom of heaven, and I am entrusting its keys to you."

**6. Corporate:** Ambassadors—"So we are ambassadors for Christ, God making his appeal through us. We beseech you on behalf of Christ, be reconciled to God" (2 Cor. 5:20). **Individual:** Ambassador—"I am an ambassador in chains" (Eph. 6:20). **Lord's Relationship:** Christ/God—See above (2 Cor. 5:20).

It should be obvious that on the day of Pentecost Peter preached the message of reconciliation when he told the people to "repent ... for the forgiveness of ... sins" (Acts 2:38). It is also clear that this was to be the work of the Church: "that repentance and forgiveness of sins should be preached in his name to all nations, beginning from Jerusalem" (Luke 24:47). Thus, Christ's ambassadors were His Church doing the work He sent the Church to do in His name.

**7. Corporate:** Household—"So then, as we have opportunity, let us do good to all men, and especially to those who are of the household of faith" (Gal. 6:10). **Individual:** Householder and Servant—"Therefore every scribe who has been trained for the kingdom of heaven is like a householder who brings out of his treasure what is new and what is old" (Matt. 13:52). **Lord's Relationship:** Master—"His master said to him, 'Well done, good and faithful servant; you have been faithful over a little, I will set you over much; enter into the joy of your master'" (Matt. 25:21).

Paul's instruction to Timothy further verifies that the household of God is the Church: "You may know how one ought to behave in the household of God, which is the church of the living God, the pillar and bulwark of the truth" (1 Tim. 3:15).

**8. Corporate:** Priesthood—"But you are a chosen race, a royal priesthood" (1 Pet. 2:9). **Individual:** Priest—"To him who loves us and has freed us from our sins by his blood and made us ... priests to his God and Father" (Rev. 1:5–6). **Lord's Relationship:** High Priest—"Therefore, holy brethren, who share in a heavenly call, consider Jesus, the apostle and high priest of our confession" (Heb. 3:1).

The priesthood bears responsibility for worship and service, and perhaps one of the most powerful things to consider is the place where they serve. They would logically serve in the spiritual house—in the temple itself. Since we have seen that both of these figures are identified as the Church, then the living caretakers and godly representatives of the structures are also the Church.

**9. Corporate:** Flock—"And I have other sheep, that are not of this fold; I must bring them also, and they will heed my voice. So there shall be one flock, one shepherd" (John 10:16). **Individual:** Sheep—"I am the Good Shepherd. The good shepherd lays down his life for the sheep" (John 10:11). **Lord's Relationship:** Good Shepherd (same verse).

In one sense, the figure of the children of God as sheep is the least flattering of all the terms used, being a cut below even servant or slave. In that respect it is probably the strongest illustration of subjection or subordination. Sheep are stupid, but they know how to follow. They are all right as long as they are following the shepherd instead of a deceiver. As sheep, that is our strongest virtue—fixing our eyes upon Jesus. The flock is clearly a direct equivalent of the Church, as Paul told the Ephesian elders: "Take heed to yourselves and to all the flock, in which the Holy Spirit has made you overseers, to care for the church of God" (Acts 20:28).

### Organic Terms

**1. Corporate:** Branches, and **Individual (inferred):** Branch—"I am the vine, you are the branches. He who abides in me, and I in him, he it is that bears much fruit, for apart from me you can do nothing" (John 15:5). **Lord's Rela-

**tionship:** Vine (same verse).

This is the only place in the entire New Testament where Christ's followers are compared to vineyard branches. In the extended passage (vv. 1–17), Jesus begins by telling His disciples that His purpose and His Father's purpose for the branches is that they bear fruit (vv. 1–2). Then He returns to the theme of their bearing fruit, obviously as branches: "You did not choose me, but I chose you and appointed you that you should go and bear fruit and that your fruit should abide" (v. 16). The verb used here, "to choose," is the verbal form of the noun that we translated as the "chosen" or "elect" in the rest of the New Testament. As we have previously seen, the elect = the Church. Since these disciples were "chosen" by the Lord in the same manner, they are the elect, and the elect are the Church.

**2. Corporate:** Olive Tree, and **Individual:** Wild Olive Shoot—"But ... some of the branches were broken off, and you, a wild olive shoot, were grafted in their place to share the richness of the olive tree" (Rom. 11:17). **Lord's Relationship:** God—"But if God did not spare the natural branches, neither will he spare you" (Rom. 11:21).

According to Romans 11:13–27, God has formed one new unit. To that which was believing Israel, He added those from the Gentiles who would receive His offer of inclusion. When that number of Gentiles is complete, the rest of nation Israel will be added to make one unified and complete unit ("olive tree"). Call this unit what you will, but it is the people of God. They are His saints. If you choose to call it the Church, then God's purpose is the same for nation Israel and believing Gentiles, since Israel, as a nation, is yet to be included in this unit. If you call it anything else, then it is greater than the Church, for the Church is included in it and supported by its roots.

**3. Corporate:** New Man—"For he is our peace, who has made us both one, and has broken down the dividing wall of hostility, by abolishing in his flesh the law of commandments and ordinances, that he might create in himself one new man in place of the two, so making peace" (Eph. 2:14–15). **Individual (inferred):** Member—"For ... the body is one and has many members" (1 Cor. 12:12). **Lord's Relationship:**

Our Peace—"For he is our peace, who has made us both one" (Eph. 2:14).

A study of Ephesians 2:11–3:6 reveals that the creation of this new man is simply another figure for the same truth that we saw in the olive tree figure of Romans 11. In the olive tree figure, the Gentile shoot was grafted into the existing root system together with the remaining believing Jewish branches to form a new kind of tree, which was then united. In the body figure, the Lord took the believers of the covenant of promises and melded believing Gentiles together with them to form one completely new man in the cross. At the end of the section, Paul says that the mystery that had existed has now been made clear—precisely that "the Gentiles are fellow heirs, members of the same body" (3:6). Then he picks up that mystery theme again and says that the plan of that mystery is "that through the church the manifold wisdom of God might now be made known to the principalities and powers in the heavenly places" (vv. 9–10). In abbreviated form Paul says that the new man (Gentile believers together with Jewish believers) is the Church and that God is going to make His wisdom known through it. Since, however, the new man is the Church, then the olive tree (its equivalent) is also the Church.

**4. Corporate:** (inferred) New Creations—"Of his own will he brought us forth by the word of truth that we should be a kind of first fruits of his creatures" (James 1:18). **Individual:** New Creation—"Therefore, if any one is in Christ, he is a new creation (creature)" (2 Cor. 5:17). **Lord's Relationship:** Life—"When Christ who is our life appears, then you also will appear with him in glory" (Col. 3:4).

What can the new creation be but the new spiritual man who is born in us at the new birth? What does this make us but a part of Christ's body? What does this mean but that we are the Church? But more of this when we look at the next, and final, organic term.

**5. Corporate:** Body of Christ, and **Individual:** Members—"Now you are the body of Christ and individually members of it" (1 Cor. 12:27). **Lord's Relationship:** Head—"We are to grow up in every way into him who is the head, into Christ, from whom the whole body ... makes bodily growth and upbuilds itself in love" (Eph. 4:15–16).

This is the most dynamic and vital of all the organic terms. The body, with its members, pulses with life, with sensitivity to its respective parts, and with purposeful objective. One can see the relationship between the body and the new creation and between the body and the new man. We have already noted the connection between that new man and the new olive tree whose branches also touch the branches of the vine. But the body also allows us to see the clearest connection between the whole (the body) and its parts (its members). And we also have the clear advantage that in unambiguous terms the Scriptures tell us that the body is the Church. We read in the Colossians epistle that Christ "is the head of the body, the church" (1:18).

**Family/Intimate Terms**

**1. Corporate:** Friends and **Individual (inferred):** Friend—"I have called you friends, for all that I have heard from my Father I have made known to you" (John 15:15). **Lord's Relationship:** Sacrificing Man—"Greater love has no man than this, that a man lay down his life for his friends" (John 15:13).

Immediately after Jesus made known to His friends all that He had heard from His Father, He tells them, "You did not choose me, but I chose you" (v. 16). We noted before, in the treatment under the vine and branches figure, that the "chosen" or "elect" = the Church. Since these disciples were "chosen" by the Lord in the same manner, they are the elect, and the elect are the Church. Thus the "friends" are also the Church.

**2. Corporate:** Race, Nation and People—"But you are a chosen race, a royal priesthood, a holy nation, God's own people" (1 Pet. 2:9). **Individual:** Son and Daughter—"and I will be their God, and they shall be my people ... my sons and daughters" (2 Cor. 6:16–18). **Lord's Relationship:** God— (same verse).

Some might wish to divide race, nation, and people, but it would seem that the terms Peter uses in 2:9 are in apposition, or are variations on the same idea. When he says, "But you are a chosen race, a royal priesthood, a holy nation, God's own people," it is not difficult to assume that race = nation = people, although one might find delicate shadings among them. The word that stands out from the rest is the word priesthood, and, therefore, it has been treated separately, but Peter is likely saying, even here, for the entire group of believers: "You form a distinct race and nation and people, and the whole lot of you are royal priests."

There are two clear indications in the New Testament that the "people" of God are the Church (by extension, the chosen race and the holy nation would also be the Church). No one would doubt for a moment that the Gentile churches founded by Paul and Barnabas on their first missionary tour belonged to the Church universal. At the council in Jerusalem, James says that God had "visited the Gentiles to take out of them a people for his name" (Acts 15:13–18). This came in fulfillment of a prophecy he quotes from Amos 9:11–12. The Gentile believers are called God's people and they belong to the Church, which makes His people the Church.

There is a further verification of this in Titus 2:13–14. In the celebrated 13th verse, Paul states that we are awaiting our blessed hope—the appearing of Christ. In the very next verse he says, "who gave himself for us to redeem us from all iniquity and to purify for himself a people of his own." It is, therefore, His people who are awaiting His appearing—the blessed hope. The Church is to be taken in that rapturous hope. The people of God, then, are the Church.

**3. Corporate:** Children—"But to all who received him, who believed in his name, he gave power to become children of God" (John 1:12). **Individual:** Son and Daughter—"and I will be a father to you, and you shall be my sons and daughters, says the Lord Almighty" (2 Cor. 6:18). **Lord's Relationship:** Father—"your Father knows what you need before you ask him" (Matt. 6:9).

The concept of the family of God is used widely throughout the New Testament, together with the idea of the spiritual, or new birth as the entrance into that family. From 2 Corinthians 6:18, which speaks of the spiritual offspring of God being his "sons and daughters," we know that the ubiquitous phrase "sons" of God is a generic term and can just as readily be rendered "children" of God. Indeed, the King James Version, in passages that refer to the "sons of God," has justifiably made widespread use of "children" to translate the Greek word uioi, which literally means "sons."

It has been the prime directive of the Church to bring lost mankind into this family. It is rather like the game of Red Rover, in which we call for an individual to "come over," and once he is captured, he becomes part of our (to him) new family and then he, in turn, helps us capture yet others. According to John 1:12, spiritual birth makes us children of God. Children are the core, or most vital part, of a household, and Paul compares this physical household to the household of God, which he calls the Church. He tells Timothy that a bishop "must manage his own household well, keeping his children submissive and respectful in every way; for if a man does not know how to manage his own household, how can he care for God's church?" (1 Tim. 3:4–5). This means that the Church = the spiritual children of God.

**4. Corporate:** (Brethren) Brothers—"But he said to them, 'My mother and my brothers are those who hear the word of God and do it' " (Luke 8:21). **Individual:** Brother—"Perhaps this is why he was parted from you for a while, that you might have him back forever, no longer as a slave but more than a slave, as a beloved brother" (Philemon 15–16). **Lord's Relationship:** Only Begotten Son—"God ... gave his only Son"/"And because you are sons, God has sent the Spirit of His Son into our hearts, crying, 'Abba! Father!' "/"For it was fitting that he, for whom and by whom all things exist, in bringing many sons to glory, should make the pioneer of their salvation perfect through suffering. For he who sanctifies and those who are sanctified have all one origin. That is why he is not ashamed to call them brethren" (John 3:16; Gal. 4:6; Heb. 2:10–11).

"Brethren," of course, is simply the sibling relationship that exists between the members of the family of God that we have just discussed. It means "brothers and sisters." Although the term is also used of the members of a physical family, and of the members of a nation (especially Israel), its use for the spiritual family of God in Scripture is usually very clearly distinguished from the other normal usages. In Acts

1:15, "Peter stood up among the brethren" to discuss the vacant apostolic ministry created by the defection and suicide of Judas. Immediately following the solving of this problem, the text states that "When the day of Pentecost had come, they were all together in one place" (2:1). That is, the same "brethren" were still together on Pentecost when the Spirit came upon them and gave birth to the Church. Then they, the "brethren," were the Church.

**5. Corporate:** Bride—"He who has the bride is the bridegroom"/"Let us rejoice and exult and give him the glory, for the marriage of the Lamb has come, and his Bride has made herself ready"/"And I saw the holy city, new Jerusalem, coming down out of heaven from God, prepared as a bride adorned for her husband" and "Then came one of the seven angels who had the seven bowls full of the seven last plagues, and spoke to me, saying, 'Come, I will show you the Bride, the wife of the Lamb'" (John 3:29; Rev. 19:7; 21:2, 9).
**Individual:** Wedding Guest and Wise (Virgins) Bridal Maidens—"And Jesus said to them, 'Can the wedding guests fast while the bridegroom is with them?'"/"Then the kingdom of heaven shall be compared to ten maidens who took their lamps and went to meet the bridegroom. Five of them were foolish, and five were wise" (Mark 2:19; Matt. 25:1–2).
**Lord's Relationship:** Bridegroom and Lamb—"He who has the bride is the bridegroom" and "Let us rejoice and exult and give him the glory, for the marriage of the Lamb has come, and his Bride has made herself ready" (John 3:29; Rev.19:7).

John the Baptist confessed, "I am not the Christ, but I have been sent before him" (John 3:28). Then he told his disciples, "He who has the bride is the bridegroom; the friend of the bridegroom who stands and hears him, rejoices greatly at the bridegroom's voice; therefore this joy of mine is now full" (John 3:29). It is obvious that John considered himself to be the friend of the bridegroom. Who, then, is the bride? According to this passage, the bridegroom has the bride. The bridegroom is identified as Christ. Whom does Christ have in such a relationship if not the Church?

Christ Himself, in answering the question about why His disciples did not fast though John's disciples did, obviously referred to Himself as the bridegroom in Matthew 9:15 (and the parallel passages in Mark 2:19–20 and Luke 5:34–35). But His disciples at that point are called groomsmen (literally "sons of the bridechamber") or more likely, and simply, "wedding guests." Obviously the bride, consisting of all the wedding guests, has yet to be prepared. It is necessary in a collective figure, like that of the Bride to find some way of seeing individual involvement and responsibility as well. For this we may not dismember the Bride and must, therefore, resort to another figure. Here it is the wedding guests. The same figure of wedding guests is used in Matthew 22:1–14, where individual involvement and responsibility are treated in the form of invitation and response and where the proper wedding garment is stressed to show qualification for the individual. The same qualification is shown for the Bride when that is used as a collective or corporate term for the Church. The Bride must be pure and have a gown of righteousness.

In Matthew 25:1–13 we see again these same themes of individual involvement and responsibility when the five wise virgins are prepared and ready for the coming of the Bridegroom. Although the virgins were attendants upon the bride, she is not in view. When the responsibility and faithfulness of the virgins is established, the Bridegroom is announced. When he comes, they go "with him to the marriage feast." No attendants are mentioned with him. The five individual wise virgins now become the corporate Bride, for at this point the individual believers have become the corporate Bride and go into the marriage feast with the Bridegroom.

Such a combination of the individual and the corporate suggested here is not unique to this passage. In 2 Corinthians 11:2, Paul says, "I feel a divine jealousy for you, for I betrothed you (plural, showing the believers as a collection of individuals) to Christ to present you (plural again) as a pure bride (singular—the corporate Church) to her (singular) one husband." Thus, both the individual and corporate relationships are seen in the one passage. This same double usage is found in Revelation 19:7–9. Verse 7 states that the Lamb's "Bride (singular, corporate) has made herself ready." But verse 8 states that her "fine linen is the righteous deeds of the saints" (plural—of the individual saints seen collectively). This is further emphasized in verse 9 where the angel states, "Blessed are those who (plural—showing the individual believers collectively) are invited to the marriage supper of the Lamb." The most extensive treatment of the Bride relationship to Christ is found in Ephesians 5:22–33, even though the term Bride does not occur. But Church and Body and Bride (wife) are all synonymous here. We are told that "Christ is the head of the church, his body" (v. 23). Paul also says that Christ had sanctified the church "that he might present the church to himself in splendor, without spot or wrinkle or any such thing, that she might be holy and without blemish" (v. 27). Even though Paul does not use the term here, so obviously is the picture that of the Bride that the first comment of nearly all major church word studies and commentators is "as a bride." Paul himself concludes this treatment by repeating a quotation: " 'For this reason a man shall leave his father and mother and be joined to his wife, and the two shall become one flesh.' This mystery is a profound one, and I am saying that it refers to Christ and the church" (vv. 31–32). That is to say, this extended picture of the relationship between man and wife (Bridegroom and Bride) is really a picture of Christ and the Church. The Bride is the Church.

> *O Church of Christ!*
> *How fair your faces;*
> *how bountiful your graces!*

# 3

## THE CHURCH AND THE TRIBULATION

*Passion*

*O Christ! You've fixed your piercing gaze on me*
*And asked, "Will you a cup of suff'ring drain?"*
*Dear Jesus, can I truly worthy be?*
*O, Lord! To live is YOU, to die is gain!*

In the previous chapter, we looked at the theme of the Church. We saw what the Church is and we looked at the variety of terms used in the New Testament that are synonymous to the Church or are the equivalents of the Church. When, therefore, we come across the term "the flock" or "saints," we know that the writer is saying church by using different terms.

But there is a further distinction to consider. The Greek term εκκλησια, from which we get our word church, is used in three different ways in the New Testament. First, it is used as an "assembly" of a civic nature (Acts 19:32, 39, 41), or of a religious nature, in reference to Israel in their Old Testament assembling: "the congregation in the wilderness" (Acts 7:38). Of approximately eighty occurrences of the word in the New Testament, the use of "assembly" or "congregation" in this sense is found no more than about five times.

A second use of the term is the gathering of a group of believers in a local "church." Many of these were small house churches and some were large groups, such as the church at Jerusalem or the church at Antioch. Many things written to or about such groups concerned only that group (for example, greetings given to the church in someone's house). Around fifty of the remaining approximately seventy-five occurrences are of this nature.

A third usage (approximately twenty-five occurrences) involves clear references to the Church universal. That is the totality of true believers worldwide. There are very few passages where we might wonder whether a local church is being considered or whether we are dealing with the entire Church of Christ. But there are as many as twenty-four instances where we are clearly dealing with the Church (universal) rather than with a church (local).

A question that has been a concern to many Christians, and one that has serious consequences relating to the lives and goals of Christians, is whether or not genuine Christians as we now know them (that is, the Church), will go through the tribulation.

By the very term itself, it is obvious that posttribulationists believe that the Church will meet the Lord at the end of the tribulation. On the other hand, pretribulationists feel that the Lord will catch up His own before the tribulation begins. One argument used by pretribulationists is that in the passages dealing directly with the tribulation period (primarily Matthew 24, Mark 13, and Revelation 6–18) the word church is never used, and that the burden of proof thus rests upon posttribulationists to show that the Church is there.

If the cause were not so serious as it relates to the relationship of the Church to the tribulation, we could simply dismiss such reasoning as specious logic and let it go at that. But because it is so serious and because the argument has been used so often by the pretribulation camp, a response will be used that should satisfy many seeking minds that have not yet looked beneath the surface of such an argument.

The temptation presents itself that we should answer in kind to such reasoning. We could say, that there is not a single instance in all of Scripture where the word church (a body of saints) is ever used in a passage dealing with the rapture. The two New Testament passages that deal with the transformation and rapture do not mention the Church in their treatment (1 Cor. 15:51–52; 1 Thess. 4:13–18). The Corinthians passage speaks of the raising of the dead and the changing of the living. The Thessalonians passage says that the dead in Christ will rise and that those remaining alive shall be caught up together with them. But nowhere does the word church appear. We all accept the fact, however (because of Paul's use of the term "my beloved brethren" in 1 Corinthians 15:58, and the use of the term "the dead in Christ" in 1 Thessalonians 4:16), that the "living" and "those remaining alive" refer to living saints in the Church and that "the dead" refers to those saints in the Church who have died before the rapture.

The Church as the universal body of Christ is only mentioned clearly about twenty-three times in the New Testament. Three of these times are when Paul mentions his persecution of the Church. Besides Matthew 16:18 (the building of Christ's Church), almost all the other references are to one's attitude either within or toward that Church, with the exception of what is said in Ephesians and Colossians. It is in these two letters (especially in Ephesians) that we are given doctrine about the Church. Colossians tells of the Church as Christ's body (1:18, 24). Ephesians tells us that Christ is made "the head over all things for the church," and "that through the church the manifold wisdom of God" is made known (1:22; 3:10). Ephesians also states that "glory in the church and in Christ Jesus to all generations" are to be given to God (3:21). We also have the extended and significant passage on the relationship between Christ and His Church stated first as His headship over her, and then fully developed as the relationship between husband and wife (5:23–32; specifically 23–25, 27, 29 and 32).

Much is said elsewhere in the New Testament about the Church by using other terms rather than "the Church" as we saw in the previous chapter. The "Church," by that name, is mentioned in Matthew, but not in Mark, Luke, or John. It does not occur in the first fifteen chapters of Romans. It is not found in 2 Timothy or Titus (where we are told of the "Blessed Hope"). Is this, therefore, not for "the Church" because those words do not occur there? It is absent from 2 Peter, 1 and 2 John, and Jude. Do we say, then, that the promises and glories there do not refer to us or belong to us because the term church does not occur there? Of course not, for equivalent terms are used that are synonymous with the term church. These terms are used in each of these books, and throughout the New Testament.

The pretribulationists believe that the Church is prominently mentioned in the book of Revelation in chapters 1–3 and then not again until chapter 22. They claim that the absence of the word church in the tribulation period of chapters 6–18 shows, by silence, that the Church is not there.

But the Church (the universal Church) is not mentioned anywhere in Revelation—not even in the first three chapters. Seven churches in Asia Minor are mentioned by name and they were not even the most important churches of the day mentioned elsewhere in the New Testament. Thyatira is mentioned once in Acts 16:14 only as the city of Lydia's origin (but not in reference to any church there). Only two of the seven are mentioned elsewhere in the New Testament in relation to the churches in those cities. The saints of Laodicea and the church in Laodicea are mentioned in the letter to the Colossians (2:1; 4:13, 15–16). Ephesus and its church not only have a letter written to them, but they are also mentioned often both in Acts and in other letters.

Aside from these two, none of the other churches are even mentioned in passing. None of the other, more celebrated, churches of the New Testament even appear by name in Revelation. Aside from Ephesus, we see none of these other churches mentioned in Acts and/or as the ones to whom epistles were written. Even more amazing is the glaring absence of the mother church of Jerusalem and the super church at Antioch. As we consider those churches that were addressed in Revelation, we are nearly forced to conclude that they were chosen simply as object lessons for the saints of all ages because of their peculiar strengths and weaknesses. It is not at all amazing, therefore, that once the object lessons have been given, these individual churches should not be mentioned again in the book, with the exception of the reminder in 22:16 that this testimony has been "for the churches."

If these churches were chosen as object lessons for the churches of that day and for the churches down through the ages (because of their strengths and weaknesses), and if they are profitable for us today, and if we are on the threshold of the tribulation, we can expect to see the same phenomenon during that period—various tribulation churches manifesting characteristics that were found in each of the historic churches of Revelation 2 and 3. Thus, it will not be surprising to find heresy in some and sound doctrine in others; immorality in some and lukewarmness and even apostasy in others; tribulation and poverty in some and the keeping, protecting power of the Lord in others.

In light of what the Church is, as shown in the previous chapter, and considering the terms that are synonymous with the term church, let us consider the identity of those who believe during the tribulation. For the most part, we will look at Revelation 6–18 and Matthew 24 (its treatment is more extensive than the Mark 13 account). We will view three different levels of identification: those terms that give impressive indications, through implication, that we are dealing with the Church; those strong terms that are convincing as equivalent terms for the Church; and finally, those terms that are overpowering in their language and logic as they cry out to us: "Here is the Church!"

### TERMS OF SOLID IMPLICATION

A. They are before the throne of God. "Therefore are they before the throne of God." (Rev. 7:15). The identification of these people is that of a "great multitude ... from every nation, from all tribes and peoples and tongues.... who have come out of the great tribulation; they have washed their robes and made them white in the blood of the Lamb" (7:9, 14). They are blood-washed believers from the great tribulation. We will refer to them again in the use of three other terms yet to come, but here it is said that they are "before the throne of God." In the New Testament there are three significant relationships for those who are before the throne of the Lord.

One is that of people who are being judged. Matthew 25:31–46 describes those who will be gathered for judgment in front of a royal throne (that of the Son) after the coming of Christ to earth, to receive either reward or condemnation. There is nothing in our passage that would even remotely suggest this relationship.

A second is that of beings who praise and worship God on His throne, as is the case in Revelation 4. These beings are the four living creatures and the twenty-four elders. No one knows who the four living creatures are and to equate them with the group in chapter 7 would be mere speculation at best. The twenty-four elders may represent both Jewish and Gentile believers, but it would seem doubtful that they are the group in chapter 7 since the tribulation is yet to begin, and the group in chapter 7 came from the tribulation.

A third would be that of people who belong to the kingdom of the one who is upon His throne and who assist Him in His reign. There are good reasons for identifying this group as such. First, we are told that "he who sits upon the throne will shelter them with his presence" (7:15). This is the language of a king caring for his own in his kingdom. Also it is known that these people have come out of the tribulation. John says, "Then I saw thrones, and seated on them were those to whom judgment was committed. Also I saw the souls of those who had been beheaded for their testimony to Jesus and for the word of God, and who had not worshipped the beast or its image and had not received its mark on their foreheads or their hands. They came to life, and reigned with Christ a thousand years" (20:4).

This kingdom feature is a distinguishing mark of the churches addressed in the first chapter: "John to the seven churches that are in Asia ... To him who loves us and has ... made us a kingdom ... be glory and dominion for ever and ever" (1:4–6). John takes up the same description in chapter 5, where the four creatures and twenty four elders sing: "Worthy art thou to take the scroll and to open its seals, for thou wast slain and by thy blood didst ransom men for God from every tribe and tongue and people and nation, and hast made them a kingdom ... and they shall reign on earth" (vv.

9–10). What is especially noteworthy about this last section is that it gives us the same description of this kingdom group as is given of the group in 7:9–15, where they are before the throne of God, namely, that they come from every people group—every tribe, tongue, people, and nation. Furthermore, when God made them a kingdom, He made them to be the kingdom of God. One cannot see that kingdom or be that kingdom without the new birth. They are a kingdom, and that kingdom is the kingdom of God, and the kingdom of God is the Church.

B. They serve God in His temple. "They ... serve him day and night within his temple" (Rev. 7:15). This is, of course, the same group we just saw under the first term: they are believers from all people groups, and they have come out of the great tribulation. The identification of those who "serve ... within his temple" is obvious. The word (λατρευω) translated "serve" means specifically "the carrying out of religious duties." They are priests. Two of the features of the kingdom that we just viewed are also features of the priesthood. First, this priesthood feature is a distinguishing mark of the churches addressed in 1:4–6: "John to the seven churches that are in Asia ... To him who loves us and has ... made us ... priests to his God and Father, to him be glory and dominion for ever and ever." John in this instance, as in the case of the kingdom, takes up the same description in 5:9–10 where the four creatures and twenty four elders sing: "Worthy art thou to take the scroll and to open its seals, for thou wast slain and by thy blood didst ransom men for God from every tribe and tongue and people and nation, and hast made them ... priests to our God."

We can carry the comparison of identification forward one more step, as we did with the kingdom group. It is especially noteworthy about this last section (5:9–10) that it gives us the same description of this priesthood group as is given of the group in 7:9–15 where they "serve ... within his temple," namely, that they come from every people group—every tribe, tongue, people, and nation. That the kingdom and priesthood group of 5:9–10, who come from every people group and the believers of 7:15, who are before the throne and serving in the temple and also come from every people group are two separate groups is nearly unthinkable. And the 5:9–10 group bears the same distinguishing marks of the Church group in 1:4–6. What can we say but that we are viewing the Church in 7:15, and, furthermore, "these are they who have come out of the great tribulation." This is the Church and they have been in the tribulation.

Finally, we saw in the chapter on the Church that Peter calls believers the royal priesthood and makes them equal to God's people (1 Pet. 2:9). And in the Jerusalem council described in Acts 15, James says that the Gentile branch of the Church is a people for God's name. The Church equals the people of God and the people of God equals the priesthood. Therefore, the priesthood is the Church.

C. They are called blessed if they keep awake. The believer is called blessed if "he is awake," since the Lord is "coming like a thief" (Rev. 16:15). This is the same language that is used for the church in Thessalonica (1 Thess. 5:1–11). They are told there that "the day of the Lord will come like a thief in the night" and they are told to "keep awake." They were obviously being told in this passage to be awake for something that they would see, since it is illogical to be awake for something that will first begin after you have left the scene. And yet in the Revelation 16:15 passage the believers are being alerted also to be "awake" in the light of the Lord's "coming like a thief." That is, the time is after the sixth bowl at the end of the tribulation and the Church is still there, and they are still being encouraged to be awake.

## STRONG TERMS THAT ARE THE EQUIVALENT OF THE CHURCH

### They are conquerors

"The accuser of our brethren has been thrown down, who accuses them day and night before our God. And they have conquered him by the blood of the Lamb and by the word of their testimony, for they loved not their lives even unto death" and "I saw what appeared to be a sea of glass mingled with fire, and those who had conquered the beast and its image and the number of its name, standing beside the sea of glass with harps of God in their hands" (Rev. 12:10–11; 15:2).

As we discovered in the chapter on the Church, the conqueror is a special breed who reflects the victory of his conquering leader, the King of kings and Lord of lords. But he also receives the privileges of the Church according to the promises given by the Lord to "him who conquers" in each of the seven churches. In each instance, the formula "to him who conquers" or "he who conquers" is used, and then the Church blessing is pronounced.

Furthermore, the Lord says "to the thirsty I will give from the fountain of the water of life without payment. He who conquers shall have this heritage, and I will be his God and he shall be my son" (Rev. 21:6–7). Two things are said of the conqueror here. First, he will have the water of life. In his Gospel, John quotes Jesus telling the Samaritan woman, "whoever drinks of the water that I shall give him will never thirst; the water that I shall give him will become in him a spring of water welling up to eternal life" (John 4:14). In other words, the Lord gives eternal life to the conqueror. Those with eternal life enter the Church. On this basis, the conquerors are the Church. In addition, God says that He will be the God of the conqueror and the conqueror shall be his son (Rev. 21:7). It was seen clearly in the Church chapter that the children of God were the core of the household of God and that God's spiritual household is the Church. On this score also, the conqueror equals the sons (children) of God, which in turn equals the Church.

**They are fellow servants**

"Then they were each given a white robe and told to rest a little longer, until the number of their fellow servants ... should be complete, who were to be killed as they themselves had been" (Rev. 6:11).

Throughout the New Testament, when the term servant is not used for literal bond slaves to earthly masters, or to an angel as a fellow servant with the Church (Rev. 19:9–10 and 22:8–9), it refers to believers who are in the Church. In Romans 6:22, in ending a well-developed theme of servanthood, Paul states, "But now that you have been set free from sin and have become slaves [servants] of God, the return you get is sanctification and its end, eternal life." I am sure we would all agree that those who are sanctified and those who have eternal life are in the Church. In like manner, Revelation opens with the words, "The revelation of Jesus Christ, which God gave him to show to his servants what must soon take place; and he made it known by sending his angel to his servant John" (1:1). In both cases "his servants" and "his servant John" are those who are in the Church of Christ.

Likewise, in the last chapter of the book there are two references to God's servants: "There shall no more be anything accursed, but the throne of God and of the Lamb shall be in it, and his servants shall worship him" (22:3); and "These words are trustworthy and true. And the Lord, the God of the spirits of the prophets, has sent his angel to show his servants what must soon take place" (22:6). In both instances the "servants" are clearly those who belong to the Church.

There is, then, no ground or reason for making the fellow servants of 6:11, who were yet to be killed in the tribulation, anything but the Church of Christ. When in the other passages it means the Church, in all fairness it must also be the Church in this passage.

**They are brethren**

"Then they were each given a white robe and told to rest a little longer, until the number of their ... brethren should be complete, who were to be killed as they themselves had been" and "I heard a loud voice in heaven, saying, 'Now the salvation and the power and the kingdom of our God and the authority of his Christ have come, for the accuser of our brethren has been thrown down, who accuses them day and night before our God. And they have conquered him by the blood of the Lamb and by the word of their testimony, for they loved not their lives even unto death' " (Rev. 6:11; 12:10–11).

As we saw in the previous chapter, this term is used for ordinary family relationships as well as for national relationships, especially regarding the nation Israel. These usages are almost always crystal clear in the setting in which they are used. In all other instances, the term refers to children of God in His spiritual family and it speaks of their sibling relationship to one another. We also saw that it was the "brethren" in Acts 1 and 2 who had gathered to fill the office Judas had vacated, and upon whom the Spirit came to forge them into the Church.

When John uses the term in his writings, with the exception of John 7 (where the physical half-brothers of Jesus are in view), he always uses it to mean fellow believers in Christ—members of His Church. Even in the other selections in Revelation this is the case. When John falls at the feet of an angel, the angel tells him that he must not do that since he, the angel, is a fellow servant with John and John's "brethren" (19:10; 22:8–9). I can find no writer who doubts that John's "brethren" are part of Christ's Church. In the other reference, John passes on his vision to the Church with the words: "I John, your brother, who share with you in Jesus the tribulation and the kingdom and the patient endurance" (1:9). Why is it, then, when we find the "brethren" suffering in the tribulation in 6:10 and 12:10–11, some want to make them something other than the Church? It is all the more baffling that they are not "allowed" to be the Church when there are other similar features they share with the "brethren" of 19:10, who are accepted by all as members of the Church. It is said that these brethren "hold the testimony of Jesus." A strikingly similar thing is said of the brethren in 12:10. They have conquered their accuser "by the blood of the Lamb" (Jesus) "and by the word of their testimony." In addition, they are called those who "have conquered." We saw under the treatment of the conquerors that they are those who have indisputable characteristics of the Church—they are given the water of life and God is their God and they are His children (21:6–7). The Church consists of the brethren.

### They are believers

"When he opened the fifth seal, I saw under the altar the souls of those who had been slain for the word of God and for the witness they had borne." / "Then the dragon was angry with the woman, and went off to make war on the rest of her offspring, on those who keep the commandments of God and bear testimony to Jesus." / "Here is a call for the endurance of the saints, those who keep the commandments of God and the faith of Jesus" (Rev. 6:9; 12:17; and 14:12).

We looked at "believers" as an equivalent of the Church in the chapter on the Church. We saw "all who believed" as a description of the newly born Church of God in Acts 2:44. But if there is a verse that serves as a formula for entrance into the Church (and multitudes of evangelicals have rightly used it as such) it is Romans 10:9: "If you confess with your lips that Jesus is Lord and believe in your heart that God raised him from the dead, you will be saved." It is a two-part formula: witness or confession, on the one hand, and faith or belief on the other. We see witness in the tribulation believers in "the witness they had borne" and in the fact that they "bear testimony to Jesus." We see faith or belief in "those who keep ... the faith of Jesus." We are saved by faith, and by it we enter the new life and the Church.

## USE OF OVERPOWERING TERMS
### (OR LANGUAGE THAT CRIES OUT, "HERE IS THE CHURCH")

**They are the Elect**

"For false Christs and false prophets will arise and show great signs and wonders, so as to lead astray, if possible, even the elect." / "And he will send out his angels with a loud trumpet call, and they will gather his elect from the four winds, from one end of heaven to the other" (Matt. 24:24, 31).

There are compelling reasons why the term elect here refers to the Church. As we search the rest of the New Testament, we can find few passages where the term refers to anything except the Church. When it does not refer to the Church, it leaves no doubt as to what is being referred to. In 1 Timothy 5:21, Paul speaks of the "elect angels" (probably to distinguish them from the fallen angels). The designation, however, is clearly to the angels and is clearly thus stated.

The term is also used elsewhere to refer to Christ Himself, as in the crucifixion scene where He is called God's "Chosen One" (Luke 23:35), or as in the cornerstone, which is "chosen [elect] and precious" 1 Pet. 2:6). Then we have it in adjective form referring to the "elect lady" (2 John 1) or the "elect sister" (2 John 13). Elsewhere in the New Testament, however, wherever it is used alone as a noun, it clearly refers to believers who belong to the Church. There must be a clear reason, therefore, to make it mean anything other than the Church in Matthew 24. Certainly it neatly fits the posttribulation position for it to mean the Church—both in verse 22 as well as in verse 31. But some pretribulationists take the word elect to refer to Israel as an elect nation.

Certainly Israel is not mentioned by name in the passage (as the angels are in the 1 Timothy passage). And we can find no New Testament passage where Israel is referred to as the elect, either by name or implication. Therefore, there must be a strong reason for departing from the accepted usage as it occurs in the rest of the New Testament. Those who approach the passage from a pretribulation position have their reason—it does not fit their prophetic pattern to have the Church in the tribulation. Therefore, the term must not mean the Church and must mean something else. If, however, it means the Church in the rest of the New Testament, it would seem that the burden of proof that it means something else here rests with those with a different point of view. Furthermore, a study of the passage itself would cause us to retain that usual usage rather than turn us toward a new and different meaning.

Though Israel is not specifically named, some still think they see Israel in the passage. There are possible references to Israel in verses 16–19 with such terms as "those who are in Judea ... him who is on the housetop ... him who is in the field ... those who are with child," but the overall context is to believers. In fact, it could even be saying "those believers who." Besides those few third-person references mentioned, most of the passage addresses His followers directly in the second person": when you see ... Pray that your flight may not be in winter ... if any one says to you ... Lo, I have told you beforehand ... if they say to you ... do not believe it." This alone should indicate that the "elect" refers to believers in Christ, as it does nearly exclusively in the rest of the New Testament. When we add verse 9, however, which begins this particular section, it becomes overwhelming: "Then they will deliver you up to tribulation, and put you to death; and you will be hated by all nations for my name's sake," that is, not because you are Israel, but because you are Christians. This personal application continues to the beginning of the next paragraph where He says: "So when you see the desolating sacrilege ... then let those who are in Judea flee" (v. 15). This may, indeed, make even the third-person references apply to believers as suggested earlier.

In that triumphant Ode to Victory in Romans 8:31–39, Paul asks the question "Who shall bring any charge against God's elect?" and then resolves the question by informing us that we have a God who justifies us, meaning that no such charge, therefore, could ever stand against us. As in so many other passages in the first fifteen chapters of Romans, he speaks here of the Church without naming it. Certainly the ones for whom God did not spare His Son; the ones whom God justified; the ones for whom Christ died and was raised up; the ones for whom He intercedes; the ones that nothing shall separate from the love of Christ; and the ones who are conquerors are surely those who belong to the Church of Christ. Interestingly, the very first thing mentioned of all the endured hardships that come to the Church, but will not separate it from Christ's love, is tribulation.

Titus 1:1–2 and 1 Peter 1:2 speak of those things relative to the elect that are the marks of union with the Church: knowledge of God, godliness, eternal life, being destined by God, sanctification by the Spirit, obedience to Jesus Christ, and sprinkling with His blood.

But the equation that says, "the elect equals the Church" is found in the hymn to the Pre-eminent Christ—the letter to the Colossians. Paul makes one of his charges, "Put on then, as God's chosen ones (elect), holy and beloved, compassion ... patience" (3:12). Still addressing the elect, he says, "above all these put on love, which binds everything together in perfect harmony" (v. 14), and then adds, "And let the peace of Christ rule in your hearts, to which indeed you were called in the one body" (v. 15). Therefore, in Paul's terms the elect were the body of Christ. To complete the equation we need only look at 1:18 where Paul states, "He is the head of the body, the church."

Thus, we can conclude: "The elect are the body of Christ. The body of Christ is the Church. Therefore, the elect are the Church."

**They are God's people**

"Then I heard another voice from heaven saying, 'Come out of her, my people'" (Rev. 18:4).

One of the most revealing studies in the New Testament concerning God's relationship to man is that of God and His people. It is clear that in the Old Testament God had a chosen people—the people of Israel. The Gentiles were outsiders, beginning with God's choice of Abraham in Genesis 12:1–3. God would make a great nation out of him and would bless those who blessed him and curse those who cursed him. This accords with the New Testament statement that Gentiles "were at that time separated from Christ, alienated from the commonwealth of Israel, and strangers to the covenants of promise, having no hope and without God in the world" (Eph. 2:12).

But even in the choice of Abraham, immediately after the notification for the benefit of the Gentiles that those who blessed Abraham (Israel-to-be) would be blessed and those who cursed him would be cursed, a curious note was added— that by Abraham "all the families of the earth shall bless themselves." There grew within Israel a fierce pride in being different from the nations, in being God's chosen people. But here and there God was saying that a change was blowing in the wind.

Sometimes He stated this subtly: "The people who walked in darkness have seen a great light; those who dwelt in a land of deep darkness, on them has light shined" (Isa. 9:2). And sometimes He said it more clearly: "All the nations thou hast made shall come and bow down before thee, O Lord, and shall glorify thy name" (Ps. 86:9); and "many nations shall join themselves to the Lord in that day, and shall be my people" (Zech. 2:11). He even stated that there would be a change in His relationship to Israel. No longer would they be His people due to birth in that nation, but they would be His people on the basis of a new covenant written in their hearts: "But this is the covenant which I will make with the house of Israel after those days, says the Lord: I will put my law within them, and I will write it upon their hearts; and I will be their God, and they shall be my people" (Jer. 31:33).

In the New Testament, this gulf, that existed between Jew and Gentile, has been bridged. The promise had been given that all nations would someday bow before the Lord. Israel had always enjoyed favored nation status with God as His chosen, covenant, people, effectively excluding the Gentiles. Then a later provision was made that a new covenant relationship would be entered into, even with Israel. We have seen in Ephesians that when Christ came into the world, the Gentiles "were at that time separated from Christ, alienated from the commonwealth of Israel, and strangers to the covenants of promise, having no hope and without God in the world" (2:12). But Paul tells us that Christ Jesus took these two people who were divided by a wall—a wall of pride on the Jewish side and of envy and resentment on the Gentile side—and in the cross broke down that dividing wall and made these two people into one new unified people ("man") in the place of the two (2:14–16). Then Paul states that this was Christ's mystery—joining believing Gentiles together with believing Israel to make the Church (3:4–6). He adds that it is through this Church that God would reveal his wisdom—even to angelic powers (3:8–10).

Throughout the New Testament, God's people are mentioned. Occasionally, reference is made to the former relationship of God to Israel. But it becomes clear that that is not the same as it used to be. After the Gospel narratives, when God's people are mentioned by God or by His point of view expressed through the New Testament writers, the people of God are seen to be the Church—believing Jews and Gentiles together. A fascinating development of this truth is seen in Paul's letter to the Romans and Peter's first letter, where these two writers quote the prophecies of Hosea: "and in the place where it was said to them, 'You are not my people,' it shall be said to them, 'Sons of the living God' " (Hos. 1:10; cf. Rom. 9:25–26); and "I will say to Not my people, 'You are my people'; and he shall say, 'Thou art my God' " (Hos. 2:23; cf. 1 Pet. 2:9–10). These prophecies were originally given to signify the return of Israel to faith and God's reclaiming them as His people. Paul and Peter, however, through the Spirit, apply this to the Church—believing Israel and believing Gentiles, as a unified body. Thus, even as it had been true that unbelieving Israel had stopped being God's people, but now became His people again through faith, so it was true of the Gentiles who had never been God's people that now, through faith in Christ, they had also become God's people.

This operation is, perhaps, nowhere more clearly developed than in the symbol of the olive tree in Romans 11:17–27, where God takes the unbelieving Jewish branches out of the olive tree and grafts believing Gentiles together with the few believing Jewish branches that remained in the tree, thus creating an entirely different and new kind of tree (the Church). And God will make the final alteration in the tree when Israel believes as a nation and is regrafted into the tree.

In Revelation, there are only two references to God's people. We have already seen the one in 18:4. The other is in 21:2–4, where John "saw the holy city, new Jerusalem, coming down out of heaven from God, prepared as a bride adorned for her husband; and I heard a loud voice from the throne saying, 'Behold, the dwelling of God is with men. He will dwell with them and they shall be his people, and God himself will be with them; he will wipe away every tear from their eyes, and death shall be no more, neither shall there be mourning nor crying nor pain any more, for the former things have passed away.' "

Not only does this equate God's people with the New Jerusalem and the Bride, but it also describes the eternal state of bliss. These are things clearly associated with the Church. If God's people are the Church in chapter 21, then His people are the Church in chapter 18, when He calls them out of Babylon before her destruction. We have previously seen in the former chapter on the Church that James calls the Gentile Church God's people (Acts 15:13–18). (Paul had not yet had the mystery of Ephesians 2 and 3 revealed to him: that the Gentile and Jewish churches would now be one Church.) Furthermore, we also saw that "His people" were waiting for the blessed hope. God's people are clearly the Church.

**They are saints**

Since there are nine separate verses that use the term "saints" in the tribulation section between chapters 6 and 18, we will not quote them all. We will only cite some representative passages: "And another angel came and stood at the altar with a golden censer; and he was given much incense to mingle with the prayers of all the saints upon the golden altar before the throne; and the smoke of the incense rose with the prayers of the saints from the hand of the angel before God" (8:3, 4); "And the beast ... was allowed to make war on the saints and to conquer them" (13:5–7); "Here is a call for the endurance of the saints, those who keep the commandments of God and the faith of Jesus" (14:12); and "For men have shed the blood of saints and prophets" (16:6). (See also Rev. 11:18; 13:10; 17:6; and 18:24.)

There are fifty-eight occurrences of the word saints in the New Testament, one use of the plural possessive saints', and one of the singular saint. Thus, the term actually occurs sixty times in the New Testament. The King James Version wrongly translates two other verses with "saints": Jude 14, where αγιας is used as an adjective, should be rendered holy myriads, rather than "10,000 saints," and Revelation 15:3, where "Kings of saints" should be translated either "King of nations" or more likely, "King of ages." The meaning is always those who believe in Christ, with two possible exceptions. One of these is Matthew 27:52, which records that following the resurrection, "many bodies of the saints who had fallen asleep were raised." Although it could possibly mean believers in Christ, it is not very likely because of the short span of His ministry (three years). Most of His adherents were "followers" or "disciples" at this point and the message of belief for forgiveness and salvation was preached basically post-Pentecost. So it seems unlikely that there would be "many" New Testament believers who could have died in the Jerusalem area by that time. It is thus much more logical to assume that these were Old Testament saints, including (but not restricted to) the followers of John the Baptist.

The other possible exception is found in Ephesians 2:19, where the believers at Ephesus are called "fellow citizens with the saints." This is almost certainly meant to be the Old Testament saints. The context itself would lead us to interpret this as believers, or the just, from the Old Testament. Paul had already clearly stated that these Ephesian (Gentile) believers were formerly "separated from Christ, alienated from the commonwealth of Israel, and strangers to the covenants of promise," but that Christ had "made them both one" (those who now know and believe in Christ were made heirs of the covenants of promise together with the members of the commonwealth of Israel—that is, believing Israel) and that He had created "in himself one new man in the place of the two." Then to these believers he says "you are no longer strangers and sojourners, but you are fellow citizens with the saints and members of the household of God." The Old Testament saints were already citizens of the commonwealth and members of the household of God and these believers in Christ had now joined with them as citizens and as members of that household.

Every other mention of the term saints in the New Testament refers to "a believer in Christ." Indeed the term equals the word brethren, as we see in Philippians, where Paul says, "Greet every saint in Christ Jesus. The brethren who are with me greet you. All the saints greet you" (4:21–22).

As the term "body" is a collective term for believers, and "members" is the distributive (or individual) term for believers in that Body, with Christ as the "Head"; and as "flock" is a common term for believers collectively, and "sheep" is the term for separate believers in that flock, with Christ as the "Shepherd," even so throughout the New Testament, "Church" is the corporate term for believers and "saints" is the term applied to individual believers in the Church with Christ as the "Lord": "and the Lord added to their number day by day those who were being saved" (Acts 2:47), or with

Christ as the "Head": "He is the head of the body, the church" (Col. 1:18).

In 1 Corinthians 1:2 and 2 Corinthians 1:1, Paul makes the terms "church" and "saints" synonymous. In the first passage he addresses "the church of God which is at Corinth ... called to be saints." Actually "to be" is supplied. The literal translation is "the church of God which is at Corinth ... called saints." In The Commentary on the Whole Bible by Jamieson, Fausset and Brown, the literal translation of this passage is "called saints" and these are further identified as "saints by calling": applied by Paul to all professing members of the church." (p.263, col. 1)

The second passage is even more striking, for there Paul not only equates the two, but also uses them in an interchangeable way: the Church is the saints and the saints are the Church: "To the church of God which is at Corinth, with all the saints who are in the whole of Achaia." Thus, when we hear of believers in Christ in Revelation who are called "saints," even though the term "church" is not used, an equivalent or synonymous word is used. (See Rev. 5:8; 8:3, 4; 11:18; 13:7, 10; 14:12; 16:6; 17:6; 18:24; 19:8; and 20:9.) (It is interesting to note that those who deny the New Testament meaning to it in Revelation 6–18, will usually grant it in 5:8, which is before the tribulation, and in 19:8, which refers to "the righteous deeds of the saints" as the pure garment covering the Bride of the Lamb after the tribulation at the marriage supper of the Lamb, while not allowing it in the intervening passages dealing with the tribulation itself.) Likewise, Paul never mentions the Church in Romans 1–15, but uses the synonym "saints" half a dozen times. Also, Titus, who speaks of the "blessed hope," refers twice to the saints, but not at all to the Church.

In Philippians 1:1, Paul addresses "all the saints in Christ Jesus who are at Philippi" rather than "the church at Philippi." In 1 Corinthians 1:1, he writes "to the church of God which is at Corinth" rather than "to the saints of God who are at Corinth." Once again, the terms are used interchangeably. In 1 Corinthians 14:33, Paul speaks of "the churches of the saints," so that the Church consists of the saints and belongs to them as the body members, even as it belongs to Christ as its Head. Indeed, they (the saints) are it (the Church). Whenever we see church it means the saints and whenever we see saints it means the Church. Why should this rule change when we encounter the term in the tribulation?

**They are the Bride**

"'Let us rejoice and exult and give him the glory, for the marriage of the Lamb has come, and his Bride has made herself ready; it was granted her to be clothed with fine linen, bright and pure'—for the fine linen is the righteous deeds of the saints" (Rev. 19:7–8).

One might ask why the Bride is being cited as proof that the Church is in the tribulation, since the tribulation ended with chapter 18 and now we see the Bride, or Church, in chapter 19. But it is only now, at the end of the tribulation, that the Church is clothed in her wedding linen. Now is the saying of Ephesians 5:26–27 come to pass, "that he might sanctify her, having cleansed her by the washing of water with the word, that he might present the church to himself in splendor, without spot or wrinkle or any such thing, that she might be holy and without blemish." The Lord has purged her through the tribulation period. She is clothed in fine linen, which is "the righteous deeds of the saints." What saints? According to the pretribulation position, all mention of the saints in the book of Revelation up to this point has meant non-Church believers during the tribulation. Now, suddenly, it is again allowed to mean Church saints, since it represents the wedding linen of the Bride of Christ.

In the New Testament, as we have seen, saints almost always means believers in Christ. The pretribulation position holds that the saints before the tribulation are raptured with the Church, whereas the saints during the tribulation will be used to people the millennial kingdom. However, 1 Thessalonians 3:13 speaks of "the coming of our Lord Jesus with all the saints." This would include Old Testament saints and all New Testament saints—both before and during the tribulation, and if He is also coming with the tribulation saints when He comes, He must have raptured them before coming.

With the Bride being clothed with the righteous deeds of the saints and with the blood of the persecuted and martyred saints having just been seen in Babylon, eight verses earlier in 18:24, we must conclude that those righteous deeds had to include the deeds of those saints just mentioned from the tribulation. The Bride was in the tribulation and now she appears "holy and without blemish" because she is "clothed with ... the righteous deeds of the saints."

**They are those "who die in the Lord"**

The apostle John states: "And I heard a voice from heaven saying, 'Write this: Blessed are the dead who die in the Lord henceforth.' 'Blessed indeed,' says the Spirit, 'that they may rest from their labors, for their deeds follow them!'" (Rev. 14:13).

The only verse in the New Testament that speaks of the rapture as such (the "catching up" of believers) is 1 Thessalonians 4:17. After saying that at the trumpet of God "the dead in Christ will rise first" (v. 16), Paul continues: "then we who are alive, who are left, shall be caught up together with them in the clouds to meet the Lord in the air." This tells about two groups who will join together in this rapture—believers who had previously died and believers who were still alive at the time of this event.

In the Thessalonian epistle, the Thessalonians are greeted in the first verse as the church of the Thessalonians. They are commended by Paul for following the example of the Judean churches by standing tall for the Lord in spite of persecution from their countrymen (2:14). These are the only two passages where the term church is used. In 4:16–17, where the rapture is described, the word is not used. The pretribulationists apply a certain test to "show" that the Church is not in the tribulation: the fact that the word church does not appear in passages that deal with the tribulation. If we applied the same test to this passage in 4:16–17, we would have to say that the rapture is not for the Church, since the word church does not appear in the passage. This would be nonsense, of course, for an equivalent term does occur. It cannot be the phrase "we who are alive, who are left until the coming of the Lord," for that definition becomes relevant only as it is tied to the expression that is equal to the Church: "the dead in Christ." Then these two groups taken together comprise the Church. We will happily grant the pretribulationists this point. It is solidly logical. We can only hope they will grant the logic of what follows.

There are at least thirty to forty occasions in the New Testament where the expressions "in Christ" and "in the Lord" are used, and they are used interchangeably. A quick example of this can be found in Romans 16 where Paul charges the Romans to whom he writes to receive Phoebe "in the Lord" (16:2), then greets "fellow workers in Christ" (16:3). He mentions Ampliatus as his "beloved in the Lord" (16:8) and Urbanus as a "fellow worker in Christ" (16:9). Then he says that Apelles "is approved in Christ" (16:10) and goes on to greet many by name "in the Lord" (16:11, 12 and 13).

John uses "the Lord" a number of times in the book of Revelation. In the opening of the book, he states that he "was in the Spirit on the Lord's day" (1:10). The meaning most scholars give to this expression "the Lord's day" is the first day of the week. It was Christ's special day, because it commemorated Sunday as the day of His resurrection. Already in the second century, Sunday was officially commemorated as "the Lord's day." So when John uses "Lord" here, he means Christ. Once again he speaks of the bodies of the two witnesses lying "in the street of the great city ... where their Lord was crucified" (11:8). In this instance, he also means Christ when he says "Lord."

Let us return to the Revelation passage we used in the beginning of this section. We read: "Here is a call for the endurance of the saints, those who keep the commandments of God and the faith of Jesus. And I heard a voice from heaven saying, 'Write this: Blessed are the dead who die in the Lord henceforth.' 'Blessed indeed,' says the Spirit, 'that they may rest from their labors, for their deeds follow them!'" (14:12–13). There are saints here continuing to die for "the faith of Jesus." Immediately following this, it says that these "die in the Lord," which means by all we have seen that they die "in Christ." The "dead in Christ" are the very ones who, according to the passage in 1 Thessalonians 4:16–

17 are going to be caught up in the rapture. But here we are near the end of the tribulation and there are still those who are going to be dying "in the Lord" or "in Christ." Since these must be taken up in the rapture, it hasn't yet happened and the Church is in the tribulation.

**They are those "washed … in the blood of the Lamb"**

"He said to me, 'These are they who have come out of the great tribulation; they have washed their robes and made them white in the blood of the Lamb' " (Rev. 7:14).

There are three separate arguments for the identity of this group, and in each case it proves that they are the Church. Any of the three should be convincing, but taken together they are conclusive.

First, the people in this group are distinguished as having "washed their robes and made them white in the blood of the Lamb," but also as having come "from every nation, from all tribes and peoples and tongues." Moreover, this group has been in the great tribulation and then come out of it. Putting the blood-washed aspect together with the idea of being composed of every people group in the world, we find this same description earlier in chapter 5, where the four living creatures and twenty-four elders "sang a new song, saying, 'Worthy art thou to take the scroll and to open its seals, for thou wast slain and by thy blood didst ransom men for God from every tribe and tongue and people and nation' " (5:9).

This group was bought by Christ's blood from every people group. Since the Church has not yet won a segment of every people group for Christ, and since there is such a group in chapter 7, it is logical to assume that the groups are part of each other. This is further corroborated by the fact that both groups are seen as a kingdom and priesthood. In chapter 5 they are "a kingdom and priests to our God," and in chapter 7 they are found "before the throne of God" and they perform religious duties "day and night within his temple."

In addition, the group in chapter 5 must also be the same group that we find in chapter 1, where we are told that Christ "has freed us from our sins by his blood and made us a kingdom, priests to his God and Father" (vv. 4–6). Once again we have the blood as the freeing agent, we are a kingdom, and we are priests. This group, however, is identified as the Church. First, John says that Christ has "freed us from our sins by his blood." John and his readers (the Church) were part of the group. Furthermore, John addressed "the seven churches that are in Asia" with these words. That is, he said that he and the churches belonged to this group.

So, to put it simply, the chapter 7 group is the chapter 5 group and the chapter 5 group is the chapter 1 group, which makes the chapter 7 group the chapter 1 group also. The chapter 1 group is the Church. The chapter 7 group is the redeemed people who were in the tribulation. Therefore, the Church is in the tribulation.

Second, what Christ has done for us by his blood is a vital part of New Testament teaching. His blood cleanses us from all sin (1 John 1:7); "we have redemption through his blood" (Eph. 1:7); and we "were ransomed ... with the precious blood of Christ" (1 Pet. 1:18–19). The word of God is able to cut discerningly between things as closely aligned as spirit and soul or bones and marrow, but we cannot have the license to divide operations of the blood and say that it does one thing for one group and a different thing for another group. In other words, if the believers in the Revelation 7 group have their robes washed white in the blood of the Lamb, they also have been cleansed from all sin, they have redemption and they have been ransomed, and these are clearly the marks of what Christ has done for the Church. If He has done it for these tribulation saints, they belong to the Church.

Finally, Scripture actually tells us directly that the prize that God has gotten with Christ's blood is the Church. When Paul spoke to the Ephesian elders in Acts, he said, "take heed to yourselves and to all the flock, in which the Holy Spirit has made you overseers, to care for the church of God which he obtained with the blood of his own Son" (Acts 20:28). It is no good to try to restructure God's word and to split nonexistent hairs by saying that He did this for the Church with Christ's blood, but that He did another and different thing for the tribulation saints with that same blood. No. What He bought with Christ's blood is the Church. He bought the tribulation saints with Christ's blood. The tribulation saints are in the Church and the Church is in the tribulation.

### They are those who claim the Lamb as their shepherd

"For the Lamb in the midst of the throne will be their shepherd" (Rev. 7:17).

The term used here for "shepherd" is the verbal form ποιμαινω (meaning "to herd, to tend, to pasture, to lead to pasture or to keep sheep"), which comes from the noun form ποιμην (meaning "shepherd"), and which, in turn, produced the forms ποιμνη and ποιμνον (meaning "flock"). The figure of being a shepherd or tending a flock is one used fairly often in depicting the relationship of Christ to the Church or of pastors as undershepherds for the Church.

So clear is the meaning of the verbal form in this verse, that there is a uniformity of agreement in word studies and modern translations. The RSV, NIV, NASV, The Living Bible, Williams, Good News for Modern Man, Concordant Literal and The New King James Version all render it "to be a shepherd" or "to shepherd." Peter was told (by the use of the same word) in John's Gospel, "Shepherd my sheep" (21:16 NASV). Then Peter himself tells his readers to "shepherd (verb form) the flock of God among you" (1 Pet. 5:2 NASV); and then that "when the Chief Shepherd (noun form) appears, you will receive the unfading crown of glory" (1 Pet. 5:4 NASV). This is important because the relationship of the Lamb (Christ) to these saints "who have come out of the great tribulation" is that of a shepherd. He is their Shepherd.

The passage that defines the Shepherd and His flock most precisely is found in John 10:1–18. He calls His followers his sheep and a fold of sheep. His relationship to them is initially that of the door to the sheepfold so that, through Him, they can enter the fold and be part of it. After that, however, He is their Good Shepherd. He is careful to tell them, however, that they are not the only fold in the flock. There are other sheep for Him to bring into their group. Bringing others into this group will create a total flock. Though there is more than one fold, there is but one flock. Anyone He brings in is part of that same flock. Not only is there but one flock, there is also only one Shepherd. If He brings in Samaritans, they are in the flock and He is their Shepherd. If He brings in Gentiles, they are also in the flock and He is their Shepherd. If He brings sheep in before the tribulation, He is their shepherd and they belong to the flock. If He is Shepherd to a group found in the tribulation, they are part of the one flock also. There is only one flock and there is only one Shepherd. The tribulation sheep belong to the same flock the disciples belong to and that we, today, belong to. We are one in Christ.

But it can be shown that the flock is none other than the Church itself. "Be on guard for yourselves and for all the flock, among which the Holy Spirit has made you overseers, to shepherd the church of God which He purchased with His own blood" (Acts 20:28 NASV). It may not come as a surprise that the word "to shepherd" here is the same word that is used in Revelation 7:17, where Christ is the Shepherd of the tribulation saints.

So, Christ is the Shepherd of the tribulation saints. He is the only Shepherd and He shepherds but one flock. The flock is the Church. The tribulation saints are in the flock. The tribulation saints belong to the Church. The Church is in the tribulation.

The argument that the Church is not in the tribulation because the word church is not found in tribulation passages is an argument that should not have to be dignified by an answer were it not for the inroads the claim has made into the rank and file of evangelicalism. On the face of it, it sounds so right. But, in essence, it is no argument. It is a magician sawing a lady in half. The term εκκλησια is a special term found in only two verses of Matthew and in none of the other Gospels. It occurs a number of times in the book of Acts regarding the founding and growth of the Church. It appears occasionally in 1 Corinthians. But even in the great resurrection-transformation chapter (1 Cor. 15) it occurs but once, relating to Paul's former persecution of it (v. 9). Ephesians specifically deals with the Church and its relationship to it head, Christ. Outside of these specialized treatments of the term, there are no more than ten verses in the rest of the New Testament where the term is clearly used of the Church universal, rather than of a local church. We depend on other terms that are synonyms for the Church. We read of believers, followers, disciples, temples, heirs, sons, children, brothers, sheep, body members, and saints to represent the same concept. Indeed at least 80 to 90 percent of the promises of the New Testament are given to us under these figures to mean the Church universal or a local assembly. Thus it is with the tribulation. It is these other terms that are used to mean the Church.

As we have seen, the same reasoning that would exclude the Church from the tribulation (because the word church does not occur in tribulation passages—especially Revelation 6–18) can be used to exclude the Church from the rapture. In none of the passages that are used by pretribulationists as the three principal rapture Scriptures does the word church appear. (See John 14:3; 1 Cor. 15:51–52; and 1 Thess. 4:13–18.) Does this mean that the Church is not to be raptured or is not in the rapture? If the argument of equivalent "church" terms is used, then that same argument can be used to show the Church in the tribulation. In John 14:3, those being addressed are those who believe in God. If that means the Church, then those saints who believe in Christ during the tribulation who "keep the commandments of God and the faith of Jesus" must also be the Church (Rev. 14:12). Paul addresses the "brethren" in 1 Corinthians 15:51–58. If that means the Church, then those tribulation "brethren" who were yet to die and the tribulation "brethren" who were accused by Satan and who conquered him by the blood of the Lamb are also the Church (Rev. 6:11; 12:10–11). In that great rapture passage in 1 Thessalonians 4:13–18, those being addressed are once again called "brethren," but then it speaks of the resurrection of the "dead in Christ." If that means the Church, then those tribulation saints who were henceforth to "die in the Lord" most assuredly are also the Church. Consistency and fairness demand that if it is the Church in the first instance, then it is likewise the Church in the second.

*Teach me, O Lord, the rewards of patience in trial!*

# 4

## TRIBULATION

### Flowers and Mortars

*The petals, whole, exude aroma sweet*
*With pow'r to lift the pilgrim on his trail,*
*To cheer him as he seeks his private grail;*
*To turn the common task to noble feat.*
*It has the pow'r to take a simple treat,*
*And then enhance its joy; transform the pale*
*And give it hue; it visits man in jail*
*And breathes a breeze of hope as it is meet.*

*But place that bloom within the mortar's womb*
*And crush those leaves, and they will win release*
*In distillate perfume whose poignancy exceeds*
*By far mere flowers' scent. Spare us the gloom*
*Of those who beg adversity to cease.*
*Give us the fragrance of the saint who bleeds!*


The tribulation is that seven-year period immediately preceding the return of Christ to earth. It is also known as the 70th week of Daniel. The second half of this period, the last 3½ years, is called the great tribulation. Since practically nothing is known about the first half of the tribulation period, when we speak of the great tribulation, we often simply call it the tribulation.

## THE TRIBULATION PRINCIPLE

Tribulation, in general, is trial or affliction that brings about suffering or distress. In this general sense it is a principle that often is applied to believers as normal or expected, due to our relationship to Jesus Christ. It is our lot in life in the natural progression of things. This was true in the first century, and it is also true today. Jesus forewarned His followers: "in the world you have tribulation" (John 16:33). Paul told some believers (just weeks after he had been stoned and left for dead at Lystra) "that through many tribulations we must enter the kingdom of God" (Acts 14:22). He also reminds young Timothy that serious believers can expect to pay a price for their faith: "all who desire to live a godly life in Christ Jesus will be persecuted" (2 Tim. 3:12).

What Jesus said to the disciples in John 13–17, and, beyond them, to believers in our day is very important. There is a small portion of what was said that applied only to them: "I am going away now, and you are sad," but principles that Jesus added apply to all believers before His return. In fact, the principles He laid down for the disciples apply to the believer today even more so than they did to them. What He outlined was trouble, sorrow, and tribulation followed by joy. He couldn't have told them that they were going through the great tribulation when He knew they weren't, but He could prepare them for the principle of tribulation so that they could be prepared for it and so that future generations could be prepared for it and also so that we could be prepared for the big one, the great tribulation, when it comes. He said, "If they persecuted me, they will persecute you" (15:20); "They will put you out of the synagogues; indeed, the hour is coming when whoever kills you will think he is offering service to God. And they will do this because they have not known the Father, nor me. But I have said these things to you, that when their hour comes you may remember that I told you of them" (16:2–4); "you will weep and lament, but the world will rejoice; you will be sorrowful, but your sorrow will turn into joy" (16:20); and "In the world you have tribulation; but be of good cheer, I have overcome the world" (16:33).

The principles are the norm for the believer and are valid

whether the persecution is small scale tribulation or the great tribulation. That principle is pain, sorrow, and death followed by joy, glory, and victory. It matters little to the individual and his fate whether he suffers and dies alone, with ten other believers or with a hundred million other believers. There will be only two major differences between tribulation in the past and the great tribulation. The scope and overall intensity will be greater, and at the same time we are being persecuted and killed, God will be pouring out His wrath against the beast and his devotees. But in the final analysis, pain is pain and death is death. And this is our lot—tribulation followed by joy—even as it was for Christ, "who for the joy that was set before him endured the cross, despising the shame" (Heb. 12:2).

In Romans 8:35–36 we are told that nothing separates us from Christ's love. We are specifically told that tribulation does not separate us. Thus, we cannot say, "If He loved us, He wouldn't let us go through this." There is an imposing juxtaposition of tribulation and subsequent glory in Romans 8:17–18. Paul rejoices in our joint heirship with Christ, "provided we suffer with him in order that we may also be glorified with him" (v. 17). He then declares: "I consider that the sufferings of this present time are not worth comparing with the glory that is to be revealed to us" (v. 18). That was the order for Christ and is the natural order for believers (Heb. 12:2). We suffer, we go through tribulation, we are persecuted, and then we are glorified, which was God's design from the very beginning (vv. 28–30). Then comes the glorious assurance of Romans 8:35–39. Nothing, no matter how severe—not tribulation, not persecution, not the sword itself (death), not even the power of angelic beings—can "separate us from the love of God in Christ Jesus our Lord."

## TRIBULATION AND THE CHURCHES OF REVELATION

The churches of Revelation were seven historical, local churches of the first century. But churches with their particular characteristics, strengths, weaknesses, and needs have continued with us throughout the centuries, and seem to be with us in a special way today.

1. **Ephesus** represents the creedal church. It has form and sound doctrine, but lacks love. This church can be found throughout the world today. Creeds without the dynamic of love are not strong enough. Therefore, she is told to repent lest her lampstand be removed.
2. **Smyrna** is the suffering, martyred church. She has been with us in varying degrees of intensity in all centuries. Today, though she can be seen somewhat in the Island World and Africa in an ever-growing dimension, her main arena seems to be the Euro-Asian theater.
3. **Pergamum** is the adapting church and is characterized by syncretism. She adapts culturally even in the area of essentials. She is told to purify herself, for she must clean up her act if she is to conquer.
4. **Thyatira** is the materialistic church. She has faith, and the work that she has done even shows an increase, as if she were outdoing herself in the latter days. But the world of commerce and goods and things have become her squalid rock. Thus, luxury and loose morals follow in her train. There is even the threat of tribulation for her. Only those who remain faithful and hold fast will conquer.
5. **Sardis** is the social, nominal church. She has a form or show of faith, but it lies asleep for the most part. She has liberal attitudes both of faith and practice. Unless her faith awakes, Christ's coming will surprise her like a thief. She must confess in true faith in order to conquer.
6. **Philadelphia** is the missionary church. She was strong in the first three centuries, but grew weak for over a millennium and now has revived in the past three centuries and is growing stronger and stronger. God has been opening door after door for her, and no one can shut them. Her strongholds are North America and, increasingly, Korea and some areas of South America and Africa. God will grant protection to these areas during the great tribulation to allow this church to complete the work of the Great Commission. They have kept God's word and name and

should hold fast or persevere and, thus, conquer.
7. **Laodicea** is the formal church—the church characterized by her form. She claims outward riches. God's assessment of her is that she is poor. He says that unless she comes up with true gold or riches, He will spit her out. Like the church at Sardis, few in her have true faith. She needs a personal experience with Christ, and thus, the invitation, "Behold, I stand at the door and knock." In order to conquer, she will have to be zealous and repent.

Not only did the problems of these early churches exist in the first century, but they have also been seen at one time or another and in one place or another down through the years since then. That similar problems exist in today's churches can hardly be debated. If we are on the threshold of the tribulation, we can look for the characteristics of those historic churches of Revelation 2 and 3 to appear in the various tribulation churches. Thus, it will not be surprising to find heresy in some and sound doctrine in others; immorality in some and lukewarmness and even apostasy in others; tribulation and poverty in some and the keeping, protecting power of the Lord in others.

The pretribulation camp would see an exception, even an exemption from the tribulation, in the case of the church at Philadelphia. They take the words of Revelation 3:10: "I will keep you from the hour of trial which is coming on the whole world," to mean that the believing Church will be raptured and, therefore, kept out of the tribulation altogether.

Although, at first blush, this verse would seem to allow the possibility of a raptured church, closer scrutiny of both the terminology and syntax of the verse would appear to make such an assumption unwarranted. There is a contrast between the two Greek prepositions απο and εκ. Both can be translated "from," but whereas απο carries the concept of a basic "from" signifying separation, εκ denotes "exit out of" something with which there has been a close connection, and it carries the idea of "from out of," "out from," or "forth from."

It is claimed that the verse promises to take the believer out of that time of trial. But it is logically impossible to remove someone out of something he was not in to begin with. It would be possible, however, to be kept from (απο) something one was never in to begin with. Furthermore, the verb used to define the Lord's activity toward the Philadelphians is not to "take" them (αιρω) away, but to "keep" them (τηρεω) out of the power of the trial.

An exact comparison of this precise contrast and language is found in John 17:15, where Christ prays to the Father for His own. He says, "I do not pray that thou shouldst take (αρης—from αιρω) them out of (εκ) the world, but that thou shouldst keep (τηρης—from τηρεω) them from (ek) the evil one." It is obvious that He is not praying that they be removed from any presence of Satan and his emissaries, but that they be kept "from out of" his power while in his very presence. It is not unreasonable to believe that part of the tribulation Church will be spared the full force of the enemy's malice while another part endures it, especially when we have seen, through the ages, part of the Church in the world suffering painfully while another part of that Church enjoys great liberty. Indeed, there are numerous instances where this is clearly seen in today's Church.

In Isaiah, the Lord speaks to His people, "Come, my people, enter your chambers, and shut your doors behind you; hide yourselves for a little while until the wrath is past. For behold, the Lord is coming forth out of his place to punish the inhabitants of the earth for their iniquity, and the earth will disclose the blood shed upon her, and will no more cover her slain" (26:20–21). These people did not leave, but simply entered their chambers and hid safely.

In the book of Revelation, this very concept is seen for Israel during the tribulation. Though much of Israel is pursued by the man of sin, a significant number of them are carried on the wings of the great eagle to a place of safety in the wilderness for that period.

How much like the history of Israel before and during the Passover! The Hebrews are safe in their chambers while death is striking the Egyptians. Indeed, as we will consider later in more depth, the whole scene of the Hebrews in Egypt typifies two things that the Scriptures seem to say about the tribulation. As many of the plagues fell on the Egyptians, they did not touch the Hebrews. If God pours out wrath on the Antichrist and his people, He can, indeed, keep it from those whom He has marked as His own. Further, while God was making His wrath felt on Pharaoh and the Egyptians, even so Pharaoh was making the lot of the Hebrews hard.

In the tribulation, as we see God punishing the Antichrist, we see the Antichrist pursuing and afflicting the saints. It is not necessarily inconsistent to see some saints paying with their heads for the testimony of Jesus while others are allowed to escape. Thus, he who endures to the end will be saved from the sword and will experience translation.

It is noteworthy that the churches of the first century were faced with these dissimilar prospects—one with suffering and the other with immunity, though both were faithful. Down through the centuries in our world, this has continued to be true. It prevails yet today. There are godless and repressive societies in our present day world where faithful believers suffer horribly and even pay with their lives. There are other free nations where true Christians are at complete liberty with hardly a suggestion of opposition. There is no compelling reason for believing that this same phenomenon will not be seen during the tribulation. The beast will have more direct influence on the Euro-Afro-Asian land mass than he will on the Western Hemisphere, Australia, and the island world. Even on his own land mass he will have great lack of respect and even open hostility, as seen in the opposition of the northern kingdom and the kings of the east. He will doubtless have even less power over those lands separated from him by oceans. It is not at all difficult to picture his extreme oppression and even execution of the saints in Europe and the contiguous areas in that land mass. Thus, a Smyrna-like church suffers. It is also easy to picture places like the United States and Australia with Philadelphia-like churches being kept from that hour of trial.

This would also explain the differing social climates existing at the same time at His return. According to Matthew 24:36–51, it will be, on the one hand, like the time of Noah before the flood. People were obsessed with food, drink, and sex (certainly God didn't destroy them for normal eating, drinking, and marrying). This would explain a fleshly lifestyle under the man of sin. It will also be a time of normal pursuits such as working in the field, grinding at the mill, and running a household. On the other hand, it will be a time when there is so much freedom (if not laxness) that a servant will have a choice of rendering faithful service for his absent master or of entering into a slovenly and even dissipated lifestyle. This can easily be reconciled with a world where the beast rules with an iron fist in one area, but has only moderate influence in another.

Our world and our experiences as pilgrims in that world is a mixed bag. In our local group, some are healed, and others, just as devout, endure suffering and die. In great social, political, or national arenas, some are free to worship, witness, and prosper, while in other communities there are those who must smuggle, struggle, suffer, and die. In Matthew 20, Jesus had an answer for those servants who complained about unequal treatment. Had they not "borne the burden of the day and the scorching heat"? And yet others had "worked only one hour" and received equal pay. He responded, "Am I not allowed to do what I choose with what belongs to me? Or do you begrudge my generosity?" (v. 15). Certainly, we all, serene or suffering, belong to Him. Why should it be thought an astounding thing that in those last days He will have those saints whom He "will keep ... from the hour of trial" while having others who will be "slain for the word of God and for the witness they had borne"? There should be two overriding truths to sustain His Body in that day: (1) the Church is one—we are united and members one of the other and will support one another by whatever means are available; and (2) "The sufferings of this present time," whether minor or major, "are not worth comparing with the glory that is to be revealed to us."

This is the pattern we see today—famine and plenty, suffering and security, war and peace all existing side by side and at the same time. We can also see it clearly at the very end of the tribulation period. Right on the heels of the bowl judgments of Revelation 16, we see the continued luxury of Babylon the Great in chapters 17 and 18.

Thus, in the world of the great tribulation we will have, side by side, both liberalism and sound doctrine; both adaptation and the keeping of God's word; both suffering and tribulation on the one hand and protection from the trials on the other. It will not be a homogeneous church, but we will feel the unity of the body. The missionary church of Philadelphia will feel the hurt of the suffering and tribulation of the church of Smyrna. Paul says that "if one member suffers, all suffer together" (1 Cor. 12:26). The writer of Hebrews instructs us to "Remember those who are in prison, as though in prison with them; and those who are ill-treated, since you also are in the body" (13:3).

## TRIBULATION SAINTS—LIKE THE EXODUS SAINTS

The situation prevailing between the tribulation saints and their enemy, the Antichrist, bears an uncanny resemblance to the situation that existed between the pharaoh of Egypt and the Hebrews preceding the time of the Exodus. During that time in Egypt, the pharaoh persecuted the Hebrews, but, at the same time, God poured out His wrath on the pharaoh and the Egyptians.

The categories of persecution by the pharaoh were quite clear-cut. In Exodus we learn that he subjected them to slavery (1:11); he made their service harder (1:13, 14); he decreed the death of their newborn sons (1:15, 16); and then he loaded even heavier work on them (5:10–14).

We know that God used ten different plagues in His attacks against Egypt: (1) water turned to blood (7:14); (2) frogs (8:1); (3) gnats (8:16); (4) flies (8:20); (5) death of Egyptian cattle (9:1); (6) boils (9:8); (7) hail and fire (9:13); (8) locusts (10:12); (9) darkness (10:21); and, finally, (10) the death of the firstborn (11:4).

In most of the plagues, God spared the Hebrews and that part of Egypt called the land of Goshen, where they lived. They were spared any involvement in plagues 4 (flies); 5 (death of the Egyptian cattle); 6 (boils: "on all the Egyptians"); 7 (hail and fire, though even the Egyptians who believed the warning also had their cattle spared); 9 (darkness); and 10 (death of the firstborn). There is no indication, however, that the Hebrews were excepted or spared from the results of plagues 1, 2, and 3 (water turned into blood, frogs, and gnats). Also it would appear that they may have been involved in plague 8 (the locusts). Though pharaoh was told that the locusts would fill the houses "of all the Egyptians" (10:6), the passage also states that "the locusts came up over all the land of Egypt, and settled on the whole country of Egypt" (10:14). But even if the Hebrews shared in this plague, they were to leave the land (laden with riches) just a few days later.

There are some striking parallels between the pre-Exodus experience of the Hebrew saints and that of the saints living during the great tribulation. The same sort of relationship that existed between the pharaoh and the Hebrews in Egypt is seen in the relationship between the Antichrist on the one hand, and the Christian saints and the Jews on the other, in the great tribulation. Actually, the Antichrist will hate these two groups: the Christian saints and the people of Israel, since they will be the only two unified groups who will stand in opposition to him. He will pursue and persecute these two enemy groups. But at the same time he is venting his malice against them, God will be waging a battle against him and his devotees. Thus, the Antichrist will be bringing tribulation upon the people of God and God will be bringing tribulation against the Antichrist and his worshipers—those who receive his mark.

Likewise, just as there were some judgments that seemingly fell on all of Egypt and others that only fell on the Egyptians and from which the Hebrews were protected, in the great tribulation there seem to be some worldwide judgments, having an effect on the world's populace in general, and other judgments from which the saints clearly are protected since they are specifically directed only against God's enemies. Another point worth noting is the fact that in Egypt there may have been Hebrews who died in (that is, during) the plagues, but there is no evidence that any of them ever died by the plagues. This is not an unreasonable expectation for the tribulation.

Another similarity is seen in the fact that God brought some plagues against the pharaoh and the Egyptians in order to influence them to change their minds and allow Israel to leave. In the tribulation, one-third of mankind will be killed by the fire, smoke and sulfur that comes from the horses' mouths, but the survivors still will not repent of their works and worship God (Rev. 9:17–21). This is very like the hardening of the heart of the pharaoh in Egypt following the plagues there before the Exodus.

Whether it issues from the similarity of the plagues in Egypt to those in the tribulation, or from the preset notion that the Church simply cannot be in the tribulation, there is a theory on the part of many pretribulation people that God will go back to dealing with believing people or the faithful in the tribulation as he did with Old Testament saints and that He will indwell only believers who have been chosen by Him for some sort of special service. If, however, they are all believers in Jesus, the whole argument of the book of Hebrews would seem to be overthrown. In Jesus we have been brought to the better, indeed the superior, way. Is God now going to accomplish His purpose by making two classes of believers? And by relating to believers in the way He did during the Old Testament era, is He not going to the lesser, and the poorer way to accomplish the great task of world evangelization? Is the Old Testament way, after all, the better way?

The first **four seals** represented by the four horsemen of deceit, war, famine, and pestilence would seem to be worldwide phenomena sent by God. The **fifth** seal appears to be a depiction of the reaction of the Antichrist. He possibly blames the saints for the four plagues God had sent. At any rate, he goes forth slaying God's saints. The sixth seal shows God's possible retaliation by the great earthquake and signs in the heavens. This is not a final wrath judgment of God, even though the people in the fearful godless herd call it that. When they make the plea to the mountains: "hide us from the face of him who is seated on the throne, and from the wrath of the Lamb; for the great day of their wrath has come," that is their assessment and interpretation, not God's (see Rev. 6:16–17). The time would yet come when heaven would speak of God's wrath about to visit mankind.

When the judgments of the **first four** trumpets come,

they would, once again, appear to be global in their effects. The burning of one third of the earth through hail, fire, and blood; the turning of a third of the sea into blood; the turning of a third of the fountains into blood; and the diminishing of the light of the sun, moon, and stars by one third would seem to be on a widespread scale. At this point, however, there appears to be a radical change, beginning with the fifth and sixth trumpets and continuing through the seven bowls. With the **fifth** trumpet, when the supernatural locusts strike, it is only against the unsealed of mankind. When the **sixth** trumpet sounds and one third of mankind is killed by fire, smoke, and sulfur, it is clear from the description of the remaining two thirds that this entire segment of mankind did not include the saints, since the remaining two thirds of the former whole "did not repent of the works of their hands nor give up worshipping demons and idols" (9:20).

The protection of the saints in the fifth and sixth trumpet judgments continues through the bowl judgments, which heaven calls "the seven bowls of the wrath of God" (16:1). The **first** bowl speaks of sores which "came upon the men who bore the mark of the beast and worshipped its image" (v. 2). The **third** bowl turns rivers and fountains into blood, but, as the angel of that bowl says to God, it is for the men who "have shed the blood of saints and prophets, and thou hast given them blood to drink. It is their due!" (vv. 4–6) The **fourth** bowl is the intensified heat of the sun for scorching men, but it is clear that these affected men are unbelievers since "they cursed the name of God who had power over these plagues, and they did not repent and give him glory" (v. 9). The **fifth** bowl is darkness specifically poured out "on the throne of the beast" (vv. 10–11). The **sixth** bowl is simply the drying up of the water of the Euphrates in preparation for Armageddon and has nothing to do with believers. The subsequent froglike foul spirits go forth only to the kings of the earth who will participate in that battle (vv. 12–16). Finally, the **seventh** bowl is the most severe earthquake in the history of humankind followed by the dropping of the heaviest hailstones on record (vv. 17–21). There is no indication of any effect of this plague on believers. Indeed, the significant result was that "men cursed God for the plague of the hail, so fearful was that plague" (v. 21). This would be the reaction of unbelievers once again, even as it was during the fourth plague. In addition there are strong reasons for suspecting that the rapture may have occurred between the sixth and seventh plagues. Toward the end of the sixth bowl plague the warning of the imminent coming of Christ found in 1 Thessalonians 5:2, 6 is repeated: "Lo, I am coming like a thief! Blessed is he who is awake, keeping his garments that he may not go naked and be seen exposed!" (v. 15). This is obviously spoken to believers on the threshold of His coming for them. This may be followed quickly by the call of the Lord: "Come out of her, my people" (18:4).

The question has doubtless arisen: "What of the plague of the **second** bowl where the sea 'became like the blood of a dead man, and every living thing died that was in the sea'?" (16:3). This certainly would seem to be a global problem. It might mainly affect the unbelievers, as the third bowl did with the bloody rivers and fountains. But even if it also impacts strongly on believers, a good parallel can be drawn between this situation and the eighth plague in Egypt, where the locusts probably covered that part of Egypt called Goshen. As it was noted above, they were leaving in a few days in the Exodus anyway, and it created no significant problem for them as a result. So it likely is, also, in this second bowl plague. If the sea life is destroyed and the saints are only to be in this period for a few days or weeks, the loss of sea life for them would be of no grave consequence.

The major point, however, in all of this is that when we reach that point in the great tribulation where God calls the judgments or plagues the "seven bowls of the wrath of God," those plagues are directed not against the earth in general, but against the throne of the Antichrist and those who worship the beast and receive his mark—those who do not believe in God and in His Christ. The pretribulation school makes a great issue of 1 Thessalonians 5:9, where we are told that God has not destined believers "for wrath." Their argument runs that the wrath of God exists in the great tribulation and, therefore, believers cannot be there. Actually, where I have used "believers" here, they use "the Church."

But the Church is not used at all in 1 Thessalonians 5. The term used there is brethren. And the term "brethren" is used of believers in the great tribulation in Revelation 6:11. Thus, even if the wrath of 1 Thessalonians 5 were the wrath mentioned in Revelation 16, God does not aim it at believers, but at unbelievers. So even here He does not destine believers to wrath. But it is actually academic, since 1 Thessalonians 5:9 itself tells us what God's wrath actually is, namely not obtaining "salvation through our Lord Jesus Christ," which is to say, God's wrath equals eternal separation from the presence of the living God.

### THE TIMES OF THE GENTILES

Harold Sevener, director of The American Board of Missions to the Jews, writes in a 1982 midyear report in The Chosen People of a conversation he had with an Orthodox rabbi on a flight to Israel. He states, "Naturally, I wanted to direct our conversation toward Christ. Thus I asked, 'Rabbi, do you hope the Messiah will soon come?' His response was both startling and heartbreaking. I sensed the awfulness of the thoughts that must have been racing through his mind as he answered, 'God forbid—before the Messiah, the Tribulation must first come!' " Sevener then goes on to say, "He was right! For Israel, before the Messiah, the Tribulation must first come."

Sevener writes again about the theme of the times of the Gentiles. Speaking of the signing of the covenant at the beginning of the tribulation, he says:

> The covenant is then broken after three and one-half years, and for another three-and-one-half-year period the man of sin, the antichrist, the Beast, will make war against Israel in an attempt to maintain his control over the city of Jerusalem (cf. Rev. 11:1,2; Matt. 24:15; Dan. 11:36–45).
>
> At the conclusion of that seven-year period, the Lord Jesus will come in power and great glory to establish His kingdom (cf. Rev. 19). Thus, the New Testament as well as the Old Testament makes it clear that the times of the Gentiles will not run out until the Lord Jesus returns to establish His kingdom at the end

of the seven-year period called the Tribulation (cf. Dan. 2:7; Rev. 19).

This is a clear assessment of the conclusion of the 'times of the Gentiles,' since Jesus stated in Luke 21:24 that 'Jerusalem will be trodden down by the Gentiles, until the times of the Gentiles are fulfilled.' Because the beast will tread down Jerusalem during the tribulation, the times of the Gentiles can't end until that treading down ends. (From *The Chosen People*, May 1985.)

Sevener says earlier in the same article:

> Jesus was put to death during this span of time called "the times of the Gentiles," so that the Gentiles themselves, along with the Jewish people, would be participants in the death of the Lord Jesus (cf. Acts 2:23; 4:26–28). And at the same time, both Jew and Gentile could participate in His salvation (cf. Acts 15:13–18; Rom. 11:25, 26).

What Sevener has placed side by side (perhaps unwittingly, for he would not agree with the logical conclusion) is the "times of the Gentiles" and the completion of the "full number of the Gentiles." These would seem, indeed, to go logically together. But, beware! This leads logically to a posttribulation position. If this "full number" is identified as the Church and also signifies the end of the bringing of Gentiles to faith in Christ as being one and the same thing, then we must note that it is not until the book of Revelation that we read that Gentiles are brought to faith from every national group and have come out of great tribulation. This would be a rational cataloging of "the full number of the Gentiles." Then at the coming of Christ to earth "All Israel will be saved" too.

## Tribulation Leads to Purifying

Certainly persecution has a purifying effect. Peter challenges us with these words: "Since therefore Christ suffered in the flesh, arm yourselves with the same thought, for whoever has suffered in the flesh has ceased from sin" (1 Pet. 4:1). Thus, for the Church, worldwide persecution would accomplish cleansing. Later in the same chapter, Peter makes a powerful statement about God's chastisement and correction of the Church. He states that "the time has come for judgment to begin with the household of God; and if it begins with us, what will be the end of those who do not obey the gospel of God?" (v. 17).

This concept of God dealing in a rigorous manner with his people, to correct them, traces back to His dealing with Israel in the Old Testament and it often included the idea of much greater severity being directed against those who were not His people. Through the prophet Jeremiah, God's message to the nations was clear: "Behold, I begin to work evil at the city which is called by my name, and shall you go unpunished? You shall not go unpunished, for I am summoning a sword against all the inhabitants of the earth, says the Lord of hosts" (Jer. 25:29).

God's judgment against Israel was modified neither by official position and responsibility on the one hand or by sex or age on the other. The sole exceptions were those who had received a special mark only because they sighed and groaned "over all the abominations" that were committed in Jerusalem. The executioners were not to spare "old men ... young men ... maidens ... little children and women" and they were to begin at the sanctuary "with the elders" themselves (Ezek. 9:4–6).

When God spoke to Israel through Amos as the people He had redeemed from Egypt, He let the people know that, precisely because they were His, He was going to discipline them: "You only have I known of all the families of the earth; therefore I will punish you for all your iniquities" (Amos 3:1–2). Once again, when the messenger was to be sent before the Lord, one of his key roles was that of purifier and refiner of those who served before the presence of the Lord, so that "then the offering ... will be pleasing to the Lord" (see Mal. 3:1–6). Then at the end of Malachi's account the wicked would be dealt with in judgment as "stubble" in His great "oven" (3:17–4:1).

Many are willing to admit that the Lord dealt thus with Israel in Old Testament days. But they raise appealing arguments against Him acting the same way against His redeemed people in the Church. After all, we have His word and covenant engraved in fleshly tablets of our hearts. We have been ransomed by Christ's very blood. He has entered our lives and the Holy Spirit lives within us, making us His very temple. And was Peter in his first letter not speaking of an early persecution that fell upon the Church? (see 1 Pet. 4:17). What can that have to do with us today?

It may well be that Peter was speaking against the backdrop of an early persecution. The context, however, will not allow us to remain in the first century alone. That there was an impending mood to the prediction cannot be denied. It evidently had not yet happened, yet Peter indicated that "the time has come for judgment to begin with the household of God" (v. 17). But what he says next shifts the time frame to the end of the time when the gospel would be offered. He asks, if judgment is to come to the Church, "what will be the end of those who do not obey the gospel of God?" The only times when this question would apply legitimately would be when the offer to obey the gospel had run its course and the full number of Gentiles had come in (Rom. 11:25). Then many will be dealt with on that basis, first, at Christ's return, and second, at the end of the millennium at the great white throne judgment. But the juncture point, the point when these two concepts of judgment (beginning with the household of God and ending with unbelieving judgment) are set in juxtaposition, is the tribulation-rapture period.

In Romans 11, Paul aims a telling blow against those who presume upon the position they have as Gentile members of the Church. When we boast of immunity to harsh treatment because of everything the Lord has done for us in the Church, we sound very much like the Gentiles who boasted that "Branches were broken off so that I might be grafted in" (v. 19). But Paul answers by saying: "That is true, they were broken off because of their unbelief, but you stand fast only through faith. So do not become proud, but stand in awe. For if God did not spare the natural branches, neither will he spare you" (vv. 20–21).

We know from 2 Thessalonians 2:3 that before Christ's return a rebellion or apostasy will come first. For the sake of clarity, so that we may know what the apostasy is and what it isn't, the Greek word αποστασια is rendered "rebellion, abandonment in relig. sense, apostasy" by Bauer, Arndt and Gingrich in their Lexicon (p.98, col.1). Thayer, in his Lexicon, gives the meaning as "a falling away, defection, apostasy" (p.67, col.1)

Verse 3 shows the condition: "unless the rebellion comes first, and the man of lawlessness is revealed, the son of perdition." The verse lacks the main clause or the clause that actually expresses result or conclusion to the conditional clause that has been given. It must be supplied in order to make sense. It is as if two people stand before a door and one simply says, "After you." That is the condition. The result has not been stated, but it is clear, nevertheless. It is: "I will go through the door." In our text it is also clear that "the day already mentioned will not come." The translations supply the missing result in various ways, but the outcome is the same. The KJV reads "that day shall not come." The RSV, NIV, and The Living Bible are virtually the same as the KJV: "that day will not come ..." The NASV reads "For it will not come unless." The Williams says, "Because that cannot take place." And Beck puts it as an understood conclusion by stating: "First there must be a revolt and...."

Of course we also know of some of the pressures from the Antichrist during the tribulation that will lead to some defections. He will constrain many to follow him and receive his mark. He will also require that mark as a basis for being able to buy and sell. Some other details of the dynamics of that rebellion are more subtle. Jesus says concerning that time that "because wickedness is multiplied, most men's love will grow cold" (Matt. 24:12). When the wickedness of the culture we live in mushrooms, it can ever so softly creep first into the thoughts, then into the desires, and finally into the lifestyles of those who name the name of Christ. The lure of Babylon with her commerce, materialism, and luxury, presented with all the hype of Madison Avenue or its counterpart, will sometimes accomplish gently what the Antichrist could not achieve with a frontal attack. So strong is her appeal even near the end of the tribulation that the Lord says, "Come out of her my people, lest you take part in her sins" (Rev. 18:4).

The church at Thyatira is a prime example. Goods and

"things" had turned her toward an accepting attitude of Jezebel and her immorality. Therefore, tribulation was coming to purify her. All seven of the churches of Revelation 2 and 3 are still with us today in one form or another. Since five of the seven churches are rebuked, it would seem that there is great need of persecution for the purpose of purifying. The persecution part of the tribulation (Antichrist versus the saints) would accomplish this very purpose and thus make the Bride without spot or blemish.

The Church will not be homogeneous in its attitudes or in its spirituality in that time leading up to His return. There will certainly be those in whom that hope burns brightly. They will be devoted and holy. It is these of whom John speaks when he considers our transformation at His coming. He says, "every one who thus hopes in him purifies himself as he is pure" (1 John 3:3). But there will also be those who "fall away." Jesus says that "because wickedness is multiplied, most men's love will grow cold" (Matt. 24:12). This alone should be enough to assure us that the word αποστασια in 2 Thessalonians 2:3 should be taken to mean "rebellion" or "falling away." Certainly that is what Jesus said for us to expect to happen. The Church today consists of both dedicated, holy believers on the one hand and those who have been seduced by wickedness and materialism on the other. I am not speaking of nonbelievers, but of carnal Christians who "will be saved, but only as through fire" (1 Cor. 3:15). In addition, there are and will be gradations of dedication and looseness in between. Somewhere and somehow this mixed bag that is the Church will have become unified or fairly homogenized at the rapture. Paul tells us that Christ "will present the church to himself in splendor, without spot or wrinkle or any such thing, that she might be holy and without blemish" (Eph. 5:27).

Since it is generally agreed by pretribulationists and posttribulationists alike that the marriage feast of the Lamb will take place shortly after the rapture, this purity must be established by that time. Paul says that each man's work will become manifest and that "that Day will disclose it, because it will be revealed with fire, and the fire will test what sort of work each one has done" (1 Cor. 3:13). Nowhere is the judgment seat of Christ (spoken of by Paul in 2 Corinthians 5:10) represented as a time of trial, or purging, or fire. Paul says that it is simply for each one of us to "receive good or evil, according to what he has done in the body." But, somewhere, the purgative effect of the "fire" in 1 Corinthians 3 must take place. If the posttribulation position is correct, "the Day" of verse 13 refers to the Day of the Lord, and the tribulation begins that day. That the tribulation is a two-way street can easily be demonstrated. God is clearly supplying tribulation for the beast and his followers during that time, but the beast is certainly supplying tribulation for the saints (persecution and martyrdom) and Israel ("the time of Jacob's trouble") at the same time.

Peter tells believers: "do not be surprised at the fiery ordeal which comes upon you to prove you, as though something strange were happening to you.... For the time has come for judgment to begin with the household of God" (1 Pet. 4:12, 17). That time has not yet come for the whole household, but the tribulation would fulfill many purposes relating to God's work in the Church. It would fulfill this prophecy. It would try the works of believers with fire. And it would purge and purify the Church so that she might be presented "in splendor, without spot or wrinkle or any such thing, that she might be holy and without blemish."

It should not appear an unthinkable scheme or even presumptuous that the Church should suffer, and suffer deeply. We are called upon in more than one Scripture to identify with Christ as a pattern in this matter of suffering. If "it was fitting that he ... should make the pioneer of their salvation perfect [complete] through suffering," how much more for the Church to be made complete through tribulation? (see Heb. 2:10). Paul tells us that "if we endure [suffer] we shall also reign with him" and that "indeed all who desire to live a godly life in Christ Jesus will be persecuted" (2 Tim. 2:12; 3:12).

Christ is going to "present the church to himself in splendor, without spot or wrinkle or any such thing, that she might be holy and without blemish" (Ephesians 5:17). In Revelation 19:7, we are also told that the bride "made herself ready." There are two things that purify us as believers. One is the Word. But that Word cleanses us only if it is applied. It does not happen automatically. Another thing that purifies us is suffering. Peter implores us: "Since therefore Christ suffered in the flesh, arm yourselves with the same thought, for whoever has suffered in the flesh has ceased from sin" (1 Pet. 4:1).

If it is not an absurd notion that the Church should suffer deeply, it should not be thought preposterous that the great tribulation should be the final vehicle of that suffering. We are told that the rebellion or apostasy will precede the Lord's return (2 Thessalonians 2:3). As a corrective to this apostasy, judgment against the Church in the tribulation would be logical in order to purify or cleanse it. Paul, in referring to that blessed hope—"the appearing of the glory of our great God and Savior Jesus Christ," states that part of His giving Himself for us was "to purify for himself a people of his own who are zealous for good deeds" (Titus 2:13–14). Note in the passage on the marriage of the Lamb that only after the tribulation is this purified Bride presented to the Lamb (Rev. 19:6–8). Furthermore, the "fine linen" with which she is "clothed" is described as being "the righteous deeds of the saints." These are the very saints that have just suffered or died in the tribulation in order to bring about this process of purification.

The next logical question would probably be: "Is the Church worldwide pure at the present time?" Few, probably, would cast a serious vote in her favor. Certainly the pull of materialism and desire have kept many believers carnal. It has already been noted that the Word has no power to cleanse if it is not personally applied. The Roman Catholic Church has seen the need for a purging of that which is base in believers. Unfortunately, they projected a post-death locale and testing to accomplish this cleansing. The Scriptures do sustain the need for purifying, but they have solved the problem here on earth rather than in Purgatory. Besides the Word, it has already been shown that persecution, tribulation, and suffering accomplish cleansing. The Church has "enjoyed" episodes of suffering through the ages, but when "the Judge is standing at the doors" (James 5:9), then that final generation must make its robes white before His appearing.

In individual experience, doubtless the most powerful incentive for getting one's spiritual house in order is when a person who knows that he will die soon faces his own mortality. This is also the typical human experience. Unless one dies accidentally or of a sudden, massive heart attack, he knows for months, weeks, or perhaps a few days before his death that he is indeed dying. This affords him the opportunity to face the Lord earnestly as the time of departure hastens on. But for the Church in the last days, alive and spiritually imperfect and incomplete, the tribulation will be able to accomplish for them what the prospect of death accomplishes for the man facing death. Indeed, then, the corporate Body of Christ will face the equivalent of death in the great tribulation itself and will thus be completed, purged, purified.

### SUFFERING OF THE BODY OF CHRIST

In the concept of suffering in the New Testament, there is also a suggestion of balance between the Head (Christ) and the Body (the Church). Peter writes: "For to this you have been called, because Christ also suffered for you, leaving you an example, that you should follow in his steps" (1 Pet. 2:21). The pattern is unmistakably set here. It is our calling to suffer. It is also consistent with the norm laid down by Christ in John 16:33 when He told His followers, "In the world you have tribulation."

It falls strangely on our ears to hear that Christ could learn maturing through suffering, but we are told that "it was fitting that he, for whom and by whom all things exist, in bringing many sons to glory, should make the pioneer of their salvation perfect through suffering" (Heb. 2:10). And a very practical outcome is noted: "because he himself has suffered and been tempted, he is able to help those who are tempted" (v. 18). This concept of a person being tested successfully and then helping others who are similarly tested forms the core of Paul's teaching on comfort in the first half of 2 Corinthians 1. In fact, the idea of my trial helping a brother as seen in verses 6–7 ("If we are afflicted, it is for your comfort ... for we know that as you share in our sufferings, you will also share in our comfort") may be one of the better clues to Paul's statement to the Colossians: "I rejoice in my sufferings for your sake, and in my flesh I complete what is lacking in Christ's afflictions for the sake of his body, that is, the church" (Col. 1:24). It would seem that in terms of suffering affliction and tribulation, Christ moves suffering and subsequent help (even subsequent glory) beyond Himself, and applies the principle to its operation through the Body for the Body.

This is clearly seen (particularly the idea of suffering followed by glory) in Hebrews 12, where the reference is again to the "pioneer" who has set us an unmistakable model. Clearly, we are to watch Him as He marks out the trail, and then follow in His steps. The writer asks us to "run with perseverance the race that is set before us, looking to Jesus the pioneer and perfecter of our faith, who for the joy that was set before him endured the cross, despising the shame, and is seated at the right hand of the throne of God" (12:1–2). In spite of the shame, He went through the trauma of the cross before accepting or realizing the joy or glory that followed. In verses 7–11 it becomes clear that we also must endure for the sake of discipline, waiting "later" for the "peaceful fruit of righteousness." This would be consistent with the principle mentioned earlier that "Christ also suffered for you, leaving you an example, that you should follow in his steps" (1 Pet. 2:21). Thus it also seems that what the Head has borne, the Body (His Church) should also bear. He did it to redeem us; we do it to honor Him.

If the principle is sound, and if the exemplar is Christ enduring the cross though despising the shame before entering into the subsequent joy, then the only logical replica for the Church would be a symbolic Gethsemane-Calvary-entombment and subsequent resurrection-glory sequence. For half a day, Christ suffered agony in scourging, suffering and dying. Following this half day, He lay helpless in the tomb for three nights and days before His resurrection. It would be exceedingly difficult to find a scenario that would fit this model for His body, the Church, unless we consider the Church going through the great tribulation—symbolic (though literal for many believers)—suffering and death for half a week (the last half of Daniel's prophetic week). This symbolic entombment is followed by the Church being resurrected-raptured at the end of this time to join, as a transfigured and transformed Body, the already glorified Head. Thus, we too would then enter into and share in His glory. Unfortunately, dispensationalists face the tribulation with the scenario that it is necessary for the Church to enter her glory before the tribulation and then enter Christ's glory after the tribulation, when He comes in His glory.

There are New Testament passages where this very sequence is shown to us. In his first letter, Peter alerts his readers to look for coming tribulation as a natural and useful event with a joyous resolution when he says, "Beloved, do not be surprised at the fiery ordeal which comes upon you to prove you, as though something strange were happening to you. But rejoice in so far as you share Christ's sufferings, that you may also rejoice and be glad when his glory is revealed" (1 Pet. 4:12–13). When the tribulation ends, the glory of Christ will be revealed. Then we shall rejoice.

Paul makes similar statements to the Thessalonians in his first letter to them. He says: "May the Lord make you increase and abound in love to one another and to all men, as we do to you, so that he may establish your hearts unblamable in holiness before our God and Father, at the coming of our Lord Jesus with all his saints" (1 Thess. 3:12–13). He states that a time is coming when the hearts of the Thessalonians would be unblamable in holiness (a glorified state), but that that time would only be "at the coming of our Lord Jesus with all his saints." That occurs when He comes to the earth after the tribulation. He made the statement even more strongly, if possible, in his second letter to the Thessalonians: "This is evidence of the righteous judgment of God, that you may be made worthy of the kingdom of God, for which you are suffering ... and to grant rest with us to you who are afflicted, when the Lord Jesus is revealed from heaven with his mighty angels in flaming fire" (2 Thess. 2:5–7). Clearly, the only time that Jesus will be "revealed from heaven with his mighty angels in flaming fire" is at the close of the tribulation. Only then, says Paul would the afflicted

Thessalonians be granted their rest.

Paul would then tell the Thessalonians that first the apostasy must come and the Antichrist must usher in the great tribulation before Christ's return to earth at the end of that time and, therefore, not to worry that the time had already come (see 2 Thess. 2:1–4). He had told them in the passages cited earlier that only then, at the end of the tribulation would their rest come. In the light of passages from the first letter, it is small wonder that he says of the second letter "Do you not remember that when I was still with you I told you this?" (2 Thess. 2:5).

Somehow there is a feeling in the pretribulation camp that it would not be a blessed hope to survive the tribulation and then be raptured without dying, and that one would be much better off to die before the tribulation begins. There is something off-center about each of these two feelings. The first fails to recognize the onus attached to dying. Human beings have endured incredible privations, have still hung on to a hope, and have shown a desire to persist even in spite of the cruelties of human "death camps." Even believers have a sense of awe in the face of this strange intruder. Almost universally we have desired to struggle through a severe lot in life as long as we can retain our integrity. Paul himself struggled with these very feelings in the early part of 2 Corinthians 5. He says, in effect, that it would be great to be with the Lord, but he would rather not have to experience death to do so—he would rather be transformed by the Lord (evidently as described in 1 Corinthians 15:51–54). It would most certainly be a blessed hope, that having struggled through the tribulation, we would now meet the Lord without going through death.

The second feeling is grievously sad; that if believers did somehow have to go through the tribulation, it would be much better for them to experience some sort of natural death before it began, rather than to go through that time. We might then ask: "Says who?" Is the "blessed hope" primarily "blessed" because it serves as an escape hatch from the tribulation? What ever happened to the concept of tribulation as the natural lot of believers? What is the significance of those being called "blessed" who die in the Lord henceforth in Revelation 14:13? Why should the disciples who had been beaten for their preaching in the book of Acts rejoice "that they were counted worthy to suffer dishonor for the name"? (5:40–41). Why does the writer of Hebrews refer to those who had suffered and died as the ones "of whom the world was not worthy"? (11:38). Where in the pretribulation scheme of things is there a viable place for "the fellowship of His suffering"?

Of course, there is a great contrast between the blessed hope of Christ's return and the idea of suffering and death in the tribulation. But it is precisely because the setting of those trials during that period is so stark, bleak, and acrid that the release and relief of His coming are so "blessed." Those who die in Christ at that time are "blessed": "Blessed are the dead who die in the Lord henceforth" (Rev. 14:13), but "he who endures to the end will be saved" (doubtless from physical death) and he, therefore, is also "blessed" (Matt. 24:13). Thus, it is "blessed" for those who die, and it is also "blessed" for those who survive.

If we must go through an ordeal in a dental chair to relieve pain in a tooth, or if we must endure the agony of an operation to emerge sound and healthy afterward, we do not look for the trial, but we look through and beyond the trial for the prize on the other side. In Romans, Paul says, "I consider that the sufferings of this present time are not worth comparing with the glory that is to be revealed to us" (8:18). We have in Christ Jesus and His cup of suffering and subsequent resurrection the perfect example and pattern for us, His Body, to take our cup of suffering in the tribulation and to be delivered at its end. For He, "the pioneer and perfecter of our faith ... for the joy that was set before him endured the cross, despising the shame" (Heb. 12:2). Christ did not look for or look forward to the cross, but rather endured it. We do not look for or forward to the tribulation, but we will endure it. He despised the shame of the cross. We will despise the shame of evil, through the beast and his agents, triumphing (even temporarily) over the King's children. But, thanks be to God, we can fix our eye on the blessed joy that is set before us.

Not only do we have the pattern of Christ's example, but

we also have a cloud of heavenly witnesses to our own pilgrim journey who already have followed in His train and imitated His example. We have the early disciples (beginning with Stephen) who were executed for their faith. We have the stalwarts of Fox's Book of Martyrs. We have believers from many repressive cultures and societies who have been slaughtered by the thousands down through the ages. There are probably no tortures during the tribulation that are worse in degree than those that God's people have, at one time or another and in one place or another, already suffered down through the ages. Only the scope is different. It will all be on a grander scale and, thus, it is the great tribulation. Because of its scope, no time has been worse. But death is also death. If one man burns to death, he is painfully dead. If he dies by burning to death with one million others in an atomic blast, he is also painfully dead. The point is that God's people have already suffered to the utmost for Him and have already died for Him. How and why am I any better than they, that I should escape that time?

## THE RESTRAINER AND READINESS

There has been much conjecture about the identity of the restrainer in 2 Thessalonians 2:6–7. The dispensational school insists that the restrainer is the Holy Spirit. Originally, they taught that He would be taken out of the world with the rapture of the Church before the tribulation. Faced with the serious problems that teaching presented, they changed the teaching. Now the assertion is that only His restraining power will be removed. If that is so, then the only function of His that will be withdrawn or taken out of the way will be His power of restraint against the power of the Antichrist so that he might be manifested. This is a sovereign power of the Spirit, independent of His presence in the Church. Indeed, all of His other offices will still be in operation. No believers can come to or believe in Christ unless the Father draw them, and this drawing was to be through the Spirit whom the Father would send in Christ's name. The illuminating power of the Spirit would remain, and His teaching power as well. He would have to continue convincing of sin, because people "do not believe" in Christ and are in need of this conviction to see a need of redemption. He would need to convince of righteousness since Christ is still with the Father according to John 16:8–11. The one concept that would relate to His restraint against the enemy would be that of "judgment." He was to convince of judgment "because the ruler of this world is judged." This force has been continually against the Serpent because of crucifixion-resurrection. Christ's heel was bruised, but so was the Serpent's head. Though it was a fatal blow, he has been in death throes until this very day. The Spirit has pressed this power against him from the day of Pentecost: "You are judged. You are a defeated foe." When this restraining power is withdrawn, Satan has the power to commence that time of trouble and to manifest himself—even to proclaim himself (in the beast) to be God.

Although this viewpoint would do no violence to the posttribulation position, there is another view that has been held by the mainstream of the Church up until the emergence of dispensational teaching in the middle of the 19th century. That view was that the restrainer was government itself. Even in the first century, under the rule of Rome, the structure of law and order has held absolute evil in check. Even in societies where the rule has been less than exemplary, government has kept the grossest of evil reigned in. Paradoxically, the privileged ruling class has usually outlawed for the populace some of the very sins that it committed. In fact, where government becomes weak and anarchy enters in, the very vacuum created by this raises a desire among the people for leadership, preferably strong "law and order" leadership. What a perfect setting for the emergence of the man of sin, when a realm without leadership cries out for a strong leader.

Actually there might even be a combination of the two views in setting the stage for the Antichrist. It may well be that the very restraints of government itself are brought about by the operation of the Spirit of God upon them. Then when, in the arena of government, He withdraws that power, that very act would most naturally result in the breakdown of government restraints and the appearance of anarchy.

Because the world actually looks to government for its leadership, it will be ill-equipped to see what is coming. Since we look to the Lord and His word, we are in a position to be prepared for that day. It should be obvious from the entire context of 1 Thessalonians 4:13–5:11 that Paul is reminding the readers to be ready for the time mentioned in chapter 5: "you know about the times and you are not going to be surprised (like the world) when they come." Some dispensationalists make too much of the word "day"—much more than the text warrants. They expect us to believe that the expression "sons of the day" means that believers are part of the day that precedes the darkness (implying a rapture before the night begins), which is much too big a leap for logic to accept. One could respond that the Hebrew concept of day and night is that of "evening and morning," where the darkness precedes the day. Thus, we would have the darkness of the tribulation followed by the dawning of the day of resurrection-rapture. In fact, a much simpler and more consistent interpretation lies in the usual meaning of day and light on the one hand and night and darkness on the other. The former refer to understanding and fellowship and the latter to lack of knowledge and enmity. Indeed the fact that the "day of the Lord" is a time of darkness for the world but of light for believers strains the pretribulation interpretation even further. A good illustration of this is found in the pillar of fire that led the Hebrews in light during the Exodus even though the Egyptians were surrounded by night. The Hebrews knew where they were going; the Egyptians didn't. Finally, the very fact that Paul warned the Thessalonians about that time showed that it had a practical value for them. If they were not to be in it, it would be irrelevant even to mention it. Since they were to be in it, it became of the utmost relevance to them.

Many sincere believers find trouble in accepting a suffering Church, when that suffering includes the tribulation. They can see no advantage for believers being alive only with the prospect of facing suffering and death. When has there ever been any earthly advantage for saints in being alive when they are being tormented and killed by antichristian forces? One does not have to be a masochist or have a death wish to have the right Christian attitude toward suffering and dying. There is a vast difference between seeking pain and death, on the one hand, and, on the other, accepting them as those who know that these are the honored lot of those who follow in their Master's steps. As Peter tells us, "to this you have been called, because Christ also suffered for you, leaving you an example, that you should follow in his steps" (1 Pet. 2:21).

The martyrs of the ages did not have any consideration for any advantage in what lay before them, but rather for That One to whom they gave their allegiance. The disciples, beaten and charged not to speak in the name of Jesus, "left the presence of the council, rejoicing that they were counted worthy to suffer dishonor for the name" (Acts 5:41). This may well be one of the most joyous responses of the tribulation saints, together with the truth of Luke 21:28: "Now when these things begin to take place, look up and raise your heads, because your redemption is drawing near." May we be delivered from the sentiment that pleads, "Let thy congregation escape tribulation," and may we dare to ask the question, "Must I be carried to the skies on flow'ry beds of ease, while others fought to win the prize and sailed through bloody seas?"

*Lord, grant grace for the Crucible,*
*That I may exult in the Crown.*

# 5

# THE MILLENNIUM AND ITS POPULATION

### Kingdom Bright

*O, noble, novel age, by sages vowed,*
*Where He shall rule, to whom our knee has bowed,*
*Where man will yield,*
*and screech of beast turn dumb.*
*For this we plead, dear Liege: "Thy kingdom come!"*

### THE MILLENNIUM

Millennialism (also called chiliasm) is the belief in the coming of the millennium, or the thousand-year reign of Christ on earth.

The belief is based on Revelation 20, which states that Christ will reign for a thousand years.

Not all believers hold this conviction. There are three basic schools of thought relating to this teaching. There are amillennialists, postmillenialists and premillennialists.

Those who are amillennial do not believe in a literal thousand years and a physical rule of Christ on earth for this period of time. They see the language of the passage in Revelation 20 as symbolic. For them, the terms are spiritualized. It is not that they do not believe that there is a millennial concept in the passage, but rather that it doesn't mean a literal period of time. Their belief stems mainly from other passages of Scripture that would indicate that judgment comes at the second advent of Christ. For example: "But the day of the Lord will come like a thief, and then the heavens will pass away with a loud noise, and the elements will be dissolved with fire, and the earth and the works that are upon it will be burned up. Since all these things are thus to be dissolved, what sort of persons ought you to be in lives of holiness and godliness, waiting for and hastening the coming of the day of God, because of which the heavens will be kindled and dissolved, and the elements will melt with fire! But according to his promise we wait for new heavens and a new earth in which righteousness dwells" (2 Pet. 3:10–13).

Later, we will look at the features of the Old Testament promises to Israel of a coming golden age. In addition to spiritualizing the time stated in the Revelation 20 passage, those who hold to the amillennial view must spiritualize these golden age promises as well. They adopt a general position that somehow all the promises given to Israel about that time of peace and prosperity simply make use of physical references to reflect the spiritual joys that believers now experience. But this does not face the problem sufficiently and consistently. It does not explain, for example, just what it means in our present day experience with Christ that Ethiopia will bring gifts to the Lord in Jerusalem (Isa. 18:7), or that there will be a pillar to the Lord at Egypt's border or a highway from Egypt into Assyria (Isa. 19:19–25). Another problem in spiritualizing the golden age language is that, during that promised age, we will have great longevity together with sin and death (Isa. 65:20). That description does not seem to fit either our present spiritual condition on the one hand, or the eternal state on the other.

The experiences that Israel had in the Exodus and in the wilderness wanderings "happened to them as a warning, but they were written down for our instruction, upon whom the end of the ages has come" (1 Cor. 10:11). We have warrant, therefore, to draw spiritual lessons from them. When Paul talks about the Old Testament system of festivals in Colossians, he says clearly that those things were "only a shadow of what is to come" (2:16–17). This is an open invitation to derive spiritual meaning from observances held in those days. But to take prophetic promises to His ancient people and to make our own spiritual likenesses of them today is an exercise we have not been invited to engage in by any New Testament passage. The fact that we enter into the spiritual blessings of our father Abraham through faith, is not the same as saying that any and all physical promises to him are ours as well.

When we turn to the Word of God, concepts should be spiritualized only if (1) the Lord has permitted us to spiritualize them; (2) the literal meaning cannot be reconciled to the broader concept of Scripture; or (3) it cannot make good sense to take it literally. We can easily arrive at the following conclusions in carrying out these tests: (1) we have been given the right, as we have just seen, to look into the festivals for spiritual realities in today's life or history; (2) we can be assured that Christ did not want us actually to exercise hatred toward our parents because of His other teachings about love and because of other New Testament teachings about obligations toward our parents; and (3) we can know that Christ did not want people to become cannibals who would eat His physical body and drink His actual blood.

Scripture is reliable in its history. Its overall message contains an undeniable letter of love, in which the Creator woos back His estranged creature. But a special place of honor within the word of God is given by the Lord Himself to those passages where He sets forth His own predictions for the days to come.

In the Sermon on the Mount, Jesus tells His followers that "till heaven and earth pass away, not an iota, not a dot, will pass from the law until all is accomplished" (Matt. 5:18). The Lord sets His own predictive word in a category infinitely removed from all others when He says, "I am God, and there is none like me, declaring the end from the beginning and from ancient times things not done, saying, 'My counsel shall stand, and I will accomplish all my purpose,' calling a bird of prey from the east, the man of my counsel from a far country. I have spoken, and I will bring it to pass; I have purposed, and I will do it" (Isa. 46:9–11). The apostle Peter felt this burden when he stated that "we have the prophetic word made more sure" (2 Pet. 1:19). And the Lord calls the book of Revelation prophecy: "the words of the prophecy"

(1:3); "the words of the prophecy of this book" (22:7, 10, 18); and "the words of the book of this prophecy" (22:19). Indeed, the angel indicates that the word of prophecy is as dependable as the message of salvation in Christ when he says, "the testimony of Jesus is the spirit of prophecy" (19:10). Therefore, let all tread lightly when walking on holy ground. If God predicts something, let us be positive that it absolutely cannot be rendered literally.

Returning to the Revelation 20 passage, we should have the right to know why the "thousand year" period is so emphatic as to be used six times in six verses (2–7). But it is clear that Satan will be bound for a thousand years and then will be released again at the end of that time to deceive the nations. Amillennialists should explain clearly what the binding and releasing mean in reference to such a stated period of time. When, even in a spiritual sense, has this ever happened in individual Christian experience or when has it happened in the experience of the Church? Furthermore, why is the destruction of the devil omitted in the description of the destruction of the beast and false prophet mentioned in chapter 19 at the end of the tribulation and only now in chapter 20 depicted as coming a thousand years later? What does this mean symbolically?

Perhaps the greatest problem for the amillennial point of view is how one goes about symbolizing or spiritualizing the Revelation 20 passage in light of certain concrete specifics of the text itself. Few would argue that Christ does not defeat His enemies literally in chapter 19 at the end of the tribulation period, or that there is no tribulation depicted before that victory. Few would argue that there is not a beast or antichrist or man of sin during that period, or that there are not believers who lose their lives for failing to accept his mark or worship him. This presents an obstacle for amillennialists. Are these martyrs who are so real before chapter 20 now suddenly symbolic in this chapter? Obviously, for them to be resurrected shows that the tribulation is over. What symbolism can a thousand years of reigning have for them following the tribulation, especially since our archenemy is to be "loosed" again after that thousand-year time? How can this first resurrection at the end of the tribulation be symbolic when the resurrection of "those who belong to Christ" at his coming in 1 Corinthians 15:23 is real?

It seems that the amillennial view shares a weakness in interpretation with dispensationalists. That weakness is picking up pieces of the mosaic and looking at them in isolation, rather than laying them next to each other for a full-blown view. For example, based on Galatians 4:4 (where Paul states that Christ was "born of woman"), it would be wrong to conclude that it was not a virgin birth because it is not stated there. What makes such a conclusion wrong is that this truth is stated elsewhere in Scripture. So, just as those with a pretribulation view omit the tribulation martyrs from the "dead in Christ" of 1 Thessalonians 4:16 (though they are mentioned in the "first resurrection" of Revelation 20:4) because they are not specifically named there, the amillennialists leave out the millennium teaching of Revelation 20:1–10 when they look at the day of the Lord concept in 2 Peter 3:10–13 simply because it is not mentioned there. But one would have just as much right to conclude that the 2 Peter passage is symbolic and the Revelation 20 passage is literal. We need to take these teachings, the teachings of the golden age, the judgment of the nations in Matthew 25:31–46 and all other teachings relating to the day of the Lord, and fit the pieces together. In other words, the day of the Lord includes the return of Christ, the judgment of the nations, the full millennial reign, the final judgment, the destruction of the present heavens and earth, and the new heavens and new earth (shown after the millennium in Revelation). If a passage, like 2 Peter, says the day of the Lord will come with fire and judgment, it has simply left that part out that relates to the millennium, and we are obligated to place it in its proper position.

The second school of thought on the millennium is that of the postmillennialists. They believe that the millennium will come first and then Christ will return to earth at the end of that time. This belief is based on the idea that the world, and specifically humanity, is improving. There have been adherents of this view as far back as Augustine in the Fourth Century A.D. It was held by many at the end of the nineteenth century and early in the twentieth century. The position suffered the loss of many followers, however, with the advent of two world wars. A recent development, that shares some of the hopes and expectations of this view, is the "kingdom now" movement. Believers are seen by them as infiltrating leadership positions, and thereby "christianizing" the world to prepare it for Christ's return. In the light of man's record and of the kinds of directions being reflected in both government and society, it seems to be an unrealistic expectation. Furthermore, because of the picture Scripture paints of man's condition and attitudes in the latter days, and because of the descriptions of the characteristics of the tribulation, few seem eager to embrace this position.

The third school of thought on the millennium is called premillennialism. Nearly all pretribulationists (who hold that Christ will rapture the Church before the tribulation) and some posttribulationists (who believe that this will take place at the end of the tribulation), share this view of the millennium. According to this view, Christ will return to the earth after the tribulation, will bind Satan, will judge the nations, and will set up His rule on the earth for a thousand years, aided by the resurrected saints. Following the thousand-year reign, Satan will be loosed and will gather an army against Christ. Christ will defeat him, and the rest of mankind will be resurrected and will face the white throne judgment. The old heaven and earth will be dissolved by fire and we will enter a new and eternal heaven and earth. This position has the advantage of accepting all the teachings regarding Christ's return (without spiritualizing some) and fitting the pieces together.

The premillennial view sees in the millennium the fulfillment of all of the Old Testament promises made to Israel about a coming golden age that would have Jerusalem as its center and believing Jews at the hub of the knowledge of God for the nations. This kingdom would be ruled over by the Messiah and His saints.

## CHARACTERISTICS OF THE MILLENNIUM

Most of the characteristics of the millennium are depicted in Old Testament prophecies with a few added from the New Testament. The majority of the Old Testament references are drawn from the book of Isaiah. He wrote more about this time and more consistently about it than any other writer. The characteristics are not intended to be exhaustive, but they are representative and give a wide spectrum of conditions during that time.

One will look in vain for any mention of a temple as one of the characteristics. There are those who feel that the new temple described in Ezekiel 40–48 is a temple in the millennial period. One could take the position that there will be an implementing of some kind of sacrificial system in the millennium as a sort of looking back at the complete sacrifice of Christ, even as we use the Lord's Supper to look back at it now. It would certainly be more sensible to spiritualize the idea of sacrifices than to spiritualize the entire golden age idea and the thousand-year concept. But a study of the passage has convinced me that sacrifice is not being outlined for the time of that golden age. The measurements of the temple itself are certainly exact. But the whole passage taken together seems to be a description of differing times and conditions. Prophecies were given in close proximity regarding Christ's suffering and reign, and the prophecies of the regathering of Israel included part of those prophecies dealing with a temporary and conditional situation on the one hand and a permanent, even eternal, situation on the other. Even so, the details of the temple and its worship patterns show rather marked differences from section to section.

It becomes obvious that the passage cannot be taken in its entirety as a millennial temple. Since the prince of that time may make "a gift to any of his sons out of his inheritance" (46:16), this can't possible refer to the ruler of the millennium, namely, Christ. Furthermore, Ezekiel tells us that "on that day the prince shall provide for himself and all the people of the land a young bull for a sin offering" (45:22). The idea that this prince could be Christ is a preposterous one, since He is himself man's sin offering and needs no such offering for himself. If we can grant this point, it should be no difficult matter to grant also that the sacrificial systems described here do not belong to the millennial kingdom either. We can find nothing in any passage clearly dealing with that golden age, the millennium, which indicates the presence of a sacrificial system, or even a temple. Indeed, in the New Jerusalem period immediately following the millennium, John tells us, "And I saw no temple in the city, for its temple is the Lord God the Almighty and the Lamb" (Rev. 21:22).

The actual mosaic of the golden age, millennial period lends itself well to a threefold division based on the concept of ruling. We discover three aspects of this: Messiah Reigns, Peace Reigns, and Justice Reigns.

## Messiah Reigns

**He will reign in Jerusalem.** "The Lord of hosts will reign on Mount Zion and in Jerusalem and before his elders he will manifest his glory" (Isa. 24:23); and "At that time Jerusalem shall be called the throne of the Lord and all nations shall gather to it, to the presence of the Lord in Jerusalem" (Jer. 3:17).

**He will be David's greater Son.** "In that day the root of Jesse shall stand as an ensign to the peoples; him shall the nations seek, and his dwellings shall be glorious" (Isa. 11:10); and "Behold, the days are coming, says the Lord, when I will raise up for David a righteous Branch, and he shall reign as king and deal wisely, and shall execute justice and righteousness in the land" (Jer. 23:5).

**He will rule in might and justice.** "Behold, the Lord God comes with might, and his arm rules for him" (Isa. 40:10); and "with righteousness he shall judge the poor, and decide with equity for the meek of the earth" (Isa. 11:4).

**He will rule in gentleness.** "Behold, the Lord God ... will feed his flock like a shepherd, he will gather the lambs in his arms, he will carry them in his bosom, and gently lead those that are with young" (Isa. 40:10–11).

**He will rule with His saints.** "And the house of Israel will ... rule over those who oppressed them" (Isa. 14:2); "Jesus said to them, 'Truly, I say to you, in the new world, when the Son of man shall sit on his glorious throne, you who have followed me will also sit on twelve thrones, judging the twelve tribes of Israel" (Matt. 19:28); and "I saw the souls of those who had been beheaded for their testimony to Jesus ... and who had not worshipped the beast or its image.... They came to life, and reigned with Christ a thousand years" (Rev. 20:4).

## PEACE REIGNS

### Peace will reign in Jerusalem

"Look upon Zion, the city of our appointed feasts! Your eyes will see Jerusalem, a quiet habitation, an immovable tent, whose stakes will never be plucked up, nor will any of its cords be broken" (Isa. 33:20).

1. Jerusalem becomes central. "It shall come to pass in the latter days that the mountain of the house of the Lord shall be established as the highest of the mountains, and shall be raised above the hills; and all the nations shall flow to it" (Isa. 2:2).
2. People come to Jerusalem to learn of the Lord. "And many peoples shall come, and say: 'Come, let us go up to the mountain of the Lord, to the house of the God of Jacob; that he may teach us his ways and that we may walk in his paths.' For out of Zion shall go forth the law, and the word of the Lord from Jerusalem" (Isa. 2:3); and "Rejoice with Jerusalem, and glad for her, all you who love her ... drink deeply with delight from the abundance of her glory" (Isa. 66:10–11).
   a) Ethiopia will bring gifts. "Ah, land of whirring wings which is beyond the rivers of Ethiopia.... At that time gifts will be brought to the Lord of hosts from a people tall and smooth, from a people feared near and far, a nation mighty and con‐quering, whose land the rivers divide, to Mount Zion, the place of the name of the Lord of hosts" (Isa. 18:1, 7).
   b) Egypt and Iraq (Assyria) will join in worship with Israel. "In that day there will be a highway from Egypt to Assyria, and the Assyrian will come into

Egypt, and the Egyptian into Assyria, and the Egyptians will worship with the Assyrians. In that day Israel will be the third with Egypt and Assyria, a blessing in the midst of the earth, whom the Lord of hosts has blessed, saying, 'Blessed be Egypt my people, and Assyria the work of my hands, and Israel my heritage' " (Isa. 19:23–25).

## Peace will reign among men

1. Their food needs will be met. "He will feed his flock like a shepherd" (Isa. 40:11).
2. They will enjoy health and healing. "And no inhabitant will say, 'I am sick' " (Isa. 33:24); and "Then the eyes of the blind shall be opened, and the ears of the deaf unstopped; then shall the lame man leap like a hart, and the tongue of the dumb sing for joy" (Isa. 35: 5–6).
3. They will enjoy great longevity. "No more shall there be in it an infant that lives but a few days, or an old man who does not fill out his days, for the child shall die a hundred years old, and the sinner a hundred years old shall be accursed" (Isa. 65:20).
4. They will own private houses and gardens. "They shall build houses and inhabit them; they shall plant vineyards and eat their fruit" (Isa. 65:21); and "But they shall sit every man under his vine and under his fig tree, and none shall make them afraid; for the mouth of the Lord of hosts has spoken" (Mic. 4:4).
5. They will not have war. "And they shall beat their swords into plowshares, and their spears into pruning hooks; nation shall not lift up sword against nation, neither shall they learn war any more" (Isa. 2:4; Mic. 4:3).

## Peace will reign in nature

1. There will be rivers in the desert. "Remember not the former things, nor consider the things of old. Behold, I am doing a new thing; now it springs forth, do you

not perceive it? I will make a way in the wilderness and rivers in the desert" (Isa. 43:18–19).
2. The desert will blossom like a garden. "The wilderness and the dry land shall be glad, the desert shall rejoice and blossom; like the crocus it shall blossom abundantly, and rejoice with joy and singing" (Isa. 35:1–2); and "For the Lord will comfort Zion; he will comfort all her waste places, and will make her wilderness like Eden, her desert like the garden of the Lord; joy and gladness will be found in her, thanksgiving and the voice of song" (Isa. 51:3).
3. All wild animals will become tame. "The wolf shall dwell with the lamb, and the leopard shall lie down with the kid, and the calf and the lion and the fatling together, and a little child shall lead them. The cow and the bear shall feed; their young shall lie down together; and the lion shall eat straw like the ox. The sucking child shall play over the hole of the asp, and the weaned child shall put his hand on the adder's den. They shall not hurt or destroy in all my holy mountain; for the earth shall be full of the knowledge of the Lord as the waters cover the sea" (Isa. 11:6–9).
4. The ground will not be cursed with thorns. "Instead of the thorn shall come up the cypress; instead of the brier shall come up the myrtle; and it shall be to the Lord for a memorial, for an everlasting sign which shall not be cut off" (Isa. 55:13).

**Justice Reigns**

1. Israel's sins will be forgiven. "Behold, the days are coming, says the Lord, when I will raise up for David a righteous Branch, and he shall reign as king and deal wisely, and shall execute justice and righteousness in the land. In his days Judah will be saved, and Israel will dwell securely. And this is the name by which he will be called: 'The Lord is our righteousness' " (Jer. 23:5–6); "And no inhabitant will say, 'I am sick'; the people who dwell there will be forgiven their iniquity" (Isa. 33:24); and "On that day there

shall be a fountain opened for the house of David and the inhabitants of Jerusalem to cleanse them from sin and uncleanness" (Zech. 13:1).
2. There will be just rule among men. "Behold a king will reign in righteousness, and princes will rule in justice. Each will be like a hiding place from the wind, a covert from the tempest, like streams of water in a dry place, like the shade of a great rock in a weary land. Then the eyes of those who see will not be closed, and the ears of those who hear will hearken" (Isa. 32:1–3).
3. Angels will be punished. "On that day the Lord will punish the host of heaven, in heaven, and the kings of the earth, on the earth. They will be gathered together as prisoners in a pit; they will be shut up in a prison, and after many days they will be punished" (Isa. 24:21–22).
4. The serpent will be punished and destroyed. "In that day the Lord with his hard and great and strong sword will punish Leviathan the fleeing serpent, Leviathan the twisting serpent, and he will slay the dragon that is in the sea" (Isa. 27:1).

There are at least four details of the Old Testament description of the golden age that are repeated in the Revelation 20 account of the thousand-year reign. The two accounts complement each other and dovetail together. First, the Old Testament prophecy declares that it is the Messiah, David's greater Son, who will reign. Revelation 20:4 says that it is Christ (the Greek form of the Hebrew term, Messiah) who reigns. Second, He will reign in Jerusalem. Revelation 20:9 indicates that Christ and His saints will be will be in "the beloved city," which is Jerusalem. Third, we have seen that angels are to be punished. In Matthew 25:41, Jesus indicated that the lake of fire was "prepared for the devil and his angels." Christ's victory at the end of the tribulation shows only that the beast and the false prophet ("these two") "were thrown alive into the lake of fire." So, it would be natural to assume, that when the devil is thrown into it according to Revelation 20:10, that his angels will join him there as well. Fourth, we were shown in the Old Testament that the serpent himself will be punished. Revelation 20:2 gives four synonyms for our great enemy: the dragon, that ancient serpent, the Devil, and Satan. We have already seen that the devil is thrown into the lake of fire at the end of the thousand years (v. 10).

## THE MILLENNIAL POPULATION—ITS RULERS

There are many areas of disagreement between pretribulationists and posttribulationists. It is refreshing to come across those areas on which we agree. Obviously, we agree that He is coming back. For those of us who believe that He will set up a millennial reign, we also agree that the general population will not have eternal bodies.

That the general populace (those to be ruled over) during this period will be mortal certainly can be sustained by verses such as Isaiah 65:20, where we learn that one dying at the age of one hundred will be thought of as having been but a child. However, there is no clear indication that the populace will be "believers" in the sense that indicates belief in Christ. Indeed, the very verse in Isaiah 65 that mentioned the "young" centenarian's death also says that "the sinner a hundred years old shall be accursed." This would argue more for an unbelieving general populace than one that believes. The fact that the knowledge of the Lord will cover the earth does not support the concept of a believing populace. It merely indicates that there will be a worldwide knowledge of the Lord.

In looking at the entire population of the millennium, we need to distinguish between those who are mortal and will be ruled over on the one hand, and those who rule over them on the other. We are in agreement that those who rule will have immortal bodies. We are not in agreement, however, over the identity of the rulers. The question arises: Who will reign with Christ at that time? Why do I ask "at that time?" Although we are seated with Christ in the heavenly places positionally at this time, there is no reigning with Christ now. The time for reigning with Christ would appear to be during and after the millennium itself. Who, therefore, will reign with Him?

There is a bittersweet irony in one of the pretribulation opinions relating to the saints found on earth at Christ's return. They hold that only the martyrs of that period will have resurrected, glorified bodies, and will reign with Christ, but not the believers who survive that dreadful time. If the tribulation believers who outlive the tribulation are not to be glorified at its conclusion, but are merely to be part of the millennial kingdom as mortals to be ruled over, it would have been much better for them to have been able to die for Christ during the tribulation. And, yet, was it not of that time that Christ said, "but he who endures to the end will be saved"? (Matt. 10:22). If being "saved" means going in a mortal body into the millennium, whereas those who could not endure until the end and were slain for their witness end up resurrected and glorified, it would appear to be much better to put one's head upon the block and not be "saved" in this manner, and thus have to wait for eventual immortality. What a pity for them to have survived and to have to remain mortal, rather than to have died and to be able to become immortal.

There is an indication in Daniel 7 that the Old Testament saints, as Daniel understood them, would possess the coming kingdom. In verse 18 he says that "the saints of the Most High shall receive the kingdom, and possess the kingdom for ever, for ever and ever." Matthew tells us that in the new world when the Son of man shall sit on His glorious throne, the twelve disciples "will also sit on twelve thrones, judging the twelve tribes of Israel" (Matt. 19:28). Paul said that it was a saying that we could accept with assurance that "if we endure, we shall also reign with him" (2 Tim. 2:12). And during the millennium there were those who "reigned with Christ a thousand years" (Rev. 20:4). Also after the millennium, "his servants shall worship him; they shall see his face, and his name shall be on their foreheads. And night shall be no more; they need no light of lamp or sun, for the Lord God will be their light, and they shall reign for ever and ever" (Rev. 22:3–5).

When we combine these facts with what we know of our relationship with Christ following the rapture, there can be no doubt that we shall be with Him during and after the millennium. We are told in John that we will be where He is, "that where I am you may be also" (14:3), and Paul says that we shall "meet the Lord in the air; and so we shall always be with the Lord" (1 Thess. 4:17). It ought to be crystal clear that He has promised us that wherever He is, there we will be with Him. During the millennium, it is said that He will be reigning on earth. He has promised us that we will reign with Him and will always be where He is. Therefore, we will be with Him on earth. The disciples will be helping in the reign over converted Israel. Nothing is said of the Gentiles, but it would seem logical that the raptured (resurrected and transformed) saints will help Him reign over the Gentile peoples at that time. So we have Old Testament saints, the twelve disciples, believers of the present age, and tribulation saints all reigning in that kingdom together with Christ. That is the unity of the saints.

### THE GENERAL MILLENNIAL POPULATION

If the saints are to reign with Christ during the millennium, who will form the general population to be ruled over? The pretribulationists argue that there will only be two classes of people during the tribulation, believers in Christ and worshipers of the beast, since "all who dwell on earth will worship it [the beast], every one whose name has not been written before the foundation of the world in the book of life of the Lamb that was slain" (Rev. 13:8).

The word all as used in this verse ("all who dwell on earth will worship it") can be misleading. If we take the "who dwell on the earth" to be (as some do) all those except believers ("every one whose name has not been written before the foundation of the world in the book of life of the Lamb that was slain"), then it would appear that only those who believe in Jesus do not worship it. It would seem to indicate that everyone who is not a believer does worship the beast.

Certainly the word all usually means "universally all with no exceptions." This is the meaning of the word as it is used in Romans 3:23: "all have sinned and fall short of the glory of God," and the context confirms that there were no exceptions. It is not always all-inclusive, however, and can be similar to our "everybody" ("everybody does this" and "everybody was at the party"). Thus, there are many occasions when the term is used in a general sense with the implication of "a great many" or "some from every group." The context will usually require that our logic render this meaning in these cases where it is general.

For example, in Luke 2:1 we read that "in those days a decree went out from Caesar Augustus that all the world should be taxed." Aside from our present knowledge that there were parts of the world that were completely unknown to the writer at that time, not even all the known world of that day was under the control of Rome. Thus, they could not even tax all of that known world.

In Matthew 2:3, we read that "when Herod heard this, he was troubled, and all Jerusalem with him." Most readers would be aware that there were many in Jerusalem who did not hear the inquiries of the wise men and who, therefore, could not be included in this general "all."

And in Matthew 3:4–5, we are told that John the Baptist "wore a garment of camel's hair, and a leather girdle around his waist; and his food was locusts and wild honey. Then went out to him Jerusalem and all Judea and all the region about the Jordan." Though John was a popular teacher, he did not attract everybody in Judea and the entire Jordan populace.

In Matthew 4:24, we are told that the fame of Jesus "spread throughout all Syria, and they brought him all the sick." It should be obvious again that reports of His works did not reach everybody who lived in Syria and that not every sick person in the area of Galilee was brought to him.

When Jesus sent the Twelve out on a mission, He said "you will be hated by all for my name's sake" (Matt. 10:22). But He had already said that some houses they were to visit would be worthy, though others would not receive them. Certainly those who were worthy and received them would not hate them.

Of course, it was not Matthew or Luke who wrote the words in Revelation 13:8. It was John. Did John in his other writings use the generalized concept of "all"? Indeed he did—in his Gospel and in all three of his letters. In John 3:26, he records the conversation that the disciples of John the Baptist had with the baptizer on the matter of Jesus also baptizing. They stated, "here he is, baptizing, and all are going to him." Not only were all the local people not going to Him, but not even all of the disciples of the Baptist were going to Him, since these very disciples obviously excepted themselves from those going to Jesus.

The Samaritan woman, amazed at the things Jesus knew about her personal life, confronted her fellow villagers with the challenge, "Come, see a man who told me all that I ever did" (John 4:29). After the personal details, she may have assumed that he knew everything about her, but it should be clear that in the few moments He talked with her that He did not cover every detail of her life.

Again, after Jesus had been to the Mount of Olives and "came again to the temple," we are told that "all the people came to him" (John 8:2). The size of the temple alone would make us realize that only a small fraction of the people in Jerusalem could fit into the temple area at one time and that we are simply dealing with a large group of people.

John even shows Jesus using the word in a non-universal way. He tells His disciples, "By this all men will know that you are my disciples, if you have love for one another" (John 13:35). Certainly many in the first century bore testimony to the love of the followers of Jesus, but most of the world of that day knew neither Jesus nor His disciples.

This use of "all" carries over to John's letters as well. In 1 John 2:16, John states that "all that is in the world ... is not of the Father," but then he enumerates the concepts that he has in mind when he discusses what that all includes.

Also, in talking about the Holy Spirit, he says that "his anointing teaches you about everything" (1 John 2:27). Doubtless the readers knew that John was speaking about spiritual matters and not about all that there was to be known in life.

In John's second letter, he begins by this greeting: "The elder to the elect lady and her children whom I love in the truth and not only I but also all who know the truth" (2 John 1). Probably the majority of believers who knew this group of believers did love them, but the majority of believers of that time likely did not know them at all.

Finally, in his third letter, John commends Demetrius because he "has testimony from everyone" (3 John 12). Demetrius may, indeed, have had a good testimony from almost all believers who knew him, but a much larger group did not even know him.

How does this apply to Revelation 13:7–8? There we are told that the beast "was allowed to make war on the saints and to conquer them. And authority was given it over every tribe and people and tongue and nation, and all who dwell on earth will worship it, every one whose name has not been written before the foundation of the world in the book of life of the Lamb that was slain." Certainly the text indicates that the beast will have adherents (even worshipers) from every people group, even as Christ will, for the beast is the great impersonator. But the context of the chapter and the wider context of the book reveal that none of the other seemingly all-inclusive concepts are really universal, but are only stated in a generalized sense. It also becomes clear that "every one whose name has not been written ... in the book of life" is not the only exception to the "all" statement.

First, the saints are warred against but certainly not totally conquered, since the section ending in verse 10 states that "here is a call for the endurance and faith of the saints." They endure and can continue to believe precisely because they are not fully conquered. In fact, in the seven representative churches of Revelation, there are those from each church who will, themselves, conquer, since a separate promise is given "to him who conquers" from each group. Furthermore, near the end of the tribulation (described in chapter 15), just before the bowls of the seven plagues, the believers beside the sea of glass mingled with fire are seen standing as conquerors of "the beast and its image and the number of its name" (Rev. 15:2).

Second, the authority given to the beast "over every tribe and people and tongue and nation" is a limited authority. Very likely, it will consist mainly of commercial or economic power in the world's marketplace, since verse 17 tells us that power for buying and selling is tied to the mark of the beast's name or number. But we see from verse 16 that the second beast is busy trying to force people to acquire such identification well after the "worldwide" authority had already been established by the beast in verse 7. Certainly, the farther away nations or people are from the center of the beast's authority (the European arena) the weaker that authority becomes. Just as the Arab oil countries would have an important impact on western lands during an oil crisis and just as that influence weakens as those lands make themselves less dependent on foreign oil, so the economic control of the beast will have less and less strength the farther away it gets from the contiguous Euro-Asian-Middle Eastern-North African land mass, which encompasses the greatest sphere of his power and influence.

Finally, after verse 8 states that all nonbelievers will worship the beast, we find the second beast going around making "the earth and its inhabitants worship the first beast" (verse 12) and killing those who refuse to worship it. No indication is even given whether those who refuse are believers or nonbelievers. In fact, we see, even at the end of the tribulation, that people other than the saints were put to death, doubtless because they would not worship the beast either. In Babylon "was found the blood of prophets and of saints, and of all who have been slain on earth" (Rev. 18:24). Even the pretribulationists see the armies of the north, the eastern bloc nations, and hordes of the Orientals moving against the Antichrist and his European Confederacy. Obviously, if they join in battle against him, they must represent a very sizable chunk of mankind that is not worshiping him or giving allegiance to him, but is actually and actively opposed to him. If Antichrist's hold over peoples on the very land mass he occupies is so very tenuous, what are we to say of those who are separated by oceans from him? The whole northern and southern hemispheres of the Americas, Australia, and the island world are certainly doubtful in terms of the strength of his authority and control. Even in the assembly of the nations to Armageddon described in Revelation 16:12–16, it is not certain that every nation is represented. But even from those that are there, there remain at home the majority of their population, millions of whom are not loyal to the beast. This very idea is fully supported by Zechariah

14:16, which states that during the millennium "every one that survives of all the nations that have come against Jerusalem shall go up year after year to worship the King, the Lord of hosts, and to keep the feast of booths." So, even when the fighting at Armageddon is over and the forces following the beast are destroyed, there remains a potential of millions upon millions of unbelieving people who have not fully given themselves (either in mark or worship) to the beast.

Thus, we have an immense pool of unbelievers to draw from to make up the general population to be ruled over during the millennium. There are pretribulationists who would have us believe that the people of the millennium are people with cleansed hearts, using as proof texts the predictions of Jeremiah 31:31–34 and Ezekiel 36:26–27, that the Lord would write his laws in the people's hearts and put His spirit in them so that they would walk in His statutes. This comes from a misreading of the texts involved and their greater contexts. To begin with, it is clear that only Israel is spoken of here. Nothing is even hinted about the Gentiles. Furthermore, even for Israel an overall pattern is developed. It is the sword followed by "grace in the wilderness," then a final gathering, and only after this—after those days—that He will write His law upon their hearts. This agrees with Luke 21:24, where Israel is led captive and Jerusalem is trodden down until the end of the times of the Gentiles, and also with Zechariah 12:10–13:1, where Israel is cleansed only after looking "on him whom they have pierced."

Now, what of the Gentiles who go into that kingdom? According to pretribulationists, as we have just noted, these must be people with cleansed hearts—saved people. They contend that this leaves posttribulationists at a disadvantage. They believe that we must somehow fit in a time when living tribulation people are given a second chance to be saved, thereby assuring a believing population for the millennium. But what if we were to say that they are not believers at all, but unsaved people who outlived the millennium without accepting the mark of the beast? Let us consider some of the things said by the prophets of Israel about that time as it relates to them. Isaiah tells us that "many peoples shall come, and say: 'Come, let us go up to the mountain of the Lord, to the house of the God of Jacob; that he may teach us his ways and that we may walk in his paths.' For out of Zion shall go forth the law and the word of the Lord from Jerusalem" (Isa. 2:3). If the nations or peoples are going up to Jerusalem to be taught the Lord's ways in those days, it sounds very much as if they do not know much about those ways and perhaps about the Lord, Himself. This does not seem consistent with the pretribulation idea that these are people with cleansed hearts who know the Lord in a personal way. Even though Isaiah 2:2 says that "all the nations shall flow" to Jerusalem, verse 3 continues that "many peoples shall come, and say: 'Come, let us go up to the mountain of the Lord.'" Not only does there seem to be this lack of basic knowledge, but there also seems to be a freedom of choice, as well as a varied interest in the Lord. It would seem that some may not even desire to increase the knowledge they already have.

Another pertinent Isaiah passage tells us that "the earth shall be full of the knowledge of the Lord as the waters cover the sea" (11:9). All this passage tells us is that knowledge of the Lord will be worldwide—there will be no part of the world to which the knowledge of the Lord does not extend. This does not mean, however, that only people with cleansed hearts will live in this kingdom. Isaiah 65:20 states that there will be death in that kingdom. There will be greatly increased longevity—one who dies at one hundred years will be considered but a child—but there will be death. This, certainly is one of the ugliest consequences of sin, but it will be there. Furthermore, the same verse says that "the sinner a hundred years shall be accursed." If his heart has been cleansed from sin, why is he yet called a sinner?

But returning to Isaiah 11, where the earth is to be "full of the knowledge of the Lord" (v. 9), we see the kingdom rule of the Messiah described: "He shall not judge by what his eyes see, or decide by what his ears hear; but with righteousness he shall judge the poor, and decide with equity for the meek of the earth; and he shall smite the earth with the rod of his mouth, and with the breath of his lips he shall slay the wicked. Righteousness shall be the girdle of his waist, and faithfulness the girdle of his loins. The wolf shall dwell with the lamb and the leopard shall lie down with the kid" (Isa. 11:3–6). In the context of His kingdom rule, there would seem to be some "wicked" there even though the Prince of Wickedness is chained for one thousand years. Then the nations shall seek the Messiah: "the root of Jesse" who shall "stand as an ensign to the peoples" (v. 10). Though there is a knowledge of the Lord worldwide, there are many nations who seek Him during this time. This accords with what we saw in Isaiah 2:3, where the nations go up to Jerusalem to learns the Lord's ways. But these are, according to all accounts mentioned, people who "seek" Him, who go to be taught His ways, and "sinners," rather than people with new and purified hearts who believe in Messiah.

Actually, the very opposite seems to be true of the general populace. We would appear to be dealing with a basically unbelieving or rebel heart on the part of these millennial inhabitants. We learn in Zechariah that "every one that survives of all the nations that have come against Jerusalem shall go up year after year to worship the King, the Lord of hosts, and to keep the feast of booths. And if any of the families of the earth do not go up to Jerusalem to worship the King, the Lord of hosts, there will be no rain upon them. And if the family of Egypt do not go up and present themselves, then upon them shall come the plague with which the Lord afflicts the nations that do not go up to keep the feast of booths. This shall be the punishment to Egypt and the punishment to all the nations that do not go up to keep the feast of booths" (14:16–19).

This last passage only makes clear sense if the population of the nations in this millennial kingdom are unsaved people who refused to worship the beast and receive his mark during the tribulation. First, they are survivors "of all the nations that have come against Jerusalem" at the end of the tribulation. This would seem to be a strange description of saints who had trusted the Lord during that time. At the end of the previous chapter, the Lord said of those who would call on His name in that period, "I will answer them. I will say, 'They are my people' " (v. 9). To switch from "my people" for those who trusted Him to "survivors" of nations pitted against Jerusalem seems too great a transition. Second, there is a consequence laid down for those who refuse to "go up to Jerusalem to worship the King." They would receive no rain. This appears completely out of character for those who know the Lord and could appreciate His rule over them after He had delivered them from their enemy, the Antichrist. But it would be a fitting description of those who, in their flesh and humanness rebelled against the beast and rejected his authority over them. Some of them now also reject the authority of their new ruler, the King. Just as rain was withheld from those in the Old Testament who did not believe and who rejected the Lord's authority, so shall it be here. Third, in singling out the family of Egypt, the Lord says that if they did not go up, the plague would come upon them. Once again, if they are a believing family, it seems inconsistent for them to refuse. But if they are unsaved rebels from the tribulation, it would be a logical response. In choosing the "plague" for Egyptian rebels, it would seem to be poetic justice. When God's people were afflicted by the Egyptians during the days of Moses, the plagues came upon the Egyptians who opposed God, but Israel was delivered.

One of the very last pieces to fall into place for me in studying the transition period from tribulation to millennium was this concept of the rebel heart. I wondered how there could be a millennial population if the world were merely divided into camps loyal either to Christ or to the beast. It was then that social and political realities in the world began to break in upon my understanding. As I considered the sweep of human history, I could find no leader who drew universal admiration, let alone obedience. Even Christ himself, with all of His miracles, did not capture dedication from the majority of His hearers. Totally aside from Christian commitment, the natural human heart is rebellious and self-centered. It is a hard fact of political and religious life that many mavericks abound who will not yield their wills to another—even when they have no personal faith—out of a fierce, if not perverse, sense of independence. The spirit of Invictus (William Ernest Henley, 1875) will live during the tribulation even as it does today. Many will stand with heads "bloody, but unbowed."

We have seen in our own country the defiance of the 1960s embodied in the halls of Berkeley. When stationed in Germany just before and just after the close of the war, I discovered that most Germans did not belong to the Nazi party. Even in the decline of the Communist power structure, we can see that even in its heyday it did not exact anything like universal dedication. In an article in the Star-News of Pasadena, California, the following was noted:

> SAN FRANCISCO—An "unusually threatening" letter from a Communist Party leader to Chinese tennis star Hu Na before she defected to the United States is a key piece of evidence in her request for political asylum, her attorney says. Miss Hu, 19, based her asylum request on fear of persecution because of her refusal to join the party and represent its leadership as a "model to youth," said her attorney, Edward C. Y. Lau. (From the *Star-News*, Pasadena, CA, March 22, 1983.)

We see a leading personality not willing to bow to the system in spite of her favored position within the country itself. The Chinese brand of Communism has proved to be much more repressive than that which was in the Soviet Union. In spite of this, they lost Miss Hu. But there are countless millions of others whom they have never gained, and we are not speaking of the Christians in that land. In the Intelligence Report of Parade magazine a report relating to this was given under From the Fact File:

> Of the 1.1 billion people in China, 48 million are members of the Communist Party, although 33,400 were expelled last year for "unhealthy tendencies." Such tendencies, explains People's Daily, the party newspaper, range from ideological inadequacy to the abuse of power. (From *Parade Magazine*, May 13, 1990.)

This means that only about 4 percent of China's population belongs to the party and over 95 percent do not, and that out of a population of 1.1 billion people, 1.052 billion refuse to receive such an identifying mark. And this in what is doubtless the most powerful Communist structure in the world.

The Antichrist will be powerful, but he will not be powerful enough to capture the allegiance of the skeptical hearts of all the unsaved—even in his own arena.

This insight makes it much easier to understand the scene early in the millennium when some would refuse to go up to Jerusalem to learn about the Lord (see Zechariah 14:17), and would have rain withheld from them, as well as the scene at the end of the millennium when Satan gathers nations to war against "the camp of the saints and the beloved city" (Rev. 20:7–9). If those who populate the millennium are saved people, it is somewhat surprising that children of believers, living with believing parents in an ideal society with justice reigning, and ruled over by the Savior Himself, would blithely rebel early in the millennium, and then at the end of the millennium rebel to such an extent and in such numbers ("their number is like the sand of the sea" [Rev. 20:8]) that they would march against the beloved city.

It is much more rational if these peoples of the millennium are unbelievers. They have been ushered into this kingdom as a result of their treatment of believers during the tribulation (as we will see in a study of Matthew 25:31–46). This had been kind treatment, because they saw the believers as fellow rebels against the tyranny of the beast. Whereas the believers withstood and defied him because of their allegiance to Christ, these "unmarked" unbelievers did not understand such nice distinctions. They withstood and defied him because they were rebels at heart, or because they resented anyone over them in a "big brother" role. They did not want to be forced or coerced by anyone.

Now in the millennium, they are once again living under the rule of a dictator—a benevolent dictator, to be sure, but a dictator nonetheless. It is not that surprising, therefore, that elements of rebellion remain in them. It is also understandable that, through the influence of their homes, their children and their children's children to the third and fourth generation (however long that will be in the millennium) should retain these rebellious attitudes. It is logical to see such offspring rallying behind Satan at the end of the thousand years.

It is also noteworthy that Satan's strategy, when he is loosed at that time, is not the frontal power play that evidenced itself in the tribulation, that the forefathers of these people resisted, but rather a design of slight-of-hand, for we are told that he "will come out to deceive the nations" (Rev. 20:7). His primary tool at that time will be that of deception. And so we have come full circle. Satan used deceit on our first parents in the first paradise to bring the first sin into the world and to end that paradise. Now he uses deceit again on the last mortals, to bring the last sin into the world to end the second paradise.

### MATTHEW 25:31–46 AND THE MILLENNIAL POPULATION

There seems to be a great deal of agreement between those who hold the pretribulation position and those who are posttribulationists that the kingdom in this passage is the millennial kingdom and that the ones who are rewarded are being ushered into that kingdom. The key disagreement lies in the identity of this group who are ready to become the citizens of this kingdom.

There are those who have used these verses down through the years to challenge believers to a sense of social responsibility. These efforts have made this perhaps the most often misused and misapplied passage of Scripture in the New Testament. Obviously, since its message is spoken to the nations at the return of Christ, it is for those living on earth at that time—not to immortalized believers. No resurrection is in view. To apply it to believers down through the ages in order to instill in them a sense of social responsibility is to miss the audience completely. There are many passages that speak to us of our social duties (see Ps. 41:1; Prov. 14:21; Luke 3:11; 14:13–14; James 2:15–17; and 1 John 3:17), but this is not one of them.

The pretribulation position states that those who are invited into the kingdom are those who have believed in Christ during the tribulation and have lived through the tribulation. My position and that of some other posttribulationists is that these are unsaved people who have come through the tribulation without receiving the mark of the beast and have given assistance to believers in their difficulties through that period.

It should be admitted at the beginning that both the pretribulation position and the posttribulation position have a problem as it relates to verse 46. It states there that the righteous will go "into eternal life." There are but two stages of eternal life. The first is when we place our trust in Christ, have our sins forgiven and pass from spiritual death into spiritual life. This takes care of our spirit or immaterial nature. Paul tells us, however, that "we ourselves, who have the first fruits of the Spirit, groan inwardly as we wait for adoption as sons, the redemption of our bodies" (Rom. 8:23). Thus, the second stage is when we pass bodily into immortality. For this, our bodies must be changed, either by resurrection or by transformation.

What kind of a problem does this present for the pretribulation position? According to them, these are people who have trusted Christ during the tribulation period. At that time of belief, they passed into life spiritually. They now go into the kingdom, but will not pass into bodily immortality until the end of the millennium. How can it be said that they now enter into eternal life?

And what of the posttribulation position in relationship to this verse? According to the identification I have given of those entering the kingdom, they are those who have aided the saints during their troubles experienced in the tribulation. They have not yet come to faith in Christ, and have, therefore, not yet passed into life spiritually. Their entrance into bodily immortality could only come at some point after that. The same problem presents itself, therefore, to my position. How can it be said that they now enter into eternal life?

Both positions are confronted with serious problems, then, as they relate to this verse. Whatever solutions we may find may seem imperfect. Whatever solutions they may find may also seem imperfect. But they are loaded down with an additional and probably insurmountable weight as well as this common problem. They must somehow also show how these millennial candidates were saved (how they entered eternal life) on the basis of their good deeds rather than on the basis of faith. Not even a hint is given of faith or that they had even a rudimentary notion that they were doing something for Christ. Their reward is based on works—what they did for these "brothers." Certainly the gospel during the tribulation can't change radically to one of works. If it did, the Galatian epistle would need to be discarded from Scripture during that time. This contradicts everything that is said in the New Testament about anyone coming to life in Christ. In other words, eternal life comes always and only as a result of faith, not of good deeds.

I wish I could say that I have a definitive answer to give in support of my position on the "eternal life" term used here. Almost all other parts of the puzzle have fallen neatly into place for me. I see three possible solutions. First, when Jesus says that the righteous enter into eternal life, it could signify that the potential is now there for them, that they now will have the opportunity to decide for Christ and life during the millennium. This, however, leaves us with the problem that they do not really enter that life at that time.

A second way of understanding it is by rendering "eternal life" to mean a long era of time. This is the original underlying meaning of the word αιωνιον through its derivation from αιων. Certainly a thousand years would qualify for an era or eon, especially in light of the promised longevity in the millennium. What weighs against this, however, is that everywhere else in the New Testament it carries the idea of life without an end. Although it is a possibility, this renders it suspect as a solution.

A third possibility is that there are two different groups called "the righteous" in the passage—one in verse 37 and the other in verse 46. The "righteous" in verse 37 are clearly, from the context, those who, during the tribulation, rendered acts of kindness to those who belonged to the Messiah. Let us consider the general concept that the Scriptures themselves use the term "righteous" in two different senses, one meaning absolutely righteous (whether being righteous in practice or by having righteousness imputed or charged to one's account) and another meaning relatively righteous.

Doubtless the term is used much more often in the absolute rather than in the relative sense. When God concluded in Romans 2:10 that "None is righteous" in this sense, He was repeating the conclusion that He had reached in

Psalm 14:1–3. The New Testament abounds with this absolute usage. To our joy, however, we who are in Christ discover that we have that very righteousness credited to us through faith. Even as Abraham believed God and, thus, was counted righteous, so we are held to be righteous through faith in Christ. Romans makes this abundantly clear in chapters 3 and 4.

Then what of relative righteousness? The concept is implied as well as clearly expressed both in the Old and New Testaments. God used both men and nations for His purposes, and in being used, they were considered His instruments or servants. In Isaiah, Cyrus of the Assyrians is called God's "shepherd" and "anointed" (44:28 and 45:1). God calls Nebuchadnezzar His "servant" in Jeremiah 27:6. When Abimelech, king of Gerar, calls himself and his people "innocent" (the same Hebrew word translated "righteous" throughout the OT) in the matter of Abraham's wife, the issue is accepted as such by the Lord (Gen. 20:4). In Ecclesiastes, the Preacher says there are degrees of righteousness even as there are degrees of wisdom (7:16). In Habakkuk, God tells the prophet that He is going to bring the Chaldeans against Israel (1:5–13). Then Habakkuk complains of seeming injustice. He asks why the Lord is silent "when the wicked swallows up the man more righteous than he." The logical extension of the use of the comparative here would indicate that the Chaldeans had a very low level of righteousness and that Israel had a higher degree of righteousness.

Does this carry over to the New Testament? It would appear so. Peter makes some interesting observations about Lot. In Genesis 18, Abraham pleads for the "righteous" in Sodom and stops at the possibility of finding ten righteous persons there. We need not debate the merits of Lot's wife or children or in-laws. But Peter calls Lot "righteous" (as much as some might question that assessment). (See 2 Peter 2:7–8.) Romans 5:7 would seem to indicate that it is possible for some who are "righteous" to be not necessarily all that "good," since Paul says there that "one will hardly die for a righteous man—though perhaps for a good man one will dare even to die."

Cornelius was a Gentile with no knowledge of Christ. Yet even before he heard the gospel and was converted, he was known as a righteous man and Peter did not contradict this assessment given by Cornelius' servants (Acts 10:22). Christ himself used it in a very general sense when he equated the "righteous" with the "good" people of the earth, saying that His Father "makes the sun rise on the evil and on the good, and sends rain on the just [righteous] and on the unjust [unrighteous]" (Matt. 5:45).

All three of the synoptic Gospels carry the same statement of Christ regarding His mission. Using the Matthew account, we hear His response to the Pharisees: "I came not to call the righteous, but sinners" (9:13). Certainly we know that He is not calling the Pharisees righteous in the absolute sense. We have too many instances recorded where He rips their hypocrisy to shreds. He did indicate that they had a sort of righteousness that was above that of the "sinners," even though that kind of righteousness may have kept them from seeking true or absolute righteousness as the sinners did.

Finally, there is a passage that has direct relevance to the passage discussed in this section. In Matthew 10:40–42, Jesus told His followers, "He who receives you receives me, and he who receives me receives him who sent me. He who receives a prophet because he is a prophet shall receive a prophet's reward, and he who receives a righteous man because he is a righteous man shall receive a righteous man's reward. And whoever gives to one of these little ones even a cup of cold water because he is a disciple, truly, I say to you, he shall not lose his reward." This sounds much like the blessing condition of the Abrahamic covenant: "I will bless those who bless you," but expanded and now applied to New Covenant saints and people's treatment of them. In the light of this, it would be appropriate that beast-defying nonbelievers during the tribulation give help and support to God's actual righteous ones and as a result are themselves called righteous (relatively) and given a righteous man's reward—entrance into the millennial kingdom.

But what of those who were the true righteous ones—the ones who are called Christ's brethren in Matthew 25? These are the believers during the tribulation, the ones to whom help and support were given. Doubtless, the disciples hearing this, recognized themselves as those who were the brethren of Christ. It would have been a natural thing for them to wonder about their status. If the helpers of the believers were to be rewarded with entrance into the kingdom, then what of the believers themselves? What would their situation be? Christ had already signified the reward of the relatively righteous ones in verse 34: "inherit the kingdom prepared for you from the foundation of the world." In the first half of verse 46, He announced the fate of those who had given allegiance to the beast and, thus, did not desire to help the believers whom the beast pursued: "they will go away into eternal punishment." There remained but one group to be considered. Nothing had been said about the disposition of the brethren of Christ, the believers, the truly righteous. In the second part of verse 46, Christ clarifies this issue by stating: "but the righteous into eternal life." And this is what the rest of the New Testament Scriptures tell us—when Christ returns, those who belong to Him obtain the redemption of their bodies, the second stage of eternal life.

There is, however, a problem with this understanding of the term. It uses two definitions of the same word in the same passage. Christ himself made just such a comparison of two different kinds of righteousness when He told the disciples that their righteousness must exceed the righteousness of the Pharisees. What it does, moreover, is to maintain the integrity of the "eternal life" concept as it is used in the rest of the New Testament.

Moving from the end of the passage to its beginning, we will first consider briefly two points. One is the concept of the "sheep and goats" and the other, the idea of the "nations." Pretribulationists believe that the use of the term sheep is an identification of the "righteous" group as tribulation believers. It is important to notice that Christ does not call the group "my sheep." Furthermore, He does not say, as one would expect if He intended to identify them as His people, "Before him will be gathered all the nations, and he will separate the sheep from the goats." Rather, He says, "he will separate them one from another as a shepherd separates the sheep from the goats." He does not use direct speech to indicate that they are His sheep or even that they are identified as sheep. He uses a simile to picture the separation in such a manner that an agrarian culture would understand it clearly.

The passage indicates that the nations are to be judged according to the way they had treated Christ's "brethren" during the period just before His return to earth. Although it deals with nations as nations, it must also include individuals as members of those nations. Thus, where a nation, as a nation, gave no help to persecuted believers through food, clothing or encouragement, but individuals within those nations did, those individuals would be treated as sheep and the rest of the nation as goats. This principle of individual responsibility, accountability, and recompense is too clearly established throughout the New Testament to be ignored. On the other hand, where a nation as a nation did assist those tribulation believers, even those members of that nation who were rather neutral or noninvolved personally may be swept into the millennial kingdom on the basis of the stand their nation had taken.

Now let us turn to the rest of the passage and see how these who enter the millennial kingdom must be unbelievers rather than saved individuals.

An unquestionable, even ironclad, indication of the idea that the people who remain alive at the end of the tribulation and go into the millennium to be ruled over by the Messiah are unbelievers rather than believers is found in a comparison of John 5:24 with this passage in Matthew: "Truly, truly, I say to you, he who hears my word and believes him who sent me, has eternal life; he does not come into judgment, but has passed from death to life."

In the judgment of the nations in the Matthew passage, those who go into the kingdom cannot be believers, since believers shall not come into judgment. There are only two judgments dealing with the issue of life or death. The judgment seat of Christ deals with rewards, but this judgment of the nations and the white throne judgment deal with life or death. Believers, according to John 5:24, do not come into either of these life or death judgments. Therefore, the ones going into the millennial kingdom in Matthew 25 must be unbelievers.

Another indication that these "righteous" are unbelieving righteous is their strange reaction to the concept regarding the good deeds they did for the "brethren." They were amazed that Christ would say that in doing these things for the brethren they were actually doing them for Him as well. They seem totally unaware that there was a union between believers as Body-members and Christ as the head of that Body. This is a fairly elementary Christian teaching. We find it written in epistle after epistle. Even the carnal Corinthian believers knew this. When Paul wrote about the concept of chastity he asked, "Shall I therefore take the members of Christ and make them members of a prostitute?" (1 Cor. 6:15). He asked this in such a natural way that it can be assumed that they were well aware of this fact—that their bodies were the members of Christ. Not only did the surprised good deed doers of Matthew 25 not know that helping believers meant helping Christ, but also the very wording of what Christ says about those believers actually removes the doers of the good deeds from the believers themselves. If these had been fellow believers, logic would call for Christ to say, "as you did it to one of the least of these your brethren, you did it to me." At the very least, Christ would have shown an identity or oneness, with the words, "as you did it to one of the least of these our brethren, you did it to me." However, His actual words were, "as you did it to one of the least of these my brethren, you did it to me." This distances Christ from the doers of the deeds just as it separates the deed-doers from the believers whom they had helped. It is a consistent picture, however, of nonbelievers who have refused the mark of the beast during the tribulation and who lend assistance to fellow nonconformists whom they see the beast oppressing.

In fact, the help that these rebel, "black market" type people have given to believers during the tribulation rather reminds one of the help given to Israel's spies by Rahab, except that she knew she was helping God's people and they were not aware that they were doing so.

There is a principle put forth in Matthew 10:40–42 that when a person receives a disciple as a guest or welcomes him, then he also shows friendship for Christ and welcomes

Him, and that he would be rewarded for it. This seems peculiarly applicable to Matthew 25:31–46—almost as if it were written for the tribulation generation. Believers understand the concept of "body life" and that what we do for our brother and fellow body member we also do for Christ, the Head. But certainly those who were hospitable in the Matthew 25 passage did not know the importance of their help—that they were actually helping Christ Himself. This corresponds precisely with what Daniel said about the distinction between those who were purified and wise (believers in Christ) and the "wicked." He said that "none of the wicked shall understand; but those who are wise shall understand" (12:10). But even though they did not understand that in showing kindness to Christians they were also showing kindness to Christ ("Lord, when did we see thee ..."), they still received their reward. Jesus says to them: "inherit the kingdom prepared for you from the foundation of the world" (v. 34).

Another critical problem arises for pretribulationists at this point. If "my brethren" are believers, and if, as pretribulationists claim, those being rewarded are believers who are being rewarded for their kindness to those called "my brethren," then we have the surprising plot of believer helping believer with no apparent knowledge that he is helping a fellow Body-member or a fellow believer. Why the division between the two groups of believers? Once again, logic would almost demand that the text would say that "you have done these things for your brethren."

But the pretribulation camp feels that it has found an answer. "My brethren" are Jews and, therefore, Christ's brethren after the flesh, or else they are that very special band of Jews—those elite believing Jews called the 144,000. This second identification presupposes that the 144,000 are evangelists who lead representatives of all the Gentile world people groups to Christ.

Because the 144,000 are believers, the same arguments developed above apply to them if they are to be considered the group called "my brethren." If those who helped them were believers, they would be Christ's brethren just as much as the 144,000, and in helping fellow believers, they could not be ignorant of the fact that they were helping Body-members and, by extension, helping Christ himself. Furthermore, it would be incredible to think that if the 144,000 did bring these believers to faith in Christ, they would not tell them that all of them were joined together as one in Christ.

Quite aside from the unsupported claim that the 144,000 are evangelists when the Scriptures do not anywhere so much as hint at such an idea, it can be shown through two separate demonstrations that Jewishness itself in no way entered into the identification of the group in Matthew 25. One of these evidences is the description Christ gave earlier in the chapter about the basis for persecution being leveled against the sufferers in the trying times to come. The second verification of the group's identity lies in the definition that Christ himself gave to the term "my brethren."

First, we know that the group described in Matthew 25:31–46, which was helped in time of trouble and is identified as "my brethren," is a group of believers because of what Christ says earlier in Matthew. He tells His believing followers that you can expect to suffer in three ways in the coming days. You will be delivered up to tribulation, you will be put to death and you will be hated by all nations (24:9). We would not argue that these things have not happened to Jews as Jews. But the important thing is the reason Christ gives for these problems coming to these people. He said—you will suffer all these things for my name's sake. Not because you are Jews, but because you belong to me and you bear my name. Because you are Christians. Because you are believers. Then He continues telling these same believers, "So when you see the desolating sacrilege spoken of by the prophet Daniel, standing in the holy place" (24:15), indicating that they, as believers, would enter the great tribulation period and suffer greatly. But this suffering would be for His name's sake, because they were believers. Because they were His brethren.

The second verification of "my brethren" being identified as believers lies in the use Jesus Himself made of the term. Even though it may be acknowledged by pretribulationists that Jesus defines "my brethren" in Matthew 12:50 as "whoever does the will of my father in heaven," they raise the objection that this identification was used thirteen chapters and two years earlier than the chapter 25 passage.

But it seems odd exegesis that will ignore the way Jesus Himself used the same term elsewhere. Does it mean that Jesus had thirteen chapters and two years in which to change His mind about what He meant by the term? We can never find Jesus using the term in any other way than to indicate believers in Him—those who are His followers. He never used it to refer to His physical half-brothers or to His kinsmen, the Jews. The incident (and its interpretation) was obviously considered so important that the other two synoptic Gospels record it as well (Mark 3:35; Luke 8:21). And what if it could be demonstrated that in less than a week after Jesus uttered the words about His "brethren" in Matthew 25, He used it again in the same way that He had in Matthew 12:50? Would that not show that that was indeed what He meant by "my brethren" also in Matthew 25?

Immediately after the resurrection, Jesus said to Mary Magdalene and the other Mary, "Do not be afraid; go and tell my brethren to go to Galilee, and there they will see me" (Matt. 28:10). Verse 16 says: "Now the eleven disciples went to Galilee to the mountain to which Jesus had directed them." We can also go to John, the other Gospel where we have the same account. Jesus says to Mary Magdalene, "go to my brethren and say to them, I am ascending to my Father and your Father" (20:17). Then the next verse reports that "Mary Magdalene went and said to the disciples, 'I have seen the Lord'; and she told them that he had said these things to her." Thus, when we find Jesus using the term (whether early in His ministry or after His resurrection), He means by it those who "do the will" of the Father, who believe in Jesus, and who follow Him.

One final word is in order regarding the group of people Jesus refers to as "my brethern." We have written at length about the group of unbelievers who did not receive the mark of the beast and who gave help to the brethren of Jesus during the tribulation as well as the group who had received the mark of the beast and who had not helped these brethren One group enters into the millenial kingdom because they helped His brethren while the other is cast into eternal punishment. They were surprised that those they helped (or did not help) were related to Jesus. Matthew has told us that this event happens "when the Son of Man comes in His glory." This can be no other time except when Jesus comes to earth after the tribulation. Where did these brethren come from? According to Rev. 20, they are believers in Christ who had been resurrected or transformed at the coming to earth of Jesus. Now, in glorified bodies, they stand with Jesus and he points to them as He says the words, "these my brethren." Neither those who helped these brethren or those who refused to help them had realized who they were. What a picture, as realization sets in! "I remember him/her. I turned away, or reported that one to the authorities." Or, "Yes, that is the rebel I helped!"

## Why a Millennium?

An honest question arises in the minds of serious followers of Christ and students of His word: "Why will there be a millennium?" Is there any reason why we cannot simply wind things up when Christ defeats His foes at the end of the tribulation? Why can we not at that point enter into the eternal state for which He has prepared us? I have dear friends in the Lord who have pondered this puzzle. It is probably one of the major reasons why some have attempted to come up with a system that effectively eliminates that period. Some may say that it is not ours to reason why. But the Lord made us thinking beings. If the Lord does not spell out a reason, however, the best we can arrive at is speculation. If we do theorize, let us take God at His Word and not bend the Scriptures, but rather allow our very imaginations to be held captive by God's principles and possible purposes.

Reason alone does not tell us why the Lord has planned a millennium. But there are some aspects and implications of the millennium that seem to make sense.

Mankind through the ages has earnestly desired a time and a place where things would be uncomplicated and peaceful. Man's very nature has manufactured excuses for his own shortcomings, and he has tended to lay blame on his environment and companions. At the height of his frustrations he has rationalized, "The devil made me do it!" If only he could live in an pure environment, things would be different.

The concept of an ideal society is an ancient one, that has nestled within our hearts for ages. The poet, the statesman, the politician, the explorer, the visionary writer, and the worshiper all have bent their thoughts and desires toward just such a dream. And they have written about it and sometimes planned it.

The poet has looked to a time relatively carefree and uncomplicated, and in nostalgia has cried out:
> *Backward, turn backward, O time in your flight,*
> *Make me a child again just for tonight!*
> Elizabeth Akers Allen, "Rock Me to Sleep" (1860)

The philosopher, Plato, showed the vision of a statesman and invented The Republic, where man would be temperate and wise, and, though rejoicing in music and gymnastics, would be supremely concerned with justice. The ideal society would be a just society.

Politicians have actually tried to make such dreams come true. Adolf Hitler set out to establish the Third Reich, where the super race of Aryans would rule the world for a millennium. Karl Marx turned a philosophy of dialectical materialism into a political quest to turn his society, and ultimately his world, into a communal system in which every person shared with his or her neighbor. Unfortunately, he forgot that the heart of every person was bent toward greed.

The explorer has at times been obsessed with the thought that somewhere, in some far off clime, is hidden the secret to happiness and long life, and so has set off to find El Dorado, or, like Ponce de León, has launched a search for the fountain of youth.

The visionary writer has created his own fantasy world where humanity is at peace and reason rules. Sir Thomas More constructed his Utopia as an island paradise where the citizens are concerned for one another and the good of the commonwealth. There is more than enough food for all and they are ruled with wisdom with no decision being rendered on the same day a problem is discovered. James Hilton built his dream castle in the air—or nearly so. High in the Himalayas he established his Shangri-La. There, "far from the madding crowd," his society enjoyed extended life of two to four hundred years in a peaceful environment with leisure to pursue the delight of music, literature, contemplation and love.

Many religious worshipers seek an earthly nirvana. We see in the New Age movement efforts to establish a commonwealth of humanity where we benefit here and now from the combined wisdom of the ascended masters. Soft music, meditation and uniting with kindred spirits are to usher in the new world.

Besides the need for love and acceptance, this longing for an ideal state may be our next deepest craving. It is a commentary on our failure to govern justly. We desire the satisfaction of ownership and the privileges that a democracy brings, but that democracy is cumbersome and its officials can be compromised and corrupted. A dictatorship is the most efficient of all rules, but all too often its leader is possessed by egomania, obsessed with a jealous clutching of the reigns of power, and consumed with malice toward any real or imagined threat to his throne.

Have these dreams found their way into our hearts accidentally? Or were they planted there by a Designer? If they were fulfilled, what would the result be? Perhaps that is the question that leads us to the answer for our first question—why a millennium?

First, it would give people the best of both worlds in terms of government. They would know the satisfaction of ownership and would be afforded privileges to match their longings and dreams. But they would be living under the efficiency of a dictator. This would, however, be a unique dictator. He would be a benevolent dictator. He would be firm, but he would be just and he would be kind. He would be uncorruptible.

On God's side, such a rule would provide for a final examination of the nature of the human heart.

After the disobedience in the garden, God promised man and woman deliverance from their alienation. The Lord left His footprints in nature, but people did not follow them, and the Lord swept all but eight of humankind away in the deluge and began anew. Even when God set up a theocratic rule over a special people whom He had chosen and when He honored them with His Shekinah presence, they turned with panting hearts to gods that were no gods, and only a remnant was faithful. Then the promised Deliverer finally came, and a fountain of grace sprang up from desert earth. God's reconciling message was available to all tongues, tribes, nations, and peoples, and there would be from each of them trophies of His love and grace. But the mass of humankind will still be outside the door. The rebel heart that sprouted in our first parents has sent its roots all the way to us today. Humans were rebels then, and they are rebels now. Our only excuse today for not being what we should be—pleasing to God—is that "conditions are against us."

Enter God. Personally. In the flesh. In residence. Exit His sworn enemies. Exit those who have pledged allegiance to His sworn enemies. Exit His archenemy. Bound. With no access to earth for one thousand years. Commence a reign of justice. Set in place just and fair governors. Establish uninterrupted peace. Allow private ownership to each citizen. Open unfettered research in physics, medicine, and aging. Solve the problems of transportation, crime, pollution, disease, food supply, and universal education. Offer universal travel to the mountain of the King. Offer free training in the studies of who He is and what He plans. Invite voluntary allegiance to the King. Continue this for a thousand years.

Loose the archenemy. Let him survey a world of natural men and women steeped in a tradition of peace, plenty, and justice—and authority. This enemy has succeeded in corrupting our primal parents, the pre-flood world and the chosen people. He has fought the Church for every soul that turned to Christ and has tormented their lives when he lost. He has even unleashed upon them the worst holocaust in the history of the planet. But now he is confronted with the millennial human. The natural millennial human of the rebel heart. Ah, but that rebel heart has been conditioned by a thousand years of the perfect society. Surely there is nothing the enemy can do to turn his head? Or her heart?

Precisely because this is the natural human of the rebel heart, the great Deceiver does turn him. Toward the beloved city. Toward the city of peace. Against the Prince of Peace. To his own destruction. And the final exam has been failed. And the human heart is proved to be, even in the most ideal of settings, "deceitful above all things, and desperately corrupt." Now human beings have finally lost, irretrievably, their last excuse. Their last shred of hope in themselves. Now they are truly and finally ripe to stand before that great white throne.

This has been a flight of fantasy. Fantasy immersed in Scripture. And hopefully not untrue to its greater design. I feel no Miltonian call to "justify the ways of God to men," but this seems a reasonable arrangement based on His work among men and women through the ages. And it does justify Him, whether He needs it or not. After all is said and done, the true heart should be so loyal to His redemptive kindness that it can hear the words, "Let God be true though every man be false" and sing its resolute AMEN!

For in the end, there will be a millennium, not because I or any person has given a reason for it, but simply because God said there would be one.

### *Blest*

*How blest the feet which tread this ground,*
*How blest the ears which hear this sound:—*
*Messiah's voice. Rejoice to dwell*
*In this blest land where all is well!*

# 6

## IMMINENCE

*Watchman*

*Make me a warning watchman on the wall;*
*A pilgrim, minding markers on the way;*
*A hand, who labors to complete His Call;*
*And then, a sentry, watching for the Day.*

### THE COMING DAY OF THE LORD

There are statements in the Word of God indicating that certain things are imminent or impending or about to happen. Probably the most noteworthy event that is proclaimed to be near or about to happen is the coming "day of the Lord." The day of the Lord stands in contrast to man's day or the "time of the Gentiles," and is characterized by divine judgment coupled with the idea of God setting things right. Therefore, before looking at the teaching of imminence itself, let us consider what the Scriptures (particularly the New Testament Scriptures) have to say about "the day of the Lord."

There is a relationship in the New Testament between "the last days" and "the day of the Lord" and between "the last days" and "the last day." "The last days" are sometimes viewed as the days since God stepped into man's historical time flow in the birth and ministry of Christ and in the birthday of the Church at Pentecost. In the book of Acts,

Peter interprets the Holy Spirit phenomenon at Pentecost as the fulfillment of what Joel said would happen in the last days (2:16–18). The writer to the Hebrews says that God "in these last days ... has spoken to us by a Son" (Heb. 1:2). Peter tells us that Jesus "was made manifest at the end of the times" (1 Pet. 1:20). And John tells his readers that "it is the last hour" (1 John 2:18). But in some places the phrase "the last days" refers to the concluding days of the time that began at the first advent. It would seem to depict those days leading up to and including the tribulation period. The apostle Paul informs Timothy that "in later times some will depart from the faith" and that "there will come times of stress" in the last days (1 Tim. 4:1; 2 Tim. 3:1). It is foretold that scoffers will arise "in the last days" and "in the last time" (2 Pet. 3:3; Jude 18).

The term "the day of the Lord," in that exact form, appears rarely in the New Testament. That day will come "like a thief" (2 Pet. 3:10; 1 Thess. 5:2); but the Thessalonian passage adds that it should not come as a surprise to believers (5:4). Paul charges the Thessalonians not to believe that it had already come, since certain things would announce its coming (2 Thess. 2:2). It obviously will be at the end of the "last days," since the sun and moon will alter their appearance at the end of the tribulation (cf. Acts 2:20; Matt. 24:29). Revelation 16:14 also places "the great day of God the Almighty" at the end of this time.

In the Old Testament, Malachi says that Elijah must come before that day (4:5). Jesus supports the idea of Elijah coming first when His disciples ask him about it, and though He states that John the Baptist was Elijah in a certain sense, He indicated that Elijah still would come (Matt. 17:10–13). As a figure of Elijah, John came before Jesus appeared. John was born a few months earlier than Jesus. John began his ministry before Jesus did. John announced Jesus. It would not seem logical for this pattern to change. When Elijah comes, he should precede Jesus and announce Him. Thus, to have Jesus come for His Church and then to have Elijah come and announce Him would seem to be an illogical pattern or sequence. Just as John the Baptist, in the spirit of Elijah, came before the Messiah to announce Him and prepare His way at His first advent, so Elijah, in person, will come before the Messiah to announce Him and prepare His way at His second advent. Finally, Peter speaks of us "waiting for and hastening the day of God" (2 Pet. 3:12). Once the tribulation ends and the millennium begins, we will be in man's day no longer, but in God's day and on His set schedule. Indeed, it is said that we can actually hasten that day. It would appear that the only way we could hasten His return and the onset of that day would be to complete the great commission.

As stated above, there is also a relationship between "the last days" and "the last day." Clear meaning and common sense would tell us that the last day comes at the end of the last days. If we had a series of final exams, the final exam would be the last in the series. And if we have a number of days in the period called the "last days," then what is called the "last day" must be the final day in that series of days. This does not restrict us to literal days as if there were sixteen solar days and this is the sixteenth. Rather, it refers to a number of significant events that happen at the close of this age. These events, where end time prophecies are fulfilled or God accomplishes His decrees, are called days.

There may be a number of events or happenings clustered together in any one of those days. For example, when the fourth seal is opened, we see death and destruction coming through a number of events (Rev. 6:7–8). There are the sword, famine, pestilence, and wild beasts all taking their toll. Likewise, when the sixth seal is opened, we have a great earthquake, the sun and moon are darkened, stars fall, and the mountains and islands are moved (6:12–17). But this is especially seen in the opening of the sixth bowl (16:12–16). There the river Euphrates is dried up, but the very drying up is a preparation for something else. It is done "to prepare the way for the kings from the east," which involves the passing of a significant amount of time before the next happening can begin. Then the dragon, the beast, and the false prophet send forth demonic spirits. These spirits perform convincing "signs" that suggest some passage of time. They also "go abroad to the kings of the whole world," which also takes time, since a demonic spirit can only be in one place at a time. Then they "assemble" those kings to Armageddon, which takes additional time. Thus we see the drying of the river, the foul spirits performing signs, these spirits going abroad into the world, and these same spirits assembling the kings—different happenings that take time to accomplish. Yet all of these happenings are part of the same "day" during the "last days."

In his message on the day of Pentecost, Peter quotes a prophecy from Joel 2:31, in which Joel speaks of "the great and terrible day of the Lord." Peter, however, translates it, "the day of the Lord ... the great and manifest day" (Acts 2:20). In other words, the day of the Lord is a great and manifest day. "Great" is a further description of that day. This is in accord even with other Old Testament prophets when they speak of that day. Isaiah speaks simply of "the day of the Lord" without using "great," but obviously refers to the time at the end of the tribulation since he says it will be at the time that the sun, moon and stars are darkened (Isa. 13:10). Zephaniah, however, also calls it "the great day of the Lord" (Zeph. 1:14). The "day of the Lord" is defined as "the great day of God" in Revelation 16:14 or "the great and terrible day of the Lord" in Malachi 4:5, and does not include the great tribulation, since it comes at the end of that time. Unless Scripture itself would indicate otherwise, we must conclude that there is but one day of the Lord, and that "the day of the Lord" and "the great day of the Lord" and "the great and terrible day of the Lord" are one and the same.

The Thessalonians were told that that day would not come until the rebellion came first and the man of sin proclaimed himself to be God in the temple (2 Thess. 2:1–4). All the other verses (except one) speak of that day coming suddenly "like a thief." But the concept of His "coming like a thief" continues up until the sixth seal at the end of the great tribulation, which would indicate that that "thief" day had not yet come (Rev. 16:15). It would then place it as the "great day of God" at Armageddon in the preceding verse (v. 14). All the references either clearly express or imply that that day deals with a final judgment. The only verse not speaking of that "coming thief" aspect of the day is 2 Peter 3:12, where we are enjoined to be "waiting for and hastening the day of

God." The martyrs under the altar during the fifth seal were eager for judgment to come to avenge their "blood on those who dwell upon the earth," and they were told to wait or "rest" awhile until the number of martyrs was complete (Rev. 6:9–11). God's day begins when man's day ends at the close of the tribulation and "waiting" for the "day of God," that is, waiting for the day of judgment (Rev. 16:14), would make sense if we were living in the tribulation leading up to that day, but not if we were rejoicing in Christ's presence because we had been raptured before that period began. More will be said later on how that day could actually be "hastened" by us.

But among all the "days" belonging to the "last days" there is a "last day." This "last day" is also the "last day." This would indicate that the other days came before it and that it comes at the end of the "last days." Therefore, if the "last days" include the great tribulation, which they obviously do, the "last day" comes at the end of the great tribulation. Since the "day of the Lord" also comes at the end of the great tribulation, then either the "last day" and the "day of the Lord" are one and the same "day," or the "day of the Lord" is included in the "last day."

The phrase "last day" is only used in the New Testament. The expression does occur in Nehemiah 8:18 (of the number of days the law was read to the people), but not in the end times sense. In the usage of the New Testament, the "last day" is equivalent to resurrection/judgment. But since there is one resurrection/judgment for the believers and another for unbelievers, there is, in effect, a "last day" A and a "last day" B. This is, however, not an imaginary or arbitrary division. The Scripture itself makes such a distinction: "And many of those who sleep in the dust of the earth shall awake, some to everlasting life, and some to shame and everlasting contempt" (Dan. 12:2). Paul points out the same division: "at his coming those who belong to Christ. Then comes the end, when he delivers the kingdom to God the Father after destroying every rule and every authority and power" (1 Cor. 15:23–24). This identical separation is shown in Revelation 20, after the tribulation, where we see the "first resurrection" in verses 4–6 and the second one in verses 11–15.

A similar distinction is made for the term "last day" in its association with the resurrection/judgment concepts. The stress is on judgment when it is used of the second resurrection. James, in speaking to rich oppressors, states: "Your gold and silver have rusted, and their rust will be evidence against you and will eat your flesh like fire. You have laid up treasure for the last days" (5:3). Even though "last days" is used, we recognize this time of judgment as being at the very end of the last days and, therefore, being on the last day. This is supported by John, when Jesus says to those who reject Him, "He who rejects me and does not receive my sayings has a judge; the word that I have spoken will be his judge on the last day" (John 12:48). Even though the stress is on judgment, we know from the passages quoted above that this judgment is at the time of the second resurrection (see Dan. 12:2; 1 Cor. 15:23–24; Rev. 20:11–15).

When "last day" is used with reference to believers, the stress is on their resurrection, although we know that it is accompanied with a special judgment, for Paul says that "we must all appear before the judgment seat of Christ" (2 Cor. 5:10). The pertinent point here, however, is the timing of believer resurrection. It is at the "last day," or at the end of the "last days," which means at the end of the great tribulation. When Lazarus had died and Jesus told Martha that her brother would rise again, she stated: "I know that he will rise again in the resurrection at the last day" (John 11:24). Evidently the Jews had reached the conclusion from the studies of the Old Testament that believer resurrection would be at the last day: "For I know that my Redeemer lives, and at last he will stand upon the earth; and after my skin has been thus destroyed, then from my flesh I shall see God" (Job 19:25–26). Martha shared this belief. Jesus did not offer any correction to her view. If we only had this passage to go on, we might infer that He agreed with that position.

But we need not draw an inferred conclusion. Jesus Himself clearly and unmistakably stated that the resurrection of believers would indeed be at the "last day." On an extended discourse on the bread of life in John 6, Jesus says four separate times that believers would be raised "at the last day." He says, "this is the will of him who sent me, that I should lose nothing of all that he has given me, but raise it up at the last day" (v. 39). In the next verse He says that "this is the will of my Father, that every one who sees the Son and believes in him should have eternal life; and I will raise him up at the last day" (v. 40). In verse 44 we read: "No one can come to me unless the Father who sent me draws him; and I will raise him up at the last day." Finally, after making the shocking statement that "he who eats my flesh and drinks my blood has eternal life," He continues, "and I will raise him up at the last day" (v. 54). Thus, we have the word of Jesus on it: our resurrection will be "at the last day."

This accords with what Peter tells us about our salvation when he says that it is "ready to be revealed in the last time" (1 Pet. 1:5). But there are many verses that speak of the completion of our redemption in, on or at "the day of our Lord Jesus Christ" (1 Cor. 1:8); "the day of the Lord Jesus" (1 Cor. 5:5; 2 Cor. 1:14); "the day of Jesus Christ" (Phil. 1:6); and "the day of Christ" (Phil. 1:10; 2:16). The things mentioned in these verses occur at the time of resurrection and glorification, and that resurrection takes place "at the last day." The "day of the Lord" also happens at the close of the great tribulation, and, therefore, also occurs on "the last day." The terms that have "Christ" or "Jesus" in the formula "the day of ..." are not synonymous with the phrase "the day of the Lord," since "the day of Christ" has to do with His dealings with His own, whereas "the day of the Lord" concerns His dealing with unbelievers. They both occur at the same time (on "the last day"), however, and are, therefore, part of the same event. They are simply different aspects of that event that happen at the same time.

## OLD TESTAMENT PROPHECY

The concept of the day of the Lord did not begin in the New Testament, but in the Old Testament. Not only does it first appear in the Old Testament, but the idea of that day being near also began at that time. At least five prophets in eight prophetic statements classified it as being near or even "at hand." It is said to be "near" by Isaiah (13:6), Ezekiel (30:3), Joel (1:15; 2:1; 3:14), and Obadiah (v. 15). Zephaniah says it is "hastening fast" and even "at hand" (1:14; 1:7).

These five Old Testament prophets wrote of the impending day of the Lord between 580 to 800 years before Christ was even born.

But what did these prophets mean by "the day of the Lord" in these passages? Were these merely local predictions of distress associated with the time shortly after the prediction was made? In other words, did the Lord say that judgment was about to come upon them shortly because of the conditions that made it necessary for that judgment? In this case that judgment shortly to come upon them could have been called the "day of the Lord."

Even in such instances, the local or immediate prediction and fulfillment can be seen as only partial or incomplete at best. The context itself identifies a future set of conditions that call for another fulfillment—an end time "day of the Lord" fulfillment. Thus we have a double-fulfillment prophecy. There is a near and incomplete fulfillment and a distant and complete one. We will consider these prophecies in the order listed above except for the prophecy of Joel. We will look at it first because it holds a prophetic idea that clearly relates to the day of the Lord as it is predicted for the end times and, therefore, it sets the stage for the understanding of other passages where this same idea occurs in the writings of the other prophets.

Joel wrote about the day of the Lord being near against the backdrop of the plagues of the locusts and the drought (1:15). He repeated that the day was near, but added that it was a day of clouds (2:15). Then Joel spoke of the day of the Lord but without mentioning the concept of nearness. In this passage he relayed the message of the Lord: "And I will give portents in the heavens and on the earth, blood and fire and columns of smoke. The sun shall be turned to darkness, and the moon to blood, before the great and terrible day of the Lord comes" (2:30–31). We know that this particular prophecy was for the end times, since Peter quotes it (together with verse 28 regarding the pouring out of His Spirit) in his sermon at Pentecost. Thus, the Spirit being poured out was fulfilled at Pentecost and the signs in the heavens would yet be given (they weren't given at Pentecost) "before the ... day of the Lord." Furthermore, Joel calls it "the great and terrible" day of the Lord. Every time, therefore, that we see the concept of the darkening of the sun, moon and stars relating to the day of the Lord, we know that it refers to the day of the Lord in the end times. By the time Joel states its nearness for a third time, he brings in the end time prediction that "the sun and the moon are darkened, and the stars withdraw their shining" (3:15). This places it clearly in the last days. An additional feature of interest in the verse is the use of the phrase "multitudes, multitudes, in the valley of decision!" There is confusion about the identification of the valley. That would be understandable in double-fulfillment. It may well have been the valley of Jehoshaphat for the "nations round about" Judah at that time, but it also may mean the Megiddo area in the end times in light of the darkening of the sun, moon and stars and the numbers of people suggested by the repetition of the term "multitudes."

The Isaiah prophecy in 13:6 speaks of the doom of Babylon, but verses 9 and 10 would direct us to the judgment on the Babylon of Revelation since this would happen when "the stars of the heavens and their constellations will not give their light" and "the sun will be dark at its rising and the moon will not shed its light."

When Ezekiel wrote that the day of the Lord was near, the Egyptian defeat by Babylon was certainly the focus of that prophecy (30:3). Immediately following that statement, however, Ezekiel states that it will be "a day of clouds, a time of doom for the nations." There can be little doubt that this looks forward to Armageddon where "the nations" will be defeated. If it had simply meant a few neighboring nations that were allies of Egypt, then we would fully expect to find the mention of "those who support Egypt" in verse 6 to appear in verse 4 instead of "the nations," which was the more general term and referred to the Gentiles overall.

Obadiah looks beyond the destruction of Edom to the end time day of the Lord when the prophet says that that day is "near upon all the nations" (v. 15).

Finally, Zephaniah is admittedly referring to the day of judgment about to fall upon Judah in 1:7, but when he returns to the day of the Lord theme in verse 14, it is the nearness of the day of the Lord in the last days that is in view since it is called "the great day of the Lord." This is the description used of the coming day of Armageddon in Revelation 16:14, where it is called "the great day of God the Almighty."

In addition to these five prophets, Malachi also mentions the day just referred to by Zephaniah. He calls it "the great and terrible day of the Lord" (4:5). This would also make it the day of Armageddon. But Malachi does not refer to it as the other prophets do as being something that is "near." Instead he passes on to us the message given to him by the Lord who said, "I will send you Elijah the prophet before the great and terrible day of the Lord comes." Whereas the others spoke of that day as near or impending, Malachi says that there is something that must take place first.

What can we conclude from what the prophets said in the Old Testament about the end time day of the Lord? First, we hear that it was imminent or near. Second, we learn that something was going to precede that day. Since that day would not occur until the second coming of Christ (when it was actually being spoken of as "near" as long ago as 580 to 800 years before Christ's first advent), we must conclude that nearness or imminence has a different meaning to God than it does to man. To God, who sits in His heavens in eternity, there is no past, present, and future. To Him who saw His Son as the slain Lamb of God before the foundations of the earth were laid, the end of man's day and the beginning of His day is near, even at hand. To man, however, forced into the mold of time and restricted within its boundaries, it is yet a long time away with certain predicted events to take place within time before that day arrives.

## New Testament Teaching

The New Testament continues the teaching on the day of the Lord begun in the Old Testament and it has some similar things to say about that day. But it also adds some new elements, which indicate that that "near" day is even nearer, suggesting that the Lord's people take a certain attitude in the light of its approach. Let us consider briefly at least seven things that the New Testament tells us about the day of the

Lord.

First, like the Old Testament, it says that the day of the Lord is at hand. Romans 13:12 states that "the day is at hand," and James even indicates that "the Judge is standing at the doors" (5:9).

Second, we are warned that there will be a suddenness to the coming of that day. Paul tell the Thessalonians that "the day of the Lord will come like a thief in the night," and that "when people say 'There is peace and security,' then sudden destruction will come upon them" (1 Thess. 5:2–3).

Third, we are told that we should watch. In the short passage on the man going on a journey in Mark 13:32–37, Jesus charges his disciples no less than three times to "watch" in the light of particular uncertainties relating to that hour. Paul tells his readers in Rome that "it is full time now ... to wake from sleep" (Rom. 13:11).

Fourth, even as the Old Testament said that something would precede the day of the Lord (namely, the coming of Elijah [Mal. 4:5]), the New Testament indicates that there are at least four things that will precede that day.

1. Elijah still must come. Even though Jesus suggests that there is a sense in which Elijah had already come (obviously, John the Baptist), He also uses the future tense to say that he still must come when He said Elijah indeed "does come" and "is to restore all things" (Matt. 17:11–13).
2. The man of sin must stand in the holy place. Jesus told His followers to watch for this (Matt. 24:15); and Paul said this must happen before the day of the Lord would come (2 Thess. 2:2).
3. According to Jesus, there must first be a worldwide preaching of the gospel. He stated that "this gospel of the kingdom will be preached throughout the whole world, as a testimony to all nations, and then the end will come" (Matt. 24:14).
4. The tribulation and accompanying signs at its end must take place first. Jesus says, "when you see all these things, you know that he is near, at the very gates" (Matt. 24:33). Since the last period of time He talked about before this statement was the tribulation

and its closing events, that must be included in "all these things."
5. We cannot pinpoint the time of that day to the very day and hour. According to Matthew 24:36, "of that day and hour no man knows." This is said in the setting of the tribulation about which Jesus had just spoken. As an example, the delay of intervening events could be seen in a master who will accomplish certain things on a trip before returning. We may not know the day or hour of his return, but we can know when he will not return—namely, before the unaccomplished events happen.
6. There is to be the fulfilling of the "sorrow before joy syndrome." This means that a pattern has been established where trial and suffering come first and joy lies on the other side. One looks through and beyond the trial to joy, and enduring the trial sets the stage for the joy to be impending. Christ is the perfect example and pattern: "who for the joy that was set before him endured the cross, despising the shame" (Heb. 12:2). Thus, when we consider a troublesome tooth, the realization of satisfaction and soundness lies on the other side of the dentist's office.
7. There is a time frame that can be measured or marked off. According to Hebrews 10:25, we are not to be neglecting "to meet together, as is the habit of some, but encouraging one another, and all the more as you see the Day drawing near."

## THE TEACHING OF IMMINENCE

We will look at these precursors or forerunners to the day of the Lord more in detail later. They are mentioned in rough form here to set the stage for developments concerning the teaching of imminence in the days of the apostles and in the first century or so, and then as it has unfolded in the relatively recent history of the Church.

When we look at the early Church, we discover an area on which the pretribulationists and the posttribulationists are in agreement: those brethren in the first and second centuries held to a posttribulation rapture of the Church. To us in the posttribulation camp it is not surprising, since the Scriptures themselves do not indicate a break at the beginning of the tribulation, although one is seen in the middle (the revealing of the man of sin) leading into the great tribulation.

For the average pretribulationist, however, such a belief by the early Church produces problems. Some have a problem with the fact that these believers did not see a break between the rapture and the coming of Christ to earth. Perhaps we could conclude from this that the early Church saw no logical reason to contemplate or create such an intervening period. Only those beginning with a pretribulation-rapture mindset would see the necessity for such a period. In other words, if no necessity is seen for the Church to have seven years together with Christ before His return to the earth, no need is developed for a rapture at the beginning of the tribulation. If, however, one begins with the assumption that the rapture will occur before the tribulation, then it is obvious that the question "why?" should be asked in order to come up with some logical reasons for such a timetable. That the rapture/coming should be one basically united event or two segments of the same basic event was no problem to the early Church and should not be to us, unless we have locked ourselves into a system that demands such a separation and then must attempt to explain or justify it.

Many in the pretribulation camp have difficulties with the fact that the postapostolic fathers thought they were in the great tribulation when persecutions arose against the Church, and, as a result of this, looked for an impending return of Christ. This troubles the pretribulationists in two ways. First, this pattern of posttribulationism seems to differ from the brands that are seen today. Second, they cannot comprehend why these fathers thought they could be in the tribulation when so many of the promised signs and prophecies had not been fulfilled first. As to the first point, what if the idea of these brethren (that one could look for an imminent rapture/second coming if one were in the great tribulation) has nothing either unscriptural or illogical about it? Then, even if it is different from many forms of posttribulationism around today, why not reclaim it and develop it in the light of current events and of our own timeframe? The concept of an imminent return during the great tribulation actually represents a biblically accountable and responsible Christian approach to the concept of imminence. This brings us to the second point of unfulfilled signs.

There is an impending aspect to the day of the Lord taught in Scripture. However, there is also a teaching that certain events will happen before that day—the fall and demolition of Jerusalem and the temple, sundry catastrophes on a global scale (wars, famines and earthquakes), false Christs, the preaching of the gospel in all cultures of the world, and the great tribulation itself. Since the early Church had seen the fall of Jerusalem in a.d. 70, experienced catastrophes, heard claims of false Christs, assumed that the inhabited earth (as they knew it) had been evangelized, and, the final straw, felt that they were now in the great tribulation, it was natural that they should now look for an impending rapture and second advent.

There are things we can understand today that they did not consider then about fulfillment. Even as certain understanding about the Suffering Servant only came during the generation in which He lived (an understanding predicted in Isaiah 52:13–15), so today we can understand things related to the latter days that first- and second-century Christians did not understand in their day. This "understanding" when "the time of the end" comes was predicted for us "upon whom the end of the ages has come" (1 Cor. 10:11). The coming of the fierce anger of the Lord in the latter days (where is this more applicable than to the great tribulation?) and the national conversion of Israel at that time are both predicted in Jeremiah: "The fierce anger of the Lord will not turn back until he has executed and accomplished the intents of his mind. In the latter days you will understand this. At that time, says the Lord, I will be the God of all the families of Israel, and they shall be my people" (30:24–31:1). In this passage, however, it is significant that our understanding of these things was to come at this time—"in the latter days" themselves. A similar prediction was made by Daniel, where the Lord said: "the words are shut up and sealed until the time of the end. Many shall purify themselves, and make themselves white, and be refined; but the wicked shall do wickedly; and none of the wicked shall understand; but those who are wise shall understand" (Dan. 12:9–10).

Many Bible scholars will doubtless have noted that there are many things in the Revelation, as well as in other prophetic Scriptures, which were a puzzle or seemed vague thirty to forty years ago, but which are clear today. Most of this enlightenment is traceable not to added years and maturity, but rather to the tenor of the times. One might have trouble remembering, for example, what his or her thoughts were forty years ago when reading in Revelation 1:7 that "he is coming with the clouds, and every eye will see him." Since the development and use of synchronous satellites, transmission of events anywhere in the world and reception everywhere in the world have become so commonplace that we barely pause at this verse today.

We have another advantage, that of intervening history. That is, since the time of the early Church, we are able to look back and see things that they did not or could not see from their vantage point. They dealt with a come and go presence of Israel in the land, even after a.d. 70. Only after about a.d. 300 was there a complete exodus from the area. Therefore, the concept of Israel being there (after a fashion) created no great problem in relationship to a need for an Israeli presence in the land. But after a.d. 300 we are able to look back and say that Israel truly had to be brought back as a nation. We would likely even extend the time back to a.d. 70.

Another historical advantage we have over the early Church fathers is our knowledge of the extent of the world. They knew basically the Roman Empire and some other areas of Asia, Europe, and Africa. But, in addition to other areas of Asia and Africa that they were not acquainted with, they had no inkling of North and South America and Australia as well as most of the island world. Therefore, when we consider the evangelizing of the whole world, we realize that it is a much broader task than they ever dreamed of.

Now, we have already seen Israel reborn as a nation, and the people in the land. When we see the world (tribes, tongues, peoples, and nations) reached for Christ and ourselves in the great tribulation, then we shall be back to the position where the early Church fathers thought they were and we can have their form of posttribulationism again. But this time the conditions will indeed be complete and we can look for an imminent rapture and return of Christ.

Returning to the early Church fathers, let us be fair to them in the light of their understanding of their day. They found themselves (as they supposed) in the great tribulation itself. Since this was the last thing to happen before the second advent, it was not too surprising that they should accept a partial fulfillment of a prophecy as a fulfillment sufficient to meet the requirements, nor was it surprising that they should have made short shrift of other predictions that may not have been fulfilled. A similar phenomenon occurred during the ministry of Christ in a reverse pattern. Because of Roman oppression, scribes looked almost exclusively at the messianic prophecies that spoke of the powerful deliverer to come and ignored those dealing with the Suffering Servant, thereby failing to recognize the Messiah when He came.

Furthermore, when pretribulationists charge the early Church fathers with making little effort to resolve the conflicts that arose in their point of view, they overlook the fact that they themselves have unresolved conflicts. They have made some changes. When it became troublesome to maintain the early teaching that the restrainer in 2 Thessalonians 2 was the Holy Spirit, they altered the teaching to say it was only His restraining power in the world that would be removed. But they still choose not to address certain areas of difficulty. They seem studiously to ignore the olive tree account of Romans 11, especially the concept of believing Israel becoming part and parcel of the rest of the tree that existed before the inclusion of Gentile believers. This unity is never dealt with. How a "last trump" of the Rapture can precede the seven trumpets of Revelation is not seriously considered either. Other conflicts (such as the mission of the Church and the purifying of the Church) are also left unresolved. When a problem of time arises, such as the need for time to rebuild the temple prior to the man of sin defiling that temple and proclaiming himself to be God within it, that time can always be found for them in the first half of the tribulation. They are forced, of course, into this solution because of the overriding importance attached to the teaching of imminence (that is, Christ can come at any time—even today—and, therefore, nothing must take place before He comes) or that doctrine would be damaged or destroyed as a concept that is relevant for the immediate present.

It is at this point that the present-day pretribulation teaching has its most serious problem. Everything has been swallowed up in the position of prominence taken by imminency. Because He can come at any time, the reasoning goes, therefore nothing needs to happen before that time. But whereas the pretribulationists are able to look back to those first two centuries and see the error of that position (there were prophetic events yet to happen before the stage could be set), they are not able to gain such a perspective relative to their own age. That is to say, they could see that Israel must be a nation again. They could see that the climate must be there for a revived Roman Empire. They could see the need for an army of the north that would be a serious and powerful threat to Israel. They could see that there had to be an eastern power capable of fielding 200 million troops. They could see all these things as necessary for fulfillment in the first two centuries for imminency to apply. Or, at least, they could see that the early fathers did not deal with such a conflict.

What they cannot see, however, is that they face a similar problem today. First, with any admission that anything happened in the second millennium that was necessary to set the stage for the rapture (e.g., Russia becoming a mighty nation, China becoming a populous nation, Europe being adaptable to the resurrection of Roman power, and Israel becoming a nation again), they leave the door open to the possibility of other things being prerequisites as well. Indeed, I well remember hearing just such pronouncements. Such and such had happened, and now Christ could return at any time. I clearly recall the air of triumph in the camp when the news was flashed in 1948 that Israel had joined the community of nations. Now, we were told, the rapture could occur any day.

Just as the charge is made that the early Church fathers

failed to resolve the tension between believing that Christ could return at any moment and the fact that many prophetic events had to take place before He could return, the pretribulation camp has this very same problem today. Jesus had said that the gospel would first be preached in all the world and gave just such a command. This is supported in Revelation by the announcement that people will be redeemed from every people group before His return. This camp simply solves that problem by separating believers into two groups—believers before the tribulation belong to the Church and those during the tribulation do not. Jesus said to watch for the man of sin. This camp dispenses with that by saying that it doesn't apply to us, since we will be gone before that. Jesus issued a word of watchfulness and preparation for the tribulation itself and that a trumpet would sound at the end of it. This camp says that neither this nor any other event must happen first, for then the rapture could not happen today. Thus, imminence has become the all-powerful norm and ruler in every interpretation of the signs of the times.

Just how has a large segment of the evangelical Church parted company in recent times with the expectations of the early Church in relationship to the expectation of Christ's return (that is that if we are in the tribulation, we can expect His coming momentarily)? Around 1830, Darby began developing the rudiments of a system that would later be known as dispensationalism. In developing this teaching, he proposed the concept that the Church would not go through the tribulation, but would be raptured before it began. This brought a heady excitement to those who were exposed to this idea. It brought attention back to the concept of the nearness of the day of the Lord. And thus it continued pretty much for the rest of the 19th century. This continued to be a key theme as prophetic conferences were held both in England and in the United States. Prayer was raised earnestly for His kingdom to come. Much preaching was done on the signs of His coming. Moving into and through the first quarter of the 20th century, as some signs were perceived as being fulfilled (especially a war on a worldwide scale), the idea of nearness evolved into extreme nearness. Then in the second quarter, especially as certain signs were fulfilled or shown to be realizable, there was a steady shift from extreme nearness to the full concept of imminence in the modern sense of an "any day—even today" possibility of His coming. In the second half of that century this became, among dispensationalists, the cornerstone of their teaching. It may have begun as the tail of their system, but now it wags the whole creature. Relative to the signs Jesus gave for us to recognize the approaching of that day, their position is "no prophetic sign needs to be fulfilled before the rapture."

Not only has this form of imminence become a full-blown doctrine, but in some groups it has become a touchstone or even a litmus test. It is even for some a test of fellowship. I know of one former professor who became persona non grata in churches where he had formerly spoken, once it was established that he did not hold this teaching. I know another professor who was not accepted by a mission organization for precisely the same reason. There is a sad touch of irony here. Today, men like William Carey, Henry Martyn, and Alexander Duff could be refused by this same group, since they believed that the gospel had to be preached in all the world before Christ's return, and therefore (by the extension of logic), His return was not imminent. Doubtless their mentor, Jonathan Edwards, would also have been denied, since they learned such things from him.

## THE TIME OF CHRIST'S RETURN

Now let us return to the seven things mentioned earlier in the chapter, which the New Testament says will be characteristic of the time just before Christ's return. By way of review they were: (1) the day is at hand; (2) it will come suddenly; (3) we should watch; (4) certain things will precede it: (a) Elijah's coming; (b) the revealing of the man of sin; (c) the preaching of the gospel in the whole world; and (d) the tribulation; (5) we will not know the day or the hour of His return; (6) there will be a suffering followed by joy mentality; and (7) it will be a measurable time. We will now consider in more detail the seven points we just touched on briefly.

First, the day of the Lord is at hand. As we saw earlier,

there is a heightened sense of the nearness of that day in the New Testament compared to the Old Testament: "the night is far gone, the day is at hand" and "the Judge is standing at the doors" (Rom. 13:12; James 5:9).We also need to remember the tremendous difference regarding imminence or even "nearness" when viewed from God's throne in heaven as He sits in eternity, and when viewed from earth and time-bound humanity's perspective. With God, a thousand years may be as a day, but with mortals, a thousand years is as a thousand years.

The dispensational position tends to confuse the concepts of "nearness" and imminence. They are not the same. Nearness means that it could happen "soon," which is a relative term, especially in the light of the distinction already noted between the vantage points of God and human beings. Imminence, on the other hand, means that it could happen "now," and fails to take into account all of the signs that were given as events preceding that day. Indeed, even in the three Scriptures that dispensationalists or pretribulationists hold to be the principal Scriptures showing the rapture, one hunts in vain for a teaching of imminence or even of nearness. In John 14:3 and 1 Corinthians 15:51–52 it is not even vaguely hinted at. Some may think they can see it in the Corinthians passage, but they are confusing imminence and suddenness. This will be addressed when we consider the idea of suddenness in the next section. In 1 Thessalonians 4:13–18 there is not even a shadow of a suggestion of imminence.

Furthermore, where imminence is stated as a principle in Matthew 24:32–51, His coming was based on a timeframe that included the great tribulation experience, for he said that we would know He was near when we saw "all these things," and He had just finished discussing the great tribulation, which would have to be included in "all these things."

Second, there will be a suddenness to the coming of the day of the Lord. Paul declares that it will come like a thief in the night (1 Thess. 5:2). But in the very next verse we learn that this holds true for those who are "in darkness" and not to the brethren, for Paul says, "But you are not in darkness, brethren, for that day to surprise you like a thief" (5:3). Thus, unbelievers, because they are in darkness, will be surprised;

believers walking in the light will not, even though they will not know the day or the hour. For one thing, we won't know when the last person in the last people group is reached for Christ. For another, the days will be shortened on our account. But we may have a fairly close estimate of a season or month.

Some who name the name of Christ will be surprised. The slothful servants or churches are not going to be alert and watching. The church at Ephesus is warned: "You have abandoned the love you had at first. Remember then from what you have fallen, repent and do the works you did at first. If not, I will come to you and remove your lampstand from its place, unless you repent" (Rev. 2:4–5). The Pergamum church had some who held the teaching of Balaam and the Nicolaitans, which had led them into immorality. They were warned to "Repent ... If not, I will come to you soon and war against them with the sword of my mouth" (Rev. 2:16). To the church in Sardis the Lord declared, "If you will not awake, I will come like a thief, and you will not know at what hour I will come upon you" (Rev. 3:3).

Just as the dispensational position at times fails to see a clear distinction between "nearness" and imminence, so, also, they sometimes confuse the ideas of imminence and "suddenness." Some tend to think that imminence can be found in the resurrection chapter in 1 Corinthians 15. But this would only be true if imminence and suddenness were synonymous terms. They are not. Imminence means that something can happen now, without delay. Suddenness means that when something does happen, its occurring breaks in upon us in a flash—instantaneously.

For example, there are some things in life that normally happen by process: "Rome wasn't built in a day." There are others that happen in a flash or in an instant: "the earthquake struck at 9:01 a.m." There are still others that may happen either way. On the one hand we may say that "she grew to love him," but that "for him, it was love at first sight." A nation may have gone through a long and drawn out process to be recognized as a nation. Israel could be "born in a day" when the UN voted affirmatively to accept her as a nation in 1948. Thus it could be with the resurrection. It could happen by bodies being reformed by a process as it happened in Ezekiel 37, or as Elijah stretched himself upon the dead child three times in 1 Kings 17:21–22, or as Adam was originally "formed" by the hand of God. Or it could be sudden, as it was when Christ issued the command "Come forth" at the tomb of Lazarus. What we are told of our resurrection/transformation is that it will happen as suddenly as a twinkle flashes in the eye of an individual—it will be an instantaneous event rather than a process. There is a difference between a dentist saying, "When you come to my office, I'll have that tooth out in a minute," meaning that it will be done quickly, and the same dentist saying, "You won't know when it is going to happen, but at any moment you can expect me to jump on you and pull out your tooth."

Thus, there is a distinction that should be made regarding the return of the Lord as it relates to indefiniteness and suddenness on the one hand (not knowing exactly when He will return and the prospects of it happening abruptly when that time does come), and imminence on the other (the idea that He could come at any time—even today). The former should be our attitude now; the latter, when we are well into the great tribulation with the predicted events already fulfilled.

If someone should go abroad with the announcement that the time of his return was indefinite, but that some events would take place before his return, then we would not know the exact time of his arrival (day or week). But if he had said that before he came back he would send an associate and also that a certain business deal must first be finalized, there would be something that we would know. We would know when he would not come back. We would know that he could not return until the conditions he had set down were fulfilled. Jesus said that an associate would come first. In answer to a question about Elijah coming first, He affirmed that statement in Matthew 17:11. Also He told them that there was a certain "deal" that had to be completed first, namely the preaching of this gospel "throughout the whole world" (Matt. 24:14). He did not say how long after Elijah came or how long after the completion of the gospel work He would return, but we can know that before these things He will not return. Not knowing "the day or hour" does not mean that we might not know the year. Not knowing when it will be doesn't mean that we can't know when it won't be.

Third, we are commanded to watch. In Mark 13:32–37, the Lord gave His disciples this charge three times. The figure is used of a master preparing to return to his house at an unknown and unannounced hour. His servants should not be asleep "lest he come suddenly" and find them in that state. Therefore, they are encouraged to watch. Both in this passage and the synoptic passage in Matthew 24:36, Christ indicates that no one (including the angels)—not even the Son Himself—knows the day nor the hour when it will take place. But it doesn't broaden the time of awareness or expectation beyond "day" and "hour." If either word were used alone, we might easily generalize it or spiritualize it, but with both terms used together, we are pretty well forced to take it literally.

So, when Jesus told His disciples in Matthew 25:13, "Watch therefore, for you know neither the day nor the hour," He did not say that they might not have a general idea of the nearness of that event. It is neither dangerous nor unbiblical to put an event before the coming of Christ. In fact, it is more dangerous and more unbiblical not to put things before that coming that were put before it in the New Testament Scriptures themselves. Jesus Himself said that "this gospel of the kingdom will be preached throughout the whole world, as a testimony to all nations; and then the end will come" (Matt. 24:14). Immediately following that, He told His followers to be on the lookout for the appearance of "the desolating sacrilege ... standing in the holy place." Paul echoed this very "lookout" mentality in relation to the same event when he wrote the Thessalonians, who were troubled about "the coming of our Lord Jesus Christ and our assembling to meet him" (2 Thess. 2:1). He said that "that day" (and he obviously equates in this passage "the coming of our Lord Jesus Christ and our assembling to meet him" with "the day of the Lord") would "not come, unless the rebellion comes first, and the man of lawlessness is revealed" when he "takes his seat in the temple of God, proclaiming himself to be God" (2:3–4). So Jesus Christ Himself places two major events before that day: the revealing of the Antichrist (also stressed by Paul) and the completion of the great commission in the evangelizing of the entire world.

In looking for signs preceding His return, care should be execised. Indeed, many have fallen into a trap in their eagerness to apply "watch" with regard to world events. An oil crisis hits and the mideast is front page news. There are four times as many earhquakes as there were in the last 5 years. Babylon becomes a thriving, important city. The nations in the European theater reaches a total number of 10. In each instance, authors are found climbing out of the woodwork, "proving" that it is "show time." Some are disappointed when the EU reaches 11 nations. In such "watching," it is necessary to add the concept of "waiting." When God's time comes, the European theater will be right where God had planned it all along. In watching for signs, let us concentrate on the signs that the Scriptures told us to expect as the ones which woud usher in that day.

When Jesus told His followers to watch, it was not done in a vacuumlike setting. They were not told to look into a vacant sky while waiting. The disciples at the Ascension were discouraged from doing that very thing. Even though they had asked about the setting up of the kingdom, they had been told even before His crucifixion to be on their guard about the coming of false Christs. This meant that there would be a period of time before His return (Matt. 24:4–5). They were given a series of signs, so that they might watch and see that day approaching or drawing near, and they were assigned a task they might work at to speed the approach of that day.

Fourth, four things will precede the day of the Lord. In the very lifetime of the apostles, signs that Jesus predicted as events that would happen before His return were already fulfilled. The temple was destroyed, and, for all practical purposes, the prophecy of Luke 21:23–24, that the Jews would again be dispersed, was also fulfilled. Many dispensationalists presently grant that certain conditions that now exist (Israel as a nation, Russia as a military power, China as a populous country, and Europe as a confederation) had to be in place before we could expect the return of the Lord.

And yet, before any of those significant signs, I was listening to preachers and evangelists proclaim that now (in the light of whatever the current development was) Jesus could return at any time. The only thing that keeps them from admitting that anything else must happen first is the imperial decree of imminence. But there are really at least four things indicated by the Scriptures themselves as preceding that day:

**1. Elijah must come.** The Lord first announced this four hundred years before the first advent of the Messiah and said it would come "before the great and terrible day of the Lord" (Mal. 4:5). That day would not come for at least 2300 to 2400 years later. Man did not know this, but God obviously did. From His perspective in eternity the day was imminent (according to His witness through other Old Testament prophets); from a human perspective in time, it was a long way off, and God accommodates us by revealing what will precede that day so that we can have a point of reference against which to measure it. Thus, while for God imminence applies now, for humanity it applies (practically) only to that generation when Elijah comes.

This may give encouragement and hope to us now, but its relevance in terms of imminence or immediacy applies only to that generation in which the conditions are first fulfilled. Thus it was with the first advent. There were prophecies about the coming of the Messiah. Many Jewish maidens must have thought with longing how marvelous it would be to bear this Promised One. But Daniel spoke of a period of sixty-nine prophetic weeks (483 years) leading up to the cutting off of this Prince or anointed one (Messiah), and, therefore, this hope could only actually apply to a maiden who was alive in that generation at least four hundred years later (Dan. 9:24–26). So with the coming of the day of the Lord, the concept of imminence from man's perspective could only apply or be relevant in a practical way after Elijah came. This is true not only for the Elijah prophetic sign, but also for the other three signs that precede His coming.

As we saw earlier, even though Jesus indicated that John the Baptist was the promised Elijah, He also said that Elijah "is to come" yet (Matt. 11:14). And when he said that in John the Baptist "Elijah has already come," He also said that he "does come" and "is to restore" (future tense: αποκαταστησει) all things (Matt. 17:11–13). Thus, we have a case of double fulfillment in the coming of Elijah. John the Baptist came in the spirit and power of Elijah and fulfilled the prophecy partially (Luke 1:17). But the complete fulfillment is yet to come, and until it does, "the great and terrible day of the Lord" will not come yet. As was noted previously, the expression "the great day" of the Lord is also found in Revelation 16:14, where we see the three foul spirits "who go abroad to the kings of the whole world, to assemble them for battle on the great day of God the Almighty." We are told, therefore, that that day will not come until Elijah comes first.

**2. The man of sin must stand in the temple or holy place.** The first prediction of this came in Daniel 9:27, where he is called the one who "makes desolate." Jesus spoke to His disciples about this, saying, "So when you see the desolating sacrilege spoken of by the prophet Daniel, standing in the holy place (let the reader understand), then let those who are in Judea flee to the mountains" (Matt. 24:15). It is important to note that when He addressed them as "you," He was talking to them first as believers, rather than as members of the Jewish nation, and second as part of the Church of Jesus Christ rather than simply as Jews who happened to be believers. We know this because He said that the things done against them would be for His "name's sake," that is, because they belonged to Him, not because they belonged to Israel. (v. 9). Further evidences appear earlier in Matthew. After Peter's great confession, "You are the Christ, the Son of the living God," we read that "From that time Jesus began to show his disciples that he must go to Jerusalem and suffer many things from the elders and chief priests and scribes, and be killed, and on the third day be raised" (16:16, 21). Now, in chapters 24 and 25, He prepares them as the Church that will be in a few days time, since at the end of this speech we learn that the last Passover and His crucifixion are but two days away (26:1). Thus, when He says, "when you see ... ," He is speaking to the Church, and specifically to the Church as it will exist when the man of sin stands in that holy place at the beginning of the great tribulation.

Paul also uses this dramatic and traumatic event as a marker for the Church to watch for (2 Thess. 2:1–3). He is clearly writing to Gentile believers as members of that Church. Earlier in this chapter as we studied the "day of the Lord" (regarding judgment) and the resurrection of believers at "the day of Christ," we noted that both of these events take place on "the last day" at the end of the great tribulation. And this is precisely what Paul reminds these believers to consider. That day will not come until the man of sin is revealed first. In other words, the man of sin will stand in the temple and proclaim himself to be God (v. 4), and some time after this, events of gathering to meet Him and final judgment will take place. Therefore, one doesn't have to be concerned that these events have happened already, since the man of sin hasn't been revealed yet. Then Paul reminds them that they had already been taught this: "Do you not remember that when I was still with you I told you this?" (v. 5). The lesson should be clear: watch for the man of sin to make himself clearly known by his blasphemy in the temple. Then start looking for the coming of the Lord.

**3. There must be a worldwide preaching of the gospel.** The key text for this prerequisite is Matthew 24:14: "this gospel of the kingdom will be preached throughout the whole world, as a testimony to all nations; and then the end will come." Since "the end" would be the end of the tribulation and the end of man's rule, and the beginning of God's rule, and since the resurrection is at the end ("on the last day"), Jesus is actually telling His followers when He will come back—after the gospel is preached worldwide. At this point, however, imminence becomes a problem for the camp of the pretribulationists. They are caught on the horns of a dilemma. There would seem to be some common sense rationale for some future planning. They want to work for the Lord. After all, He told them to do so. He also gave the "commission." But there is this thing called imminence. What if He came back today? How can we make meaningful plans? How can we even plan to complete the work of missions if He might interrupt it in the middle? This creates a serious tension between "Shall I?" and "Will He?" But perhaps the signals are being misread.

If the New Testament message stated clearly or even strongly suggested, "Witness for me as much as seems practical, though you will have trials and difficulties, but be constantly watching, for I could return at any moment," then there would be genuine relevance for such a tension in our lives today. Our manner of life and our priorities would be quite different, however, if, on the other hand, the message read as follows: "You will see certain early signs pointing to my return, but there will be two momentous signs more important than any others. My Archenemy will reveal himself clearly and introduce a time of terrible suffering in the world. But more significantly, the task I gave you will be completed and the gospel will have reached the entire world—go therefore. And when you see these things being fulfilled, know that the time is drawing near and lift up your heads, for you will not know on what day or at what hour I will return." Then we would be consumed with the thought of finishing His commission. All other things would be secondary in the light of this all-important priority. We can do little about the man of sin, except to withstand him. We can do much to fulfill the great commission. We can dedicate the totality of our beings, time, and resources to it. We don't need to know the exact time of his coming if we know His program and know our part in it. We can do the work at the same time we are watching the patterns that He predicted. Indeed, when we consider the Great Comission given by Christ in Matt. 28:20, the Savior Himself predicted how long He would be with the incipient Chuch. It was not promised up until the time of trouble, but "to the end of the age." The present age does not end with the beginning of the tribulation, but with its end.

If an important person set off on a journey, stating that the time of his return would be uncertain, but also adding that before then certain things would happen (a representative of his would come first, a different government would be in power, and that he would also buy out a particular company), we would be negligent in not watching the indicators while awaiting his return. Even if we did not know exactly when he would return, we would know two important things.

We would know that he would not return before those things happened and we would also know that his return was imminent when those things were fulfilled. And thus it is with the return of Christ. When those things He spoke of are fulfilled, then the teaching of imminence begins to apply. Indeed, we ourselves may hasten that day by fulfilling the great commission. But His return can be marked in its progression by the fulfilling of the things He pronounced as conditions, and thus we can measure His approach according to Hebrews 10:25, where we are encouraged not to be neglecting "to meet together, as is the habit of some, but encouraging one another, and all the more as you see the Day drawing near."

The concept of planning for a full life while living with the idea that Jesus could return today can lead to distortions. Indeed, it has already led to some. Whether directly or indirectly, it has led to the teaching that there is nothing that must happen or that must be done in the world before the return of Jesus for His Bride. If this is true, then the great tribulation does not have to come first, and I do not have to be prepared either spiritually or physically for it. As a consequence of this "bailed out" philosophy, some carry "escapism" into the practical concerns of their everyday lives. When they face painful or distasteful situations, they sometimes (only half jokingly) look for the Lord's possible return to save them from the consequences. Some have put off that full planning of their lives temporarily and some permanently, in anticipation of the rapture. Others have set their eyes and minds so on the heavens in such expectation that they have ignored their responsibilities in the world. Admittedly, these have not planned their lives as if they would live them fully, for the opposite principle (He may return at any time) has become so strong that it overpowered this one.

Much more serious, however, is the ability of this philosophy of imminence to emasculate the power of the great commission. Just as we are "bailed out" of the great tribulation, even so we are "bailed out" of our responsibility to complete the task of reaching the whole world with the gospel message. If nothing must happen before the return of Christ, then we don't have to preach the gospel everywhere first. With this responsibility removed, we are confronted with many options. We can work hard at missions. We can work at missions when it seems convenient. We can play at missions work. We can ignore missions entirely.

A grave question that remains, however, is whether Christ intended for the great commission to be completed by His Church before His return. If not, it would seem that a simple "tell people about me when you have opportunity" would have sufficed. If He did intend for every area of the world—every people group—to be reached before His return, there would seem to be two ways of understanding the situation. First, perhaps He did intend for it to be done, and He made its completion dependent on us, but He can come back before it is done. In this event, if Christ does rapture the Church before the work is done, then the Church has failed in the task that He set for her to do. The gates of Hades have prevailed against her, for if this was her task and Satan kept her from accomplishing it, he has won out and prevailed against her. Second, perhaps He intended for it to be done, and made it dependent on us, but He will not return until it has been done. In that event, His return is not imminent now and can only reach a state of imminence when that precondition is first fulfilled. Accordingly, the responsibility rests squarely upon our shoulders now. We cannot exercise an accommodation of a Lord Chamberlain and declare "peace in our time" and leave the burden of war to a future generation. It is our battle and our burden today. We can hasten the return of Christ. We can bring back the King.

As we measure our progress in that direction, we need to consider that the Scriptures indeed show a time when there will be redeemed souls from all people groups of the world. In the book of Revelation, heavenly voices sing to the Lamb: "Thou wast slain and by thy blood didst ransom men for God from every tribe and tongue and people and nation, and hast made them a kingdom and priests to our God, and they shall reign on earth" (5:9–10).

Who are these ransomed ones? The whole description would signify the Church. It is almost word for word the description given to the Church in chapter 1, that He "loves us and has freed us from our sins by his blood and made us a kingdom, priests to his God and Father" (4–6).

What is the timeframe in 5:9–10? Have these believers already been ransomed before what follows (that is, before the tribulation)? Or is this predictive—speaking of the completion of the number of ransomed ones to come (in the tribulation)?

If it is present and they are already redeemed before the tribulation, then we are faced with something that must happen before the tribulation can take place and, therefore, also before the rapture, for if these are raptured as those who are already ransomed, then they must be ransomed before they can be raptured. But we have not yet reached every tribe and tongue and people and nation for Christ. Therefore, He cannot return "now" (imminently).

It could, however, be predictive. There are certainly precedents in Scripture for displaying in advance that which was to come. The Suffering Servant of Isaiah 53 is a prime example. Also, Peter tells us that Christ was "a lamb without blemish or spot" who "was destined before the foundation of the world but was made manifest at the end of the times for your sake" (1 Pet. 19–20). If the Revelation 5:9–10 passage does speak of the completion of the number of the ransomed ones to come, then many of those ransomed ones are found in the tribulation and the Church is still on earth during the tribulation. Indeed, the description of these as ones coming from every people group (tribes, tongues, people, and nations) shows a remarkable correspondence to the description of that group in Revelation 7:9–17, who were "from every nation, from all tribes and peoples and tongues" and who had "come out of the great tribulation" and "washed their robes and made them white in the blood of the Lamb." Since this multitude will be reached, we cannot carelessly assume that the work will get done by someone else, some other time. Now is the time and we are the workers.

One can see inconsistencies at times in the reasoning of some who hold the pretribulation position when they walk on pragmatic or practical ground. This is especially true when it relates to the work and program of the Lord. There is much to be done. There is a burden to see work for the Lord progress toward a goal. But idealistically this must run headlong into the wall of imminence, particularly as they express it: "Jesus may come today" and "There is nothing that needs to happen before the rapture."

On July 18, 1985, Hal Lindsey told Paul Crouch (in the middle of the PTL program) that he felt the Lord would delay His coming until he (Lindsey) and Paul had a chance to finish some of their work for the Lord. Moreover, earlier in the program he stated clearly that he believed the Lord would not return until the Church, and particularly the Church in America, experienced strong persecution for the Lord. If a pretribulationist can believe the Lord would delay His coming because of the work the Lord had given him to do, why can he not accept the premise that the Lord will delay His coming because of the work He has given the Church to do, namely the great commission? This would be to take Matthew 24:14 at face value: "And this gospel of the kingdom will be preached throughout the whole world, as a testimony to all nations; and then the end will come."

There are two directions in which we can lift our eyes—to the horizon or to the heavens. After His encounter with the Samaritan woman, Jesus was offered food by His disciples. He said, "I have food to eat of which you do not know.... My food is to do the will of him who sent me, and to accomplish his work. Do you not say, 'There are yet four months, then comes the harvest'? I tell you, lift up your eyes, and see how the fields are already white for harvest" (John 4: 31–35). Christ had to accomplish the Father's work. We have to accomplish Christ's work—the completing of the great commission. Until we do, the only legitimate view we have the right to focus on intently is the view of the horizon—the harvest field. The time will come when harvesting is in its final stages. In the parable of the fig tree, after talking about the great tribulation, Jesus said, "So also, when you see all these things, you know that he is near, at the very gates" (Matt. 24:33). In a parallel passage in Luke, He said, "Now when these things begin to take place, look up and raise your heads, because your redemption is drawing near" (21:28). Then—when we see the signs described coming to pass, including the great tribulation and the final stages of world evangelization—we may properly lift up our eyes vertically,

# The Tribulation Church

to the very heavens, for then, and only then, our "redemption is drawing near." In our generation, those who gaze heavenward saying, "Lord, today?" could profit from the question of the angelic messengers at the Ascension: "Why do you stand looking into heaven?" Let us now fix our gaze intently on the harvest field.

**4. The great tribulation, including its accompanying signs, must run toward its end.** In Matthew 24:3 the disciples asked Jesus, "what will be the sign of your coming and of the close of the age?" In answering that question, Jesus proceeded to compress world events into a one- to two-day timeframe (with the Lord and His plan for the world, a thousand years is as a day) by comparing the program of God to the last day or two of the human birth process. He mentions four signs that would begin the whole process. Two are human tragedies growing out of the deception and greed of the human heart. First, many false Christs would appear and lead many people astray (v. 5). Second, there would be wars and rumors of wars, finally pitting nation against nation and kingdom against kingdom (vv. 6–7). Then there would be a proliferation and scattering of two natural disasters. First, there would be famines, and second, earthquakes (v. 7). The multiplication of these four tragedies and disasters Jesus calls "the beginning of the birth-pangs" (v. 8).

It is worth noting, however, that the Lord said these were but the beginning of birth pains. Any mother will tell us that the initial contractions clueing her to the onset of the birth process are hardly in the same arena as that intense crucible she endures immediately preceding and during the time of birth itself.

Is there later in Matthew 24 anything that would indicate a more intense time than that of the four adversities mentioned in verses 5–8? Immediately following the birth pains statement, Christ says that His followers will be delivered up to tribulation, be put to death and hated by all nations because of His name's sake (v. 9). In addition to other things, He states that there will be a falling away, but that "this gospel of the kingdom will be preached throughout the whole world, as a testimony to all nations," before the end can come (vv. 10–14). Then He says, "So when you see the desolating sacrilege ... let those who are in Judea flee" (vv. 14–16).

Then at the end of His description of the period of the great tribulation, He states that "when you see all these things, you know that he is near, at the very gates" (v. 33). Certainly the "all these things" that He described included the great tribulation, since He had just finished talking about it. Jesus had said that we were not to be led astray by those who declared "the time is at hand!"(v. 8). But in the corresponding passage in Luke 21:20–37, He said that certain things must happen first. After having spoken about coming tribulation events, He said, "when these things begin to take place, look up and raise your heads, because your redemption is drawing near." (v. 28). Thus, we look for our redemption against the backdrop of the tribulation, and we can see it as a traceable or markable approaching event. This corresponds with Hebrews 10:25. We are to "encourage one another," and especially so as we "see the Day drawing near." Therefore, to carry the figure of birth pains even further (according to other things said in Matthew 24), the revealing of the abomination of desolation could signify dilation and the fulfillment of the great commission, the moment of delivery: and "then the end will come."

Actually, there are prophetic events in the Matthew 24 account that come at the end of the great tribulation but must be part of this whole birth process. The darkening of the sun and moon (v. 29) comes after, or at the end of, the tribulation. This is the event quoted by Peter in Acts 2:20 as something that must happen before the day of the Lord (cf. Joel 2:30–31). Furthermore, at the end of the tribulation there will be a trumpet sound and the gathering of the elect (Matt. 24:31).

After these words about the tribulation and its end, Jesus said that "this generation will not pass away till all these things take place" (v. 34). But in order for that generation not to pass away and to see these things, the Church must also see them from the inside (that is, from the earth) and to go through them—including the great tribulation. Earlier in the chapter, Jesus spoke to His followers: "Then they will deliver you up to tribulation, and put you to death; and you will be hated by all nations for my name's sake" (v. 9). He adds, "So when you see the desolating sacrilege spoken of by the prophet Daniel standing in the holy place" (v. 15). Finally, after the description of the great tribulation period, He says, "So, also, when you see all these things you know that he is near, at the very gates" (v. 33). The concept of "all these things" must include the great tribulation period He had just spoken of. He spoke these things to the disciples (the incipient Church) in answer to the question of what they should look for at His coming and of the close of the age. They are the same "you" of verses 4–8 when they would look at preliminary signs. Thus, they would see these preliminary signs, but when they saw the great tribulation period (and the gospel preached in the whole world), they would have seen all these things and could know that He was near, indeed "at the very gates." It is then that the teaching of imminence becomes relevant for the Church.

Paul also sounded a word of warning in anticipation of the last days and the great tribulation (1 Cor. 7:26–31). He even clearly sounded a note of imminence for that time. Whether or not he himself anticipated that time as looming on the immediate horizon is, in a sense, immaterial. God gave him the message, and he penned it. Just as Old Testament prophets wrote messages they may not have understood, Paul did the same. What he wrote was for our information: the believers who are living on the threshold of those days. It is interesting that Paul did not write of the urgency of imminence in relation to the resurrection and rapture in chapter 15, but rather in respect to the great time of trial. In other words, we need to consider imminence not from some idea that the rapture could occur at any time in some vague kind of vacuum, but because we are going to have to deal in a practical way with the tribulation we are about to enter.

In this passage Paul speaks of a time of distress in light of which believers should not make any radical changes in their life commitments. There is more evidence to suggest that it was something he saw on the horizon (about to happen) than something they found themselves in right at that time. Even though the RSV and NASV render the term "the present distress," they both add as a footnote the alternate "or impending." Indeed both the Bauer, Arndt & Gingrich Greek-English Lexicon of the New Testament and the Thayer Greek-English Lexicon of the New Testament list this concept as the preferred rendering of this verse (Bauer, Arndt & Gingrich: impend, be imminent, p. 266; Thayer: close at hand, p. 217). In verse 28 there is no grand significance in the fact that the term "worldly troubles" uses the same word elsewhere rendered "tribulation." It may be suggestive. What is significant is the fact that Paul uses the future tense, "will have worldly troubles." If it were a present distress, the married would already be having such troubles and a more appropriate comment would be "those who are married have worldly troubles, and I would spare you that." Rather he says he would spare them troubles they will have if they find themselves in a married state, which they have time now to avoid. In verse 29 he states that "the appointed time has grown very short," and recommends a radical outlook in the face of this observation. The cumulative effect of these statements is a feeling of portent. If Paul anywhere in this letter sounded a note of imminence, it is here, not in chapter 15. If he felt that at any time they could enter this great distress (whether or not he named it the tribulation), then the Corinthians fully expected to go through that time before the resurrection.

As that day draws nearer, the words of Paul will have found their relevance for the Church. Through the direction of God's Spirit he was preparing the Church for the concept of the great tribulation and imminence. That word was for us as we stand on the threshold of the tribulation. He told us that "the appointed time has grown very short; from now on, let those who have wives live as though they had none, and those who mourn as though they were not mourning, and those who rejoice as though they were not rejoicing, and those who buy as though they had no goods, and those who deal with the world as though they had no dealings with it. For the form of this world is passing away" (vv. 29–31). Then, there must be a change in our outlook toward familial relationships, toward occasions of natural mourning and joy, and toward our connection with material things. Our normal national and social responsibilities will also be altered. It will be a day of pressures, to be sure. But what a day for unity it will also be—to feel, finally, the oneness of that Body Universal. To know what the issues and ties are that really matter. Perhaps as the early Church was noted for the resurrection greeting: "He is risen" and the response: "He is risen indeed," our universal word of greeting will reflect our new knowledge that He is standing at the door as we say and respond with a single word: "Maranatha"—Our Lord Come!

**5. We cannot know the exact day or hour of Christ's return.** In Matthew 24, Jesus had told the disciples that two momentous events were to precede the end of this (man's) age and His coming. The gospel would be preached worldwide (v. 14) and the great tribulation would be ushered in by the man of sin (vv. 15–21). At the end of that tribulation the Son would appear and a trumpet would sound for the gathering of the elect (vv. 29–31). Then He gave parables and instructions that would show what their activities should be. The preaching of the gospel to the ends of the earth was their work. He compared this to servants doing the work of a household (vv. 45–51) and servants entrusted with talents that should be invested for their master (25:14–30). In other words, in the light of the first momentous event, they were to be doing (completing) the work their Master gave them to do. But they were also to be on the lookout for the second momentous event. In the parable of the fig tree immediately following the discourse on the great tribulation and its conclusion, he told them to be on the lookout for it. He had already said, "So when you see the desolating sacrilege" (24:15); and now He says, "So also, when you see all these things," which includes seeing the man of sin in the holy place and the great tribulation itself, "you know that he is near, at the very gates" (24:33). The word is not "when you see some of the preliminary things," but "when you see all these things."

But in the midst of looking at these signs, they were to begin looking for something else. When they saw these things, particularly the completion of the great commission and the onset of the great tribulation, they were then to start looking for His return. Then "you know that he is near, at the very gates." In fact, He gave an entire parable devoted to watching for that return when He taught them about the wise and foolish maidens, some of whom were prepared and some of whom were not (25:1–13). They were told to watch. He issues this warning both at the end of this parable (v. 13) and in an entire section devoted for the need to watch (24:36–44). In the context of the fulfilling of the two great signs (the commission completed and the great tribulation), He not only tells them to watch, but also that at that time they should watch with bated breath, for "of that day and hour no one knows" (24:36); and, therefore, they should then live with a sense of imminence. Also He will come "at an hour you do not expect" (v. 44). Since our world is a sphere, how could anyone know the hour they were to expect Him? For some it will be dawn, for others that same moment will be noon, for still others it will be evening and for some it will be midnight. Some will be working in the field (morning and midday work), some will be grinding at the mill after the gathered grain has been brought in (mid- to late-afternoon and evening work), but the maidens waiting for the bridegroom are seen in sleep, even though some of them are, indeed, ready (cf. 24: 40, 41; 25:5). Thus also, in this bridegroom parable, the motto is WATCH: "for you know neither the day nor the hour." The word watch is appropriate because we have seen the signs He gave us to watch for, and now there remains nothing else to watch for except His impending return.

**6. We will see the "sorrow before joy" principle fulfilled.** The pattern was established by the Savior in Passion week: trial, suffering, death, and resurrection. So, trial and tribulation were established as the pattern for believers. Jesus told His disciples: "In the world you have tribulation," but He assured them immediately that He had "overcome the world" (John 16:33). In fact, the very process of seeming defeat held within it the power of victory because of the joy of resurrection that followed. Thus, when John looks for the one who is worthy to open the scroll and is told that it is the "Lion of the tribe of Judah" who has conquered, who is the only worthy one, he turns to look (Rev. 5:5). Instead of seeing a lion, however, he sees "a Lamb standing, as though it had been slain" (v. 6). The primeval promise of Genesis 3:15

was fulfilled in both parts in an inseparable manner. The bruising of the heel of Jesus, the seed, was, at one and the same time also the bruising of the head of Satan, the serpent. Jesus was thought to be conquered, but Satan was irrevocably conquered. So it is for the believers in the tribulation. The enemy thinks he has conquered them when the beast "was allowed to make war on the saints and to conquer them," but they are seen as ones "who had conquered the beast and its image and the number of its name" (Rev. 13:7; 15:2). So the pattern established by Jesus is also realized in the saints, and Paul can say, "I consider that the sufferings of this present time are not worth comparing with the glory that is to be revealed to us" (Rom. 8:18).

If we must go through an ordeal in a dental chair to relieve pain in a tooth, or if we must endure the agony of an operation to emerge sound and healthy afterward, we do not look for the trial, but we look through and beyond the trial for the prize on the other side. We have in Christ Jesus and His cup of suffering and subsequent resurrection the perfect example and pattern for us, His Body, to take our cup of suffering in the tribulation and to be delivered at its end. For He, "the pioneer and perfecter of our faith ... for the joy that was set before him endured the cross, despising the shame" (Heb. 12:2). Christ did not look for or look forward to the cross, but rather endured it. We do not look for or forward to the tribulation, but we will endure it. He despised the shame of the cross. We will despise the shame of evil, through the beast and his agents, triumphing (even temporarily) over the King's children.

One day as I drove to my teaching assignment, I had a vivid and visual object lesson concerning imminence. On my route I would reach a hilltop where I could look down to the traffic signal a half mile away where I made a right hand turn to my parking area. Usually I got into the right hand turn lane early, preparing for my turn. This day, however, there was a city truck parked in that lane some fifty yards before the light, effecting some sort of repairs. I could have gotten into the turn lane early, as usual. But it would have been pointless and futile. As soon as I came to the truck, I would have to leave the turn lane to go around the truck. Only after passing the truck would getting into the turn lane be effective or practical for me. So it is with imminence and the rapture. The turn lane is imminence. The truck is the combination of events that must come (world evangelization and the tribulation) before imminence can be practically applied. If we get into the lane too early, it will not help us reach our goal. If we recognize the obstacle, we can prepare for it and use the lane effectively when we get there. And only then will the lane be practical for us.

But what of "the joy that was set before him"? So long as Christ still faced the cross, He could not look for an immediate joy. At that point, He could only look beyond the cross to that joy. Only as He endured the cross, did there exist an impending joy. Even so it is for the Church of Christ. So long as we still face the tribulation, We cannot look for an immediate hope. At this point, we can only look beyond the tribulation to that hope. Only as we endure the tribulation, will there exist an impending hope. Thus, there is a difference between looking for the return of Christ (beyond the ordeal) and looking for the imminent return of Christ (during the trial itself).

**7. The last days will be measurable, so that we can trace them or mark them in their progress toward their conclusion.** We see this concept of measuredness in Hebrews 10:25, that believers should be found "encouraging one another, and all the more" as they "see the Day drawing near." This concept perfectly fits the posttribulation scheme of the rapture. We follow the program to its conclusion and watch for His return for us in the latter part of the tribulation whose sequence has been given to us. If we accept the pretribulation artificial division in time between Christ coming "for" His saints and "with" His saints, then we need to decide whether the "Day" spoken of is a rapture before the tribulation or Christ's coming to earth after it. If we choose a rapture before that seven-year period, we would be told by this verse that it is accompanied by traceable signs beforehand. If our last sign was the nationhood of Israel in 1948, then we have been wandering for more than forty years in a signless, trackless wilderness and the admonition simply doesn't make sense for us today. If, on the other hand, it were to refer to the Day of Christ's return to earth at the end of the seven years of tribulation, it would be addressed to those who are in that tribulation. Since this letter is obviously addressed to the Church, the choices for the pretribulation school at that point would be either to deny their own position or to deny the implications of this verse. The verse clearly suggests a sort of marking pattern. One thing follows another, and in that progression, one can see the goal approaching or the light at the end of the tunnel. To hold an "any day" approach now without these measurable things passing in review would make this passage nearly meaningless.

Paul said that the day of the Lord would not come until the rebellion and the revealing of the man of sin came "first" (2 Thess. 2:3). Thus, these things would precede the day of the Lord, which closes out the tribulation. Therefore, the Thessalonians need not be upset by a false report that that day had already come and that they had somehow missed it. They would not have to guess whether the day had come and gone. They would see it coming. Once the man of sin has been revealed, the great tribulation begins and is clearly defined in terms of how long it will run. That limitation is marked off for us in three different terms: 3 1/2 years (a time, times and half a time), 42 months (3 1/2 years x 12 months) and 1260 days (42 months x a 30-day prophetic month), and these three obviously agree completely with one another.

But whereas the end of that time is clearly defined once it has begun, the time of its beginning does not seem to be set in concrete. As in the Old Testament certain judgments were delayed through spiritual awakening (as we see in the book of Jonah), so there is some suggestion that the countdown to the onset of that last 3 1/2 years might be flexible. According to Matthew 24:20, Christ speaks of the flight of Judean believers at the very start of that time (when the man of sin is standing in the temple). There He encourages His followers by saying, "Pray that your flight may not be in winter or on a sabbath." It does not seem logical that He would enjoin them to pray for a situation's timing that could not possibly be altered. This should also help us to understand that we can actually set a goal of hastening the onset of God's Day by completing the commission that Christ gave to us. How else can we fulfill what Peter said when he spoke of us "waiting for and hastening the coming of the day of God"? (2 Pet. 3:12). It would also explain the fact that what is interpreted by some as a delay in Christ's return is actually an accommodating delay so that the work of reaching the world for Christ can be accomplished, since God is "forbearing ... not wishing that any should perish, but that all should reach repentance" (2 Pet. 3:9). Even the end of that time is not set in stone, since Jesus, in Matt. 24:22, said that "for the sake of the elect those days will be cut short." We cannot know by how much, but what a clear indication for those counting days that it cannot be calculated to the day or the hour. That is true imminence!

With the pretribulation position, however, the time of the rapture is unconditional. That is, it could occur at any moment with nothing whatsoever seen as a precondition or as a necessary intervening or preceding event. This is a set position of pretribulation teaching. Imminence is the cornerstone of the building. One must conscientiously ask the question "How far back in history can we go to reach the point where imminence did not apply?" Because Christ said He would return at an hour when His followers did not expect Him, could He have returned five days after His ascension? That would have made null and void the promised coming of the Spirit in His place to teach about Him. Could He have come the day after Pentecost? Then the commission to spread the message throughout the world would not have been begun, let alone realized. Could it have been before the destruction of Jerusalem and the temple? In Matthew 24, Jesus had predicted this event as well as the signs relating to His coming and "the close of the age." Then this prophecy would not have been fulfilled. Furthermore, the canon of our New Testament Scriptures—the very revelation of God—would not have been completed.

If we can see those early times as periods in which the teaching of imminence was not relevant as a present and practical truth, could this same principle hold true in recent times? Many, if not most, pretribulationists would not have considered the year 1000 or even 1900 as times when imminence as an "any-moment" concept was applicable. There are those of their number who feel that Israel had to exist as a nation, that Russia had to be capable of being a military power, that an army of the east had to be capable of fielding two hundred million troops, that there had to be some sort of confederacy in Europe, and that communications had to be so advanced that an event of importance could be seen by everyone in the world at the same time. And in those assumptions they are right. It is regrettable that they cannot also see that signs were given to us purposely as indicators of that approaching rapture and that those signs (especially the finishing of the great commission and the beginning of the great tribulation) have not yet been realized. And there is no crime in recognizing that His coming is being purposely delayed until they are realized.

The servant in Matthew 24:48 wasn't guilty because he said "my master is delayed," but because this belief led to slothfulness. The Lord does not teach that such a belief automatically leads to slothfulness. That particular servant was guilty because of his worldly attitudes and activities—beating fellow servants and eating and drinking with the drunken. If a servant thought that the Lord was delaying His coming because the great commission had not been completed and more of the world had to be reached yet, and, as a result of that belief, he was busy working for the evangelization of the world, he would most assuredly not be a wicked servant. He would be a good and faithful servant.

Beliefs have consequences. Chamberlain's "peace in our times" announcement during World War II caused Britain to relax its guard and it set the stage for Nazi conquests. Winston Churchill's "blood, sweat and tears" prediction caused Britain's citizens to tighten their belts and laid the foundation for ultimate victory.

In the Old Testament, God issued stern warnings about false prophets. He warned the people not to listen to the bearers of false hope. In Jeremiah 29, the prophet had to undo the harm that had been done by the prophet Hananiah who encouraged the people not to worry by predicting peace and restoration to the land within two years (see Jer.28:3).

Jeremiah had to tell them that they must prepare for a seventy-year exile and hardship.

Earlier God had warned the people, "Do not listen to the words of the prophets who prophesy to you, filling you with vain hopes; they speak visions of their own minds, not from the mouth of the Lord" (23:16). He later said that "a whirling tempest" would "burst upon the head of the wicked," and that "in the latter days" they would "understand it clearly."

Beliefs have consequences, and strong beliefs produce profound consequences. Almost all those who hold to the pretribulation position, do so in innocence and kindness. But, all other things being equal, and for the believer committed to this teaching (often with great subtlety), it eviscerates the power of the gospel—especially as it relates to completing the great commission. With the realization that nothing must be done to bring on the rapture, and when challenged with producing a reason for finishing that work, in the deepest subconscious level of logic, the question must somehow arise: WHY?

On the other hand, a posttribulationist with a powerful conviction that Christ will not come for His Church until His commission is complete, must, if his or her heart is pure and is controlled by the love of Jesus, have a consuming passion to bring to pass the burden left to the Church by the Master. That person will burn with a desire to bend every effort to that goal, and will look for the road signs the Master gave in following that path.

*Lord, teach me that working and waiting are wedded.*

# 7

## THE WRATH OF GOD

### Bane and Blessing

*Thou—awesome, holy, righteous God of flame*
*Which burns unquenched in wrath 'gainst all thy foes—*
*Didst on the tree in grace efface my blame;*
*Didst dub me "just" and "son" when He arose.*

There are two Greek terms that are translated into English as "wrath." These terms are θυμος and οργη. There are at least three good reasons for making a distinction between the terms when translating them into English rather than simply translating them both "wrath."

First, there are three verses where the two terms appear as separate qualities or emotions. In Romans 2:8 they are listed as two of the actions of God that are coming upon unbelieving and disobedient mankind. In Ephesians 4:31 and Colossians 3:8 they are mentioned separately as human qualities that the redeemed person should "put away."

Second, there are three verses where the two terms are used in combination. Revelation 14:10 speaks of the individual who worships the beast as drinking "the wine of God's wrath, poured unmixed into the cup of his anger." In speaking of the judgment of Babylon, it is said that she will "drain the cup of the fury of his wrath" (16:19). When Jesus wars against the nations, "he will tread the wine press of the fury of the wrath of God the Almighty" (19:15). In the 16:19 and 19:15 passages we have a double genitive for the two words—of the fury of his wrath. It is obvious in these three Revelation passages that one would need to find alternate words for the two Greek words (θυμος and οργη) often translated "wrath," since it would present an awkward redundancy to speak of "God's wrath, poured unmixed into the cup of his wrath," or of someone draining "the cup of the wrath of his wrath." The older KJV as well as the more modern translations (RSV, NASV and NIV) all present major problems in translating the two words consistently, but that will be covered later.

Third, there is a contrast seen by lexicographers in the way the two words are generally used in the New Testament. Thayer's Greek-English Lexicon of the New Testament describes θυμος as "passion, angry heat ... anger forthwith boiling up and soon subsiding again," whereas "οργη, on the other hand, denotes indignation which has arisen gradually and become more settled." Bauer, Arndt and Gingrich's Greek-English Lexicon of the New Testament shows some inconclusiveness in dealing with θυμος because it mixes together references to man's anger on the one hand and God's on the other, although it gives passion or passionate longing as the primary meaning of the word, which would indicate the short term or passing nature of the word. But it is clearer in its treatment of οργη as it relates to God's wrath, and states that it is more often "to be expected in the future, as God's final reckoning with evil" and "is a legitimate feeling on the part of a judge." It is this οργη wrath of God that has to do with final judgment and vengeance, as is seen in Romans 12:19, where Paul appeals to his readers to live peaceably with all men, saying, "Beloved, never avenge yourselves, but leave it to the wrath (οργη) of God; for it is written, 'Vengeance is mine, I will repay, says the Lord.' "

As one takes these primary considerations into account and studies the usages of the two words in relationship to God throughout the New Testament, it becomes clear that when each is used alone of God's feelings and dealings, θυμος is used of short-term punishments upon man's body or environment, while οργη shows His final judgment, particularly as it relates to man's final judgment.

It is unfortunate that these basic distinctions have not been better reflected in the translations of θυμος and οργη as they relate to God and His dealing with man. It is like reading a treatise about the greed of man, part of which deals with his rapacity and part of which deals with his miserliness. If we constantly saw the word rapacity whenever man's greed was being viewed as a predatory, forcible grasping of that which was not rightfully his, in order to have it for his own, and if, just as consistently, we saw the word miserliness when man's greed was being considered as a hoarding of his present wealth or a stingy clutching of what he now owned, even though it resulted in his own discomfort, we would have no problem in keeping the two separate. But if first one, and then the other was referred to as greed, it would only tend to muddy the waters and would lead to unnecessary confusion.

This is precisely the sort of problem we have in the translation of these two Greek words for "anger" and "wrath." Even Webster's second college edition of the New World Dictionary of the American Language recognizes in English two separate meanings of the word wrath: 1. "intense anger; rage; fury" and 2. "any action carried out in great anger, esp. for punishment or vengeance." This becomes a glaring problem when the two words appear together in a verse. In Romans 2:8, when it speaks of God's future dealings with man, θυμος is translated as fury and οργη as wrath. Then in Ephesians 4:31 and Colossians 3:8, when human believers are told to put away evil traits, the θυμος, which in Romans 2:8 was God's fury, now becomes man's wrath, and the οργη, which in Romans 2:8 was God's wrath, now becomes man's anger.

Even though we might concede that an attribute in God may have dimensions that go beyond a similar quality in human beings, this confusion carries over even in dealing with these terms when applied only to God and His dealings when the two terms are used together. John says the one who worships the beast and receives his mark "shall drink the wine of God's (θυμος) wrath, poured unmixed into the cup of his (οργη) anger" (Rev. 14:10). Yet a switch of translation is made when those same words occur together in 16:19 and 19:15. In 16:19, "God remembered great Babylon, to make her drain the cup of the (θυμος) fury of his (οργη) wrath." In 19:15, at the great battle, Jesus "will tread the wine press of the (θυμος) fury of the (οργη) wrath of God the Almighty." Thus the θυμος of God is rendered His wrath in 14:10, but changes to His fury in 16:19 and 19:15; and His οργη in 14:10 is His anger, but becomes His wrath in 16:19 and 19:15.

If we had a single English word that meant "wrath which results in final judgment" (the biblical concept of God's οργη), it could solve our problem. Perhaps a two-word combination, "wrathful judgment" would serve as well if it were understood that we were dealing with wrathful final judgment or ultimate judgment and not a punishment in time, such as a plague (or θυμος type) judgment.

First Thessalonians 5:9 has become a classic defense for the pretribulation position. Their teaching seems logical enough. It runs as follows:

1. Paul assures us as believers that "God has not destined us for wrath."
2. But we read in descriptions of the great tribulation that God's wrath will fall upon the world.
3. Since the Church is not destined for wrath, we cannot be in the world when this happens.
4. Thus, the rapture occurs before the tribulation begins, and we are spared from this wrath.

But there is a fatal flaw in their position at the very beginning, since the promise has been pulled out of its context in order to make it apply to the tribulation. Unfortunately, some of them would see that we are spared from that short time of wrath rather than from ultimate wrath itself. Indeed, the passage does begin with the day of the Lord, but it ends with ultimate destiny. The word destined should be a tip-off itself. It is a rather grand word to use for coming temporal and physical plagues, but by the time we see the two ultimate and contrasting destinies in the verse, there can be no doubt left as to the meaning of the word.

Aside from all consideration of which "wrath" the verse means (θυμος or οργη), the immediate context (indeed the very verse in which it is used) is clear, even in the English text, about which wrath Paul is talking about. The complete verse states: "For God has not destined us for wrath, but to obtain salvation through our Lord Jesus Christ" (1 Thess. 5:9). When any statement is made about a condition that is followed by the opposite of that condition or situation, we must interpret the first condition by comparing it to the opposite condition. For example, if we are to consider the meaning of "dumb," we must analyze the setting in which it is used. If it is used with a contrasting opposite, our problem is solved for us. If someone should say, "You are not dumb, but you simply choose not to talk," then we know that the dumbness has to do with speaking. If, however, one should say, colloquially, "You are not dumb, but one of the smartest people I know," then we know that the dumbness has to do with intelligence. Such is the case with the "wrath" used in 1 Thessalonians 5:9. We are given the contrast or opposite in the very sentence in which the word occurs. If "God has not destined us for wrath, but to obtain salvation through our Lord Jesus Christ," then the wrath spoken of here must be the opposite of the salvation that we are to obtain. The only legitimate contrast or opposite of obtaining salvation through Jesus Christ is not receiving that salvation, and that, in turn, means being separated from Christ eternally in the place called "the lake of fire." Thus, even by using the English text alone, the wrath spoken of in this verse refers to the ultimate and eternal judgment of God. He has not destined us for such judgment, but for its very opposite—for obtaining His glorious salvation through Christ.

Therefore, when we take the entire context into consideration and especially the verse in which wrath is found, and add to that the natural and logical force of the word but, we are left with little choice but the following understanding: "We are headed for troublesome times, as you know. They will come as a great surprise to those who are in darkness, but not to you who are sons of light. Therefore, let us be alert and armed for that day with spiritual protective weapons like faith and love and that great hope we have—salvation. That is our greatest assurance. God's ultimate destiny for us is not wrath. Quite the contrary, it is salvation through our Lord Jesus Christ. Whether we are alive when He returns or whether we have died, eternal life with Him is our destiny." Any other meaning of wrath than ultimate wrath (eternal separation and punishment) is belittling to the opposite (salvation) stated in verses 8 and 9.

The punishment involved in the outpouring of the plagues of the tribulation found in Revelation is fierce. But it is short and it is physical. To equate that with the wrath from which we are to be saved makes wrath a very weak and shallow specter. The wrath of 1 Thessalonians 5:9 and Romans 5:9 is surely much more dreadful than that (as much as one might wish to avoid even that). God's wrath from which we are saved is both spiritual and eternal. If wrath were only short and physical, man could produce similar pains. Death in a nuclear holocaust would be horrible. So would being boiled in oil. The ancient water torture is dreadful. Space would almost fail if we were to mention the gruesome aspects of man's inhumanity to man. It would, indeed, include mental and psychological anguish, which man has learned to produce both psychologically and chemically. Yes, God's punishment could be worse, even when it is physical and mental and merely temporal. But it is this very contrast that is illustrated in the New Testament when speaking about the true wrath of God—the wrath that is both spiritual and eternal.

In Luke 12:4–5, Jesus said, "I tell you my friends, do not fear those who kill the body, and after that have no more that they can do. But I will warn you whom to fear: fear him who, after he has killed, has power to cast into hell, yes, I tell you, fear him!" Since only God has this power, He is the one to fear, and precisely because His wrath goes beyond the body and time and reaches to the soul and eternity. Hebrews 10:31 echoes this warning: "It is a fearful thing to fall into the hands of the living God." After the beast and the false prophet and then, later, Satan are cast into the lake of fire, we read that "if any one's name was not found written in the book of life, he was thrown into the lake of fire" (Rev. 20:15). This is the wrath of God, and it is from this that we will be saved. To be denied the very presence and blessing of God is truly hell. Any other punishment pales by comparison. Salvation is not escape from the tribulation. And wrath is not the tribulation plagues. Salvation is glory with Christ, eternally. Wrath is ignominy and separation from Him, eternally.

Considering which Greek word is used in 1 Thessalonians 5:9 leads to the same conclusion. The word is οργη, the word that is used to show God's final or eternal judgment. Thus, whether using the English translation or the Greek word, the meaning comes out the same. God has not destined believers for eternal judgment, but has destined us instead for salvation.

The rest of the New Testament shows a consistent use of οργη as a final judgment when used in reference to God's wrath. The parallel passages about the preaching of John the Baptist in Matthew 3:7 and Luke 3:7 show multitudes, including even many Pharisees and Sadducees, coming to him for baptism. John poses the question "Who warned you to flee from the wrath to come?" The context makes clear what John's message of God's wrath was all about. It was not about a temporal plague to come, but about eternal judgment. In the Matthew passage he said the Lord would "clear his threshing floor and gather his wheat into the granary, but the chaff he will burn with unquenchable fire" (v. 12). In the Luke account he said, "the axe is laid to the root of the trees; every tree that does not bear good fruit is cut down and thrown into the fire" (v. 9). To complete the use of God's οργη wrath in the Gospels, John 3:36 might well serve as a proof text of what this particular wrath is: "He who believes in the Son has eternal life; he who does not obey the Son shall not see life, but the wrath of God rests upon him." Just as in 1 Thessalonians 5:9, the opposite of God's οργη wrath is given in the very verse where this wrath itself is mentioned. Here we are clearly told that the opposite is "eternal life," thus making this wrath (which presently rests upon the disobedient or unbelieving) eternal condemnation.

In the book of Romans no fewer than six verses treat this wrath: "the wrath of God is revealed from heaven against all ungodliness and wickedness of men who by their wickedness suppress the truth" (1:18). We would search the Scriptures in vain to find anything that would suggest that God reserves a temporal or physical or plaguelike punishment for such perversion. Obviously, the just recompense is final judgment. Indeed, in a similar kind of situation, Christ suggested that a physical punishment would be much preferred by such offenders rather than God's final punishment when He said, "it would be better for him if a great millstone were hung round his neck and he were thrown into the sea" (Mark 9:42). Paul uses the term twice to refer to hypocritical judges who are committing the very sins that they condemn in others: "by your hard and impenitent heart you are storing up wrath for yourself on the day of wrath when God's righteous judgment will be revealed" (Rom. 2:5). Not only does God's day of this wrath come at the end, but also the very fact that it has been stored up down through the ages by all the centuries of such hypocritical judges indicates that it cannot come through a plaguelike punishment in any given generation—not even in the last one. Otherwise, only that individual generation would have suffered such plaguelike wrath since they would be the only ones alive on earth in that generation. As it is, all of these false judges since the middle of that first century will partake of that wrath.

Romans 5:9 indicates that since "we are now justified by his blood, much more shall we be saved by him from the wrath of God." At the very least, it would be a trivializing of the concept of end-time blessing to suggest that our present justification will be overshadowed by the idea of escaping plagues or physical pain and suffering. Much more understandable and appropriate is this idea: though our justification at the present time is wonderful, how much more wondrous and blessed will be the fact that we will escape final judgment altogether and enter eternity glorified. How much more fitting is what Paul says when he declares that even "the sufferings of this present time are not worth comparing with the glory that is to be revealed to us" (Rom. 8:18). This same contrast between wrath and destruction on the one hand and mercy and glory on the other is used again in Romans 9, where Paul uses the wrath term twice: "What if God, desiring to show his wrath and to make known his power, has endured with much patience the vessels of wrath made for destruction, in order to make known the riches of his glory for the vessels of mercy, which he has prepared beforehand for glory?" (vv. 22–23). It should be clear that the contrast is not between plague punishment and escape from it. It is between "destruction" and glory (or eternity in glorified bodies). That the destruction is eternal rather than temporal and physical is clear from the fact that God "has endured with much patience the vessels of wrath made for destruction." This He has endured down through the ages until the final judgment. Thus, we escape not temporal and physical pain or punishment, but this final and spiritual judgment, and we gain its counterpart—eternal and incorruptible glory.

The final passage in Romans that treats this divine wrath is found in chapter 12: "Beloved never avenge yourselves, but leave it to the wrath of God; for it is written, 'Vengeance is mine, I will repay, says the Lord.' No, 'if your enemy is hungry, feed him; if he is thirsty, give him drink; for by so doing you will heap burning coals upon his head' " (vv. 19–20). The fact that divine vengeance is tied to οργη wrath implies a time of waiting until the end.

This eternal judgment comes only at the end of the tribulation and at the end of the plague judgments. When the martyrs of Revelation 6:10 call out "O Sovereign Lord, holy and true, how long before thou wilt judge and avenge our blood on those who dwell upon the earth?" they are "told to rest a little longer, until the number of their fellow servants and their brethren should be complete, who were to be killed as they themselves had been." Thus, the final vengeance (God's) will come at the end of the tribulation after the last tribulation saint has been killed.

In Ephesians 2:3, we find that before our rebirth "we were by nature children of wrath, like the rest of mankind." This is like an echo from John 3:36, where the wrath of God rests upon the world of the disobedient. Certainly humankind outside of Christ throughout the ages does not face plaguelike wrath from God, but just as surely it does face His final judgment wrath. Indeed, this very concept of the children of disobedience facing the wrath of God is given in

Paul's other reference to God's wrath in this Ephesians letter: "Let no one deceive you with empty words, for it is because of these things that the wrath of God comes upon the sons of disobedience" (5:6). And the preceding verse establishes for us that this wrath is the final judgment wrath of God, since it gives us the opposite of this wrath: "no fornicator or impure man, or one who is covetous (that is, an idolater), has any inheritance in the kingdom of Christ and of God" (5:5). Either we have inheritance in His kingdom, or we face eternal judgment wrath.

We have already seen which wrath Paul was talking about in 1 Thessalonians 5:9, the verse that is used as the dispensational proof text for the idea that the Church is spared the tribulation since God's wrath is seen in the tribulation. First Thessalonians 1:10 also makes mention of the coming wrath, stating that Jesus "delivers us from the wrath to come." Although not as clear as the other passages treated above, the context makes a contrast between the former life of the Thessalonians when they served idols, and their present life since turning to God and serving "a living and true God." There would seem to be an implication that the idols had no power to save from any ultimate judgment, but that the living God could and would accomplish just such a deliverance. Further strength is given to such an interpretation when we consider that in the other two passages in this letter Paul uses οργη and applies it to eternal judgment. We have already seen this in 1 Thessalonians 5:9. In the remaining passage this is also the clear meaning. In the second chapter, Paul speaks of "the Jews, who killed both the Lord Jesus and the prophets, and drove us out, and displease God and oppose all men by hindering us from speaking to the Gentiles that they may be saved—so as always to fill up the measure of their sins. But God's wrath has come upon them at last!" (14–16). We can conclude that God did not strike them dead with some plague then, since they continued at that time to "displease God and oppose all men." We can also see that the RSV translators were not completely happy with their own translation, "at last," since they added a footnote about the translation, indicating viable alternatives: "Or completely, or for ever." Those particular Jews had obviously become hardened in their opposition to the Christ and to His truth and God's eternal or "for ever" wrath was now upon them.

In the letter to the Hebrews, this term is used twice. In both instances (3:11 and 4:3) it is a quotation from Psalm 95:11: "Therefore I swore in my anger that they should not enter my rest." At least two elements of the text of Hebrews indicates that the rest spoken of is eternal rest for the believer and not simply an entering into the promised land of Canaan. First, the author of Hebrews translated the "not" of Psalm 95:11 as never in both passages: "They shall never enter my rest." This "never" places the possibility of God's rest for them even beyond death. He is evidently speaking of the eternal rest of God. That this is not merely speculation is borne out by the second element of the text, that is, the explanation of this rest given by the author in the chapter 4 passage. He states that "if Joshua had given them rest, God would not speak later of another day. So then, there remains a sabbath rest for the people of God" (vv. 8–9). He had already said that the rest spoken of was completely a matter of faith, that it did not benefit those Hebrews "because it did not meet with faith in the hearers," but that "we who have believed enter that rest" (vv. 2–3). He also says that "those who formerly received the good news failed to enter because of disobedience" (v. 6). So, we are dealing not with a temporal, physical, plaguelike punishment, but the eternal destiny judgment of God.

The concept of a merged wrath (a future wrath realized in a present condition of already standing under that wrath) is clearly seen in the teaching of John 3:18 and 36. Verse 18 tells us that "he who does not believe is condemned already, because he has not believed in the name of the only Son of God." In one sense, he does not have to await ultimate condemnation—he stands condemned already. Verse 36 carries the idea a brooding step further when it states, "he who does not obey the Son shall not see life, but the wrath of God rests upon him." Although Ephesians 5:6 says that the wrath of God is coming on the sons of disobedience, we are told here that it sits upon his shoulder like a ravenous vulture awaiting its victim's last breath. It is a sword of Damocles held in place by a single hair. It is like a man who has decided against using the exit in a building that is condemned to imminent destruction. Thank God for His grace, which has put the door there, but it is the essence of condemnation to the man who does not use it.

We come now to the critical passages in Revelation. After all, they deal directly with the tribulation period, since they cover chapters 6–19. The first two are found in succeeding verses in 6:16–17, after the opening of the sixth seal. Beginning in verse 15, as a result of the great earthquake and the signs in the heavens, "the kings of the earth and the great men and the generals and the rich and the strong, and every one, slave and free, hid in the caves and among the rocks of the mountains, calling to the mountains and rocks, 'fall on us and hide us from the face of him who is seated on the throne, and from the wrath of the Lamb; for the great day of their wrath has come, and who can stand before it?' " But who are the speakers here? In the preceding seal, the martyrs had suffered at the hands of "those who dwell upon the earth," which is a typical expression for the unredeemed. There is every reason to believe that the crowd calling out in craven fear in verse 16 are those fearful unsaved. There is no good reason to think that they are believers who are afraid of their Lord. This is strictly a human opinion about the situation these people find themselves in, and can no more be depended on to be God's assessment than the speeches of Job's comforters could be assumed to represent the mind of God.

Even though the term that they use for the wrath of God is οργη, or "final judgment" wrath, there is no warrant or excuse for accepting their interpretation of the events as God's interpretation. To them it may seem as if the ultimate end has come upon them. Little do they realize that this is but the beginning of God's temporal and physical punishment (His θυμος wrath) and that they haven't seen anything yet.

The term is next used with the blowing of the seventh trumpet, where the twenty-four elders, after thanking God, say, "The nations raged, but thy wrath came" (11:18). If we were to ignore the context, we could believe that this kind of wrath has come upon the earth before the end of the tribulation. But a reading of the entire verse assures us that this is a prophetic statement that looks beyond the close of the sixth trumpet (which preceded this trumpet) to the very end of the tribulation itself. The complete verse reads, "The nations raged, but thy wrath came, and the time for the dead to be judged, for rewarding thy servants, the prophets and saints, and those who fear thy name, both small and great, and for destroying the destroyers of the earth." We know that the judging of the dead is a future event after the tribulation and that this fits the description of this form of wrath. The rewarding of the Lord's servants would hardly be complete without the marriage of the Lamb, and this does not occur until the final bowl plagues are ended. The destruction of the destroyers is not realized until Babylon is dealt with and the Lord triumphs at Armageddon, and both of these take place at the end of the tribulation. In effect, what is said here is stated as an accomplished fact, even though it looks beyond the bowl judgments to come to the end of the tribulation itself. It is similar to believers being chosen in Christ "before the foundation of the world" or to Christ being destined "like ... a lamb ... before the foundation of the world but ... made manifest at the end of the times." (Eph. 1:4; 1 Pet. 1:19–20).

This ends the occurrences of the οργη wrath of God with the exception of three passages, but those are very special passages, since they combine the concepts of His θυμος wrath and His οργη wrath. We will return to those verses after we have considered the use of God's θυμος wrath in the New Testament.

Actually, God's θυμος wrath occurs only in the book of Revelation and only during the tribulation. It could be called God's plague wrath or God's short-term, temporal punishment wrath. It is confined to seven verses. Three of these are the verses mentioned above where it occurs together with God's οργη wrath. Before considering those special verses, let us look at the other four. They are found clustered at the end of chapter 14, in 15 and at the beginning of 16.

The last of the seven trumpets has sounded and an angel with a sickle has been told to gather the clusters of the vine of the earth since its grapes are ripe. "So the angel swung his sickle on the earth and gathered the vintage of the earth, and threw it into the great wine press of the wrath of God; and the wine press was trodden outside the city, and blood flowed from the wine press as high as a horse's bridle, for one thousand six hundred stadia" (14:19–20). Chapters 12, 13, and 14, coming between the close of the trumpets in chapter 11 and the beginning of the bowls in chapters 15 and 16, seem to be a sort of interlude between the plague series, where some general or comprehensive information is given. The passage just cited is either partly or wholly symbolic. Certainly the sickle, the vintage of the earth, and the wine press are symbolic. Generally, when a passage begins so strongly symbolic, it continues to be symbolic. We would expect the symbolism to continue with wine coming out of the wine press, but here the Lord interprets for us by announcing that blood came out of it. Thus, it is obviously a physical judgment of God upon His enemies. We are not sure of the amount of blood involved. We are told that it was as high as a horse's bridle (about five feet) and reached a distance of sixteen hundred stadia (two hundred miles). That would make it a river of blood, but how wide a river we do not know, which is all the more reason to look at the entire passage as symbolic except for the realization that the wine was actually blood. A winepress would produce a fairly narrow stream, but, nevertheless, a narrow stream five feet high and two hundred miles long still represents a lot of blood and a lot of death. It cannot be said with any certainty whether the passage is talking about a special judgment of God or whether it represents the total amount of blood already shed in the previous plagues or the total of the blood that will be shed in the bowl plagues or whether it is a comprehensive look at the blood already shed together with that which will yet be shed. What is certain is that it is a temporal and physical (plaguelike) judgment. This is what θυμος judgment is all about.

The next three instances of this plague judgment follow in rapid succession and all refer to the seven bowls of the wrath of God or the seven last plague judgments: "Then I saw another portent in heaven, great and wonderful, seven angels with seven plagues, which are the last, for with them the wrath of God is ended" (15:1). John notes that "one of the four living creatures gave the seven angels seven golden bowls full of the wrath of God who lives for ever and ever" (15:7). This is followed immediately by what John then heard: "Then I heard a loud voice from the temple telling the seven angels, 'Go and pour out on the earth the seven bowls of the wrath of God' " (16:1). Immediately following this, the bowls are poured in succession upon the earth with no significantly noticeable delay between them.

Certain things are worthy of note regarding these θυμος judgments of God.
1. They are physical judgments against human bodies.
2. Their target is unbelievers and followers of the beast.
3. They apparently are not poured out solely to punish, but also to attempt to gain repentance among those being punished, since the commentary is made after both the fourth and fifth bowls that the sufferers did not repent, but, rather, cursed God.
4. They are temporal and last for a relatively short period of time.
5. They are not eternally planned and eternally enduring judgment such as we have in the οργη wrath of God. They are more akin to God's judgment predicted against the Amorites when their iniquity would become complete (Gen. 15:16), or against the nations in the promised land during the times of the judges when God would endure the conditions no longer and would raise up a Hebrew judge to punish a wicked people.

Another noteworthy fact about these judgments is that this series of bowl judgments completes the θυμος judgments of God. In 15:1 we were told that these "are the last, for with them the wrath of God is ended." Any judgment to come after them will be of another kind—the οργη wrath of God. Also, if they are the last θυμος judgments, others of the same kind of judgments had come before them. That group would include the trumpet judgments that just preceded the bowl judgments. It would also include the opening of the seven seals, although the fifth seal is not a judgment per se, but a promise of a judgment to come. It would even include the sixth seal, since that judgment has all the earmarks of a θυμος judgment, even though it was misinterpreted by the fearful earth dwellers who thought it was the end and that God's οργη judgment had come.

A final fact for our consideration is the focus of the last two plagues, which come at the end of the great tribulation (16:12–21). The sixth bowl concerns itself with Armageddon and the preparations for that battle. The seventh, or last bowl, deals with God's judgment of Babylon (16:19). This brings us to those three special passages where God's θυμος or temporal wrath is used together with His οργη or eternal wrath.

In 16:19, we read that "God remembered great Babylon, to make her drain the cup of the fury (θυμος) of His wrath (οργη)." The same construction is used in the account of God's judgment at Armageddon, that the Lord "will rule ... with a rod of iron; he will tread the wine press of the fury (θυμος) of the wrath (οργη) of God the Almighty" (19:15). No doubt the use of the two terms in combination indicate an intensifying of the concept of God's wrath at this point, as Bauer, Arndt and Gingrich suggest. But one should also not overlook the fact that in these two last judgments God's temporal judgment and eternal judgment combine. They happen basically at the same time. Just as there was a judgment of the throne of the beast in the fifth bowl judgment (16:10), there is also one against the forces he controls at Armageddon in the sixth bowl (16:14 and 19:15), and of Babylon, the mercantile luxury system he controls, in the seventh bowl (16:19 and 18:21).

But we need to go to the first verse in which the two kinds of wrath are used together in order to get a perspective on why they are both used in the same setting. After an angel is seen in midheaven proclaiming the gospel, another angel comes to announce the approaching fall of Babylon, "saying, 'Fallen, fallen is Babylon the great, she who made all nations drink the wine of her impure passion.' And another angel, a third, followed them, saying with a loud voice, 'If any one worships the beast and its image, and receives a mark on his forehead or on his hand, he also shall drink the wine of God's wrath (θυμος), poured unmixed into the cup of his anger (οργη), and he shall be tormented with fire and sulphur in the presence of the holy angels and in the presence of the Lamb'" (14:8–10). Temporal fairness is served when the rebellious beast worshipers both in Babylon and Armageddon come face to face with the physical consequences of their fatal choice; eternal justice is served by their immediate assignment to hell following their temporal judgment. It is like the fate of King Zedekiah when Nebuchadnezzar passed sentence on him: "They slew the sons of Zedekiah before his eyes, and put out the eyes of Zedekiah" (1 Kings 25:1–7).

There is another Scripture passage in which we can see the combination of the temporal and eternal judgment of the rebels. In the judgment of the nations in Matthew 25:31–46, those who are called unrighteous are the beast-marked survivors of Babylon's judgment and the beast-marked nationals in the homelands of the soldiers arrayed against the Lord at Armageddon (Rev. 19:19). If they owed allegiance to the beast, it would be altogether natural for them not to give any help or comfort to those who belonged to Christ during the great tribulation (that is, to his "brethren"). It is said at the end of that passage that "they will go away into eternal punishment." Since they would seem to be physically alive at this judgment (nothing is said about any type of physical death to the contrary), they may be cast bodily into hell, suffer physical death by the fires of hell, and then enter spiritually into the suffering described in Revelation 14:10–11, where they "shall be tormented with fire and sulphur in the presence of the holy angels and in the presence of the Lamb. And the smoke of their torment goes up for ever and ever; and they have no rest, day or night, these worshipers of the beast and its image, and whoever receives the mark of its name." This would be very like the fate of King Zedekiah and would be a realization of the warning Christ gave: "And do not fear those who kill the body but cannot kill the soul; rather fear him who can destroy both soul and body in hell" (Matt. 10:28). Only the Lord has the power to cast into hell. He can either destroy both physically and spiritually in hell itself or kill the body now and cast the soul into hell later: "But I will warn you whom to fear: fear him who, after he has killed, has power to cast into hell; yes, I tell you, fear him!" (Luke 12:5).

We now can draw certain conclusions. First, God has not destined the believer to the eternal wrath of hell, or separation from Him, but to the glory of eternal salvation. The Word sets these two eternal destinies in opposition to each other on a number of occasions. This is the wrath He promises to keep us from. Second, His plague wrath is directed against rebels—the disobedient and unbelieving. He can single out the unbelievers and seal the believers. Third, when He strikes nature, there may be occasions of inconvenience or suffering as a byproduct even for believers, just as the opposite has been true through the ages that He sends His rain on the just and on the unjust. Thus, if water is poisoned and the fish die, nobody eats the affected fish. Fourth, the beast and his followers are the target of the plague wrath of God, but Jews and Christian believers are the targets of the wrath of Satan and the beast. So it was in the Egypt of the Exodus that the Hebrews were the focus of Pharaoh's wrath while Pharaoh was the focus of God's wrath. So it shall be in the tribulation. Not only is the beast furious at believers then, but the wrath of Satan himself is also directed against them. This is clearly stated for us: "But woe to you, O earth and sea, for the devil has come down to you in great wrath ... Then the dragon was angry with the woman, and went off to make war on ... those who ... bear testimony to Jesus" (Rev. 12:12–17). But just as surely, the beast and his kingdom and his followers are the target of God's (temporal) wrath at that time. The first bowl is poured against "the men who bore the mark of the beast" (Rev. 16:2), and the fifth bowl is poured "on the throne of the beast" (16:10). Thus, it becomes the great tribulation for the saints because of Satan's wrath, and it becomes the great tribulation for the beast and his followers because of God's wrath.

The fullness of God's ultimate wrath is detailed in Revelation 14:9–11: "If any one worships the beast ... he also shall drink the wine of God's wrath, poured unmixed into the cup of his anger, and he shall be tormented ... for ever." This is the true wrath of God and we are saved from it. Our life is hid with Christ in God. When Christ who is our life appears, then we also will appear with Him in glory.

*Thank you for the security of your eternal fortress which no foe can breach.*

# 8

## DISPENSATIONALISM AND THE TIMES OF THE GENTILES

### *Priceless Grace*

*What awesome grace: redeem a Gentile race;*
*'Twixt us and Jacob, bid the conflict cease.*
*What whelming love: Your lovéd Son abase;*
*Upon the tree unite us; be our peace.*

Two major schools of thought in the interpretation of Scripture are covenant theology and dispensational theology. A covenant is a compact or agreement between two parties. When a covenant regards God and man, God enters such an agreement for man's benefit. In the Old Testament the basic concept is that of binding one to a duty or service toward the other. In the New Testament the idea is that of a unilateral enactment made by one with absolute power. The other party could accept or reject it, but could not change it.

Covenant theology is the concept that all of Scripture is divided into two covenants: the covenant of works and the covenant of grace. Even though the covenant of works existed for a time (outwardly), the new covenant (of grace) was eternal and was promised even while the old was in operation. The old covenant was administered by Moses, a servant; the new covenant was revealed in Christ and is better than the old since it was being administered by the Son.

Theologically, a dispensation is the concept of God's plan

or scheme. Covenant theologians would see two dispensations—the old (Mosaic, mainly) and the new (Christian). Dispensational theologians would see more—traditionally seven dispensations.

Dispensational theology is the belief that God has at different times tested man in different ways in respect to obedience to some specific revelation of the will of God. They see seven such dispensations: innocence, conscience, civil government, promise, law, grace, and the kingdom. Although these divisions are not found as such in the New Testament, dispensationalists claim that the distinctions come from "rightly dividing the word of truth."

We will not consider dispensationalism in the entirety of its teachings, but we will look at it in terms of its attitudes in four different areas: first, as it regards the Scriptures; second, as it regards "rightly dividing the word" relating to times; third, as it regards "rightly dividing the word" relating to terms (and in a special way as that relates to Jews/Gentiles/Church and the tribulation and the times of the Gentiles); and, finally, as it regards their concept of the rightness of their theological position.

## THEIR ATTITUDE TOWARD SCRIPTURE

### Their attitude regarding inerrancy

Fortunately, the dispensational school holds a high view of Scripture and its reliability. They hold firmly to the inerrancy of the word of God. Some might feel that they are somewhat rigid in some of their approaches, but if one is to err, it is better to err on the side of the angels. What becomes disturbing to us who hold a posttribulation view is the idea within their fold that because those who deny inerrancy are posttribulationists, therefore, those who change from a belief in pretribulationism to a belief in posttribulationism might also change to a denial of inerrancy as well.

It is an unfortunate implication that there is some sort of equation between the phenomena of posttribulationism on the one hand and the denial of Scripture on the other. One could doubtless also say that practically all liberal scholars believe in social concerns (carried to their extreme in "the social gospel"). It does not naturally follow, however, that within the Christian scheme of things social concerns are wrong.

If one were to take a poll of the entire world of Christendom that believes in inerrancy, it might also show that the majority of these believers are posttribulationists too. It may be that the majority of the prisoners in our country like apple pie, but this doesn't mean that there is a criminal streak in the rest of the population who happen to like apple pie.

Furthermore, those who do deny inerrancy, may find it easy to dismiss the dispensational position, since it is only inferred at best, whereas so much is said in the Scriptures about the tribulation that they must somehow deal with it, and the logical conclusion is that it will happen just before Christ's return.

I am sure there are those who have changed from the post position to the pre position just as there are those who change from pre to post, but the overwhelming majority of those who began as pretribulationists and became posttribulationists (this is certainly true of those I am acquainted with), retain their high view of Scripture. It is regrettable that we are somehow seen as defectors. The idea of defecting can be used for those who no longer trust the Scriptures, but surely it is unfair to think of a change from pretribulationism to posttribulationism as defection. It suggests an unwarranted pride in pretribulationism to assume that the position is clearly defined in Scripture and, therefore, inspired doctrine. We who have been in that position and have moved to posttribulationism (while retaining our lofty view of the inspired Scriptures) may regard it more as graduation than defection. Let us be kind and fair. I know of ministers and Christians leaders who happened to be pretribulationists in their orientation to eschatology who had moral lapses, but I would not presume to conclude that it was not uncommon for people who held that view to be corrupted morally.

In the cases of those who do change from the pretribulation position to posttribulationism and who also defect in their commitment to the inerrancy of Scripture, the position of pretribulationism itself may sometimes have to share some of the responsibility. Unfortunately, even a scholar can at times be a "weaker brother." If he is a "Bible believer" and becomes disillusioned with a position he considers no longer tenable, he could (although it is rationalizing rather than being "logical") also become somewhat disenchanted with the Scriptures his fellow Bible believers use in support of what is, to him, an insupportable conclusion. It is like the child whose parents tell him both about Santa Claus and the Lord Jesus. Because he feels disillusioned with his parents when he discovers that what they told him of Santa was a hoax, he may transfer serious doubts to the Jesus story they also told him.

### Their attitude toward the spiritualizing of Scripture

All readers and scholars of the Scriptures spiritualize them in some areas. Few of us would presume to believe that Jesus was a door or a road or bread in any literal sense. Problems and disagreements arise when some parts or ideas are spiritualized that should have been accepted literally. Pretribulationists are not free from spiritualizing certain words or phrases or passages—especially when a literal rendering does not fit their position. But they charge us with heavy spiritualizing, particularly in regard to the prophetic Scriptures.

This charge holds a special fascination for me. It was precisely this tendency that I found in the pretribulation position (and in dispensational teaching at large) that caused me to become disenchanted with that system of eschatology. Dispensationalism specifically spiritualized the meaning of descriptions applied to an entire multitude of believers during the tribulation period. They took these descriptive terms, which throughout the New Testament meant the Church, and made them mean an entirely new group during the tribulation. As I studied the Scriptures (without any bias against their position—after all, it was at that time, my position too), I discovered more and more problems that I could not solve, and that were not addressed by proponents of my pretribulation system.

The more I searched for answers, the more I was drawn to consider other basic approaches. With the passing of time, I found that more questions were resolved from a posttribulation position than from a pretribulation position, until I reached the point where almost everything fit from the posttribulation vantage point and very little fit from my former pretribulation point of view.

One passage that is consistently ignored by the pretribulation position is the olive tree account found in Romans 11, where the unity of Jewish and Gentile believers is stressed and where Paul states that all Gentile believers must come in before Israel's national conversion. Only a closed system like dispensationalism could shut out the Gentiles who believe during the tribulation from being included in this unified whole.

## "RIGHTLY DIVIDING THE WORD" RELATING TO TIMES

### Kingdom rules and regulations

Certain teachings of the New Testament, including most of the teachings of the sermon on the mount in Matthew 5–7, are applied by dispensationalism to a different time—the time of the kingdom age in the millennium. For example, Jesus says, "You have heard that it was said to the men of old, 'You shall not kill; and whoever kills shall be liable to judgment.' But I say to you that every one who is angry with his brother shall be liable to judgment; whoever insults his brother shall be liable to the council, and whoever says, 'You fool!' shall be liable to the hell of fire" (5:21–22). Rather than accepting the possibility that Jesus was making use of hyperbole to show the seriousness of our responsibilities to our brother, they would interpret this to mean that capital punishment would be used against anyone in the millennial kingdom who used such words against his brother. They would not have such ideas apply to us in the here and now. The wider context of the Matthew passage, however, should predispose us to accepting our responsibility to our brothers at the present time. Following the statement about calling a brother a fool, Christ said, "So if you are offering your gift at the altar, and there remember that your brother has something against you, leave your gift there before the altar and go; first be reconciled to your brother, and then come and offer your gift" (5:23–24).

**Prophetic order of events**

Dispensationalists have no serious problem with the order of prophetic events that face the world. They claim to have a prophetic unity in their end-time beliefs. This is one of the features that make the system attractive. But the real reason for their unity is found in the teaching of imminence, and that is why they have no serious problem—because they take the Church out of the world before the prophetic times of real difficulty begin. They can actually disagree rather radically on end-time events after the rapture and it does not matter. Jesus could come at any time—even today—and, therefore we need not be concerned about the order of what is going to happen after we are gone. If we conjecture the order one way and it comes out another way, it has not affected us.

On the other hand, for those of us who believe that we will actually be living during those prophetic times of trouble, the order of events is of serious consequence. We are sometimes charged with having no unified system of order regarding the second advent and what immediately precedes it and what immediately follows it. One question that might legitimately be raised, however, is whether we are required to have all the details worked out in advance, even though we are dealing with earnest matters.

Since there are some events relating to the second advent that the Scripture itself does not fit clearly into a given sequence slot (for example, the judgment seat of Christ), it is presumptious to suppose that we know what the Lord did not choose to tell us in that order. The best we can do is to be clear where the word seems clear and to admit conjecture beyond that point.

A possible order, in the light of what we can know, could be as follows:

1. The building of the temple

2. The onset of the 70th week of Daniel by a pact made between the man of sin and Israel (possibly a secret pact)
3. The first half of the tribulation (which may produce nothing by which to note that we are in that period)
4. The man of sin (the abomination which desolates) enters the temple, defiles it, proclaiming himself to be God
5. The beginning of the second half of the tribulation—the great tribulation period
6. The flight of the Jews from Jerusalem
7. The events of Revelation 6–15, including:
   a) Conversion of a Jewish remnant as first fruits (144,000)
   b) Conversion of the last full number of Gentiles ("from every nation, from all tribes and peoples and tongues")
   c) The scroll and trumpet judgments
8. The beginning of the bowl judgments and imminence relevance
9. The first six bowls
10. Imminence relevance reaches "critical mass" and the rapture occurs:
    a) God calls His people out of Babylon.
    b) All dead saints are resurrected and living saints are transformed.
    c) All saints meet Christ in the air and are there with Him for a matter of hours or a few days.
    d) The judgment seat of Christ
11. The seventh bowl
12. The marriage supper of the Lamb
13. Christ descends to earth "with all His saints"
14. Christ defeats the armies at Armageddon and Satan is bound
15. The judgment of the nations with righteous unbelievers invited into the millennial kingdom (Matt. 25)
16. The millennial rule of Christ and all His saints

This order, however, is fairly flexible. Some elements are solidly in place. Obviously, the first half of the tribulation precedes the second half, and, just as obviously, the building of the temple must come before that temple can be defiled. But there are many intangibles. There are some events that can fit just as easily in two or three different slots. For example, the temple could be built before the 70th week of Daniel—that last seven-year period, or it could be built sometime during the first half of that period. The attack of the armies of the north (omitted from the list) could come before the entire seven-year period, during the tribulation itself, or (most likely) near the end of the millennium. It would seem logical that the judgment seat of Christ would come before the marriage supper of the Lamb, but both of these could take place in the air before the descent of Christ to earth, or after He actually sets foot upon the earth.

Of extreme relevance in this entire matter is the importance of not running ahead of the Lord. Most students of the word will agree that we understand so much more today about the book of Revelation and prophecy in general than we did thirty years ago. Some things that simply did not make sense then are perfectly clear to us now. Furthermore, those who, at that time, made wild conjectures about those elements were shown to be foolish in their imaginations. Let us learn from their mistakes. And let us learn the lesson of Jeremiah 30:24, where the time of tribulation was predicted. The prophet said, "The fierce anger of the Lord will not turn back until he has executed and accomplished the intents of his mind. In the latter days you will understand this." As the days close in upon us, things will become clear. Some things the Lord may make known to us weeks, months, or even years before they happen. Others He may reveal to us as they are ready to break in upon us. Let us wait before the Lord, but let us also wait on the Lord.

## "RIGHTLY DIVIDING THE WORD" RELATING TO TERMS

### The rapture and His coming

When such terms as appearing, revelation, and coming are used in the New Testament to refer to the return of Christ, dispensationalists take great pains to pass these through a strainer to keep the rapture intact and separate from any binding relationship to these terms. Posttribulationists see the rapture and Christ's coming together, because they appear together in the New Testament. Paul says to believers in Thessalonica that God is going "to grant rest with us to you who are afflicted, when the Lord Jesus is revealed from heaven with his mighty angels in flaming fire" (2 Thess. 1:7). Thus, Christ will grant His rest to believers when He is actually revealed from heaven. And Paul tells the Corinthian believers that "at his coming those who belong to Christ" will be resurrected (1 Cor. 15:23). This tells us that the time of His coming and the resurrection occur together. Dispensationalism would like to draw a comparison between our expectations regarding the return of Christ today with the expectations of those who awaited the Messiah's coming in fulfillment of the Old Testament prophecies. In the actual fulfillment of those Old Testament promises, they reason, the prophecies themselves actually materialized into two separate advents of Christ. They see the New Testament prophecies in the same light. Though we see concepts of His coming and the rapture associated with each other, they contend, they are actually two distinct events separated by seven years.

This parallel overlooks a critical difference. We have been given a clear Spirit-inspired New Testament to show us the difference between the prophecies of the Old Testament regarding the first and second coming of Christ. No corresponding God-given inspiration is granted to dispensationalists so that they might "rightly divide the word" to show a separation between rapture and coming of Christ. Lacking this, when the concepts occur either together or interchangeably, logic asks us graciously to accept the union.

**The 144,000**

There is mention of the 144,000 in only two passages—both in the book of Revelation. In 7:2–8, we are told only two things about them. They are sealed in the forehead as servants of God for protection in the tribulation, and twelve thousand of them come from each of the twelve tribes of Israel. In the second passage (14:1–5), we are told only a little more about them. They were a special cadre of Jewish believers—they were pure and they were truthful. The Lord gave them a special song that only they could sing. It is not said that they are the only Jews redeemed in the tribulation period, but they are mentioned as being redeemed as a special Jewish group. They "have been redeemed from mankind as first fruits for God and the Lamb" (v. 4). This would make them the official forerunners of nation-Israel, which will come to redemption at the return of Christ (according to Zechariah 12:10–13:1). This is all we are told about them, and, without Scripture to support it, anything said about them beyond this would be pure speculation.

Dispensationalists would see in them more than this, however. They look at the multitude of tribulation believers from every nation, tribe, people, and tongue who have washed their robes in the blood of the Lamb who are described in Revelation 7:9–17, and because this group is mentioned right after the 144,000, they conclude that the 144,000 have brought them to faith in Christ. They make of them flaming evangelists after the order of a modern-day Billy Graham. It is understandable that they would want to perceive them this way. According to their position, the Church is raptured before the tribulation, and now there appear 144,000 believing Jews as well as multitudes of believers from every people group in the world. Somehow this almost unbelievable turn of events must be explained. The 144,000 proves to be the straw they grasp. They are mentioned before the vast Gentile multitude in Revelation 7:2–8, but there is no warrant for making them the source of that Gentile multitude. There is not even a hint of such a connection. Only a grasping for a solution to so many coming to faith after the Church was gone could cause one to light upon them as a possible answer. They are never called evangelists, and it is never even suggested that they might be such.

**Divisions or distinctions between Jew/Gentile; Church/saints; and tribulation/times of the Gentiles**

Those who hold to a posttribulation rapture see God's

ultimate goal for Jews and Gentiles as the same—He wants to make them one in Christ. Also, we would see the Church and the saints as being the same group. The saints from the Old Testament times, the saints from Pentecost to the tribulation, and the saints in the tribulation are joined together in a unified whole. Finally, we see the tribulation time as the time when the final Gentiles are brought to Christ. Thus, we would see the "times of the Gentiles" coming to an end only at the end of the tribulation itself: "Jerusalem will be trodden down by the Gentiles, until the times of the Gentiles are fulfilled" (Luke 21:24). We also see the time of the "full number of the Gentiles" coming into the Church of Christ corresponding to the same timeframe, since believers from all people groups will believe during the tribulation (Rev. 7:9–17). We see nation Israel, which comes to Christ only at the end of the tribulation, doing so right after the last of the Gentiles are added (Rom. 11:25–26).

Dispensational theology, however makes key distinctions between Jews and Gentiles once the tribulation begins. According to them, the Church is gone—having been raptured. So, in the tribulation they see unbelieving Jews distinguished from unbelieving Gentiles on the one hand, and believing Jews distinguished from believing Gentiles on the other. God has stopped dealing with the Gentile and has begun again to focus on the Jew as a Jew. This would make it impossible for the Church to be in that time of tribulation (since in the Church there is no distinction between Jew and Gentile), which would make a rapture of the Church before then necessary.

This points out a key weakness in the dispensational system—an inflexibility that locks God into a box that is not of His making. All seven dispensations are tied with neat ribbons with abrupt beginnings and conclusions. At times, allowances are made for some ordinances that existed under an old dispensation continuing under a new dispensation. But the dynamic of God's dealings with man is much more complex than that, even if we did have seven neat economies. There is a foreshadowing, at the very least, of some of the supposed principles of one era (or dispensation) within another.

Ostensibly the dispensation of civil government began with Noah. To assume that there was no civil government before Noah would be presumptuous. Aside from the brief story of Cain and Abel, almost all of the history of the "dispensation of conscience" or "self-determination" is taken up with childbirth and death, until Genesis 6 tells us that "the wickedness of man was great." There is, therefore, little space devoted to culture and lifestyle. We do read, however, that there were (organized?) crafts or guilds. Jubal was "the father of all those who play the lyre and pipe" and Tubal-Cain "was the forger of all instruments of bronze and iron" (Gen. 4:21–22).

It is of interest that verse 20 tells us that Jubal "was the father of those who dwell in tents and have cattle," since it follows verse 17, which tells us that Cain, the very firstborn of mankind "built a city" and even named it—after his son, Enoch. Thus, cities, with some probable form of government, preceded by many centuries the establishment of the "dispensation of civil government."

Also, long before the "dispensation of Israel under promise," the principle of promise or oath or covenant affects Israel-to-come (and, through her, the world) in the prophetic word concerning the seed of the woman (the coming Messiah/Savior) in Genesis 3:15. This same principle of promise affects the entire world in the Genesis 9 rainbow of promise that the world would never again be destroyed by a flood.

Not only is there this foreshadowing of a fuller development of these concepts in future eras, but there is also found in other cases an overlapping of two elements in a period that has been designated as belonging to one of those elements. Sometimes (if one accepts the traditional dispensational schematic) this overlapping even leapfrogs (or leaps over) an intervening dispensation. For example, in the dispensational system, the number 3, 4, and 5 dispensations are civil government, promise, and law. But the concept of civil government (as in the "dispensation of civil government") may seem somewhat weak under Abraham, Isaac, and Jacob (in the next "dispensation of Israel under promise"). And yet, at times during the "dispensation of Israel under law" (two dispensations removed from "civil government"), it shows itself in varying degrees, not only in intertribal disputes (which tribes are for bringing back King David, and which are against), but in the breakup of the original kingdom into Israel and Judah with separate and often conflicting governments. (In the "dispensations," it doesn't seem that God always ordered them to be such. Did He order human beings to live by conscience?)

Perhaps the clearest instance of overlapping (including the concept of leapfrogging) is our own experience of living in two eras at the same time. We live in the "dispensation of grace" or in the "Church age" and, at the same time, we already live (in some senses) in "eternity future." We are on earth, but we are "in Christ" (though Christ is in heaven). Indeed, we are already made to "sit with him in the heavenly places." We are a redeemed people even while we await "the redemption of our bodies" in the rapture. Even while we are citizens down here, we are "fellow citizens with the saints and members of the household of God."

Therefore, to suggest that God must completely remove the Church before dealing with Israel as a people, is an interesting—but unnecessary—position. We have already seen that even according to the dispensational scenario, God has had segments or principles of one "dispensation" at work in the midst of another. In fact, during the "law" dispensation we have an amazingly powerful "promise" (the keynote of another dispensation) of the approaching "grace" (still another) dispensation when God says: "Behold the days are coming ... when I will make a new covenant with the house of Israel and the house of Judah, not like the covenant which I made with their fathers ... but this is the covenant which I will make ... I will put my law within them, and I will write it upon their hearts" (Jer. 31:31–33).

When we move from the Old Covenant of Law to the New Covenant of Grace, it was an abrupt transition only in principle when the Messiah was "cut off." In practice, it was more of a graduated transition, with a strong overlap. John the Baptist, himself part of that transition, declared that "the axe is laid to the root of the trees," but the Lord was a long time in the hewing. Though the transition began with the miraculous harbingers of the coming King—Gabriel, the star and the angelic hosts—the overlap continued into the early days of the Christian Church with the differences between the Jewish and Gentile churches being only too obvious. It is true that in God's view there were no divisions in Christ— neither Jew nor Greek, male nor female, bond nor free. But for years there were clear-cut distinctives in the two groups. There were requirements in the Jerusalem church that were not sought in Antioch. Indeed, in Acts 18 and 19, first Apollos had to be brought up to speed in doctrine (having known only the baptism of John) and then the disciples of John at Ephesus had to be baptized into Jesus to enter the New Covenant era. Ultimately, Christianity became basically Gentile in orientation, and the few Jews who were converted adapted to a Christianity steeped in Gentile culture.

The tribulation is a unique period. Not even the dispensationalists look at it as a separate dispensation, but rather as the completion of the 70 weeks of Daniel, which they also do not consider a separate dispensation. Since the first 69 weeks were under the "Law," this presents a problem. But it is only a problem if one insists that the covenant of grace is a parenthetical "dispensation" exactly between the 69th and 70th weeks of Daniel.

The 70th week of Daniel (the last seven years of that prophetic period of 490 years) is also clearly a time of God focusing on and dealing with the Gentiles. He uses this time to finish His dealings with them because the "times of the Gentiles" extends as long as Jerusalem is trodden under their feet, and that does not end until the tribulation itself ends (Luke 21:24 and Rev. 11:1–3).

The nation of Israel is not saved until Messiah returns (Zech. 12:10–13:1), and the full number of Gentiles will be brought in before that time (Rom. 11:24–26). Since Gentiles are still "coming in" during the tribulation, God is still dealing with the Gentiles in the matter of evangelism through that seven-year period.

Since there have been so many foreshadows, transitions, and overlaps in God's dealings with man in those "dispensations," and because of the uniqueness of the tribulation period, there appears to be no scriptural reason why this same period of time cannot be used by God both for the completion of His Church (basically in terms of Gentile conversions) and for the preparation for full acceptance by the Jews and the coming of the millennial kingdom. Indeed, there is strong scriptural support for just such a position.

The commission for the preaching of the gospel was based on a three-pronged offensive—to the Jews in "Jerusalem and in all Judea," then to "Samaria" (the Jewish half-breeds), and finally "to the end of the earth." Jerusalem was reached dramatically at Pentecost, and the spread to all Judea was rapid. Only shortly after this beginning, Samaria was introduced to the gospel by Philip, followed with confirmation by Peter and John. Then the outreach to the Gentiles was begun at Caesarea when Peter introduced Cornelius to Christ, and it was continued by the missionary journeys of Paul, who understood the commission to be the bringing of "salvation to the uttermost parts of the earth" (Acts 13:47). And down through the corridors of the centuries, the Church has continued that journeying without yet reaching "the end of the earth."

There is no indication that the first-century world was fully reached with the gospel. The closest suggestion of such a claim would probably be found in Romans 10:18 where Paul says, "But I ask, have they not heard?" and then responds, "Indeed they have; for 'Their voice has gone out to all the earth, and their words to the end of the world.' " But he uses a quotation from Psalm 19:4, that nature's voice has declared God's glory in the whole world. If that were fulfilled in the time of the author of that Psalm (David), it certainly doesn't refer to the spread of the gospel message. Furthermore, Paul later states in Romans that he made it his "ambition to preach the gospel, not where Christ has already been named," lest he "build on another man's foundation" (15:20). He also writes in 2 Corinthians (in a letter probably written in the same year that Romans was written): "We do not boast beyond limit, in other men's labors; but our hope is that as your faith increases, our field among you may be greatly enlarged, so that we may preach the gospel in lands beyond you, without boasting of work already done in another's field" (10:15–16). Thus, he still looked forward to reaching unreached areas.

So God is not finished with the Church and He is not yet finished with Israel as Israel. But He accomplishes both goals during that 70th week. He purifies and completes the Church in terms of Gentile believers and begins the conversion of Israel through a startling new remnant that foreshadows the conversion of Israel as a nation.

According to the figure of the olive tree in Romans 11, "a hardening has come upon part of Israel until the full number of the Gentiles come in" (v. 25). Immediately after this announcement, Paul concludes: "and so all Israel will be saved" (v. 26).

Although the Church has not yet reached "the end of the earth," we discover as we go into the tribulation period that the job gets finished. We see in Revelation 7 "a great multitude which no man could number, from every nation, from all tribes and peoples and tongues" who had "come out of the great tribulation" and had "washed their robes and made them white in the blood of the Lamb" (vv. 9, 14). The full number of the Gentiles finally is brought into the olive tree and God has done the work He set out to do among the Gentiles.

But there is that other group presented to us just before we view this vast multitude. We see twelve thousand from each of the twelve tribes of Israel. These 144,000 also are Christians, but they are "fulfilled Jews." Revelation 14 tells us that they are "redeemed" ones who "follow the Lamb." But they are special in the sense that they are the first new branch to be grafted back into the olive tree, and although Israel as a nation is still steeped in unbelief, these are "first fruits of God and the Lamb" (Rev. 14:4) to indicate that the rest of that harvest (Israel as a nation) is to follow very soon—"and so all Israel will be saved."

This national redemption will take place after the tribulation, when "every eye will see him, every one who pierced him; and all tribes of the earth will wail" (Rev. 1:7). This account is taken from Zechariah 12:10-14, which tells of a Jewish mourning—national and family by family: "when they look on him whom they have pierced, they shall mourn for him, as one mourns for an only child, and weep bitterly over him, as one weeps over a first born." Following the description of this family-by-family mourning, we read that "on that day there shall be a fountain opened for the house of David and the inhabitants of Jerusalem to cleanse them from sin and uncleanness" (13:1).

Previously, we noted that down through the centuries (after the first) Jewish believers were basically assimilated into the Christian Church as a Gentile-culture church. Only recently, we have begun to see the spirit of that "first fruits" group of 144,000 revealed in a growing number of recent Jewish converts. Although obviously a part of the body of Christ, they also are keenly aware of that special relationship, which, originally in the first-century Church, showed the melding of the Old Covenant into the New. Their services make broad usage of those messianic "shadows" of the Old Testament. They rejoice in the fulfilling of those types in the Messiah in a dynamic sense only hinted at in their Gentile Christian counterparts. One can see this clearly in such groups as the Chosen People Ministry and Jews for Jesus. Indeed, they refer to themselves as "completed Jews."

Thus, there is no inconsistency in the fact that the number of Gentile Christians is being completed at the same time that Jewish acceptance is being prepared for. According to the olive tree figure, it becomes a logical necessity.

It is wise to avoid unnatural divisions in looking at God's dealing with people. By looking at certain verses, we could conclude that He deals with us by segregated groups, but this could be done only by ignoring the wider context of Scripture. For example, dispensationalists may feel they have found such a division in 1 Corinthians 10:32, where Paul charges the Corinthians to "Give no offense either to Jews or to Greeks or to the church of God." But the reason for the distinction between Jews and Greeks in the Corinthian passage is clear from the context. There was one set of cultural patterns among the Jews and another among the Greeks. In neither case was the believer to give offense. In fact, even in the Church of God (where the law of liberty superseded these cultures), offense was not to be given.

We cannot ignore this context. God's division today is believers and nonbelievers, the saved and the lost, the redeemed and the condemned, light and darkness. Indeed, God will bring back the Jews as a people, but, when He does, it will be as part of all of the redeemed people. By ignoring the context, we can easily make a case for God dividing the world into the five categories in Acts 1:8, as the commission is given to take the gospel to Jerusalem, all Judea, Samaria, and the ends of the earth. Then we would have unbelieving Jerusalem Jews, unbelieving non-Jerusalem Jews (all Judea), nonbelieving Samaritans, and nonbelieving Gentiles in addition to the fifth group—believers from all of these other groups.

In the tribulation itself we do not see these divisions. At the opening of the fifth seal, we see "the souls of those who had been slain for the word of God and for the witness they had borne," who were told "to rest ... until the number of their fellow servants and their brethren should be complete" (Rev. 6:9, 11). There is, here, no Jew/Gentile distinction. In Revelation 12:17, after the dragon had been prevented in his pursuit of "the woman who had borne the male child," he "was angry with the woman and went off to make war on the rest of her offspring, on those who keep the commandments of God and testimony to Jesus." It is obvious that "the woman who had borne the male child" is Israel (whether believing or not). On the other hand, "the rest of her offspring ... those who keep the commandments of God and bear testimony to Jesus" are certainly believers and no differentiation is made as to their Jewishness or non-Jewishness.

Paul clearly includes both Gentile and Jewish believers in father Abraham, when he says in Romans that Abraham "received circumcision as a sign or seal of the righteousness which he had by faith while he was still uncircumcised. The purpose was to make him the father of all who believe without being circumcised and who thus have righteousness reckoned to them, and likewise the father of the circumcised who are not merely circumcised but also follow the example of faith which our father Abraham had before he was circumcised" (4:11–12). Thus there are no grounds for making the believing offspring of the woman here either Jewish or non-Jewish. They are merely the ones who "bear testimony to Jesus." In Revelation 13:7, we learn that the beast "was allowed to make war on the saints." Here, also, there is no designation of Jewish saints or Gentile saints, but the group is simply "the saints." What God has joined together, let no man put asunder.

## THEIR ATTITUDE TOWARD THE RIGHTNESS OF THEIR POSITION

### The posttribulation position is diverse

There is a good deal of diversity among posttribulationists, and it is not surprising, given the diversified events in the day of the Lord itself, and especially in the light of the "timing" of the rapture in relation to the Lord's actual and physical touching down upon the earth. Much of the "agreement" among pretribulationists is in the areas where premillennial posttribulationists also agree with them—the events of the great tribulation period, the fact of the resurrection/rapture, the coming of Christ to earth and the millennial reign.

But aside from that, it is simply not true that a beautiful and sweet unity exists overall in the pretribulation camp. Some of them have rendered the Greek word αποστασια in 1 Thessalonians 2:3 "the departure," and have interpreted the apostasy in this way as the departure of the church. However, this view is not generally shared by even the majority of pretribulationists. Early in dispensational teachings it was taught that the Spirit was taken completely out of the world with the Church, but this has been modified by most pretribulationists since those early days. Many explain that the vast missionary outreach during the tribulation comes about because the 144,000 Jews are flaming evangelists, while others hedge on this explanation. It is true that they are in agreement that the Church is to be raptured before the great tribulation, but even here we sense a lack of unity. Some hold that the tribulation will immediately follow the rapture, while others see a sizable or indefinite interval coming between the two events.

Sometimes an issue is made of "counting up" posttribulationists. Numbers alone are not always significant. In the early days and years of Christianity, believers were certainly vastly outnumbered by unbelievers, but that did not make unbelief right. Also, when it comes to eschatology, non-evangelicals today may have views on the end times that do not rely on the authority of Scripture, and they may outnumber evangelicals. But if they do, that mathematical advantage would not make them right in respect to the end times. I do not know that any survey has ever been taken among evangelicals to discover their views on eschatology. If it were, and if the majority were posttribulationists, this numerical superiority would not make the position correct. I suspect, however, that because of the Bible School movement (which had its roots in dispensational teaching) and its influence on the evangelical movement in our country, there may be more in the pretribulation camp than in the posttribulation camp (my early belief was determined by such a dispensational pastor). But, once again, numbers don't determine truth. Logic under the control of Scripture must be the determining factor (the Scripture under the control of logic produces sects). Therefore, it would be significant to discover the ratios of sincere evangelicals who started out in one position and ended up in the other through studying the Scriptures, and who yet retained their evangelical identity. Because of my interest in end time events and particularly the return of Christ, I have spoken to many evangelicals about the subject. I have found scores of people who have changed their views from pre- to posttribulational. I have yet to meet one who began as a posttribulationist and through studying the Scriptures changed to the pretribulation position. To me, this speaks eloquently.

**There is widespread belief in the pretribulation position**

Dispensationalists acknowledge rather freely that this teaching is a rather new belief, which first surfaced in Church history around 1830. They feel, however, that its widespread acceptance now must be accounted for on the basis of biblical verification. Otherwise why would so many sincere Christians hold this position today?

One does not doubt that many pretribulationists are convinced that they are basing their views on the Bible. But when the average person grows up within the framework of a particular bias or point of view, it is generally a natural consequence that as they read the Scriptures, they reconcile those passages that deal with the subject area in question as far as possible. Thus, before Martin Luther came along, the laity took the church's teaching on indulgences for granted, and the hierarchy in its study of Holy Writ found verses or passages that would seem consistent with such a teaching. Also, one glance at the cults is enough to show that their adherents accept what is taught them—usually without question—while their scholars find support from the Scriptures for their positions. And let us be open enough to admit that even cults and sects (especially those that thrive) have their intellectuals and scholars.

The claim is made that pretribulationism's widespread acceptance now is an indication that it has a biblical basis, because it first surfaced as a teaching only around 1830. One can point to many false teachings that have won many adherents and shown phenomenal growth in a century of time. Thus, growth and acceptance are not necessarily dependable signs of biblical soundness. The false teachings of some groups have placed those groups outside the Church of Jesus Christ because of serious departure from sound teaching on the person of Christ. Others have stayed within the mainstream of Christianity because their doctrinal departure has been trivial or in an area essential neither to the person of Christ nor to the teaching of salvation. So it was in the first century. The church in Pergamum held the Lord's name fast and did not deny His faith, even though the teaching of Balaam and the Nicolaitans was permitted. Those at Thyatira exhibited "love and faith and service and patient endurance," but tolerated the teaching of Jezebel.

When people are loved and accepted for who they are, this itself will often draw masses of people to a movement, and that even in a short period of time. We need only look at the 1960s and the "love children." That movement was short-lived, however, because it had no sound and logical system behind it and it lacked a sound and credible philosopher around whom the people could rally.

The teaching of dispensationalism had much to recommend it in its origins. It arose in the mainstream of Christianity and remains to this day in that mainstream. It remains adamant in the central truths of the person and work of Christ and in the gospel message. It is, therefore, not to be considered a cult as those groups that depart from this core. Indeed, it has much more to offer than faithfulness to central Christian truth. It is characterized by love and has developed a strong missionary zeal. Its weakness is another zeal that it has shown—an unflagging zeal for an even now imminency and a rigid (if not ironclad) system of seven (no more, no less) dispensations into which God is locked in His workings.

When the system began to develop under Darby around 1830, it was rather rough hewn. There are probably few who would consider Darby a scholar. But there were those who took up his teaching who were scholars, and they spread and systematized his teaching. This particularly grew out of his concept of a rapture before the tribulation. Perhaps the strongest and most widespread influence in the acceptance of this teaching was the printing of the Scofield Reference Bible. The growth of the Bible School movement owed much to this publication. This has been followed more recently by the rise of dispensational seminaries. Given the framework mentioned above of sound doctrine in core truth, love demonstrated, and missionary zeal, it was not difficult to understand a widespread acceptance of this teaching among evangelicals. This is especially true in the light of the attractive package offered—we shall escape the pain and trial of the great tribulation and we can expect to see our Savior at any time (even today). What a bright and cheerful promise! Small wonder the teaching gained acceptance.

The Spirit works in wondrous ways in the life of a child of God. He equips the spirit of the believer with His gifts in order to nurture the Body of Christ and to multiply its members. But the gifts of the Spirit, even when operating effectively through His vessels, do not confer holiness upon the life of those vessels. That is left to a burning within the heart of those vessels for purity and Christlikeness and an act of will to surrender to that holiness. We certainly can see this truth (that the gifts of the Spirit do not confer holiness) reflected in the church at Corinth. No church had received more of the manifestations of the gifts of the Spirit, but neither was any church to which Paul wrote embroiled in more carnality than the church at Corinth.

The Spirit also bears His fruit within the open and willing heart of the child of God. The Spirit's operation in bearing fruit is distinctively separate from His operation in conferring His gifts. The Spirit is the determining force in the gifts—He "apportions to each one individually as he wills" (1 Cor. 12:11). The believer is the determining force in the fruit of the Spirit. He can choose to bear as much fruit as he desires by yielding himself to the control of the Spirit of the holy God. It becomes a heady and liberating experience—to be overwhelmed with love and joy and the other manifestations of that fruit. But as glorious as the experience of this filling may be, it does not bestow an automatic grasp of that which is sound and true in doctrine or teaching. As loving and kind as the "elect lady" of 2 John was, she had to temper that love with discernment and firmness when someone would come who did not "abide in the doctrine of Christ," and she had to be warned not to "receive him into the house or give him any greeting." In both Thessalonian letters, Paul could commend the Thessalonians for their love and faith (1 Thess. 1:3; 2 Thess. 1:3). But in 2 Thessalonians, he had to beg them not to be shaken in mind by supposing that the day of the Lord had come and the believers had been assembled together to meet Him already, since certain things would have to happen first (2:2). Indeed, he challenged them by asking, "Do you not remember that when I was still with you I told you this?" (v. 5). Thus, the fruit of love did not protect their minds from anxiety regarding teaching. And so it was that at Berea, "these Jews were more noble than those in Thessalonica, for they received the word with all eagerness, examining the scriptures daily to see if these things were so" (Acts 17:11). So it takes an open and searching mind to clarify sound teaching. Thus, the fruit of the Spirit no more protects one against error than the gifts of the Spirit protect one from sin. So it is not amazing that a group such as the dispensationalists can exhibit the fruit of the Spirit and even show great missionary zeal and yet be mistaken in the area of eschatology. Let us search all the Scriptures together and take them in their clear and systematic totality on the subject.

*Grant me, Lord, John's love, James' holiness, the Bereans' diligence!*

# 9

## Prophecy (Fulfilled and Unfulfilled)

### Covenant

*From ancient Ur, God chose a man,*
*Bade him depart, forsake his clan,*
*And seek a land, as yet unknown,*
*Then vowed him it should be his own.*

*So, down the corridors of time,*
*When Jacob's sons within that clime*
*Prevailed, then failed, their lot reversed—*
*They were uprooted and dispersed.*

*But God has sworn they should return,*
*Possess the land; that tribes should learn*
*From them, and God should sovereign reign.*
*That day SHALL dawn—His vow's not vain.*

### The Fullness of the Time

Galatians 4:4 tells us that "when the time had fully come, God sent forth his Son, born of woman, born under the law." When Jesus came to earth during the first advent, He came to a prepared time and a prepared world. Travel and communication through the Roman road system, the bankruptcy of human philosophy, the sterility of Jewish legality, and the use of a common language were but a few of the factors preparing His way. Dozens of prophecies began to be fulfilled. Many of them were fulfilled through the eagerness of the Roman political system as it set out to make itself the power of the world and to spread its influence even by using another language and culture (that of the Greeks) to cement its control over its farflung empire. They were not considering God and His glory, but He can use even the wrath of men to praise Him.

When Christ returns, in His second advent, the time will have fully come once more. Once again man will proudly, and in some cases greedily, accomplish goals and open new doors, and those goals and those doors will be used by God for His purposes. Through man, in many cases, the way will have been prepared and prophecies will have been fulfilled.

Some years ago, many eyes in the world were focused on the year 2000. There was a special fascination with the transition from one millennium to the next. The question was raised whether the Lord might return at that time.

Precisely this belief was held by many. It was also held by many of the Christians who lived in the closing decades preceding the year 1000. There is an astounding difference between the climate of the year 1000 and our time in the prophetic arena, however. That time was in an era often referred to as the Dark Ages, so named to illustrate the general feeling that it was a time "distinguished" by intellectual stagnation, cultural decline, and ignorance. It is said to have started with the end of the Roman Empire in a.d. 476. Some believe that it did not end until about a.d. 1350, but almost all agree that it lasted at least until a.d. 1000. The only "prophetic" thing going for the period was the possibility that there was a renewed Roman Empire. It is generally conceded that the original one closed at about a.d. 476. There are differing opinions regarding the beginning of the Holy Roman Empire. Some felt that it began with Charlemagne in a.d. 800, while others felt it originated with the crowning of Otto in a.d. 962. Some, however, could have felt that, in this empire, the old Roman Empire had been revived. Beyond that, there was nothing. There was no Israel. There was no east with a staggering population. There was no Arab unity. There was no convenience of communication—news of anything noteworthy in the world could only crawl at the speed of a horse or a sailing vessel. Today, we have all of those other necessary situations (Israel as a nation, the eastern masses, the Arab identity and mass, worldwide communications) in addition to the empire.

One further difference is the activity of the Church. Before the close of the first millennium, the Church was marking time at best. There were many monasteries devoted almost exclusively to copying the Scriptures and to study and meditation. Just before 2000, the Church was interested in serving its members, but also in spreading the message of the gospel.

Some felt that looking expectantly at the year 2000 was unrealistic because there were things that needed to happen first, or that decades or even generations might pass before His return. Actually there is not a great deal that needs to happen in order for that day to arrive, and, although it could be delayed several generations, it would seem very strange. For almost two millennia nothing striking had happened in the arena of prophecy. Then in a period of some forty to fifty years we experienced numerous key elements falling together into a readable mosaic just at the end of that second millennium. Israel is a nation with millions of its people having returned to the land. There is a powerful European confederacy. There is an eastern horde capable of fielding 200 million troops. There has been a communication explosion that allows the entire earth to see an event together at the very time it happens. It is possible that some of these things could dissipate and later form again. It is possible that most or all of them could simply remain on a sort of holding pattern for generations to come. Knowing the pattern of political and social flux that is the norm in our world, however, this would seem improbable. When one adds to the present picture the capability we have developed of blowing ourselves apart many times over and the fact that vain, corruptible, greedy, power-hungry, defensive man is the human cushion between security and the button, it would seem highly unlikely that several generations would come and go before the fullness of time.

Aside from the resurrection of Christ, fulfilled prophecy

is the single most convincing element in Christianity that sets it apart from world religions and makes it the trustworthy communication of God's message to humanity. In relation to prophecy and the return of Christ, we will consider three classes of prophecy that set the stage for His actual coming. The first class of prophecies relates to those things that have already happened and are presently set in place. The second category has to do with those prophecies that are partially fulfilled or are in the process of being fulfilled. The final order of predictions concerns prophecies that have not yet been realized and that must be fulfilled before the actual return of Christ.

## PROPHECIES FULFILLED AND IN PLACE

### Israel is in the land as a nation

Often the Lord had told Israel that she would be scattered among the nations as a result of her sin and waywardness, but also He had often told the people the day would come when He would gather them from the nations and bring them back to the land. Jeremiah 29:14 is typical of the many verses to proclaim this promise: "I will be found by you, says the Lord, and I will restore your fortunes and gather you from all the nations and all the places where I have driven you, says the Lord, and I will bring you back to the place from which I sent you into exile."

The birth of Israel was arranged in such a way that many see it as a fulfillment of the words of Isaiah 66:7–8: "Before she was in labor she gave birth; before her pain came upon her she was delivered of a son. Who has heard such a thing? Who has seen such things? Shall a land be born in one day? Shall a nation be brought forth in one moment? For as soon as Zion was in labor she brought forth her sons." The scattered people of Israel suffered greatly before and during their return to the land following World War II. They struggled for existence for years in the land and they fought when their enemies attacked. But they were not a nation and they wanted to be one. Then on November 29, 1947, Resolution 181 was drafted by the General Assembly of the United

Nations. The resolution called for recognition of Israel as a nation in the world community of nations. On the very day the vote was taken, Israel was born as a new land among the other lands of the world. When the vote was being taken it reached the point where one more vote was needed for the acceptance of the resolution. At the very moment when that next "yes" vote was voiced, signifying acceptance, Israel was brought forth as a nation, fully recognized as such by the other nations of the world.

### There is now a European Confederacy

In the book of Daniel certain prophecies were made having to do with the end times, before the return of Christ. There we read that "after the sixty-two weeks, an anointed one shall be cut off, and shall have nothing; and the people of the prince who is to come shall destroy the city and the sanctuary. Its end shall come with a flood, and to the end there shall be war; desolations are decreed. And he shall make a strong covenant with many for one week; and for half of the week he shall cause sacrifice and offering to cease; and upon the wing of abominations shall come one who makes desolate, until the decreed end is poured out on the desolator" (9:26–27).

Most commentators agree that the anointed one who is cut off is the Messiah at His crucifixion. The people who destroyed the city and the sanctuary can only be the Romans under Titus in a.d. 70. It is said of the prince who is to come that he will make a strong covenant with many for one week and then for half the week he will cause sacrifice and offering to cease. Some hold that "the prince to come" is the Messiah, but this would not seem to fit Daniel's description, since the people this prince belonged to had to be Roman, because it was a Roman destruction of Jerusalem. Therefore, the man had to be a Roman prince, not a Jewish prince. This sacrificial defilement found a fulfillment in Antiochus Epiphanes, but that was only a partial fulfillment and we await a more complete fulfillment in the person of the Antichrist or man of sin. We know this because Jesus said we would yet see "the desolating sacrilege spoken of by the prophet Daniel, standing in the holy place" (Matt. 24:15), and Paul says that there will be a revealing of the man of lawlessness, "the son of perdition, who opposes and exalts himself against every so-called god or object of worship, so that he takes his seat in the temple of God, proclaiming himself to be God" (2 Thess. 2:3–4).

But this man will be Roman, since it was his people who destroyed Jerusalem and the temple. And he will be a prince or ruler. Therefore, there must be a Roman or European power in which he rules. Today that power exists in the European Economic Community.

In the closing days of World War II, when I served with our armies in Europe, and afterward in the army of occupation, I was acutely aware of the enmity that existed between the allied European nations and the axis powers of Italy and Germany. Later, when I served some years with Greater Europe Mission in Germany (1956–1962), my wife and I experienced this continuing animosity. It was felt that it was too strong ever to allow for any kind of genuinely close associations. But Europe later came together, even though it was an iron/clay union.

The union grew, however, and the October 19, 1987 issue of Time noted in a report on Economy and Business that Europe had moved from a 42 percent world export market in 1980 to 46 percent of the world market in 1986. It has since become, in most respects, truly a United States of Europe, and they implemented a common currency. This power rivals that of the U.S.A. and Russia. Some feel she will actually be more powerful than both. To call it a restoration of the Roman Empire is by no means an overstatement.

**The Eastern hordes are in place**

After the sixth trumpet, we see an army of 200 million by the river Euphrates (Rev. 9:13–16). There are some who connect these troops with the kings of the east at the sixth bowl, since the angel there dries up the river Euphrates to "prepare the way for the kings from the east" (Rev. 16:12). Whether or not the two groups are the same is a matter we will have to hold in abeyance until we are closer to the time, but at least in our day, for the first time, the eastern powers, and particularly China's millions, possess the capability of fielding such a large body of troops.

**Worldwide communications have been established**

In Revelation 1:7 John says of the returning Christ, "Behold, he is coming with the clouds, and every eye will see him." This represented no problem to a first-century audience. The world as they understood it was flat. If Jesus were to return over Jerusalem, they could simply look in that direction and see Him. When the world became aware of the fact that the earth was round, such a worldwide viewing presented real difficulties. In order for a worldwide viewing to take place under such circumstances, light and vision would have to be able to bend around the earth, and in so doing, also be magnified. Or Christ would have to arrive slowly in a polar orbit in order to cover the entire viewing area of the ground below. Or the earth would have to become a transparent magnifying glass. Today, however, since the deployment of numerous synchronous satellites, we are able to take such an announcement for granted, since we are able to see anything that occurs anywhere in the world just at the time it happens. It will be a simple thing to focus cameras on the clouds above Jerusalem so the entire world can view it.

**The United States is the air power of the "great eagle"**

There have been many doomsayers regarding the fact that there is no mention of the United States in prophecy, and these people contend, therefore, that we will be a "nothing" nation during the last days and will have no impact upon the world then.

Doubtless, people from the United States will be among those from the west mentioned in Matthew 8:11, where Christ states that "many will come from east and west and sit at table with Abraham, Isaac, and Jacob in the kingdom of heaven." But quite aside from that, the conclusion that any nation not named in the end times is of no importance in the world scheme of things is simplistic at best. Though God's divine purposes are more important to me than national pride, there seems to be no purpose served by summarily throwing in the scrap heap any modern nation that does not get specific mention in the prophecies regarding the end times.

There are no direct end-time references to many of today's nations, besides the U.S.A., though some may cover significant portions of land mass—Canada, Brazil (indeed, the entire Western Hemisphere), Australia, and New Zealand. Some may even be politically or economically important—Canada, Japan, and South Africa.

A perusal of prophetic writings relating to the end times would seem to indicate that the geographic arena involved in those prophecies is confined to the Euro-Middle East-Asian-North African land mass. In terms of indirect references to America, however, it is hard to find a better meaning for the "great eagle" of Revelation 12:14 than America. Certainly, Rome, in her day, had the eagle as her symbol. But today, of the nations that make use of the eagle as a symbol, only America is a great power. This passage says that "when the dragon saw that he had been thrown down to the earth, he pursued the woman who had borne the male child. But the woman was given the two wings of the great eagle that she might fly from the serpent into the wilderness, to the place where she is to be nourished for a time, and times, and half a time" (Rev. 12:13–14).

Unless one takes this passage literally and expects to see a monstrous eagle capable of flying tens or even hundreds of thousands of Jews to the wilderness and safely, then it must be seen in a figurative or symbolic way. Since it is not described as a great eagle, but as the great eagle, it likely refers to a group or nation. In the day in which we live, there is but one great nation that is symbolized as an eagle. Even as Russia is the great bear, the United States is the great eagle.

During the days of challenge and confrontation between Russia and America following the end of World War II, the Russians tried to deny America access to West Berlin by closing down the rail lines and the highway system leading to that city. The whole world was witness to America's peaceful solution to the problem. In a massive display, fleet after fleet of aircraft were shuttled to and from Berlin and a new term was added to our vocabulary: airlift.

In the winter of 1985, in the early days of that year, a report came out of the New York Times News Service under the caption:

### US Joins in Airlift of Jews
### Secret Operation was Directed by the CIA

In a secret operation, the United States on Saturday completed the evacuation of virtually all the Ethiopian Jews who were left in Sudan after an Israeli-sponsored airlift was halted, administration officials said.

The Central Intelligence Agency was in charge of the operation, which also involved the State Department and the Air Force, the sources said. In a three-day period, 800 people were flown by C-130 Hercules transports to Israel, they said.

Thus, four factors point to the United States being the eagle that will fulfill the prophetic statement of Revelation 12:14. First, America is the only great world power today that is symbolized by the eagle. Second, she remains the only major power that maintains her friendship with Israel and that firmly defends Israel's right to sovereignty. Third, she is the only power that has demonstrated a successful massive and sustained airlift. Fourth, she has already committed herself to a successful mission of airlift to an entire segment of the Israeli people.

In addition to the five fulfilled prophecies mentioned, some see two others that will be mentioned in passing. They are: (1) the existence of present-day Babylon; and (2) the existence of a powerful army to the uttermost north of Israel.

There is in Iraq, a city of Babylon. Only time will tell what will happen to it. Some contend that it will be destroyed in the end times in fulfillment of the predictions (in Revelation) of God's judgment on Babylon. There is some basis for such a contention, since Isaiah said that the destruction of Babylon "will be like Sodom and Gomorrah ... it will never be inhabited or dwelt in for all generations ... no Arab will pitch his tent there" (Isa. 13:19–20). Since these prophecies are yet to be realized, it could be destroyed in such a manner in the end times. The most important part of the predicted destruction of Babylon, however, is the fact that Babylon, in its wider context, represents the world of luxury and commerce, but that could certainly include the present-day city of Babylon as well.

The second present-day condition some see as fulfilled prophecy deals with the existence of a world power to the extreme north of Israel with an army capable of moving in force against Israel. They see this as the setting of the stage for the invasion described in Ezekiel 38 and 39. They believe that this will happen before the return of Christ, either before or during the tribulation.

As one reads the description of that invasion, however, it would seem more logical that this is the same invasion that is mentioned toward the end of the millennium in Revelation 20:7–9. First, it is the same ruler (Gog) who is involved and it is the same land (Magog). Further, the description of their destruction is the same. Ezekiel 38:22 says it will be by the raining of "fire and brimstone," and Revelation 20:9 states that "fire came down from heaven and consumed them."

Although it is possible that these armies could be destroyed twice in the same manner (once around the time of the tribulation and another at the close of the millennium), a single destruction seems more logical. This is especially true in the light of the description of Israel in the Ezekiel passage when these armies come against her. It does not seem in any way to fit present-day circumstances. They certainly could not fit Israel during the time of the tribulation. The main problem lies in the fact that when the attack takes place, Israel will be "restored from war," and will "now dwell securely" (Ezek. 38:8). She will be a "land of unwalled villages" and a "quiet people who dwell securely, all of them dwelling without walls, and having no bars or gates" (v. 11). In addition, it states that these troops will come against Israel "riding on horses" (v. 15). Today, if northern armies attacked, they would use tanks, personnel carriers, and planes. In the millennium they will not manufacture weapons of war. Swords will be fashioned into pruning hooks and they will not learn war. They will not have tanks and armored personnel carriers. But they may raise herds of horses in the millennium and use them in battle toward the end of that time.

## Prophecies Partially Fulfilled Or in the Process of Being Fulfilled

These are prophecies that Christ predicted would come before the end. He said:

For many will come in my name, saying, "I am the Christ," and they will lead many astray. And you will hear of wars and rumors of wars; see that you are not alarmed; for this must take place, but the end is not yet. For nation will rise against nation, and kingdom against kingdom, and there will be famines and earthquakes in various places: all this is but the beginning of the birth-pangs.

Then they will deliver you up to tribulation, and put you to death; and you will be hated by all nations for my name's sake. And then many will fall away, and betray one another, and hate one another. And many false prophets will arise and lead many astray. And because wickedness is multiplied, most men's love will grow cold. (Matt. 24:5–12)

In these prophecies, all of the conditions have been fulfilled on a small scale down through the ages. But they are being intensified in these last days. For example, tribulation was to be the lot of His followers. In the last days, however, this standard tribulation would expand into the great tribulation. Let us examine seven predictions He made that have come to pass formerly, but are being intensified in our day.

### False Christs and false prophets will arise

Even as early as the end of the first century, John wrote that "the spirit of antichrist ... is in the world already" (1 John 4:3). There have probably been few generations since then that have not seen either a false Christ or a false prophet. In our day they have seemed to proliferate. Unfortunately, Californians have been exposed to more than their share of them. On a small and extremely unconvincing scale there was a Charles Manson. In a more serious vein and on a worldwide scale there are Rev. Moon and the promised New

World Messiah who will communicate with each person in his native tongue. All of this, of course, prepares for the ultimate imitation—the Antichrist himself.

**There will be wars and rumors of wars**

There has been no century without warfare. These wars, however, ultimately were to involve nations pitted against each other and kingdoms fighting against other kingdoms. It is difficult to find any significant periods of peace in the last century, and the world has been rocked by two wars of such a wide range, that they have been called (and justly so) world wars, since they involved most of the strongest nations and kingdoms of the world. We have done well in preparing the world for the ultimate battle at Armageddon.

**There will be famines**

There have been many periods where one nation or area has been afflicted by famine while almost all of its neighbors were enjoying bumper crops. In recent years, there have been an unusual number of crop failures and famines in Ethiopia and other African countries. There has seemed to be a discouraging frustration about our inability to render meaningful help to these suffering people, and it has been compounded when supplies sent to the countries end up under the control of repressive rulers and all too often never get into the hands of the needy.

**There will be earthquakes in various places**

Earthquakes down through the centuries have been as ubiquitous as the poor. Jesus said, "you always have the poor with you" (Matt. 26:11). Earthquakes go back thousands of years in recorded history and it has seemed that we have always had them with us also. In the Scriptures, the first recorded earth movement of a violent nature is found in Numbers 16:30–32. There are Bible commentators who see this as an earthquake. Splits or fissures opened up in the earth, and Dathan and Abiram plunged to their deaths as a result of their revolt against the leadership of Moses. If it was a violent earthquake, it is interesting that it came as punishment for such rebellion. At that time the Lord said that He was doing a new thing.

It may well be that predictions of earthquakes coming upon the earth signify the approaching judgment of God. All the major quakes that we have seen—including the San Francisco quakes of 1906, the Himalayas quake of 1958, and the recent quakes in China, Mexico City, Chile, Haiti and Japan—will pale into insignificance when the truly great shake strikes after the opening of the sixth seal (see Rev. 6:12-17). So severe will it be that the unsaved will interpret it as the wrath of God and of the Lamb.

There are some who doubt that there has been an increase in earthquake activity in recent years. As we have said, it seems that earthquakes have always been there. But since the 1930s, since the introduction and use of the Richter Scale, we have had an accurate way of measuring and monitoring quakes throughout the world.

It is noted in Hal Lindsey's Countdown magazine that Lindsey had contacted the National Earthquake Information Center located in Golden, Colorado to get data only on earthquakes that could be considered "major" (6.0 or greater) in the last hundred years. The results were both enlightening and startling.

> Lindsey found that between 1880 and 1890 there was one major quake. Between 1890 and 1900 there was one major quake. Between 1900 to 1910 there were three. From 1910 to 1920 there were two. From 1920 to 1930 there were two. From 1930 to 1940 there were five. From 1940 to 1950 there were four. From 1950 to 1960 there were nine. From 1960 to 1970 there were 13. Then from 1970 to 1980 there were 46. From 1980 to 1989 there have been 51.
>
> (From Countdown, vol. 4, no.10, December 1989)

It is notable that in the first two decades of the use of the Richter Scale nothing out of the ordinary was happening. The first significant changes came in the 1950s and 1960s. But what happened in the 1970s and 1980s was nothing short of astounding.

**There will be suffering and death for believers**

In John 16:33 Jesus announced to the disciples what they could expect in this life as His followers: "In the world you have tribulation; but be of good cheer, I have overcome the world." The normal course of events for them would include both tribulation and final victory. But in the Matthew 24:9 account He also forewarned them that they would face both hatred and death.

Down through the decades and centuries and even for two millennia, in various places, His followers have lived out this expectancy and have died in fulfilling it. Foxes' Book of Martyrs is brimming with the accounts of those who counted not their lives dear, for the sake of their Savior. In the 20th century we saw John and Betty Stam in China and the five missionary husbands in South America (who reached out to the Aucas), place their very lives on the altar of love. And there have been many others.

This general tribulation will culminate in the great tribulation, which will not be different in intent, but only in scope and intensity. That is to say, persecution and death will still be the intent, but whereas hundreds and even thousands of us have been suffering and dying up until now, then we will have hundreds of thousands and perhaps millions suffering and dying with us.

### Wickedness will be multiplied

It has been the common lot of the older generation of a society to view the antics of the younger generation with a somewhat jaundiced eye. "What is the younger generation coming to?" and "When I was young ..." have become mottos that the older use to keep the younger in their places. But at times we read such complaints of a particular generation only to discover that these complaints came from a generation that lived centuries ago.

When we say such things today, does that mean that we are simply repeating the age-old protests of a Geritol generation? Hardly. There is actually a great difference today. Certainly the younger generation, in its very development, must press at the boundaries of parental sheltering to break out into a sense of its own independence. But there has been a dramatic shift in the basic pattern of "youth presses at boundaries, youth becomes independent, youth matures, the maturing ones recognize the boundaries set by their elders as practical, the newly arrived matured generation directs their young within these boundaries."

Recent generations have evolved in a new direction. Rather than falling into the pattern of their own parents (who became like their parents before them), they have carried their newly found independence into other arenas. They have broken free of parental restraint and have now turned to other restraints and continued their demands for freedom in the direction of these other restraints. It has become a challenge. It has become a quest. What was a search for freedom from their parents has now become a revolution against the constraints of "morality," religion, and society. Because they now have positions in education, politics, the arts, and the sciences, they are actually able to effect "liberating" changes.

And so it is that today is different. Things that were spoken of in whispers in the dark one or two generations ago are shouted in the light of the television cameras today to an audience that no longer feels a blush of shame. Scenes that could only be seen by sneaking into a "dirty" theater years ago, are seen in the "legitimate" theater, on cable television, or for the price of a video rental today. In some communities people bar themselves in their dwellings to escape the ravages of gangs. Segments of society that hid from the public in days past militantly demand their rights as a minority group today. Today the public can no longer demand of their leading officials that they stay true to their vows of marriage or that they lead a life free of substance abuse. And so it is that wickedness has multiplied. And it will continue to multiply into the great tribulation, and then it will call for a law-and-order leader who will promise a safe and regulated society again.

**Most men's love will grow cold**

In the history of the Church, there have been times of general coldness, such as the Middle Ages produced. At other times, there have been periods of great warmth and fervor such as the world saw in the new Church following Pentecost. At most times there have been situations where love was shown in one area (sometimes through the renewal of a revival), while a callous coldness existed in another. In our days there exists a threefold pull toward coldness. The multiplied wickedness that we just looked at has a desensitizing effect on many. The science that has revolutionized our way of life sterilizes the warmth of affection. The appeal of luxury and merchandising woos the heart toward a new love. As we move into the tribulation, wickedness and science will combine in the man of sin, and Babylon will embody the glorifying of luxury and merchandising. People will be coerced by the man of sin and enticed by Babylon. The heart that is not bound by the love of Christ will grow cold.

## PROPHECIES YET TO BE FULFILLED

### Elijah must come

Malachi 4:5 declares that the Lord would send "Elijah the prophet before the great and terrible day of the Lord comes." Jesus suggested in Matthew 17:11–12 that there was a sense in which John the Baptist was Elijah, but He also said that Elijah "does come," yet. This is covered in the chapter on Imminence. According to Revelation 16:14–16 and 19:19, Armageddon is that "great day of God the Almighty." Most conservative scholars see Elijah as one of the two witnesses in Revelation 11. That would be an ideal time for him to fulfill that prophecy.

### Impact will be made by the man of sin

a) *He makes a pact with the nation of Israel.* Earlier in the chapter in our consideration of prophecies that had already been fulfilled, we examined the fact that "there is now a European confederacy." We looked at the Daniel 9:26–27 passage. That passage states that the prince who was to come (the man of sin or Antichrist) would make a strong covenant with many (probably with Israel) for one week and that in the middle of that week he would break that agreement by causing sacrifices and offerings to cease.

Will this pact made by the Antichrist with Israel, which he breaks in the middle of the week, be an open or a secret pact? It is not unusual in our day for secret pacts to be made. There is evidence that the United States and Japan made such a secret treaty in 1960. On April 7, 1987, the Pasadena *Star-News* carried the following story from the N.Y. Times News Service:

> WASHINGTON—Japanese communists, searching in the Library of Congress here, have uncovered documentary evidence of a secret agreement that permits the United States to take nuclear arms into Japan.
>
> The visiting members of the Japanese Communist Party found a telegram referring explicitly to the accord, a "transit agreement" that was appended as a top-secret document to the 1960 United States-Japan mutual security treaty.
>
> The Japanese search team had long assumed the existence of the agreement, which had been reported in the news media since 1971 on the basis of a national security study memorandum dating from 1969.
>
> In the case of each such report, however, State Department and Japanese officials, who feared the political backlash remaining from the atomic bombings of 1945, flatly denied the existence of the accord.

In fact, there is good reason from Scripture to suppose that the pact made by the Antichrist with Israel is a secret pact. Certainly the kind of pact implied, if made common knowledge to the world through the media would alert us immediately to the identity of the man of sin. But Jesus told His followers, "So when you see the desolating sacrilege spoken of by the prophet Daniel, standing in the holy place (let the reader understand), then let those who are in Judea flee" (Matt. 24:15–16). Certainly if the followers of Jesus knew of the pact, they could count three and a half years from the signing of the pact and prepare to leave before that time arrived. Furthermore, Paul states that before the day of the Lord came, the man of sin must first be revealed, and that he will take "his seat in the temple of God" (2 Thess. 2:3–4). The very fact of a revealing is an indication that it was a mystery or was hidden before it was revealed. The blatant revealing in the temple would let the followers of Christ know exactly who the Antichrist was.

b) *The temple must be built.* Simple logic tells us that if the temple is to be defiled by the man of sin, then the temple must first be there. There is no temple there now. A number of Christian travelers, including Harold Sevener and Hal Lindsey have given reports about the projected building of the temple and the idea that such building will not interfere with the Dome of the Rock site. In terms of something to look for, this is something quite tangible and verifiable. The temple will be built.

c) *The temple will be defiled by the man of sin.* This is predicted by Daniel in 9:26–27, by Jesus in Matthew 24:15 and by Paul in 2 Thessalonians 2:3–4. It is dealt with in the chapter on Imminence. This is the time when all who desire to know, will indeed know exactly who the Antichrist is.

d) *The apostasy must come.* This goes hand in glove with the revealing of the man of sin in 2 Thessalonians 2:3–4, and its tendencies will precede that revealing. It is put side by side with the revealing of the man of sin as an indication that we are rapidly approaching "the coming of our Lord Jesus Christ and our assembling to meet him" mentioned in verse 1. It is the final fulfillment of the prediction made by Jesus that "many will fall away" and that "most men's love will grow cold" (Matt. 24:10, 12).

e) *The great tribulation must come.* When Jesus spoke to His disciples of certain events that would precede His coming, he stated that "when you see all these things, you know that he is near, at the very gates" (Matt. 24:33). He had just finished speaking of the events of the great tribulation, so it must naturally be included in the "all these things" that He referred to. He gave these details to curious disciples and for our benefit as those days approach. We can ignore these teachings and these details only to our own disadvantage and hurt. Those teachers and scholars and writers who choose to slight or omit these things or leave them to chance or even simply to leave them to the Lord himself, do so at great peril. The Lord, when asked by His followers about that time before the end, far from chiding them for curiosity or lack of trust, not only gave them details that He deemed important, but enjoined them to watch.

There is no other timeframe spoken of in Scripture—whether it concerned the time when it was given, or time past, or future events—that so exactly and with such varied terms spelled out the amount of time involved in the completion of so many and so varied prophecies. In one place it is called "a time and times and half a time" (one year plus two years plus half a year) or three and a half years. In another place it is called "forty-two months." In another it is measured at "1,260 days." Based on the thirty-day prophetic month, forty-two months equal exactly 1,260 days. The tribulation period is covered in the chapter on Imminence, but is dealt with even more at length in the Tribulation chapter.

**The gospel must be preached throughout the whole world to every nation**

This is the commission that was given to Christ's disciples. It is apparent from Revelation 5:9 and 7:9–14 that every people group will be reached. This is dealt with in the chapter on Imminence, but is developed even more thoroughly in the chapter on The Great Commission. This is the central sign that towers above all others and is the clearest prophecy of all that must be fulfilled. Christ himself stated that it was an absolute necessity before the end that the disciples had asked about and were anticipating would come. Israel may be regathered in the land. Political powers may be in place. False Christs may parade before us. Wars may rage around us. Nature may make its powers felt. We may be offered up for Christ's sake. We may see wickedness run rampant in the streets. We may huddle together for warmth in the face of love that has chilled in others. But the fulfilled commission is the fulcrum upon which the rapture-return balances.

*Lord, sharpen our eyes to read your signposts!*

# 10

## THE OLD TESTAMENT FEASTS

In the midst of Paul's letter to the Colossians, the Lord reveals a mysterious relationship between certain Old Testament practices and Christ (2:16–17). The ancient festivals, new moons, and sabbaths "are only a shadow of what is to come; but the substance belongs to Christ." The festivals or feasts of Israel are described for us in Numbers 28 and 29 and also in Leviticus 23. In addition, there is a detailed account of the Passover feast in Exodus 12. The new moons were celebrated as new beginnings, since the beginning of the Hebrew months came not according to astronomical calculations in general, but rather according to when the phase of the moon reached its new beginning or "new moon" phase, or every 28 or 29 days. The sabbaths were days of rest, which usually came on the seventh day of the week, thus ending the week. There were, however, special days that were set aside as holy rest days. These may have come on any day of the weekly calendar, but they also were special rest days and, therefore, were also called "sabbaths."

Let us, however, return to the feasts or festivals. Although the Exodus account of the Passover gives us the details of that feast, and the Numbers account gives us some of the details of the other feasts not found in the Leviticus account, it is the Leviticus account that mentions all seven of the feasts and puts them in their chronological order of observance for the year. Since Paul says that Christ is the substance of these festivals, which are but the shadow, many have made comparisons of these feasts as types to Christ and His work as fulfillments or antitypes. Some would see the spring feasts of Passover, First Fruits and Pentecost as fulfilled in the first advent of Christ and in the same time allotment covered in the Old Testament festival year. An exceptionally strong case can certainly be made for such an idea, especially since some of the comparisons are made by the New Testament itself. They make an additional proposal that the fall feasts of Trumpets, Day of Atonement, and Booths will be fulfilled at Christ's second advent. The case might not be quite as strong for this idea, since the New Testament does not speak clearly as it does for some of the spring feasts. This is understandable, however, since Christ's first advent was already history when the New Testament supported a fulfillment view. But there are strong enough details given in the New Testament, which adapt themselves readily to such an interpretation, even for the fall feasts, and since the passage in Colossians states that Christ is the substance or fulfillment of the feasts, we would appear to be on safe ground when we consider how that might be the case. Though I have a natural tendency to draw back from improper spiritualizing, since I saw this abuse of Scripture in my younger days, in this case it is almost as if the Lord issues an invitation to do so properly. He says that the Old Testament shadows or symbols in the feasts stand for realities or substance in Christ. It would seem to be honoring to the Lord to look for that substance or the meaning of the shadow.

First, we will consider the spring feasts of Passover, First Fruits, and Pentecost to see how they were brought to fulfillment by the ministry of Christ in His first coming. Then we will look at the fall feasts of Trumpets, Day of Atonement, and Booths to see what we could reasonable expect to see in having them fulfilled when He comes again. Even though the Sabbath is mentioned first in Leviticus 23, there are good reasons for considering it last in our study. Therefore, we will begin with the first of the spring feasts.

### *Passover*

*The paschal lamb is slain, the blood applied,*
*The 'venging angel sees, and passes by.*
*The Lamb of God has lived, been judged and died.*
*The righteous Judge accepts, and draws us nigh.*

The Passover is documented in far more detail in the Old Testament than any other feast. Furthermore, more direct, as well as indirect, comparisons are made in the New Testament between Christ (and His suffering and death) and the Passover than are made between Him and any other feast. We will consider some of the more significant aspects of the Passover as it relates to Christ and His ministry during Passion Week.

In the Exodus 12 narrative the central figure is that of the lamb. Each family (or if the family was small, two families would join together) had to kill its own lamb. Then the blood had to be applied, using hyssop, to the two doorposts and the lintel of their house. (The unprotected firstborn—in houses where the blood was not applied—would die). When the feast was later celebrated, the blood would be represented by cups of wine. The lamb was to be roasted and eaten. None of it was to remain until the morning, and no bone of the lamb was to be broken. The lamb was to be eaten with unleavened bread and bitter herbs. When the feast was later celebrated, there would be three pieces of matzo or unleavened bread. The middle piece, the "Aphikomen," would be broken in half. The first half would be broken in pieces and distributed to all to eat. The second would be hidden and then brought back at the end of the feast. The bread was to be unleavened to represent the haste with which they left Egypt. The bitter herbs were to illustrate the affliction they suffered at the hands of the Egyptians. The entire feast was to be celebrated as a memorial, looking back to the fact that their firstborn were passed over because of the protecting blood.

The pattern of animal sacrifice pre-dates the law. Even as far back as Abel, we see his sacrifice of a lamb as an acceptable sacrifice (Gen. 4:4). Noah's sacrifice of animals was so acceptable to God that He vowed never to send such a widespread flood again (Gen. 8:21). Job offered animal sacrifices for his sons in case they had sinned (Job 1:5). There were, of course, in the Passover lamb seeds of the entire sacrificial system, where lambs and other animals would be offered to the Lord for the sins of the people. In addition to the idea of sacrifice, however, there was also the concept of substitution. The soul that sinned was to die, but in this arrangement the animal could die in the place of the sinner. So it was that when John the Baptist sees Jesus coming toward him, he calls Him "the Lamb of God, who takes away the sin of the world" (John 1:29). Paul specifically identifies Him as "our paschal lamb" (1 Cor. 5:7).

As the blood of the Passover lamb had to be applied to the entrance of the house, so the blood of Jesus, the Lamb of God, has to be applied to us. We are freed (Rev. 1:5), washed (Rev. 7:14), cleansed (1 John 1:7), ransomed (1 Pet. 1:18–19), redeemed (Titus 2:14), and obtained (Acts 20:28) with the blood of that sacrifice when we personally apply it to our lives (John 3:16). When Jesus gave His discourse on the bread of life (John 6), He stated the need for personal appropriation of His blood so strongly ("unless you eat the flesh of the Son of man and drink his blood, you have no life in you; he who eats my flesh and drinks my blood has eternal life" [vv. 53–54]) that many of His own disciples were offended by it and drew back from following Him (see vv. 60–61, 66). When Jesus instituted the Lord's Supper, He established the wine in the cup as a symbol of His own sacrificial blood, saying, "This is my blood of the covenant, which is poured out for many for the forgiveness of sins" (Matt. 26:28).

It is easy to see the concept of grace in this substitutionary death of the lamb. In essence, the message during the first Passover was: "The firstborn must die. However, if a lamb is slain, I will accept its spilled and applied blood in the place of, and instead of, the life of the firstborn." Who could or would refuse such a gracious offer? But there remained the matter of the actual carrying out of this transaction. The blood still had to be applied. It was no good having a dead lamb on one's hands if the blood did not get from the lamb to the doorway. If no blood was seen on the doorposts and lintel as covering a particular house, there would be a dead man in that house in the morning. The word was, "The blood shall be a sign for you, upon the houses where you are; and when I see the blood, I will pass over you" (Exod. 12:13). How difficult was it for the Hebrews to carry out this condition? They had to pluck some hyssop, dip it in the blood, and sprinkle it on the doorway with the hyssop. This was indeed a fortunate choice as an applicator for the Hebrews. Not only was it ideal for sprinkling because of its shape, but a bush would grow multiple clusters of hyssop. Most important, it was readily available to all who wanted it. If the substitution of the lamb's blood represents grace, the applying of it with hyssop signifies faith. Just as anyone could apply the blood with hyssop, so anyone can turn, in simple faith, to the Lamb of God in acceptance of His gift. According to John 1:12, "to all who received him, who believed in his name, he gave power to become children of God." Thus we had the wedding of grace and faith spoken of in Ephesians 2:8: "For by grace you have been saved through faith."

Even as the blood had to be applied, so it was with the flesh of the lamb of the Passover. It also had to be eaten (or assimilated) personally and totally. None could be left until the morning and no bone of it could be broken. In His message on the bread of life in John 6, not only did Jesus speak of the need to drink His blood, but also of the necessity of eating His flesh. After all, the discourse was mainly about bread—something to be eaten. He said, "Unless you eat the flesh of the Son of man and drink his blood, you have no life in you; he who eats my flesh and drinks my blood has eternal life" (vv. 53–54). Likewise in establishing the Lord's Supper, Jesus called the matzo, or unleavened bread, His body when He said, "Take, eat; this is my body" (Matt. 26:26). The unleavened bread became the symbol of His flesh or body.

Thus we have a strange admixture in the Passover/Last Supper of the significance of the death of the lamb. The flesh of the lamb was to be roasted—it was a sacrifice, a substitute for sin—and God's fire of judgment must burn it. But the bread was unleavened, and in the New Testament leaven stood for sin, so the Lamb was also sinless. What better picture could we have of that unfathomable sacrifice as described in 2 Corinthians 5:21: "For our sake (substitution) he made him (sacrifice) to be sin (the flesh of the lamb burned in judgment) who knew no sin (the unleavened bread), so that in him we might become (substitution) the righteousness of God"?

The flesh of the lamb of the Passover was not to be left in the house until the morning. Not only can we see in this the need to appropriate the Lamb of God completely, but this was also prophetically fulfilled at the time of the crucifixion: "Since it was the day of Preparation, in order to prevent the bodies from remaining on the cross on the sabbath (for that sabbath was a high day), the Jews asked Pilate that their legs might be broken, and that they might be taken away" (John 19:31). It was ordered regarding the paschal lamb that no bone of it was to be broken. This was also fulfilled as prophecy in the crucifixion: "So the soldiers came and broke the legs of the first, and of the other who had been crucified with him; but when they came to Jesus and saw that he was already dead, they did not break his legs" (John 19:32–33).

Bitter herbs (strong enough to open the tear ducts) were to be eaten with the Passover meal. This reminded the Hebrews of the bitterness of their slavery in Egypt. Today, appropriating the Lamb of God is often preceded by repentance (sometimes accompanied by tears) as converts are reminded bitterly of their sins and their former slavery to the world. In Luke 24:47, the resurrected Christ commanded His followers "that repentance and forgiveness of sins should be preached in his name to all nations."

In the eating of the unleavened bread at the Passover, the middle matzo was broken in half. The first half was broken and distributed to all present and the other half was hidden, then brought out again at the end of the meal. In the Trinitarian formula the Son of God is the middle name given. As He blessed and broke the bread at the Lord's Supper, He said that it was His body broken for us. But His broken body was hidden in the tomb for three days and then, like the hidden half of the unleavened bread, brought out again in glorious resurrection.

Finally, the Passover feast was to be observed as a memorial. Obviously, it looked back to the Lord passing over the protected houses of the Hebrews where the blood had been applied. In a way it also looked forward to the coming sacrificial system, in which a lamb (or other animal substitute) would be sacrificed for sin. But especially it looked forward (even though the people didn't understand it) to the Lamb of God, who would not only take their sins away, but would also make an offering for the sins of the entire world. When Jesus transformed His last Passover into the Lord's Table, He also established it as a memorial. It began by looking back to the Passover. But once instituted, it became a new memorial. And as the trusting Old Testament Jews looked forward unknowingly to His sacrifice when they, in faith, made their offerings, so now the disciples of Jesus would look back on this night and on His death whenever they celebrated the Lord's Supper, and they would look forward to His coming so they could eat it anew with Him in His kingdom.

### *First Fruits*

*The first fruit sheaves before the Lord they wave,*
*To praise Him for the coming harvest tide.*
*Messiah rises—firstborn from the grave—*
*The pledge of resurrection for His Bride.*

The Feast of First Fruits is described in Leviticus 23:9–14. It was an occasion of joy, thanksgiving, and promise. The earliest grain to ripen in Israel was barley, which ripened three weeks before the wheat. A sheaf, or loose bundle of it, was brought to the court of the temple. After the grain was ground in a mortar, incense would be sprinkled on it. The precise directions for the preparation of this offering were given in Leviticus 2:14–15: "If you offer a cereal offering of first fruits to the Lord, you shall offer for the cereal offering of your first fruits crushed new grain from fresh ears, parched with fire. And you shall put oil upon it, and lay frankincense on it; it is a cereal offering." Then the priest would lift it up, and wave it as an offering before the Lord, pointing it toward the four points of the compass. The purpose of this wave offering was that the people might find acceptance (Lev. 23:11). According to Deuteronomy 26:1–11, it was also an occasion of thanksgiving, not only for being brought out of Egypt and oppression, but also for being brought into the land God had promised them. And it was a time of thanksgiving for the beginning of the harvest (v. 10) and the promise of the rest of the harvest to come.

The Old Testament ties the offering of first fruits in this feast closely together with the feast of Pentecost that followed. The two were even linked together by the principle of first fruit offerings, and the New Testament illuminates this connection, but we will look at that more in detail when we cover the feast of Pentecost.

In addition to the relationship in the New Testament between First Fruits and Pentecost, a connection can also be traced in those writings between First Fruits and Trumpets as it touches upon suffering, but in particular as it relates to resurrection. The Feast of Trumpets follows Pentecost, and we will cover the specifics of those connections when we come to the Feast of Trumpets.

The basic concept of Christ as the first fruits in the New Testament is that He is the foundation for that which has Him as its source or center. He is the guarantee or promise of that which follows. Just as the barley was the first grain to ripen and just as the first of the ripened barley was used in the wave offering, even so Christ had no progenitors or forefathers in what He began. He was both the beginning and the fountainhead, which produced all that followed in the stream. The two areas in which Christ is such a first fruits offering are the Church and the resurrection. In some of the figures there is necessarily some overlap, since it is the Church that was begun by the power of His resurrection and it is the Church that will be raised up by that same resurrection power.

As we will see in the feast of Pentecost, there is a first fruits offering there that is related to the first fruits offering during the Feast of First Fruits. Even though the first fruits figure is not used in the New Testament in connection with Christ and the Church, other symbols that carry forth that relationship are used. A case might be made for the figure of the vine and its branches. In John's Gospel, Jesus says, "I am the vine, you are the branches. He who abides in me, and I in him, he it is that bears much fruit, for apart from me you can do nothing" (John 15:5). Not only does the vine come first and support the branches that come later, but it produces those branches and only through its power do they produce their fruit.

The more significant figure, however, is that of the cornerstone and the stones that grow out of it and rest upon it. The Old Testament spoke prophetically of this cornerstone. The psalmist says, "The stone which the builders rejected has become the head of the corner. This is the Lord's doing; it is marvelous in our eyes" (Ps. 118:22–23). Isaiah adds, "Behold, I am laying in Zion for a foundation a stone, a tested stone, a precious cornerstone, of a sure foundation" (Isa. 28:16). In an account carried in all the synoptic Gospels, not only did Jesus quote the psalm, but He made it clear that He was that stone and that the chief priests, scribes, and elders to whom He spoke were rejecting Him (cf. Matt. 21:42; Mark 12:10–11; Luke 20:17). The meaning was also all too clear that He was predicting that God would make Him the head of the corner. So clear was the meaning to these hearers that they tried to arrest Him.

In Acts 4, Peter and John were arrested for preaching the resurrection. The next day they had to appear before the rulers, elders, and scribes. Peter reminded them of their rejection of that stone (v. 10). But he also coupled the resurrection of Christ (v. 10) with the fact that Christ had now become the head of the corner (v. 11). Peter had no delusions about who he was and who Jesus was in the building of the Church that grew on that foundation. In 1 Peter 2:6–7, Peter cites both the psalm and the Isaiah passages. It is evident that Peter knew that Christ was the foundation. Even though Jesus said that Peter was a rock upon which the Church would be built (Matt. 16:18), Peter obviously placed himself with his readers when he said "Come to him, to that living stone, rejected by men but in God's sight chosen and precious; and like living stones be yourselves built into a spiritual house, to be a holy priesthood" (1 Pet. 2:4–5).

This very concept of the Messiah as a living, growing stone can be found in Nebuchadnezzar's dream in the book of Daniel. In his dream, as he looked at the great image, he saw "a stone ... cut out by no human hand, and it smote the image on its feet of iron and clay, and broke them in pieces; then the iron, the clay, the bronze, the silver, and the gold, all together were broken in pieces, and became like the chaff of the summer threshing floors; and the wind carried them away, so that not a trace of them could be found. But the stone that struck the image became a great mountain and filled the whole earth" (Dan. 2:34–35).

Even though the apostles and prophets may, in one sense, be considered foundational in the building of the Church, Paul is careful to point out the supremacy of Christ as the cornerstone upon which they rest (Eph. 2:20). But also he shows that same growing power described in 1 Peter and Daniel, that in Christ "the whole structure is joined together and grows into a holy temple in the Lord" (v. 21). He further points to the preeminence of Christ in that building in 1 Corinthians 3:11: "For no other foundation can any one lay than that which is laid, which is Jesus Christ." The closest the language of the New Testament comes to the first fruits idea relative to Christ and the Church, however, is in Romans 8:29, where Paul says that the believers whom God "foreknew he also predestined to be conformed to the image of his Son, in order that he might be the first-born among many brethren."

While Christ as the first fruits of the Church is implied in the New Testament, Christ as the first fruits of the resurrection is stated explicitly. The same "firstborn" idea that was used of Christ and the Church applies to Christ and the resurrection in Colossians. Paul says that Christ "is the head of the body, the church," and that He is also "the first-born from the dead" (1:18). He is also called "the first-born of all creation" (1:15). This tends to flavor the term firstborn with the meaning "source." Certainly when we consider the prologue to John's Gospel (1:1–5), we conclude that Jesus, the Word, was not created, since He already was "in the beginning," which would be before the creation of anything. Furthermore, the same prologue shows us that nothing was ever created except through Jesus, the Word. These two thoughts taken together are convincing arguments for understanding "source" as the best meaning of the term firstborn in Colossians 1.

But Christ is actually called "first fruits of those who have fallen asleep" in 1 Corinthians 15:20–23. Thus, He is the primal or original resurrection (glorified resurrection) on the one hand (v. 23), and the source of our resurrection (v. 21) on the other. He is the first fruits in the order of resurrection and in the origin of resurrection. Paul says that "if we have been united with him in a death like his, we shall certainly be united with him in a resurrection like his" (Rom. 6:5). He also links our resurrection inseparably with Christ's: "He who raised the Lord Jesus will raise us also with Jesus," and "If the Spirit of him who raised Jesus from the dead dwells in you, he who raised Christ Jesus from the dead will give life to your mortal bodies also" (2 Cor. 4:14; Rom. 8:11).

As the source or origin of our resurrection, it is sometimes stated that Jesus Himself will raise our bodies. Four times in John 6 Jesus says of those who believe in Him: "I will raise him up at the last day" (vv. 39, 40, 44, and 54). In fact, there was a sense in which, as God, He raised His own body from the dead. He said, "For this reason the Father loves me, because I lay down my life, that I may take it again. No one takes it from me, but I lay it down of my own accord. I have power to lay it down, and I have power to take it again; this charge I have received from my Father" (John 10:17–18). Of the crucifixion it is stated that Jesus Himself "yielded up his spirit" (Matt. 27:50), and He said, "Father, into thy hands I commit my spirit" (Luke 23:46). Then after the resurrection, when the women went to the tomb and heard the announcement of the angel, his message was not "He has been raised," but rather, "he has risen, as he said," and "he has risen from the dead" (Matt. 28:6–7). We are in the hands of Him who is the resurrection and the life. Though it is not Scripture, the saying is scriptural and true: "because He lives, we shall live also."

Not only did Christ fulfill the concept of the first fruits in the resurrection, but other facets of the Feast of the First Fruits were also fulfilled in Him. The wave offering itself was fulfilled in the resurrection, but in preparation for the festival wave offering, the grain was first ground in a mortar and parched with fire. So Jesus was first bruised and crushed and passed through the fire of judgment. From Gethsemane to betrayal, to arrest, to desertion, to trial, to scourging, to mocking and, finally, to Calvary and becoming the sin of the world, forsaken and alone, He was in the maw of the mortar.

After the grain was crushed in the mortar, incense was sprinkled on it. This would make it a sweet smelling offering. Since the wave offering was made so that the people might find acceptance, the offering itself had to be acceptable. Hence, the acceptance of the offering would indicate that the people had found acceptance. This very principle is stated in Romans 11:16: "If the dough offered as first fruits is holy, so is the whole lump; and if the root is holy, so are the branches." When Jesus was taken from the cross by Joseph of Arimathea, Nicodemus came with myrrh and aloes and they put the spices in the linen cloths as they bound the body of Jesus (John 19:38–40). Then they placed His body in the tomb. This was all that they could do. The wave offering lay dormant in the bowl.

In order for the ground grain, now sprinkled with incense, to become a wave offering, it had to be lifted up or raised by the priest to be waved before the Lord. Jesus, our Great High Priest, as we have already seen, raised His own body from the grave. As He raised it, it was immediately acceptable to the Lord. Indeed the very raising of it was at the very same time the acceptance of the offering. As we have already seen in John 10:18, Jesus had power to lay down His life and to "take it again." In fact, He said He had received this very "charge" from His Father. And so it was that the act of raising His body became the acceptance. As Paul stated in Romans 4:25, He "was put to death for our trespasses and raised for our justification." The waving and acceptance of the wave offering were to be "on the morrow after the sabbath." (Lev. 23:11). This signifies the beginning of a new week, but, more significantly, also a new beginning between the Lord and the people. On the first day of the week, Jesus raised Himself and, thus, the wave offering of first fruits. This was God's acceptance of His offering and of us, as we are in Him. So indeed He was "put to death for our trespasses and raised for our justification."

As the raising of the wave offering was predictive of the resurrection of Christ's offering, so the manner of the waving was predictive of the extent of the acceptance of that offering. The wave offering was not only waved before the Lord, but was also pointed toward the four points of the compass. Because the disciples of Jesus had asked Him about the sign of His coming and of the close of the age, He had to tell them that the gospel would be preached in the whole world before the end (Matt. 24:3). But after His resurrection He made it clear to them not only that it must be preached worldwide, but also that they were the ones to undertake that preaching mission. Then He pointed this wave offering to the four points of the compass when He said they would be His witnesses "in Jerusalem and all Judea and Samaria and to the end of the earth" (Acts 1:8). His wave offering was acceptable to the Father for all men everywhere, and whoever accepted that message would be acceptable to the Father and would become His child.

Finally, that offering was one of thanksgiving for being brought out of Egypt and into the land of promise, as well as one of thanksgiving for the beginning of the harvest and the promise of the later completion of the harvest. By the offering of Christ, we not only passed from death to life, but we have changed kingdoms and citizenships. Egypt signified bondage; Canaan, liberty. Paul tells us that God "has delivered us from the dominion of darkness and transferred us to the kingdom of his beloved Son" (Col. 1:13). We who were "alienated from the commonwealth" are now "fellow citizens with the saints and members of the household of God" (Eph. 2:12, 19). Also, in Christ we are thankful for the beginning of the harvest. We are thankful already for the down payment, since "he has put his seal upon us and given us his Spirit in our hearts as a guarantee" (2 Cor. 1:22). And, as Paul assures us, this very Spirit "is the guarantee of our inheritance until we acquire possession of it" (Eph. 1:14). Thus, the Spirit brings us full circle to the promised harvest based on the first fruits, since He has promised that "if the Spirit of him who raised Jesus from the dead dwells in you, he who raised Christ Jesus from the dead will give life to your mortal bodies also through his Spirit which dwells in you" (Rom. 8:11).

### *Pentecost*

*They bring as gifts two loaves with leaven raised,*
*As tokens reaped and formed from harvest field.*
*The Spirit comes. In sundry tongues God's praised.*
*And now the Jewish/Gentile Church is sealed.*

    The Feast of Pentecost was to be observed fifty days following the Feast of First Fruits, which was celebrated on the morning following the Sabbath. The counting of the fifty days was to begin with the counting of the Feast of First Fruits as the first day of that count. Thus, when they counted seven weeks and came to seven Sabbaths, they were at day 49, which was a Sabbath. Then the next day, the fiftieth, was the day of Pentecost, which was (like the Feast of First Fruits) also on the first day of the week. Once again, as in the Feast of the First Fruits, this was a new beginning. The Lord was going to do a new thing, which was related to and grounded in the truth of First Fruits. Indeed there was to be a first fruits offering in this feast also. In fact, so closely were these two feasts entwined, that the Numbers 28:26–31 account of Pentecost begins by calling it "the day of the first fruits."

    As the Feast of the First Fruits took of the very first fruits of the ground, the Feast of Pentecost took from the spring harvest itself. Pentecost came just over one and a half months after First Fruits and the wheat did not begin to ripen until nearly a month after the barley, which was used for the wave offering in First Fruits. Thus, we are dealing with the harvest as such when we reach Pentecost. There was a wave offering at Pentecost also and it was called a first fruits offering. It is significant that this "first fruits" was offered on the day following the Sabbath or on the first day of the week, indicating another sort of new beginning. This offering, then, has a dual character. It is a fruition or completion of what began in the original First Fruits, since it came at harvest time, but it is itself a new beginning, since it came at the beginning of the week and was also a "first fruits" wave offering.

    In what way was the harvest offering of Pentecost a completion (perhaps realization might be a better term) or fruition of what began in the First Fruits offering? As we noted earlier, in the resurrection of Christ the cornerstone was laid. He was that beginning or foundation or first fruits of the Church. Living stones were added to that cornerstone and there was now a living, growing building. That was the realization of what began at the open tomb. But there was also a sense in which this adding or building was in itself a new beginning. Just as the Feast of Pentecost was at the beginning in earnest of the major spring harvest (which is why another "first fruits" wave offering could be made), this building of the Church was only the beginning of the overall harvest. The realization of the original First Fruits at Pentecost was itself a beginning. The Commission was given in Acts 1:8 to reach "Jerusalem and ... all Judea and Samaria and ... the end of the earth." The apostles were just now beginning to reach the first strategic location. It was but the first point of the compass.

There are some significant facts about the first fruits wave offering of Pentecost that distinguish it from the wave offering of First Fruits and that show relevance to the Church. The first (the First Fruits wave offering) was ground grain; the second (the Pentecost wave offering), fully baked bread. The first was in a bowl; the second, in loaf form. The first was sprinkled with incense; the second, baked with leaven. The first was a single bowl; the second, in the form of two separate loaves.

As the first offering was ground grain, so Christ went through the crucible of trial, suffering, and death. The second offering was fully baked bread and this fit the picture of the new body, the Church. First, 120 received power when they were baptized with the Spirit according to the prediction Jesus made to them. The Church was actually born in the upper room before Peter ever stood up to preach. When he did preach, three thousand more were added to the already existing Church (Acts 2:41). They were a living organism. Though they were individual parts (individual bits of meal), they comprised one common loaf or whole.

The first offering was offered in a bowl with all the evidences of the grinding intact. When Jesus rose from the tomb, He still bore in His body the marks of His passion and death. He even showed these to the disciples after the resurrection to assure them that He was indeed their Master and not a specter. The second offering was in loaf form. The Church was a united whole. The Spirit within them was a common bond that joined them together in a single body, even if they were individual members. They presented an even smooth texture and unity. Or as Acts 2:42 states it, "they devoted themselves to the apostles' teaching and fellowship, to the breaking of bread and the prayers." It is fascinating that though they, as the Church, were an unbroken, whole loaf, they broke bread to remind themselves of the sacrifice of Christ's broken body.

The first offering was sprinkled with incense. Incense was used in the temple to fill the holy of holies. Incense was part of the holy items cared for by the priests (1 Chron. 9:29). Christ's life was bracketed near its beginning and at its end with incense. The wise men brought gold and incense (frankincense and myrrh) to the young Christ child, and Nicodemus brought incense for preparing the body of Jesus for burial. Jesus carried the fragrance of holiness with Him from the cradle to the grave. In this sense, we can look at the feast before First Fruits (Passover) and identify Jesus not only with the Passover lamb, but also with the pure, unleavened bread. So the unblemished lamb, the unleavened bread, and the incense on the meal all combine to speak of the holiness and sinlessness of Christ. On the other hand, the loaves of the Pentecost first fruits wave offering were baked with leaven. Even though the Church was a united organism, even though it was a whole, even though it was indwelt and joined together by the Holy Spirit, even though it was built upon the perfect cornerstone, it was made with flawed ingredients. The leaven in the loaves typifies the sin in the lives of those who are transformed into an acceptable loaf. The loaf of the Pentecost wave offering is acceptable because the meal of the First Fruits wave offering was already accepted. Thus, the Church embodies those who had been individual sinful beings who are now transformed into a pure and spotless Bride.

Finally, the wave offering of First Fruits was a single bowl. Christ was the unique paschal lamb. He was the only begotten Son of God. He was the sole sinless one. He was the once-for-all offering of Hebrews 9:12. According to Peter's speech in Acts 4:12, "there is salvation in no one else, for there is no other name under heaven given among men by which we must be saved." The Pentecost wave offering consisted of two loaves—both leavened. In the Old Testament, Israel prided herself on being the chosen people of God. The rest of the world consisted of the Goyim or Gentiles. These nations were out there somewhere on the periphery and were little better than dogs. But God had planned all along that they not stay out there. Ephesians 3:4–6 states that though it had been a mystery, the Gentiles were to be fellow heirs and members of the same Body. The former chapter told how God had taken the two former men (Jews and Gentiles) and in the cross had made them one new man (vv. 14–18).

Jesus, before He ascended, had given a clear Commission that all nations were to be reached. He had even told His disciples during His ministry with them that even though they were in His fold, He had "other sheep, that were not of" that fold and that He "must bring them also," and that there would be but "one flock, one shepherd" (John 10:16). So there were two loaves, and they were both leavened. Paul clearly showed in Romans 1–3 that sin was universal both among Gentiles and Jews. At the Feast of Pentecost two loaves were waved, one of tradition and one of promise. On the day of Pentecost, in the upper room, the Jewish loaf was waved and accepted. A short time later in Caesarea, in the home of Cornelius, the Gentile loaf would be waved and accepted. But God had long ago already joined the two loaves together in one united wave offering, just as the Son of God had joined the two folds together in one flock.

### *Trumpets*

*The New Year dawns; the trumpet call resounds,*
*And joy prevails at what is new begun.*
*We rise, transformed—the final trumpet sounds.*
*We joy—renewed in likeness to His Son.*

The spring feasts covered nearly two months from the

beginning of the first feast (Passover) to the end of the last feast (Pentecost). Then there is a gap of three to four months until the beginning of the fall feasts. The spring feasts are a unit, in which one feast grows or blends into the next. So it is with the fall feasts. But the two groups are separated from each other by a clearly defined break. Nowhere is that interval more pronounced than it is in the historical fulfillment of the feasts as prophecy. The spring feasts were fulfilled nearly two thousand years ago in the exact amount of time that those feasts covered in the festival calendar. When the Feast of Passover began, Jesus was tried and crucified. He arose on the Feast of First Fruits on the very first day of the week when it was celebrated. Fifty days later, on the Feast of Pentecost, the Jerusalem Church was born. Now the gap between the two has stretched, prophetically, to nearly two thousand years. When prophecy again begins to materialize in the fall feasts, we can expect it to follow the pattern of fulfillment that was seen in the spring feasts. That is, they should all be fulfilled consecutively, once they begin, in the same number of days that those feasts covered in the festival calendar. This would be the most natural of expectations, unless we look at their fulfillment from a vantage point of a pre-accepted (pretribulational) system that is superimposed on the feasts and that demands another gap as part of its doctrine.

The question that may arise at this point is whether the prophetic fulfilling of the next scheduled feast (Trumpets) better fits the pattern of a pretribulation rapture or a posttribulation rapture. If the Feasts of Trumpets is, prophetically, the rapture, or if it includes the rapture (and most—whether pretribulationists or posttribulationists—who see the feasts as God's prophetic program being fulfilled in the Church would agree that it does), then one should certainly consider how God worked in the spring feasts. As we have already noted, God worked in the framework of those feasts on a day for day fulfillment. The number of days that was used to fulfill the feasts prophetically in Christ and the Church was identical with the days required to celebrate the feasts originally. Just as the spring feasts flow into one another, so, also, the fall feasts flow into one another. So we can assume that the same day by day timetable of the celebration of the fall feasts would once again be used in fulfilling those feasts prophetically, even as it was in the spring feasts. There are no internal arguments against this position. The only opposition comes from imposing a condition from the outside. If we say that the Church cannot go through the great tribulation and that Trumpets and the rapture come next, we must insert a seven-year interval somewhere in the fall feast schedule and find a place somewhere in one of the feasts for that tribulation. Some may see it as the Day of Atonement following the Feast of Trumpets. We will consider how valid such a theory is when we look at the Day of Atonement as the next feast.

Before further consideration of the celebration of the Feast of Trumpets itself, it may be interesting to note that there were two silver trumpets that were constructed specifically for this feast as well as for other appointed feasts and special occasions. Numbers 10:1–10 tells how these horns should be made and for what occasions they should be used. When both trumpets were sounded, it meant that everybody should assemble. When a single trumpet blew, only the leaders and the heads of the tribes were to gather. When the people were at war against an invader, the trumpets were to be sounded as a reminder to the Lord to save His people from their enemy. They were to be sounded at the beginnings of their months, which meant at the new moons (since each month began on a new moon). They were to sound over the sacrifices and offerings as a "remembrance." And the Lord instructed the people: give the trumpet sound "on the day of your gladness." If the Feast of Trumpets is next in the schedule of fulfilled prophecy, each of the details just mentioned would seem to play a part in God's trumpet festival for the Church.

Rabbinic teaching regarding the Feast of Trumpets adds an interesting sidelight about the people who would live in the end times and be involved in this feast. By the time of Christ, it was held in the teaching of the rabbis that God, in His coming judgment, would divide the world into three groups. There would be the righteous, who would be judged first. Then, nine days later, on the Day of the Atonement, there would be a judgment for the unrighteous and also for the third group, which was neither wholly righteous nor totally unrighteous. Though this was not spelled out in the Old Testament itself, the idea of God's books ("the book of the living" [Ps. 69:28]; and "thy book" [Exod. 32:32–33]) and the idea of appropriate judgment were found there. This also would seem to be a concept that will be fulfilled during the Lord's trumpet festival.

Finally, if the Feast of Trumpets is a completion or fulfillment of what happened during the Feast of First Fruits, we might do well to look at a full picture of just how Christ was the first fruits. We have already seen in Pentecost how He was the first fruits of the Church. We also have seen how clearly He was the first fruits of the resurrection. But let us consider what He experienced before He was lifted up (the resurrection) and see if that earlier pattern has relevance for the Church in the Feast of Trumpets also.

Looking first at the rabbinic tradition, which does reflect the order of judgments in the New Testament, we see that those who are wholly righteous will be judged first—at the judgment seat of Christ. This judgment is not for condemnation. That was settled long ago for us who believe. When Paul contrasted the legacies left by Adam and Jesus, he says, "the judgment following one trespass brought condemnation, but the free gift following many trespasses brings justification" (Rom. 5:16). He follows that by stating, "There is therefore now no condemnation for those who are in Christ" (Rom 8:1). Jesus Himself expressed the same truth when He said, "he who hears my word and believes him who sent me, has eternal life; he does not come into judgment, but has passed from death to life" (John 5:24). When we stand before the judgment seat of Christ, it will be for rewards for the deeds done in the body (2 Cor. 5:10).

The next judgment, nine days later, according to this tradition, would be of those who are totally unrighteous on the one hand and of those who are neither completely righteous nor completely unrighteous on the other. The great white throne judgment will not happen until a thousand years after the judgment seat of Christ. But there will be a judgment of the nations when Christ has returned to earth and sits on His throne to begin His millennial reign (Matt. 25:31–46). This judgment will be to separate the totally unrighteous from those who are neither completely righteous nor completely unrighteous, but who are called "righteous" in comparison to the unrighteous. The unrighteous will be sent into eternal punishment, because they did not help Christians (those whom Jesus called "my brethren") during the great tribulation. Elsewhere in Scripture we see why they did not help—they received the beast's mark and worshiped him and hence were enemies of the Christians (Rev. 14:9–11). Those called "righteous" are more righteous than the other group, because they did not receive the mark of the beast and they helped the Christians (as fellow rebels) in the time of their need during the tribulation. Thus, they are not completely unrighteous. But they are not completely righteous either, since they did not believe in Jesus. This is why they are so surprised that Jesus said they gave help to Him when they helped His "brethren," the Christians. These comparatively "righteous" ones will be rewarded for the service they rendered to Christians during the tribulation by being allowed entrance into the millennium as mortal citizens.

In the instructions given for the sounding of the silver trumpets noted earlier, the trumpets were also used to serve "for remembrance" (or as a "memorial" as the Hebrew word is translated elsewhere) over the sacrifices and offerings. There are only two feasts that were instituted as memorials and each related to a special sacrifice or offering. In Exodus 12:14, God said that the Passover "shall be for you a memorial day." The very nature of the Passover makes it clear why it was a memorial day. The people were to look back to their deliverance from the pharaoh and Egypt and from slavery and death through the sacrifice of the Passover lamb.

The only other feast that is spoken of as a memorial is the Feast of Trumpets. We have seen that one of the very purposes of the trumpets was that they be sounded as a memorial over sacrifices and offerings. It is of great significance that this feast would be a memorial in God's prophetic purposes. When Jesus instituted the Last Supper, He did it as a memorial of sacrifice. It already looked back to the memorial sacrifice of Passover. Jesus was the perfect Passover Lamb slain for the sin of the world. But He instituted it as a memorial of His sacrificial death—even while He was still alive and with the disciples. Whenever they celebrated that feast, they would be "remembering" His death. But there was a codicil or appendix to His instructions, for He told them, "I shall not drink again of this fruit of the vine until that day when I drink it new with you in my Father's kingdom" (Matt. 26:29). Paul echoed this thought when he spoke of the Lord's table and said, "as often as you eat this bread and drink the cup, you proclaim the Lord's death until he comes" (1 Cor. 11:26). Now a memorial trumpet—the last trumpet—sounds. The Church is caught up to be with the Lord. Once again, the followers of Jesus gather around the Lord's table. But this time the Lord of that table celebrates the feast with them, as He eats and drinks with them new in His Father's kingdom.

The trumpets were also to be blown when the people were at war against an invader. This alarm was to remind the Lord to save His people from their enemy. We see from Revelation 18:4 that God's people are in Babylon during the great tribulation, for the heavenly voice calls, "Come out of her, my people." We know that the beast is an invader (even invading God's own temple) pursuing God's people as an enemy. We know that Satan, the dragon, is cast down from heaven and pursues God's people in great fury (Rev. 12). The trumpets need to be blown. Let God be reminded to save His people.

But in the fulfillment of the Old Testament feasts, God accomplishes the fulfillment. For the Passover, He gave the Passover Lamb. For First Fruits, He accomplished the resurrection. For Pentecost He supplied the power and essentials for the birthday bread that was the Church. And for the fulfillment of Trumpets, He will Himself furnish the trumpets. In essence, He will remind Himself. There will be seven trumpets to sound in the midst of that terrible time, and with each one He will remind Himself of the plight of His people. By the time we reach the fifth trumpet we see that this is aimed at those who are not sealed by God. When we reach the sixth trumpet we note that it was aimed against the idolaters of the age, and the implication is that the other trumpets were also focused on the unbelievers, even if they affected some believers as well. Therefore, with each trumpet that sounds, God, in effect, also reminds His people that they will shortly be saved from their enemy.

But can this people of God in this great tribulation be identified as the Church? If the concept of first fruits is consistent, then it is the Church. Christ was the first fruits of the Church. This was fulfilled as a beginning at Pentecost. Christ is the first fruits of the resurrection, and that resurrection comes during Trumpets and it is the Church that is resurrected. But before the raising up of the first fruits offering, that offering was crushed and parched with fire. This Christ fulfilled in His suffering and death. If He fulfilled the resurrection of first fruits for the Church, and if the Church realizes the completion of that in Trumpets, then the symbolism of the preceding crushing or suffering should also be realized. That is, if He fulfilled the crushing and parching of first fruits for the Church in His suffering, then the Church will also realize the completion of crushing and parching, or suffering, during Trumpets. Certainly, somebody suffers during the tribulation—those who are believers in Jesus. If this is not the Church, how grossly inconsistent that a group of believers that is not the Church should reflect the realization of His sufferings, but that the Church reflects the realization of His resurrection.

Because the feast is called "trumpets" (plural), it could be these seven trumpets of Revelation that sound in the tribulation. On the other hand, it could signify the rapture, based on the term "a memorial" (the Last Supper), since the Lord said He would not eat or drink the memorial supper with them again until He ate and drank it new with them in His Father's kingdom. In light of the plural term "trumpets," however, it is most likely a combination of the two. Hence, it would indicate the seven trumpets of the tribulation followed by "the last trump" of the rapture. Obviously, in order to qualify as the last trump, it would have to follow the other seven, but the eight together would be a natural combination, even as Christ's resurrection on the first day of the week suggests a new beginning added to the week (Sabbath) of His passion and death. Further support is given to the seven and one idea by the fact that the Feast of Trumpets was on the first day of the seventh month. It was the only feast to begin on the first day of the month and, as such, called for the blowing of the trumpets, since new moons (and each month began on a new moon) were celebrated by the sounding of the trumpets. In each case we get eight as a concept of new beginnings. In Christ's case, there was the week of passion, death, and entombment—seven days. But after the Sabbath, He arose on the first day of the week (7 + 1). In the case of the Church, after seven days (or a sabbath) of tribulation (also represented by the seven trumpets), there is another (eighth) last trumpet signifying the first day of the rest of our lives with a new beginning in resurrected, immortal bodies. Even the structure of the weeks is similar. Christ's passion week began without threat (the triumphal entry and the cleansing of the temple), but was broken in the middle by the betrayal, trial, and crucifixion. The week (seven years) of the tribulation begins with rather normal events. People may even be saying, "Peace. Peace." But in the middle of that week, the man of sin is revealed and the great tribulation (the symbolic "death" of His Body—the Church) begins. And after the last half of this week (three prophetic days + (= three years +), this is gloriously followed at the last trumpet with the resurrection of His Body, the Church.

As we place Christ's experience on a line in front of the experience of the Church (His Body) and use as a central point death and resurrection (of Christ, the Head, first, followed immediately by that of His Body, the Church) we see an amazing radar graph. His passion week followed this pattern: glory (the triumphal entry), judgment (the cleansing of the temple), and transformation (death and resurrection). Beginning with the great tribulation, we have the mirror image for His Body, the Church. We have symbolic death (real for some of the Body) and then resurrection at the last trumpet, followed by judgment (the judgment seat of Christ and the judging of the nations), and then glory (the millennial reign).

Finally, there is another amazing fulfillment in the rapture of the Bride of Christ when it is compared to the purposes for which the silver trumpets were made. When both trumpets were blown for assembly, all the people were to assemble. But when only one of the two trumpets sounded, only the leaders and the heads of the tribes were to gather—a select, elect group. When the last trump sounds, not everyone will be summoned—only the elect of the Lord. Five wise virgins will be called, but five foolish ones will not. The last and exciting note on when the trumpet sound should be heard was that it should be "on the day of your gladness." We search the Old Testament in vain to find the expression "the day of gladness," except in one place. In the Song of Solomon, in the section covering the praise of the bride, the announcement of the coming of the bridegroom is made: "Go forth, O daughters of Zion, and behold King Solomon, with the crown with which his mother crowned him on the day of his wedding, on the day of the gladness of his heart" (3:11).

Thus, the son of David comes for his bride and it is "the day of the gladness of his heart." How fitting that the only other mention of "the day of the gladness of ... heart" is an occasion for trumpet sound. On the Feast of Trumpets, the trumpet will sound, and the bridegroom, the greater Son of David, will come for His Bride. What for Him will be "the day of the gladness of His heart" will also be for us, His Bride, "the day of the gladness of our heart." What more appropriate Old Testament expression for what the New Testament will call "our blessed hope, the appearing of the glory of our great God and Savior Jesus Christ" (Titus 2:13).

### Atonement

*His ancient folk afflict themselves and trust*
*Their prayers are heard. But hope is not in view.*
*They look on Him they pierced. Then grieve they must.*
*Cleansed Nation Israel is born anew.*

Following the schematic of the feasts, the Day of Atonement follows the Feasts of Trumpets. Therefore, it would come next on the prophetic calendar after Trumpets. Pretribulationists who hold to a prophetic fulfillment of the feasts, for the most part see the Feast of Trumpets as the rapture and nothing more. This means that they must look for the tribulation somewhere else if it is not during Trumpets. Since the Feast of Booths is so obviously related to the millennium, the only place left to put the tribulation is on the Day of Atonement. Since both pretribulationists and posttribulationists alike would agree that by now the Church is raptured (during Trumpets), the Day of Atonement must refer to atonement for nation Israel. For the Church, atonement has already been realized. There are major arguments, however, against the Day of Atonement for the Jews occurring during the great tribulation.

First, this would imply that the atonement is dependent upon, or at least related to, the affliction that they experience. It has long been a misconception on the part of many devout Jews that they are not only the whipping boys of humankind, but also for humankind. An accepted interpretation of Isaiah 53 is that Israel is that suffering servant and that she suffers for the nations. When the Jewish atonement comes, however, it will come because they have finally turned in faith to embrace their Messiah in acceptance.

Second, the Day of Atonement does not indicate affliction for the people from an external force, such as an enemy. It does not even suggest affliction from God. It clearly states, instead, that the people should afflict themselves—"and you shall afflict yourselves" (Lev. 23:32). The responsibility for their affliction was upon them. This is consistent with the offer of redemption through the Messiah down through the ages. On the day of Pentecost, at the first expounding of the gospel message, when the hearers cried out, "Brethren what shall we do?" the first word of Peter's answer was, "Repent." Then, in faith, their sins could be forgiven. Thus, before Israel's national redemption, there must first be a national repentance. To require self-affliction of each individual is to prepare them for cleansing. We will see in the following reason how perfectly this self-affliction fits another timeframe rather than that of the tribulation.

Finally, atonement for the Jews as a nation does not come during the tribulation, but after it. Suffering comes for them during the tribulation. Trouble comes then. Pain comes. Death. But not atonement. Zechariah 13:1 clearly states when Israel will be saved: "On that day there shall be a fountain opened for the house of David and the inhabitants of Jerusalem to cleanse them from sin and uncleanness."

That is the day of their national atonement. And just what is that day? The preceding verses indicate that it is when "they look on him whom they have pierced" (Zech. 12:10). Revelation 1:7 says that will be when He comes "with the clouds and every eye will see him." And what is Israel's response to seeing Him whom they have pierced? "They shall mourn for him, as one mourns for an only child, and weep bitterly over him, as one weeps for a first-born ... each family by itself ... and their wives by themselves ... and all the families that are left, each by itself and their wives by themselves" (Zech. 12:10–14). What a perfect example of the self-affliction that was demanded in the Day of Atonement. So, although Israel is afflicted by the beast during the tribulation, they do not afflict themselves until after the tribulation when they look upon the Pierced One and recognize Him as their Messiah. Only then is the fountain of cleansing open for them, as it has been open for all others who repented before them.

It may well be, however, that the external affliction of the tribulation will prepare the hearts of Israel for an expectation of the Messiah as their one hope of deliverance, so that when they do look upon Him they will recognize Him as the Messiah whom they had rejected, and, because of this, afflict themselves to prepare for a national acceptance and cleansing. There is a curious verse in Hebrews, at the end of the 9th chapter: "Christ having been offered once to bear the sins of many, will appear a second time, not to deal with sin but to save those who are eagerly waiting for him" (9:28). We rightly apply the latter part of the verse to the blessed hope of those who belong to Christ. The completion of our salvation will come with His coming. After all, according to Romans 8:23, we who know Him "groan inwardly as we wait for adoption as sons, the redemption of our bodies."

But may there not also be an application for Israel as a nation if their hearts have been prepared to look for the Messiah as they never have before, so that they, too, "are eagerly waiting for him"? In Charles Dickens's Great Expectations, we feel with Pip as he learns the true identity of his benefactor. To say that that revelation was a shock would doubtless be understating his emotions. Imagine Israel longing for their Messiah. He comes and He is the stone that they had rejected. Furthermore, they had cried out for His execution. They had demanded crucifixion. Through the Romans they had pierced their King and Messiah. In the Passover God had spared their firstborn. At Golgotha they condemned God's only begotten. Now they see Him with seeing and knowing eyes, and the truth crushes them. He stands before them and they afflict themselves and weep as a mother weeps at the death of her firstborn. But that very self-affliction, that deep repentance, prepares them for atonement. He had appeared the first time to pay for their sins as well as ours. Now He can "appear a second time ... to save" the house of Israel "who are eagerly waiting for him."

And that is the message of Romans 11 in Paul's olive tree theme. Israel, predominantly, as a nation, was broken off the olive tree. Almost all of her branches were gone because of unbelief. We believing Gentiles were graciously grafted into the tree together with the few believers from Israel who remained. But, "all Israel will be saved." This would fulfill the very prophecies God had made concerning them: "The Deliverer will come from Zion, he will banish ungodliness from Jacob" and "this will be my covenant with them when I take away their sins." But for nearly two thousand years they have been seeking atonement in the Day of Atonement. Sadly, they have sought salvation without a savior; atonement without an acceptable sacrifice. What glorious result there will be, on the day they look on Him whom they have pierced and recognize Him as their sacrificial Lamb! Then, in joy, they will realize their final Day of Atonement. And the olive tree will be complete.

### Booths

*With branches green their booths they build, and muse*
*On leaving desert wastes for promised land.*
*Messiah comes. The Pilgrim turns and views*
*The Kingdom come. 'Tis now as He had planned.*

The Feast of Tabernacles, or Booths, was the final festival

of the year. It had a twofold purpose. First, the people were told: "You shall dwell in booths for seven days; all that are native in Israel shall dwell in booths, that your generations may know that I made the people of Israel dwell in booths when I brought them out of the land of Egypt" (Lev. 23:42–43). It was a reminder, therefore, of that forty years spent in the wilderness, living in temporary dwellings. Second, it was a time of celebrating the end of fall harvest. In fact, it was also called "the feast of ingathering." In Exodus 23:16, the people were instructed: "keep the feast of ingathering at the end of the year, when you gather in from the field the fruit of your labor." So, it was a curious mixture of remembering the time before they came into the land when everything was temporary on the one hand, and of celebrating with joy and thanksgiving at the bounty produced within the land now, on the other.

The celebration of joy was commanded for this feast: "You shall rejoice before the Lord your God seven days" (Lev. 23:40). For special occasions of rejoicing, the people of Israel used special praise songs, much as we, today, might use special praise songs. Their songs were taken from the book of Psalms. They specifically used Psalms 113–118, which were called the Hallel Psalms. Hallel means, appropriately, "praise." Our word hallelujah means praise (hallel) (be ) to (lu) Jahweh or Jehovah (jah being a shortened form).

By the time of Christ, two outstanding practices had developed in the celebration of the Feast of Tabernacles in the temple service. One was the water ritual, where water would be brought from the Pool of Siloam and poured into the basin below the altar. The other was the lighting of the temple, both by pilgrims carrying torches to the temple and by the lighting of the golden candlesticks in the temple. Very likely, one reason for the development of these practices was the references to water and light found in the Hallel songs that the pilgrims sang during the feast, year after year. In Psalm 114:7–8 they sang, "Tremble, O earth, at the presence of the Lord, at the presence of the God of Jacob, who turns the rock into a pool of water, the flint into a spring of water." Then, in 118:27 they also sang, "The Lord is God, and he has given us light. Bind the festal procession with branches, up to the horns of the altar!"

Not only did the people sing about water from the rock, but they were also especially conscious of water at the end of the harvest. When the harvest was in, it was time to enter into the rainy season. Without a bountiful rainfall, there could not be a bountiful harvest next year. They depended upon the Lord for His supply. Even as He made water come from the rock, He must now make the heavens drop rain. A water ritual would do two things. It would thank Him for the water that produced their present harvest, and it would beseech Him for abundant rain for next year's harvest.

When Jesus went to the Feast of Tabernacles in John 7, He issued an invitation and made a promise. This was on the last day of the festival and the most significant day for the water ritual, since the feast would now be ended and it was the final appeal to the Lord for His blessing of rain. John records that on that "last day of the feast, the great day, Jesus stood up and proclaimed, 'If any one thirst, let him come to me and drink. He who believes in me, as the scripture has said, "Out of his heart shall flow rivers of living water" ' " (vv. 37–38). He was promising not only an abundant supply of water to those who believed in Him, but also nothing less than an individual and unending supply. They had been looking to God for water. Jesus stood before them and promised water—flowing "rivers of living water." Such a promise could come only from God. This significance of the claim was not lost on them (vv. 40–41). Some felt that He must be God's promised prophet. Others were convinced that this was none other than the Christ Himself—the Messiah.

It is almost impossible to miss the connection between Psalm 118:27 and the Feast of Tabernacles. Its instruction was to "bind the festal procession with branches, up to the horns of the altar!" The "festal" procession was obviously a procession during a feast, and the Feast of Tabernacles was the only one to use branches. But the first half of that verse said, "The Lord is God, and he has given us light." It is very understandable, therefore, that the priests should have developed this into a Tabernacles' symbolism of light flooding the temple, as the Lord's house, to show that the Lord is the source of promised light.

Unfortunately, the passage covering John 7:53–8:11 (the story of the woman caught in adultery) intrudes into the text of John at this point in most translations. The translators admit that most of the ancient and best texts do not have the story here. It likely belongs in Scripture, but not here. The very context itself shows that it is not part of this text. The woman and Jesus were left alone (v. 9), and yet immediately following His command to the woman alone, "go, and do not sin again" (v. 11), Jesus "spoke to them " (v. 12). This makes it a continuation of the text of 7:52, where the officers had left the feast to report to the chief priests. Then, immediately following that report, we switch back to the feast where Jesus was still with the Pharisees who were present there as well (8:12).

Then, right after making his offer of rivers of water (7:38), Jesus spoke to them again, saying, "I am the light of the world; he who follows me will not walk in darkness, but will have the light of life" (8:12). When He was challenged by the Pharisees to establish authority for making such an audacious claim, He told them that the Father supported His testimony, and that He was equal to the Father. They wanted to arrest Him, but "his hour had not yet come" (v. 20). It would not come until the spring feasts of the following year.

The disciples were concerned about details of the setting up of the kingdom and asked questions accordingly. James and John wanted to secure a place at His right and left hand (Matt. 20:20–21). The disciples wanted to know what things would announce His coming to reign (24:3). Peter might have thought that the kingdom was beginning at the mount of transfiguration (17:4), when he suggested setting up booths, since the Feast of Booths was the festival that was a symbol of the kingdom and Messiah's reign. Certainly, when the disciples were with Jesus just before the Ascension they thought He might be establishing the kingdom at that time (Acts 1:6).

At the beginning of Passion Week, even the multitudes were looking for the kingdom and were acknowledging Jesus as the King, the Son of David. Even though they were preparing for the celebration of Passover at that time, at His triumphal entry to Jerusalem on Palm Sunday, they combined two other feasts and saw Him and this triumphal event as the fulfilling of both. They saw Him as ushering in the Day of Atonement as they cried out, "Hosanna to the Son of David! Blessed is he who comes in the name of the Lord! Hosanna in the highest!" (Matt. 21:9). Salvation or atonement was a part of the Day of Atonement. "Hosanna" means Save now or Save Lord. This cry of the crowd is taken from Psalm 118:25–26: "Save us, we beseech thee, O Lord! O Lord, we beseech thee, give us success! Blessed be he who enters in the name of the Lord! We bless you from the house of the Lord."

But they were also celebrating the Feast of Booths, which followed the Day of Atonement. Their actual celebration of Atonement and Booths would not have come until the fall, whereas Passover, which was nearly upon them, was the first of the spring feasts. They brought their tender branches and cast them before Him. This was part of the Feast of Booths, and they, therefore, were seeing this as the realization or fulfillment of the festival, or the beginning of the millennial kingdom under the Son of David. But, as we have noted, His time (and hence the time of the kingdom) had not yet come.

We see an interesting sequel to the Hosanna scene of Matthew 21 in chapter 23. The "triumphal" entry to Jerusalem is over. It is just before Passover and the Last Supper and betrayal and crucifixion. Jesus looks on the city of Zion and laments, "O Jerusalem, Jerusalem, killing the prophets and stoning those who are sent to you! How often would I have gathered your children together as a hen gathers her brood under her wings, and you would not! Behold, your house is forsaken and desolate. For I tell you, you will not see me again, until you say 'Blessed is he who comes in the name of the Lord' " (23:37–39). They had just said those very words. But they did not come from the heart. They were not repentant. They were not seeking atonement. They had not enshrined Him as the Son of David on the throne of their hearts. They were not ready to follow Him into a righteous millennium. Their time had not yet come. Thus, His time had not yet come.

But when He comes, and Israel has been reborn in the

Day of Atonement, the Feast of Booths will be realized. The pilgrims will be reminded that their wandering days are over and that all of their dwelling places in the past were temporary booths, like a fleeting dream. The arid places will be no more, as they enter the promised kingdom. The era of disappointment in human dominion will cease as they step into the golden age of a righteous rule and prosperity. Strife and conflict will be past, and harmony will cover the earth.

Not only did the Feast of Tabernacles feature booths for a reminder of wilderness wanderings, but it also served as a joyous celebration of the end of the fall harvest—the final ingathering of the year. The saints of the Old Testament have been gathered. The saints of the New Testament from Pentecost through tribulation have been assembled. Now nation Israel is cleansed and banded together with them all as the last of the ingathered harvest. And they are all joined together with the "first fruits" to rule and reign with Him in this glorious kingdom for a thousand years.

### Sabbath

*Their calm is blest, but then they fail His test,*
*And soon forget the God who called them out.*
*For God's own Bride there's yet a Sabbath rest,*
*All banished now are stress and strain and doubt.*

Numbers are, for some people, a wasteland—dry and barren. For others they are a puzzle. To a few they are a fetish. Numerologists find significance in nearly any number. There are even Bible numerologists who find meaning (usually hidden, except to the initiated) in nearly every number found in the Bible. For the most part, there is little significance to most numbers found in the Scriptures, unless God gives a particular meaning to them or the Word itself suggests that they are somehow special. If John informs us in Revelation that the number 666 is ominous and charged with danger, we may ignore that to our own peril. But most numbers should be taken at face value. If we read in Deuteronomy 3:11 that Og, the King of Bashan, had an iron bedstead nine cubits long and four cubits wide, we should not use those numbers in order to psychoanalyze the king. We should simply conclude that he may have been very tall or else he had one of the earliest king-sized beds on record, and let the matter rest at that.

Some numbers, whether in Scripture or outside of Scripture, are what might be called "natural" numbers in terms of being memorable or important in their own right. The three that suggest themselves as naturals would be the numbers 1, 2, and 10.

The importance of the number 1 can hardly be overstated. It is exclusive. It is the beginning or foundation of all that follows. It is unity. It is indivisible in terms of wholeness. We have one head, one mouth, and one heart. In the Old Testament Scriptures it was the foundation of Israel's faith as found in the Shema in Deuteronomy 6:4: "Hear, O Israel: The Lord our God is one Lord."

The number 2 is only secondary in relationship to number 1. It is the basis of all dualism as we find it in nature or in logic, in parallels or in contrasts, in angles or in angels. It is the basis of marriage and family, and of the language of computer science. We have two arms and hands, two legs and feet, two eyes and two ears. In the world we are confronted with good and evil, light and darkness, positive and negative. It is the basic foundation of choice itself.

The number 10 forms the base for nearly all calculations in the world of numbers today outside of the language of computer science and its cousins. In fact, America is one of the few nations in the world that has not officially adopted the metric system of measurement (measuring distance, weight, and so on, in multiples or divisions of 10). Long ago man looked at his hands and began reckoning amounts by giving a different name to each of his fingers as he counted. Then he developed names to signify repetitions of the process, and mathematics—base 10 was off and running. It is small wonder, therefore, that this became one of our "naturals."

We would expect, in the Scriptures, that these natural numbers would show up in volumes appropriate to their natural importance. And that is what happens. The other numbers, with two or three notable exceptions, decline in frequency as the numbers increase in size. Combining both the cardinal forms of the numbers (one, two, three) and the ordinal forms (first, second, third) we see the following pattern: 1 (2208); 2 (944); 3 (641); 4 (400+); 5 (300+); 6 (200+); 7 (549); 8 (100+); 9 (81); 10 (312); 11 (42); 12 (208); 13 (26); 14 (47); 15 (42); 16 (26); 17 (16); 18 (33); 19 (7); 20 (202). Numbers 1 and 2 appear in volumes that would be anticipated. So does number 10, following declines in 8 (100+) and 9 (81). From 13 to 19 we have a random variation in volumes between 7 to 47. Number 20 takes a jump, but this is a combination of the natural 10 multiplied by the natural 2. Proof that this was looked upon as a "natural" is the fact that the Hebrews did much of their reckoning on the basis of "scores" or 20s. If we were to use that term also, we would add at least 130 more to the 202 already mentioned.

The number 3 presents a possible variation to the pattern. This is, however, a bit "iffy." We might have expected to see a drop to about 500 in the light of what follows (4 = 400+; 5 = 300+; and 6 = 200+), but the true significance of 3 is first clearly revealed in the New Testament. As much as we cherish the teaching of the triune God, this is not spelled out for us in the Old Testament—neither in language nor in numbers.

We do have a clear example of unusual or extraordinary volume, however, when we come to the number 12. Following the volume 42 of the number 11 and the volume range of 7 to 47 of numbers 13 to 19, we should have expected something in the 7 to 47 range. The volume 208 goes far above what we might have expected. Its significance goes beyond the twelve months of the year. The choice of a people of twelve tribes for God's special people in Old Testament days and the choice of twelve disciples in the New Testament for the founding of Christ's Church are the obvious factors of distinction for the number.

The final meaningful number is 7. Nestled between number 6 with 200+ occurrences and number 8 with 100+, we would expect to see a volume somewhere in the 150 range. Instead, we see an astounding 549 usages of the number. But there is another word that is used that has not been included even though it is based on the seventh day, or end, of a span of seven days. It is the word sabbath. It means "to rest, to cease, to put an end to." It came on the seventh, or last, day of the week. This term is used around 170 times in addition to the number 7 itself, giving us a total of more than 700 usages of the concept.

To say that observance of the sabbath day was important in the Old Testament would be something of an understatement. There were two symbols given to Israel to show that they were God's chosen people. One was circumcision. The other was the Sabbath. Circumcision was not put in the Ten Commandments (it was, after all, a strictly male rite). Sabbath observance was (it was for everybody). The desecration of this Fourth Commandment was as serious an offense as murder. The people were thus instructed: "You shall keep the sabbath, because it is holy for you; every one who profanes it shall be put to death; whoever does any work on it, that soul shall be cut off from among his people" (Exod. 31:14).

All Sabbaths were rest days, days to keep holy unto the Lord. There were four Sabbaths in the Old Testament economy. First, there was the Sabbath that was the seventh or last day of the week. Second, there were the special Sabbaths, special feast days, that could fall on any day of the week. Third, there was the Sabbath year. Every seventh year was a Sabbath year, when the ground was to lie fallow—to receive its year of rest. Fourth, there was a Sabbath of Sabbaths of years. After seven Sabbath years had past (49 years), the next, or 50th year was the year of Jubilee. The entire land would have rest. Property rights would be restored. Slaves would be freed.

In New Testament days, both in the ministry of Jesus and the writings of the apostles, the Sabbath was not imposed on believers—at least not the rabbinical additions to Sabbath observance. Jesus proclaimed Himself Lord of the Sabbath and taught that doing good deeds was a proper way of honoring the day. At the council of Jerusalem in Acts 15, though some things were expected of the new Gentile believers, Sabbath observance was not one of them. The other Commandments, in one form or another, find support in New Testament admonitions, but no one was to be judged on the basis of "a festival or a new moon or a sabbath" (Col. 2:16).

Indeed, early in the first-century Church, the practice of assembling together, breaking bread, preaching, and taking collections on the first day of the week instead of the seventh was begun (Acts 20:7; 1 Cor. 16:2). The new day of worship was appropriately called "the Lord's day" in remembrance of the Lord's resurrection on that day (Rev. 1:10). Barnabas, writing in the first century, said, "We keep the Lord's Day with joyfulness, the day on which Jesus rose from the dead." Justin Martyr, in a.d. 135 wrote, "Sunday is the day on which we all hold common assembly ... and Jesus Christ our Saviour on the same day rose from the dead." Thus, rather than being a later development in Church history, it was practiced from the earliest days.

But does the Sabbath have any relevance for believers either now or in the future? Indeed. Just as the three spring feasts of Passover, First Fruits, and Pentecost had their fulfillment at our Lord's first advent, and as the three fall feasts of Trumpets, Day of Atonement, and Tabernacles will be completed at His return, even so the perfect and final and eternal Sabbath will be realized when the true Feast of Tabernacles ends after a thousand years.

In the prophetic alignment of the feasts in Leviticus 23, the Sabbath is listed first. At first glance this seems curious. Was the Sabbath fulfilled in the ministry of Jesus first, before He fulfilled Passover? He said He came to fulfill the Law. Did He fulfill the Sabbath Law for us? Is that why believers are not obligated to observe it now? But if He fulfilled the Law, why are we still obligated not to kill, steal, and commit adultery? Perhaps we need to look for another reason. If the Sabbath is listed with the feasts, it would seem logical to assume that it must also, somehow, be fulfilled. Is it a carrot dangling at the end of a stick? Perhaps this is closer to being a valid idea than the concept that it has already been fulfilled.

Leviticus 23:2–3 sets the stage for the feasts, but as we examine this text, it also shows us an end or a goal. The Lord told Moses, "Say to the people of Israel, The appointed feasts of the Lord which you shall proclaim as holy convocations, my appointed feasts, are these. Six days shall work be done; but on the seventh day is a sabbath of solemn rest, a holy convocation; you shall do no work; it is a sabbath to the Lord in all your dwellings." Then the very next verse begins: "These are the appointed feasts of the Lord." In other words, the Sabbath was not technically included in the feasts. Otherwise, it should have read: "These are the other appointed feasts" or "These are also appointed feasts." Rather than being listed as a feast in verse 3, it says that before the celebration of the Sabbath there would be six days in which work was to be done. Only after those six days would the Sabbath be held.

But then, in sequence, there is a chronological listing of exactly six feasts. If we accept these at all as prophetic feasts awaiting fulfillment (and we certainly have already seen fulfillment of the three spring feasts), then verses 2–3 become clear. The six feasts are six prophetic days in which work was to be done. Only after the six days, on the seventh, would we reach the "sabbath of solemn rest." Therefore, the Sabbath also will be prophetically and eternally fulfilled, but only after the first six days have seen the completion of the work that was to be accomplished in them.

This is consistent with the fact that believers are not under obligation right now to observe the Sabbath. It is consistent with the fact that we celebrate worship and praise on the first day of the week, since the resurrection of Jesus was on the first day. That also makes a statement. As long as we honor Him on the first day, we are looking at a work week and a work schedule. We are concerned, not with rest, but with work. We have a job to do; a task to complete. The rest of the week must be finished first, before we can enter into that rest.

But this is also consistent with what the New Testament has to say about a future Sabbath and the believer. The first seven or eight verses of Hebrews 4 describe spiritual rest for the believer, the one who has been laboring in vain in his former life. But in verse 9, the writer mentions the Sabbath for the first time. There is also a Sabbath rest "for the people of God."

We have already received the spiritual rest described

earlier, but the Sabbath rest yet "remains ... for the people of God." In other words, there is still a rest out there for believers—a Sabbath rest. It has not yet come, but it is being reserved for us, it still remains—waiting for fulfillment. When the last trumpet sounds, we will complete the fourth work day. That will be followed quickly by day five, when nation Israel finally finds atonement. Then we will begin the one-thousand-year sixth day, which begins with a reminder of our temporary dwelling in booths. Then, when the millennium ends and Satan is defeated and the books are opened and all things are resolved and Christ Himself rests when He "delivers up the kingdom to God the Father after destroying every rule and every authority and power," we also, finally, will enter with Him into that glorious and eternal Sabbath rest (see 1 Cor. 15:24).

## LEVITUCUS 23 AND PSALM 118

There seems to be an amazing parallel between Leviticus 23 and Psalm 118 as it relates to the prophetic fulfillment of the six feasts and the Sabbath rest. One or two of the comparisons may appear a bit vague, but most of them are singularly clear as we look at Psalm 118.

**Passover: the suffering and death of Christ.** "Out of my distress I called on the Lord (v. 5); All nations surrounded me (v. 10); on every side (v. 11); like bees, they blazed like a fire of thorns (v. 12); I was pushed hard, so that I was falling" (v. 14).

**First Fruits: Christ's resurrection and victory over death.** "Hark, glad songs of victory (v. 15); I shall not die, but I shall live (v. 17); he has not given me over to death" (v. 18).

**Pentecost: the birthday of the Church.** "This is the gate of the Lord; the righteous shall enter through it (v. 20); The stone which the builders rejected has become the head of the corner. This is the Lord's doing; it is marvelous in our eyes" (vv. 22–23).

**Trumpets: the resurrection and rapture of the Church.** "This is the day which the Lord has made; let us rejoice and be glad in it" (v. 24). (Compare Numbers 10:10—

there was to be a trumpet sound "on the day of your gladness.")

**Day of Atonement: atonement or salvation for nation Israel.** "Save us (Hosanna), we beseech thee, O Lord! O Lord, we beseech thee, give us success!" (v. 25).

**Tabernacles: a reminder (through the building of booths with branches) of our former temporary dwelling as we now enter the millennial kingdom.** "Blessed be he who enters in the name of the Lord! We bless you from the house of the Lord. The Lord is God, and he has given us light. Bind the festal procession with branches, up to the horns of the altar!" (vv. 26–27).

**Sabbath: the eternal Sabbath rest for God's people.** Even as Leviticus 23 begins with the Sabbath idea, this psalm also begins with it (v. 1). In this psalm, however, it also ends with this eternal state. "O give thanks to the Lord, for he is good; for his steadfast love endures for ever!" (v. 29).

*Lord, let me work the rest of my days,*
*till I can rest the work of my days!*

# 11

## THE UNITIES

### ONE

*The SHEMA hear! "The Lord our God is one"—*
*Forever mere, though Father-Spirit-Son.*
*From Greek and Jew, He's ONE man now begun—*
*No longer two, and nevermore undone.*

    God has established certain indivisible unions or units in the Scriptures. There is one God. There is one Satan. There is one heaven and there is one hell. God is that way and He has made Satan and hell and heaven that way. They cannot be split or divided. God-given unities are like that. When God welds a seam, they labor in vain who strive to undo it. One of these unities is the way God solved the problem of reconciling sinful men to Himself.
    Ever since the fall, God has dealt with man in forgiveness on the basis of faith and blood sacrifice rather than multiple dispensations. Man's relationships and societal surroundings may have been different, but God's principles of forgiveness have been steadfast. Even under the "law," God didn't forgive through the law. If someone had been perfect under the law, he would not have needed forgiveness to be acceptable to God. No one was perfect, but if he trusted God in the matter of the blood sacrifice, he was forgiven, pending the perfect sacrifice of the Lamb of God.

The division of history into a given number of dispensations is arbitrary at best, and unnatural, illogical, and unwarranted at worst. These divisions are forced upon dispensationalism by the stand it begins with: a pretribulation rapture. If the Church is to be taken before the tribulation, then God must deal differently with man during the tribulation. Further, by extension, He must have dealt with man in different ways at other times. Scofield found seven divisions or dispensations: innocence, conscience, civil government, promise, law, grace, and the kingdom. It is obvious that this particular division was made in order to reach the magic number seven. Not only are some of these particular divisions debatable, but there is also no more warrant for some of them than there is for some replacements or additions. For example, why not have a dispensation of the wilderness? Or why not make two dispensational divisions under "government"? Why not a dispensation of judges and another of kings since they were so very different in their structures and applications? Why not a dispensation of bondage (the Hebrews in Egypt)? How about a dispensation of captivity? There had been nothing like that before in God's relationship to Israel. Why not a special dispensation of the seventy weeks? And another for the tribulation itself?

The unity of faith and blood sacrifice as God's way of dealing with man in forgiveness is but one of the unities that is shattered by the dispensational method of interpretation. Pretribulationism takes at least eight other unities of the Scriptures and fractures and destroys them by dividing each into two or more parts. Those unities are: the work of the Spirit; the saints; the sheep and the shepherd; the fullness of the Gentiles and the times of the Gentiles; tribulation wrath; Christ's coming; the trumpets; and the resurrection. Let us look closely at each of these unities.

## THE UNITY OF THE WORK OF THE SPIRIT

Since most of the other unities are dealt with at some length elsewhere in the book, a great deal of detail will not be necessary in those cases. But a challenge has been laid down by the pretribulation position regarding the work of the Holy

Spirit in the lives of believers. It has not been touched on elsewhere. Therefore, it is necessary to go into sufficient detail to lay the objection to rest. In short, the position of pretribulationism on this subject is that the Spirit will deal differently with believers during the tribulation than He does now with the believers in the Church. This is, for them, a logical division since they believe the Church will be gone by then—having been raptured before that time begins. The major area of difference in the Spirit's work, according to them, is that in the tribulation He will not baptize believers— He will not indwell them. They believe that there is no possible way of proving that He will do this.

The pretribulation position shows at this point a critical weakness, which it labors unsuccessfully to overcome. The New Testament does teach that those who believe in Jesus are indwelt by the Spirit, that they are placed into the Body of Christ at the time of belief, and that this Body is the Church. What does one do, then, with those who believe in Jesus during the great tribulation? If one is a pretribulationist, he says that things change radically at a pretribulation rapture—the Church is gone and the accompanying indwelling of the Spirit is also gone. But he does this to try to make some rime or reason out of a position that must somehow account for those troublesome believers who appear during the tribulation. In some way they must be shown to be different from all those other believers who disappeared with the Church before the tribulation began. Otherwise they are part and parcel with the Church, and the same Spirit would be inhabiting them as belongers to the whole of the Temple. They also would have to be united somehow with the former group (the Church). If the Spirit does not indwell these believers, the pretribulationist can use them to be the population of the millennium. However, when one considers their claim that there is no indwelling of tribulation believers by the Spirit, one wonders why the cart has been put in front of the horse. It is as if one went to a court of law with the burden of having to prove he is innocent. If believers are indwelt by the Holy Spirit, and if there are believers in the tribulation, the burden of proof lies with pretribulationists. It is really their responsibility to prove that believers at that time are not indwelt by the Spirit.

Furthermore, if we use the pretribulationists' rules for establishing the concept that tribulation believers are not indwelt by the Holy Spirit, we should, in fairness, be allowed to apply the same rule elsewhere in the New Testament. That is, if it is not expressly stated that the Holy Spirit indwells a group of believers or that He baptized them into the body of Christ, then He does not indwell them. Let us apply this rule to the rest of the New Testament.

The fact that Jesus would baptize with the Holy Spirit is stated in Matthew (3:11), Luke (3:16), and John (1:33). Jesus Himself told the disciples to wait in Jerusalem for that event (Acts 1:4–5). This was fulfilled in Acts 2 when the 120 disciples were baptized with the Holy Spirit and enabled to speak in other tongues. We do not read of the Holy Spirit coming on any believers again until Acts 8 when the Samaritan believers receive Him. The next instance of the Holy Spirit being poured out is in Acts 10 where Cornelius and his family receive Him. These three instances are in keeping with the evangelistic order stated by Christ in Acts 1:8: (1) Jerusalem (and all Judea), (2) Samaria, and (3) the end of the earth (Gentiles). They are also consistent with the charge Jesus gave to Peter when He gave him "the keys of the kingdom" (Matt. 16:18). Peter was the leader of the brethren, and the kingdom is opened to the Jews through this office given to him (Acts 1:13–15; 2:14). It is not until Peter goes down to the Samaritans that the keys are used again and they receive the Holy Spirit (Acts 8). Thus, the kingdom is opened to the Samaritans. Then it is Peter who is first sent to the Gentiles, and he uses the keys to the kingdom a third time (Acts 10). The Gentile church is born. Thus, the three major "peoples" of the world are ushered into the kingdom: the Jews, the Samaritans, and the Gentiles.

The only other account in Acts of a "baptism" of the Spirit is in chapter 19 when Paul finds some "bridge" believers. They were disciples of John the Baptist and did not know of Jesus and the Spirit. John had led them part way out of the Old Testament, but they needed to come off the bridge that John represented and come into the New Testament experience, and, therefore, the Spirit came to them as well when they were baptized into Jesus.

There is no other account in Acts of this act of the Spirit. There is the "filling" again of those who had already received the Spirit. Even on the day of Pentecost when three thousand "were added" and on the days following when "the Lord added to their number day by day those who were being saved," the indwelling of the Spirit is not mentioned (2:41; 2:47). When five thousand "who heard the word believed," we hear nothing about the indwelling of the Spirit (4:4). If it were not for the speech by Peter to the council of Jerusalem, we would not have the information that God had given the Holy Spirit "to those who obey him" among those Jerusalem believers (5:32).

Throughout the rest of Acts when the gospel is preached and people believe, not a word is added about the Spirit indwelling those believers. Even those churches that have become familiar to us (because of the epistles written to them) lack any word in Acts about the indwelling of the Spirit when those churches were being founded or revisited. We only get that as teaching about the Spirit in the corresponding epistles. But when we read about them in Acts, there is nothing: the Galatians in 16:6; the Philippians in 16:12; the Thessalonians in 17:1; the Corinthians in 18:1; and the Ephesians in 18:19.

When we go on to other communities in Acts where there are believers, but where there is no doctrinal epistle written to them, there is a complete lack of any word written about the indwelling of the Spirit. We find in chapter 13, Salamis (v. 5), Paphos (v. 6), Perga (v. 13), and Antioch of Pisidia (v. 14); in chapter 14, we see Iconium (v. 1), and Lystra and Derbe and the surrounding country of Lycaonia (v. 6); in chapter 15, Phoenicia (v. 3); in chapter 16, Phrygia (v. 6; see also 18:23), and Troas (v. 8; see also 20:6–12); in chapter 17, Beroea (v. 10), Caesarea (v. 22), and Achaia (v. 27); and in chapter 21, Ptolemais (v. 7). Are we to conclude that the consistent lack of a clear statement regarding the indwelling of the Spirit in these believers means that they did not possess the Spirit? When we study 2 John, 3 John, James, and 2 Peter, no hint is given that the believers to whom these letters were written were indwelt by the Holy Spirit. Should we then apply the pretribulation rule and say that because there is no direct statement there, the Spirit does not indwell them? In chapters 2 and 3 of Revelation, when the seven churches are addressed, none of them has listed the indwelling of the Holy Spirit as one of their identifying marks. Even if we exclude Ephesus because an epistle was written to them explaining the sealing of the Spirit, that leaves Smyrna, Pergamum, Thyatira, Sardis, Laodicea, and even noble Philadelphia without an indication of the indwelling Spirit. Are we to assume that the Spirit did not live in those believers?

The answer is obviously "no!" There are too many passages dealing with the concept of the indwelling Spirit that clarify His work and the identity of those whom He indwells. When we study the extended passage in Romans 4:22–5:5, for example, we learn that those who believe in God and the risen Christ and who rejoice in their sufferings have the Holy Spirit given to them and that He pours love into their hearts. Then Paul confirms that "anyone who does not have the Spirit of Christ does not belong to him," by which we must gather that if anyone does belong to Him, he must have the Spirit of Christ (Rom. 8:9). Otherwise we would have some belonging to Him with His Spirit and others belonging to Him without His Spirit. Paul adds that "if the Spirit of him who raised Jesus from the dead dwells in you, he who raised Christ Jesus from the dead will give life to your mortal bodies also through his Spirit which dwells in you" (Rom. 8:11). And he informs us that the Spirit intercedes for the saints (Rom. 8:26–27).

Paul further tells the Corinthian church that we who were washed and sanctified "were justified in the name of the Lord Jesus Christ and in the Spirit of our God." (1 Cor. 6:11). He claims that "no one can say 'Jesus is Lord' except by the Holy Spirit." (1 Cor. 12:3). In his letter to the Galatians he clearly gives the reason for the Spirit being given to us: "because you are sons, God has sent the Spirit of his Son into our hearts" (4:6). To the Ephesians he proclaims, "In him you also who have heard the word of truth, the gospel of your salvation, and have believed in him, were sealed with the promised Holy Spirit" (1:13). The apostle John makes the point that "All who keep his commandments abide in him, and he in them. And by this we know that he abides in us, by the Spirit which he has given us" (1 John 3:24). He reiterates the thought by saying, "By this we know that we abide in him and he in us, because he has given us of his own Spirit" (4:13).

As we put these statements together and apply the law of collation to them, we understand that because those churches in Acts and Revelation and those readers of 2 and 3 John and of James and 2 Peter truly believed and were children of God, that the Spirit baptized them into the body of Christ, indwelt them, sealed them, led them, poured love into their hearts, interceded for them, helped in their justification, helped them claim "Jesus is Lord," assured them of their abiding in Christ, and will one day bring life to their mortal bodies.

But the same principles of the operation of the Spirit of God must also apply to those believers found in the tribulation. If their description fits what is said in the rest of the New Testament about those who possess the Holy Spirit, then the Holy Spirit indwells them just as He does those other saints mentioned above. In a statement of logic and in the application of its conclusion, if we have a situation where the condition X always produces the result Y, then when we come upon the existence of X, we will always be able to say with assurance that Y also exists. For example, let X represent the temperature we call absolute zero. Then let Y represent the ceasing of all molecular motion (freezing). This does not mean that whenever we get freezing (Y) that it was always caused by absolute zero (X). That would be putting the cart in front of the horse. We may get water to freeze (result Y) at a comparatively warm +32°F. Thus, result Y may not always find its source in cause X. However, if we have absolute zero, −459.67°F (cause X), we will have freezing in any matter. That is to say, where cause X exists, result Y will always exist also.

This applies to truths written about the Holy Spirit in the New Testament. If the word says that given condition X, the result will be Y, then we are able to depend on that. But before looking explicitly at truths that have to do with the

Spirit indwelling believers, let us exam first His other operations and the settings that produce those operations.

The Holy Spirit regenerates the believer upon the beginning of his faith and actually is the force through Whom the person is drawn to that faith in Christ. John claims that all "who believed ... were born ... of God" (1 John 1:12–13), but that the Spirit is the medium in that regeneration, stating that "unless one is born of ... the Spirit, he cannot enter the kingdom of God" (3:5–8). In terms of men being drawn to faith, the entire Godhead is involved in that process, but the Spirit is the agent (actually the Spirit in and through other believers—viz. the Church) through Whom the work is done. Jesus declared that no one comes to Him "unless the Father ... draws him" (John 6:44). He also states: "I, when I am lifted up from the earth, will draw all men unto myself" (John 12:32). But the conviction and the voice is that of the Spirit working through the Bride, the Church. Christ told His disciples that the Counselor would come to them, and then He would "convince the world (through the Counselor Who is in them) concerning sin and righteousness and judgment" (John 16:7–11). And, finally, John states "The Spirit and the Bride say, 'Come,'" and that the invitation is open to "let him who is thirsty come, let him who desires take the water of life without price" (Rev. 22:17). So it will also be in the tribulation. When men come to faith, the Father and Son will draw them through the work of the Spirit moving through those who already believe—when the Spirit and the Bride say "Come." And when they believe, they will be born of God, but that regeneration will be through the person of the Spirit—they must, of necessity, be "born of the Spirit." If it is a rule that belief is followed by birth of the Spirit (as John 1 and 3 tell us), then that will not change in the tribulation.

A further reference to the Spirit assisting in witnessing to the truth of Christ is found in 1 Corinthians 12:3, where Paul states that "no one can say 'Jesus is Lord' except by the Holy Spirit." This obviously goes beyond a simple recognition of the identity of Christ—the demons could recognize Him (as they did on more than one occasion, stating to Him that they knew that He was the Holy One of God)—and undoubtedly refers to bearing witness to this central truth, to His glory. It probably included the promise given to the disciples that the Spirit of their Father would be "speaking through" them (Matt. 10:16–20). That promise doubtless extended to all who would be dragged before officials to give an account of their faith. Just as the Spirit spoke through the disciples under fire and to those saints down through the ages in proclaiming Jesus to be Lord even in the face of opposition, it also holds true of those tribulation saints who lift Christ up in His redemptive Deity. When John saw the angel opening the fifth seal, he "saw under the altar the souls of those who had been slain for the word of God and for the witness they had borne" (Rev. 6:9). We also see the dragon making war "on those who keep the commandments of God and bear testimony to Jesus" (Rev. 12:17). This witness is accomplished through the assistance of the Spirit. In fact, it is of interest to note that nowhere in Acts or the epistles can we find anyone filled with the Spirit (or exhorted to be filled with the Spirit) who had not first received the Spirit through saving faith and been baptized by Him into the body of Christ. The concept of boldness to witness is seen as a consequence of the filling of the Spirit (Acts 4:31). Indeed the work of witnessing itself is associated with the baptism of the Spirit, for the Holy Spirit would come upon the believers and they would "receive power" and be Christ's "witnesses ... to the end of the earth" (Acts 1:8).

The concepts of spiritual washing, sanctifying, and justifying are joint efforts between Christ and the Holy Spirit: "you were washed, you were sanctified, you were justified in the name of the Lord Jesus Christ and in the Spirit of God" (1 Cor. 6:11). Note that this work was in the name of the Lord Jesus Christ. He did more than just set the stage for these operations in our lives. He paid for them and thus secured them for us. But they were accomplished in our lives, they were effected in us (they took place experientially in us) "in the Spirit of God" Himself. It is too much to suppose that that operation could be done by the Spirit as an outside power or influence. Our own experience bears witness to His inner working in these areas—the Spirit as indweller, if you will. Paul seems to suggest it as an internal operation: "There is therefore now no condemnation for those who are in

Christ Jesus. For the law of the Spirit of life in Christ Jesus has set me free from the law of sin and death" (Rom. 8:1–2). The Spirit of life works not in an exterior fashion upon us, but in an internal way on our own spirit.

And yet these very same operations of the Spirit can be seen in the tribulation saints. Revelation 7:9–17 describes those saints "who have come out of the great tribulation," and, thus, were in that time frame on earth. The Spirit's work of washing can be seen in them in verse 14, where the elder states that "they have washed their robes ... in the blood of the Lamb." This redemption by blood and cleansing is described as a mark of the Church (Acts 20:28). The passage speaks of "the church of God which he obtained with the blood of his own Son." These tribulation saints were the recipients of this activity.

Not only has the Spirit washed these believers, but He also has justified them: "They have washed their robes and made them white in the blood of the Lamb." (Rev. 7:14). This is nothing less than justification. Paul tells us that "we are now justified by his blood" (Rom. 5:9). Obviously if they have made their robes white in His blood, they are thereby justified.

In addition to the Spirit's washing and justifying these believers, He also sanctifies them. The same blood that justified believers (Rom. 5:9) also sanctifies them, and it does so through the operation of the selfsame Spirit: "For if the sprinkling of defiled persons with the blood of goats and bulls and with the ashes of a heifer sanctifies for the purification of the flesh, how much more shall the blood of Christ, who through the eternal Spirit offered himself without blemish to God, purify your conscience from dead works to serve the living God" (Heb. 9:13–14). It is also worth noting what terms are used of believers in the tribulation period (see Rev. 6–18). Two that stand out in terms of overall New Testament usage are "brethren" and "saints," since these two are used more than any other terms in the New Testament. In general, "brethren" is used of those who are members of the family of God and is sometimes substituted with "sons" (or in the singular as "son"). On the other hand, the term "saint" is used to indicate an individual member of the

Church or Body of Christ (since "the body" and "the church" are synonyms [Col. 1:18]). The plural form "saints" is really a substitute for "church," whether the Church universal ("the Spirit intercedes for the saints" [Rom. 8:27]) or an individual church as a local body of believers ("To all the saints in Christ Jesus who are at Philippi, with the bishops and deacons" [Phil. 1:1]). Since, in the original, the term "saint" means one who is dedicated or consecrated to God and the cognate verb "sanctify" means to make holy or dedicate or consecrate, we could call the process "saintifying" and mean the same thing. In Revelation 6–18 (the tribulation), whereas "brethren" is used twice, "saints" is used no less than ten times in eight separate chapters. So it is that the Spirit is at the work of sanctifying (saint building) the believers of the tribulation.

What of the work of the Spirit that we call the indwelling of the believer? Let us examine the conditions that result in or are accompanied by the indwelling of the Spirit according to the New Testament Scriptures. Probably most believers (whether pretribulationists or posttribulationists) would agree that there are terms in the New Testament that indicate His indwelling even though different phrases may be used. For example, when it says that the Holy Spirit was to come upon the disciples in Acts 1:8, this would indicate His indwelling of them in that same process. There are three phrases in Acts 8:14–19 that all refer to the coming of the Spirit upon the Samaritan believers, which would also mean that those believers were indwelt by the Spirit as well. Those phrases are: "it had not yet fallen on any of them" (v. 16); "they received the Holy Spirit" (v. 17); and "the Spirit was given" (v. 18). Therefore, if we should find the phrases elsewhere relating to the work of the Spirit in believers, we can know that He also indwells those believers. Another phrase that would be a synonym for being indwelt by the Spirit would be to "have the Spirit" as we find in Romans 8:9: "anyone who does not have the Spirit of Christ does not belong to him." Thus "having" or "possessing" the Spirit would be the same as Him "possessing" or "indwelling" us.

A relationship is also established between the indwelling of the Spirit and the resurrection of the believer in whom He dwells. Paul says that "if the Spirit of him who raised Jesus from the dead dwells in you, he who raised Christ Jesus from the dead will give life to your mortal bodies also through his Spirit which dwells in you" (Rom. 8:11). It should come as no surprise that the Spirit should be the agent of the resurrection when Paul tells us in the resurrection chapter (1 Cor. 15) that that body will be "raised a spiritual body" (v. 44). If the resurrected body is a spiritual body, and if the Spirit Himself raises that body, and if the basis of His raising that body is that it belongs to Him (because He dwelt in that body), what is to be said of those martyred saints in Revelation 20:4? There is no Scripture dealing with the resurrection that even remotely hints at an alternate method of believer resurrection. Because there is no indication to the contrary, we must conclude that this is the same kind of resurrection, with the same basis. Indeed it is not only the same kind, but it is the resurrection itself.

When we compare the two Scriptures (Rom. 8:11 and Rev. 20:4), there is one remarkable similarity in what happens to the bodies in each passage. In the Romans passage, at the resurrection, the Spirit will "give life" to the bodies. In the Revelation passage, the believers "came to life." It is not just that the latter passage uses the verb form of the word "to live" and the former the noun form "life" drawn from a contracted form of that verb, but that they draw on that concept at all rather than saying that the Spirit (in Romans) "will raise" those bodies, and that those saints "rose" or "rose from the dead" (in Revelation). Instead, the Romans passage not only says that the Spirit "will give life to your bodies," but also that He "will give life to your mortal bodies." There are two ways a body can be a mortal body. It can be a dead body (one that has already died), or it can be a body destined for death (on its way to eventual death, but still alive). In other words, this passage shows the work of the Spirit in resurrecting those already dead and transforming those who still live. This corresponds with the 1 Corinthians 15:52 passage indicating that "the dead will be raised imperishable, and we shall be changed." It is also consistent with 1 Thessalonians 4:16–17, where "the dead in Christ will rise first; then we who are alive, who are left, shall be caught up together with them." It fits with what Jesus tells Martha when He says, "he who believes in me, though he die, yet shall he live, and whoever lives and believes in me shall never die" (John 11:25–26). But the same concept can be seen in the Revelation 20:4 passage. Two groups of believers "came to life." The NASV translation shows the distinction between the two groups. If parenthetical identifications are supplied, the relationship becomes even clearer: "And I saw the souls of those who had been beheaded because of the testimony of Jesus and because of the word of God (the tribulation martyrs), and those who had not worshipped the beast or his image, and had not received the mark upon their forehead and upon their hand (those believers who had not died and had outlived the tribulation); and they (both the dead and the physically alive) came to life and reigned with Christ for a thousand years." If this resurrection/transformation is compared to the description given in Romans 8:11, we see that it happens because those bodies belonged to the Holy Spirit—He indwelt them. He indwelt the bodies of the martyrs and thus resurrected them, and He indwelt the bodies of the living saints and thus transformed them. Because He indwelt them, they formed the Body of Christ—the Church.

In Romans 4:22–5:5, Paul states that those who believe in the Lord have the Spirit given to them. We have to look to the beginning of the passage to see who the audience is to whom the Spirit is given and at the end of the passage to see that it is the Spirit who is given to them. But looking at key phrases in the passage leading from recipient to gift, it reads as follows: "righteousness ... will be reckoned to us who believe in him that raised from the dead Jesus our Lord ... we are justified by faith ... the Holy Spirit ... has been given to us." There are other glorious truths in the passage, but the truth about the Spirit is clear: "to us who believe ... the Holy Spirit ... has been given." Ephesians 1:13 adds, "In him you also who have heard the word of truth, the gospel of your salvation, and have believed in him, were sealed with the promised Holy Spirit." If the Holy Spirit has been given to us, and if that same Spirit Who has been given to us has sealed us, then He dwells within us. This was true of the Church in Acts and the epistles and has been true of the

Church down through the ages since then. But it must also be true of the believers in the tribulation described in Revelation 6–18 unless overpowering Scripture shows us that it is not so, and when the word does not even suggest that it is not so, we have no reason for believing that it is not so. An angel depicts the fate of the followers of the beast, challenges the tribulation saints to endurance and calls them "those who keep ... the faith of Jesus" (Rev. 14:12). If they "keep the faith of Jesus," they believe. If they believe, they have had the Spirit given to them, and they have been "sealed with the promised Holy Spirit." If they have been given the Holy Spirit and have been sealed by Him, then He indwells them.

Paul tells the Galatians the reason that the Holy Spirit is given to believers: "Because you are sons, God has sent the Spirit of his Son into our hearts" (4:6). This presents a neat equation. God sends the Spirit of His Son into the hearts of those who are His sons. That Spirit is, of course, the Holy Spirit. If one is a son of God, the Spirit has been sent into his heart, which is the same as saying that the Spirit indwells him. We find another expression of this family equation in Romans, where Paul says that we Christians were "predestined to be conformed to the image of his Son, in order that he might be the first-born among many brethren" (8:29). Once again the equation is the Son producing or being reflected in sons. But here an equivalent term is used: "brethren." Throughout the New Testament, "brethren" is the term (followed closely by "saints") that is most often used of believers in Christ. It means the same as other synonyms—sons or children—used in the same fashion. "Brethren" is occasionally used in a family or national sense (especially regarding Israel according to the flesh), but whenever the reference is to belief, it always means sons of God. Thus, the Spirit has been sent into the hearts of all the "brethren," according to Galatians 4:6 and Romans 8:29. In addition, the Spirit leads the sons of God (Rom. 8:14). Twice in Revelation 6–18 the tribulation believers are referred to as "brethren." Near the beginning of the tribulation, the restless martyrs are told to "rest a little longer, until the number of their fellow servants and their brethren should be complete, who were to be killed as they themselves had been" (6:9–11).

These martyrs "had been slain for the word of God and for the witness they had borne." These martyrs as well as those yet to be killed were killed because they believed, thus making them sons of God (those already slain may be all the martyrs down through the ages). Near the end of the tribulation, when Satan is cast down from his access to heaven, the loud voice in heaven calls him "the accuser of our brethren" (12:10). The only logical identification of these "brethren" would be that they are believers on earth and thus sons of God, since Satan could scarcely accuse to the Lord those believers who were already dead and, therefore, resting in His presence. This should suffice, but at the marriage supper of the Lamb, the angel identifies the meaning of "brethren" when he tells John "I am a fellow servant with you and your brethren who hold the testimony of Jesus" (19:10). Therefore, the "brethren" in the tribulation in Revelation 6–18 are sons of God and have the Spirit "sent into their hearts."

Another treatment of the concept of the giving of the Spirit is found in 1 John. We have already seen to whom the Spirit is given (those who believe in Christ) and the reason why He is given (because we are in His family by virtue of being His children), but here we are told that He is given to prove the Lord abides in us. John states that "All who keep his commandments abide in him, and he in them. And by this we know that he abides in us, by the Spirit which he has given us" (3:24). He restates the idea when he says, "By this we know that we abide in him and he in us, because he has given us of his own Spirit" (4:13). John doubtless remembered the time the Savior said to him and the other disciples that He would pray the Father and He would give them "the Spirit of truth ... for he dwells with you, and will be in you" (John 14:15–18). Then He immediately added, "I will not leave you desolate; I will come to you." In other words He promised that the Father would send the Holy Spirit to be in them, but also that He (Christ Himself) would come to them in that person of the Holy Spirit. Therefore, here in 1 John, John says that the Spirit being in us proves that Christ abides in us and that we abide in Him. But what is the description of the people for whom, or in whom, this truth would be realized? John says it would be for "all who keep his commandments." Turning to those tribulation saints in Revelation 14:12 who are challenged to endure, they are described as "those who keep the commandments of God." If they keep His commandments, they abide in Christ and Christ abides in them. And to prove this to them, Christ has given them His own Spirit, which is the Holy Spirit, to dwell in them.

Then there is another passage that speaks of possessing or "having" the Spirit of Christ, which is to say again, being indwelt by the Spirit of Christ (Rom. 8:9). The verse is framed in the negative, saying that "anyone who does not have the Spirit of Christ does not belong to him," but we can also set it forth as a positive statement. We can acclaim, "Only those who have the Spirit of Christ belong to Him." If we were to state it as cause and effect, we could not say, "All who have the Spirit of Christ belong to Him" (although the other passages we have studied would support that), but rather we must state it, "All who belong to Him have the Spirit of Christ." Therefore, if we can determine that any person or group does not have the Spirit of Christ, we can absolutely affirm: "They do not belong to the Lord." But if we suppose that they do not have the Spirit of Christ, and yet they can demonstrate that they do belong to the Lord, then we are wrong, and they do have the Spirit of Christ.

In the Old Testament economy, Israel was called the people of God. But at times even they had a rather tenuous grip on that title. In Hosea 1:9 God indicated that they were not living up to their billing when He named Gomer's son "Not my people." But He looked beyond that day to a day when they would be His people in a new, more intimate way, "and in the place where it was said to them, 'You are not my people,' it shall be said to them, 'Sons of the living God' " (v. 10). But this "new people of God" relationship would not only extend to a revived Israel; it would also include those who had never been God's people (even the nations, or Gentiles), for Hosea was given the message that God would "say to Not my people, 'You are my people'; and he shall say, 'Thou art my God' " (2:23).

On the basis of the Hosea text, one might consider that this was a further message to Israel, but when we see the

Spirit interpreting the prediction in the New Testament, it becomes clear that it was a reference to the Gentiles also becoming God's people. Paul says that God called us "not from the Jews only but also from the Gentiles" (Rom. 9:24), and as proof cites the above passage from Hosea 2:23. And Peter cites Hosea again to stress the new "people of God" relationship (1 Pet. 2:10).

However, the pretribulation position claims that the Spirit does not dwell in tribulation believers. If we can demonstrate that tribulation believers are God's people—that they belong to Him—then it cannot be said of them that they do not have the Spirit of Christ, and the pretribulation position will be wrong, since Romans 8:9 says that if one "does not have the Spirit of Christ," he "does not belong to him."

In Revelation we have a view of believers "who have come out of the great tribulation" (7:9–17). These believers are "before the throne of God, and serve him day and night within his temple; and he who sits upon the throne will shelter them with his presence. They shall hunger no more, neither thirst any more; the sun shall not strike them, nor any scorching heat. For the Lamb in the midst of the throne will be their shepherd, and he will guide them to springs of living water; and God will wipe away every tear from their eyes" (vv. 15-17). With this most caring and tender and intimate of language, how can the idea even be entertained for a moment that these do not belong to the Lord? The shepherd figure alone ought to convince the hardest skeptic. Jesus Himself said that He had other sheep to bring, but that there would only be "one flock, one shepherd" (John 10:16). Surely if He is their shepherd, they belong to that one flock and they belong to Him. But the very passage itself indicates that this is a future state described here. These are no longer restless saints awaiting the consummation (as those in 6:9–11 as they lay under the altar). These are those who have reached the place of having God "wipe away every tear from their eyes." As we look to the future, we find this activity in the description of the new heaven and new earth and in the New Jerusalem, that He "will wipe away every tear from their eyes" (see Rev. 21:1–4). We also learn that "He will dwell with them, and they shall be his people" (v. 3).

But if this should not suffice, during the tribulation period there is also a call from heaven to those who belong to the Lord to come out of Babylon. The voice commands: "Come out of her, my people" (Rev. 18:4). Once the Church began and the door of salvation was opened to Gentiles as well as Jews, whenever God Himself speaks of "My people" (as He does in 2 Cor. 6:16), it refers to all of the redeemed. These tribulation people called "my people" are in that fold, and if they are God's people, they obviously belong to Him. Once again, since Romans 8:9 is true, that "anyone who does not have the Spirit of Christ does not belong to him," for anyone to say "they do not have the Spirit," is also to say, "they do not belong to Him," and since these, God's people, do belong to Him, we would say to the peril of our own credibility that they do not have the Spirit.

## THE UNITY OF THE SAINTS

In the chapter on The Church, it was seen that the New Testament calls believers saints and that the term is a substitute term for the Church. Distinctions are not made by the Scripture. Dispensationalism does make a distinction. More accurately said, they make three distinctions. They make a division between Old Testament and New Testament saints. They further distinguish between the saints before the tribulation and the saints during the tribulation. Finally, they differentiate between the saints who die during the tribulation and those who outlive the tribulation. Let us consider each of these separations of the saints.

### Old Testament saints and New Testament saints

They make a distinction between justified believers of the Old Testament and those of the New Testament. Basic to the teaching of dispensationalism is the concept that Israel is Israel and the Church is the Church and that God has a specific destiny for each. Arguments have raged on both sides of the aisle as to whether the Church is the new Israel and whether the promises and covenants given to Israel in the Old Testament are fulfilled in the Church in the New Testament. Generally, the answer of dispensationalism is "No. God has a special program and plan for Israel." Most covenant theologians would say, "Yes. The Church is the true and spiritual Israel. Those things were written for us 'upon whom the end of the ages has come.' " Depending on how one looks at it, both positions are wrong, or both positions are right. Taken as exclusive statements, both are wrong. There is more to Israel than the nation on the one hand, and there is more to God's program than New Testament believers before the return of Christ on the other. Taken in combination, both are right. God has a plan for nation Israel on the one hand, and there is fulfillment, spiritually, of many of the old promises in the new Church on the other.

Actually, the problem is resolved in a study of the Scriptures when we are guided by the New Testament teaching that there are two Israels and that in the end, the one will be melded into the other. There is a physical nation called Israel. There is, however, a spiritual people of God that is also called Israel. The first group was, though peculiarly blessed by God, for the most part, unbelieving and unfaithful. The second group was born physically into the first, but was a believing, faithful minority. They believed and sacrificed their lambs in faith, and because they believed, it was counted to them for righteousness. When Jesus, the consummate Lamb was offered, they were completed. He was the "messenger of the covenant" of Malachi 3:1 and they had delighted in that coming One.

When the Messenger of the covenant came, He brought a new covenant, but He merged the old covenant into the new. The covenant that He introduced was new because it established a perfect and completed once for all sacrifice. They who had already believed (from spiritual Israel in the past), who had had their sins "passed over" were now forgiven. But they were the true commonwealth of Israel. They were the "root" of the olive tree in Romans 11. They were the incipient Church that other Jews joined on the day of Pentecost when the gospel was preached. But most Jews (as they were in former, Old Testament days) were unbelieving. So the Master Pruner tore out the majority of the old branches and opened the good news message to the Gentiles. He grafted in these new and foreign branches. According to Ephesians 2, He broke down the wall that divided us from believing Israel and from the two made one new man. As the Spirit of Christ had been in their prophets (1 Pet. 1:11), He was now in us whether believing Jews or believing Gentiles and had combined us into one man (Eph. 2) or one tree (Rom. 11). Or as Christ said, we became one flock with one shepherd (John 10:16). This was the mystery of our joint union with the Lord Himself: Christ in us, "the hope of glory" (Col. 1:27). Although Gentiles were not descended from Israel, we now belonged to the true Israel; although we were not descendants of Abraham, in Christ we became Abraham's children (Rom. 9:6, 7). In the commission given by the Lord, Paul was sent to the Gentiles that they might find "a place among those" who were already sanctified (believing Jews) by faith in the Lord (Acts 26:18). But the promise was to faithful Jews of the Old Testament first and we joined them. Indeed, they were actually in Christ when we Gentiles in those Old Testament days were SEPARATED FROM CHRIST (Eph. 2:12). The Church is the Body of Christ, and to be in Christ = being in His Body which, in turn, = being in the Church. Paul says that we Gentile believers "like Isaac, are children of promise," and that our persecution as the spiritual by those who are fleshly is a reflection of that earlier state when "he (Ishmael) who was born according to the flesh persecuted him (Isaac) who was born according to the Spirit" (Gal. 4:28–29).

But completion of spiritual Israel is only thinkable when Old and New Testament saints are seen as joined together in the new man of Ephesians 2 or in the olive tree of Romans 11. The writer to the Hebrews indicated that, in spite of the great examples of faith in believing Israel in the Old Testament, those believers had to be completed by New Testament believers being joined together with them and that "apart from us they should not be made perfect" (11:40). How sad, if not tragic, that some now hold that we New Testament believers (who were the outsiders, now joined together with the insiders) are perfect apart from them. At least, some present day believers don't want to be in the same "man" or "tree" with those Old Testament saints.

The New Jerusalem is described as having on the twelve gates the names of the twelve tribes of Israel, and on the twelve foundations the names of the twelve apostles (Rev. 21:9–14). What a unity between Old Testament and New Testament saints. And the union is called "the Bride, the wife of the Lamb." Probably the most logical interpretation of the twenty-four elders is that they are representatives of the Old Testament and New Testament believers joined together in the presence of the Lord (see Rev. 4:9–10).

In Theomatics, a fascinating study of the numerical values of Greek letters in the New Testament, Jerry Lucas and Del Washburn point out how the combinations of the letters in given passages come out to consistent numbers that correspond with the themes they are treating. They indicate that two of the most striking passages in the Greek are two passages on this unity.

The New Jerusalem is described in chapter 21 of Revelation as being the "bride, the wife of the lamb," which we as saints are also. The complete design of the holy city is structured around all of the redeemed, which make up the Bride of the Lamb. This is why the names of the twelve tribes of the sons of Israel are inscribed on the New Jerusalem. The numbers 12 and 144 bespeak the kingdom of God and kingdom of heaven, because the saints are to reign forever with Christ. The New Jerusalem along with the saints forms that kingdom.

Now here is a marvelous truth. As we mentioned earlier in Chapter 2, the words in Greek often have different spellings. We also mentioned that each of these spellings produces a different aspect of God's truth. For this reason, Jerusalem spelled one way is 144, and spelled another way it comes out 888, the same as the theomatic value of Jesus. This demonstrates that the city, which represents the redeemed, and Jesus are unified as one. (Jerry Lucas and Del Washburn, Theomatics, p. 215)

Later on, they state:
Probably the most profound Scripture, which ties this whole design together, is found in Romans 11:17. In this passage Paul speaks of his fellow Jews and how he wanted to save some of them. In this epistle Paul was writing to the

Gentile believers in Rome, and here is what he said in verse 17: "But if some of the branches were broken off, and you, being a wild olive, were grafted in their place to share the richness of the olive tree ..." Now in this passage the branches that were broken off stand for natural Israel after the flesh. This Scripture states that the Gentile believers were grafted in their place, and that is why the kingdom of God was taken away from the Jews who rejected their Messiah and given to the true Israel. For this reason all believers in Jesus, whether they be Jew or Gentile, have been grafted in their place. "And you, being a wild olive, were grafted in their place" 144 x 27 Romans 11:17. (p. 243)

But the olive tree of Romans 11 is still not totally completed until the natural branches of nation Israel are also regrafted back into the tree when "all Israel will be saved" (v. 26). Thus, we will have all believers of the Old Testament, all Jewish and Gentile believers of the New Testament (including the tribulation believers), and believing nation Israel joined together in a living monolithic union with Christ. This is the New Jerusalem—the Bride of Christ.

## Pretribulation saints and posttribulation saints

Dispensationalism also makes a division between the saints who believe in Jesus before the tribulation and those who believe in Him during the tribulation. Although they are called by the same name ("saints") and share the same blood-washed experience (Rev. 1:5; 7:14); and although they both have the same Shepherd (John 10:11, 27; Rev. 7:17) Who said there would only be one flock and one shepherd (John 10:16), this belief separates them into "Church" and "non-Church" saints. Enough has been developed elsewhere in this chapter and in the rest of the book to assure us that they have a common bond and that they are all one in Christ.

## The saints who die during the tribulation and the saints who outlive the tribulation

According to the system of dividing the word adopted by dispensationalists, the martyred saints from the tribulation will be resurrected at the end of the tribulation and rule with

Christ for a thousand years (which is tough to get around in the light of Revelation 20:4), but they contend that the living saints, who had escaped the sword of the beast, will go into the millennium as a mortal populace to be ruled over. In response to this idea, one might feel something like Marc Anthony when he pointed out to the Roman citizens the wound made in Caesar's body by the dagger held by Brutus, Caesar's friend. He commented: "This was the most unkindest cut of all." Though we might argue with his grammar, we cannot deny the sentiment. What can we feel but pity for those unthinking tribulation sufferers? How unkind is their fate! With all of their dodging, hungering, thirsting, alienation, nakedness, illnesses, imprisonment, and steadfast loyalty to their Lord, they now are brought mortally into the kingdom as subjects. Their brothers who were executed get immortal bodies and get to reign with their Lord. How much better had it been to stick their heads in the maw of the beast and have them bitten off! Then they could say with Sydney Carton: "It is a far, far better thing that I do, than I have ever done; it is a far, far better rest that I go to than I have ever known."

An enlightening verse is seen in Revelation 15:2–3. It shows us a group "who had conquered the beast and its image" singing "the song of Moses, the servant of God, and the song of the Lamb." Moses' deliverance foreshadowed and was included in the deliverance of the Lamb, the true substance of the shadow. In the Lamb, Old and New Testament saints alike combined in one. Old and New Testament saints, not complete without each other. And not complete without the full number of Gentile believers. Yet again, not complete without believing nation Israel. But all complete in the New Jerusalem—the Bride of Christ.

### THE UNITY OF THE SHEEP AND THE SHEPHERD

As far back as the Babylonian captivity, God established the concept of a new relationship to believing Israel and a new idea of unity. He even said that there would be different kinds of sheep to form one flock and that His servant "David" would be the one shepherd to be set up over that flock: "I will save my flock, they shall no longer be a prey; and I will judge between sheep and sheep. And I will set up over them one shepherd, my servant David, and he shall feed them and be their shepherd. And I, the Lord, will be their God, and my servant David shall be prince among them; I, the Lord, have spoken" (Ezek. 34:22–24). The Lord also says that the two parts of Israel itself (northern Israel and Judah) would be reunited by their union in that flock: "My servant David shall be king over them and they shall all have one shepherd" (37:15–24).

Jesus took up this theme and declared himself the fulfillment of the one-shepherd figure (John 10:1–18). Before the final realization of the Ezekiel prophecy, Jesus indicated that there was to be a spiritual fulfillment. His followers were already His sheep. This means they joined together with believing Israel, which had gone before them in the Jewish "fold." (There would be others to be added to that fold down through the ages until—at the return of the shepherd—nation Israel itself would become believing Israel and would join the fold.) But there was another fold to be brought (v. 16). They were the Gentiles—those from the end of the earth—who would believe. Since there are such believers in the tribulation who have Jesus (the Lamb) as their shepherd (Rev. 7:17), they are part of that Gentile fold that also must be brought. And so all are included in the one flock ("So there shall be one flock"), all believing Jews and all believing Gentiles (John 10:16). And so all shall have but one Shepherd: "So there shall be ... one shepherd" (John 10:16). We are not allowed to split the flock that He united, or find a hireling or another shepherd for one part of it.

### THE UNITY OF "THE FULL NUMBER OF THE GENTILES" AND "THE TIMES OF THE GENTILES"

Those with a pretribulation point of view separate what God calls the "fullness" or "full number of" the Gentiles from what He labels "the times of the Gentiles." Each of the terms relates to God dealing in a special way with the Gentiles. The second term, "the times of the Gentiles," refers to the fact that God is allowing the Gentiles for a certain time span to "do their thing" or have control of world policy and events. We find the term in Luke's Gospel, where Jesus says that Israel "will fall by the edge of the sword, and be led captive among all nations; and Jerusalem will be trodden down by the Gentiles, until the times of the Gentiles are fulfilled" (21:24). Any peace that Jerusalem now knows, any freedom from foreign boots, will be rudely disrupted when "the nations ... trample over the holy city for forty-two months" (Rev. 11:2). This is yet to come. This will come in the tribulation period. And it will stop at the end of the tribulation when Christ returns with "a sharp sword with which to smite the nations" (19:15). So, the times of the Gentiles cease with their defeat at the end of the tribulation.

The first term, "the full number of the Gentiles," refers to that phenomenon of God accepting Gentiles into the olive tree until Israel is ready as a nation to embrace the Messiah. Paul states that "a hardening has come upon part of Israel, until the full number of the Gentiles come in, and so all Israel will be saved" (Rom. 11:25–26). Pretribulationists are fond of proclaiming that as soon as the last soul is added to the Church, Christ will return. It is accepted that, for the most part, these are Gentile believers, and some even use the "full number" concept. In order to do this, however, they must disconnect this concept from the "times of the Gentiles." That is, God can bring in the "full number" of believers, the rapture can come, the tribulation can follow, and then Christ can come back and defeat the nations (the Gentiles) at Armageddon.

This creates a problem, though. Israel will be saved when they see the one whom they have pierced, mourn over Him in repentance, and are finally cleansed from their sin (Zech. 12:10–13:1). This, however, comes at the end of the tribulation when He returns and they see Him. This scenario agrees with the fact that during the tribulation we see millions of Gentile believers (Rev. 7). These believers, logically, must be those spoken of in Romans 11 who are the last to be grafted into the olive tree before the conversion of nation Israel. Thus, the "full number of the Gentiles" also is realized at the end of the tribulation, and is part of the timetable of the "times of the Gentiles." God deals with Gentile nations in two ways until the end of the tribulation. With longsuffering, He lets them have their head to run the world as they choose on the one hand, but, in grace, holds out to them the message of love and invitation on the other. They are both part of the one package.

## THE UNITY OF TRIBULATION WRATH

There is a wrath principle in the tribulation that is a polarized unity like the positive and negative poles of a magnet. That is, during that time, the wrath of God is directed against the Antichrist and a rebelling people while, simultaneously, the wrath of the Antichrist is pitted against the saints or people of God and, through them, against God Himself. But dispensationalists divide that opposing wrath and basically discard the wrath of the beast while speaking only of wrath on the part of God. Once they have done this, they state that the Church is exempted from the wrath of God and, therefore, cannot be in the tribulation. But when God says that we were not destined for wrath, He referred to His eternal wrath. The bowls of Revelation 16 certainly describe a wrath of God, but that wrath is clearly aimed against His enemies. On the other hand, the wrath of the dragon is clearly against God's people (Rev. 12:12, 17). They, God's enemies, suffer God's wrath; we, God's people, suffer the wrath of Satan. This was the very division of wrath that existed in Egypt during the Hebrew bondage: God's wrath against the pharaoh and the pharaoh's wrath against the Hebrews. So in the tribulation these exist together and cannot be separated.

## THE UNITY OF CHRIST'S COMING

The pretribulation school is forced to divide the coming of Christ into two comings: the secret coming of Christ before the tribulation "for the saints" and the public coming of Christ after the tribulation "with the saints." A full treatment of this idea will be found in the chapter on "The Blessed Hope: The Resurrection/Rapture." A few summarizing words will suffice here. There is no indication of a secret rapture in the Scriptures. The coming of a thief comparison simply fits in with the idea of suddenness and unexpectedness and of our not knowing the day or hour of His return. Christ gives His followers a quite different concept when He tells them not to listen to reports or rumors that He has come, because when He does come, it will be like a flash of lightning seen from one end of heaven to the other (Matt. 24).

Furthermore, the clear words of Scripture lead us to belief in a one-time unified coming. At the end of the tribulation there is a resurrection, and it is called the first (Rev. 20). The apostle Paul says that after the resurrection of Christ, the next resurrection will be that of those who belong to Christ, AT HIS COMING (1 Cor. 15).

Finally, we are told that when the Lord Jesus comes, He will be coming "with all his saints" (1 Thess. 3:13). This will have to include all tribulation saints, both martyred and living. There is but one second advent.

### THE UNITY OF THE TRUMPET

Paul states directly and clearly that the raising of dead believers and the transforming of living believers will occur "at the last trumpet" (1 Cor. 15:52). Violence must be done in one of two ways to the plain meaning of the word "last" by those who hold to a pretribulation rapture of the Church. Obviously there are going to be seven trumpets that will sound during the tribulation. Then there will be another trumpet, which will blow at the end of the tribulation (Matt. 24:29–31). One way of destroying the natural meaning of "last" is to say that this trumpet is somehow different than those other biblical trumpets. But the Scripture gives no hint of distinguishing among trumpets or between trumpets. Even if one were to grant a difference between the last trumpet and the seven trumpets of judgment, it is not possible to make a distinction between the last trumpet and the one at the end of the tribulation, since they are both sounded for the gathering of God's people. The simplest conclusion is that they are one and the same.

The other way of canceling out the simple meaning of

"last" is to divide the word itself into two phases. The first phase would signify the rapture of the Church. But there is an obvious resurrection in Revelation 20:4, so there would have to be a second phase of the last trumpet after the tribulation. This kind of division has two obvious problems. First, Paul said that at the last trumpet there would be a resurrection of dead believers and a transformation of living believers. The pretribulation position can't allow this, however, since they believe that the living tribulation saints will not be transformed, but will go into the millennium in mortal bodies. Second, the word trumpet is clearly singular. We cannot have two last "trumpet." We also cannot have two trumpets that are the last trumpet. Last means last, and singular means singular.

### THE UNITY OF THE FIRST RESURRECTION

That resurrection called the "first" resurrection in Revelation 20:4 is divided by pretribulationists into at least three parts: the resurrection of the Church before the tribulation, the resurrection of the martyred saints of the tribulation, and the resurrection of the Old Testament saints (also after the tribulation). Obviously they have the same problem with the plain meaning of "first" that they do with "last" in interpreting the last trumpet. The word first can only mean the "first one in a series." Is there any other instance in the New Testament where we find a series of events that are in the same category (as here—"resurrections") where one event in that category (a particular resurrection) comes before the next to the last event, but where the speaker still calls this next to the last event "the first"? For example, given miracles #1, #2, #3, and #4, has anyone ever called miracle #3 "the first"? What this asks of reason is patently illogical. In like fashion, they divide the resurrection that Paul calls "those who are His at His coming" into a resurrection of those who belong to Christ before the tribulation and another resurrection of martyred saints (killed during the tribulation) at the end of the tribulation.

It does no good to say, as they do, that Christ's resurrection was the first. Obviously the Revelation text is talking about the resurrection of mortal believers, and this is the first. Christ was the first fruits and this group is the first resurrection. It could only occur to someone to divide this "first" into parts if he had previously already concluded that there was a resurrection of believers before this time. And that is precisely the boat pretribulationists found themselves in. Just as last means last, even so, first means first. And there is only one of each.

## UNITY

There is a unity passage that encourages in us an eagerness to "maintain the unity of the Spirit in the bond of peace," and continues by stating that "There is one body and one Spirit, just as you were called to the one hope that belongs to your call, one Lord, one faith, one baptism, one God and Father of us all, who is above all and through all and in all" (Eph. 4:3–7).

The pretribulation position takes the "one body" of verse 14 and fragments it into at least four bodies. They have the Body of Christ (the Church) raptured before the tribulation, the body of Christian martyrs who die for the Lord during the tribulation, the body of Old Testament saints, and the body of believers who live through the tribulation. They have two Spirits: one Who indwells believers before the tribulation and one Who "works" in the tribulation. Hope is divided into three starkly contrasting hopes. There is one hope for the Church—to escape the tribulation. There is another hope for the tribulation martyrs (and the Old Testament saints?)—the resurrection from the dead. There is still another hope for the saints who live through the tribulation—that they might endure the persecution without dying. There are two Lords rather than one. One is for believers before the tribulation. He forgives them in grace and gives them immortal bodies. There is still another Lord for believers during the tribulation. He calls them "blessed" for their endurance, and "rewards" them by allowing them to enter into a thousand-year kingdom in their tired mortal bodies. There are two faiths. There is a faith for pretribulation saints unto eternal life. For tribulation saints there is a faith unto a physical millennium. The baptism "with the Holy Spirit and with fire" offers a neat division. The first baptism "with the Holy Spirit" is for the Church before the rapture, and believers are thereby melded into the Body of Christ. The baptism "with fire" is reserved for the faithful after the rapture when they are plunged into the holocaust of the tribulation. There are two who can be called God and Father. One is the God and Father of a spiritual family, and His children are eternal sons of God. The other is the God and Father of an earthly clan and they become sons of the millennial kingdom.

The posttribulation position embraces the Ephesians 4 unity with open arms. For us there is one body. It is the same body Paul spoke of in 2:11–22: God reconciling "us both to God in one body through the cross." It is not just Jews and Gentiles made one in the cross, but all the blood-washed, right through those tribulation saints who had "washed their robes and made them white in the blood of the Lamb" (Rev. 7:14). We know but one Spirit. He is the Spirit Who is given to all who believe and Whose indwelling power will "give life" to our "mortal bodies" whether we believe before or during the tribulation (Rom. 4:22–5:5; 8:11). We see one hope and we joy to call it "blessed." It is the "appearing of the glory of our great God and Savior Jesus Christ" and our being forever with Him. It is enhanced in our earthly triumphs and anticipated and intensified in our trials and tribulations. We recognize one Lord. We joyfully await His second coming "with all his saints" whether they are called saints before His first coming, after His first coming, or after the onset of Daniel's 70th week. We hold to one faith. It is "the faith which was once for all delivered to the saints" (Jude 3). That faith is in the gospel of the great commission that Christ said would "be preached throughout the whole world" and that is called "eternal" as it is carried by an angel during the tribulation (Luke 24:47; Rev. 14:6). We own but one baptism. It is by the Spirit Who begat all who believe in Christ and Who joins us all to the Lord we love, regardless of when we believed. We acknowledge one God and Father. He is God and Father *of us all* **when** we believe, for whether we believe before the tribulation or during the tribulation, we all become sons of God at that moment of belief (John 1:12).

*What God has joined together,
let not man wrongly divide!*

# 12

## THE GREAT COMMISSION

*The Great Commission*

*Behold, the Mission's mystery concealed*
*And barely, dimly sensed in years of yore.*
*But lo! His purpose clearly now revealed—*
*To offer hope to earth's remotest shore.*

### THE WHOLE WORLD

The great commission was to be preached in "the whole world"—a corporate, all-inclusive view (Matt. 24:14). It was also to go to "all nations"—a separate, individualized view (Matt. 28:19).

The first offer was made to the Jews, but then to others also: to the Samaritans and the Gentiles. When Jesus sent the twelve out, He told them not to go either to the Gentiles or the Samaritans, but only to "the lost sheep of the house of Israel" (Matt. 10:5–7). This corresponds with John 1:11. He came to His "own home" (Judea) and offered Himself and His message to His "own people" (the house of Israel). But "his own people received Him not."

Among other Old Testament writers, Jeremiah foretold the widespread turning of Gentiles to the Lord: "O Lord, my strength and my stronghold, my refuge in the day of trouble, to thee shall the nations come from the ends of the earth and say: 'Our fathers have inherited nought but lies, worthless things in which there is no profit. Can man make for himself gods? Such are no gods!'

Therefore, behold, I will make them know, this once I will make them know my power and my might, and they shall know that my name is the Lord" (16:19–21). Actually the plan had always been to offer redemption to the Gentiles as well as the Jews. God simply implemented the plan within man's timeframe and toward his human state by saying first to the Jews: "Here is the Good News." Before the disciples were sent to the "house of Israel" in Matthew 10, we see Jesus healing the servant of the centurion, who was obviously a Gentile (Matthew 8;5-11). Furthermore, in the very midst of the encounter, Jesus tries to prepare His disciples for the day when all nations would be included in the offer. He said, "many will come from east and west and sit at table with Abraham, Isaac, and Jacob in the kingdom of heaven" (v. 11). The account of Jesus healing the daughter of the Canaanite woman is found in Matthew 15. Since the disciples begged Him to send her away, it was (perhaps) for their sake that He told her that He "was sent only to the lost sheep of the house of Israel." But He did heal her after proclaiming, so that His disciples could take it in, "O woman, great is your faith! Be it done for you as you desire" (Matt. 15:21–28). We don't know the exact time of the Good Shepherd discourse of John 10:1–18 in relation to this event, but in that passage He returned to the theme of lost sheep when He told His disciples, "I have other sheep, that are not of this fold; I must bring them also, and they will heed my voice. So there shall be one flock, one shepherd" (v. 16).

Jesus set up the plan for the commission in Matthew 16:17–19. The plan would include a dynamic—the building of the Church. It would also include a truth—Jesus is the Christ, the son of the living God. Furthermore, it would include a human leader or implementor—the apostle Peter. Finally, it would include an authority of access—the keys of the kingdom of heaven. The authority of access (the keys of the kingdom) was entrusted to the human leader (Peter) and not to all the apostles. When Jesus said, "I will give you the keys," He uses the singular "you" rather than the plural form. Peter would bind earthly access to the heavenly kingdom, or he would open up that access with those keys. Later, Jesus would give to all the disciples (and to us today by extension) the authority of ambassadors of reconciliation. He would say, "If you (plural) forgive the sins of any, they are forgiven; if you retain the sins of any, they are retained" (John 20:23). Because of this, we can say today to a person who rejects Christ that he is still in his sin, and to one who embraces Christ and His gracious offer, we can say with the full authority of God, "Your sins are forgiven." But Peter first had to use the keys of access in three distinct instances, on three separate occasions, as we will see later.

Jesus set up the program for the commission. John, speaking in retrospect, tells us that although Christ's "own people received him not," the offer would go beyond His "own people" (John 1:11–12). Indeed it would go "to all who received him, who believed in his name," and to them He would give "power to become children of God." Jesus had said that His followers were to "make disciples of all nations" (Matt. 28:19). He also said, "This gospel of the kingdom will be preached throughout the whole world" (Matt. 24:14). And He stated that "repentance and forgiveness of sin should be preached in his name to all nations, beginning from Jerusalem" (Luke 24:47). But it was not until His ascension that He laid down the schematic when He said to His disciples, "you shall receive power when the Holy Spirit has come upon you; and you shall be my witnesses in Jerusalem and in all Judea (first, to the Jews) and Samaria (second, to the Samaritans), and to the end of the earth (finally, to all the Gentile world)" (Acts 1:8).

In the book of Acts this pattern was followed, and in each instance it was Peter who used the "keys" to open the door of access in that precise order. Peter's leadership was seen after the ascension in Jerusalem. In the gathering of the disciples, Peter's name is mentioned first (Acts 1:13). Peter stood up to call for a replacement for Judas (1:15). And as they prayed together, the Spirit filled them and the Jewish church was born (2:1–4). Then it was Peter who stood up to open the door of access to heaven's kingdom to all Jews from various outlying regions and three thousand entered that kingdom. Thus Peter used the "keys" for the first time. Under Philip's preaching, many in Samaria believed (Acts 8:4–13). But it was not until Peter came down from Jerusalem and prayed for them that "they received the Holy Spirit" and the Samaritan church was born. So for the second time, Peter used the "keys." Then Peter was sent by a vision from God to the Gentile Cornelius and his family (Acts 10). When he preached to them and they believed, God poured out the Spirit "even on the Gentiles," and the Gentile church was born. Thus, Peter had used the "keys" for the third and final time. Henceforth, the kingdom would be open to all—to Jews, Samaritans, and Gentiles alike, and there would be one Church, one flock.

All that remains is the fulfillment of the commission. The Scriptures show that it will be done. Jesus said that the "gospel of the kingdom will be preached throughout the whole world, as a testimony to all nations" before the end would come (Matt. 24:14). More about that later. But as yet, the goal has not been achieved. In the mid 1990's, it was estimated that about 40 percent of the world, or twelve thousand "people groups" still had not been reached.

When the gospel message was opened to the Gentiles, and Paul preached to multitudes, the Jews who viewed these multitudes actually "were filled with jealousy, and contradicted what was said by Paul" (Acts 13:45). Paul responded to their hardness of heart both to the gospel and the Gentiles by saying, "It was necessary that the word of God should be spoken first to you. Since you thrust it from you, and judge yourselves unworthy of eternal life, behold, we turn to the Gentiles. For so the Lord has commanded us, saying, 'I have set you to be a light for the Gentiles, that you may bring salvation to the uttermost parts of the earth' " (13:46–47). In quoting from Isaiah 49:6 ("I will give you as a light to the nations, that my salvation may reach to the end of the earth"), Paul recognized that God had always planned to extend salvation to the nations beyond Israel.

In speaking to the council in Jerusalem, James said the Old Testament prophets "agree" with Isaiah (Acts 15:15–17). When he quoted Amos 9:11–12, he stated that God had said He would "rebuild the dwelling of David ... that the rest of men" (including "all the Gentiles") "may seek the Lord."

Then James added that "the Lord ... made these things known from of old" (v. 18). The Lord taught these things, but they were "hidden," because they were not "received" or accepted.

Thus (though the Church was a mystery—the winning of multitudes of Gentiles to salvation from everywhere in the world), this truth was there, even in the Old Testament, but it was neither understood nor accepted by Israel. God, however, had planned salvation through the Church to reach the end of the earth. So in the New Testament, the great commission calls for us to go to all nations, to the very end of the earth (Acts 1:8) and preach "this gospel of the kingdom ... throughout the whole world ... to all nations" before the end comes (Matt. 24:14).

### Mission Accomplished?

The question may arise whether that commission was ever fulfilled. We know that it is not fulfilled in our day. But what of the first century? Is there any record in the New Testament writings that it had been accomplished? There is only one passage that might suggest this in some translations. Romans 16:25–27 is a doxology to the Roman epistle. Although disputed by some, it is undoubtedly part of the letter. The difficulty comes in verse 26. The verb "made known" (γνωρισθεντος) comes at the very end of the verse. Most translations have followed the KJV and associated it with "to all nations" immediately preceding it. Thus we have: "made known to all nations." The RSV adopts the same translation at this point. But the expression "for obedience of faith to (or 'for') all nations" seems to be a unified construction that is better left unbroken. Therefore, the NIV would have a better rendering with "but now revealed and made known through the prophetic writings by the command of the eternal God, so that all nations might believe and obey him." Since "made manifest" comes at the beginning of the verse and "made known" at the end, however, the best rendering would be something like: "but now revealed through the prophetic writings by the command of the eternal God and made known so that all nations might believe and obey him."

Paul himself would contradict the KJV/RSV translations which suggest that the gospel had already been "made known to all nations." Just before this verse (Rom. 16:26), Paul had said that his ambition was "to preach the gospel not where Christ has already been named" (15:20–21). He indicates that this desire fulfills the Old Testament prophecy of Isaiah 52:15, which predicted that "They shall see who have never been told of him, and they shall understand who have never heard of him." He then said that, for this reason, he was hindered from visiting them, but that he hoped to see them on his way to Spain (possibly for the purpose of preaching the gospel again where it had not been heard). Certainly, pointing out a goal of working in unreached areas just a few verses before the statement of 16:26 would indicate without any doubt that there were a number of unreached areas.

He also told the Corinthian church, to their shame, that some people had "no knowledge of God" (1 Cor. 15:34). Then, in the second letter to the Corinthians, which was probably written in the same year as the Roman letter (a.d. 56), he told the Christians there: We have a desire to "preach the gospel in lands beyond you, without boasting of work already done in another's field" (10:16). The places Paul spoke of were in the known areas of the Roman Empire and in its borders or fringes; those areas Paul and his contemporaries were aware of in his day. In addition to the unreached areas he was aware of, there were other areas in what was to him the unknown world. There can, therefore, be no doubt: the world of that day was not reached.

Once again, the commission was "to make disciples of all nations" (Matt. 28:19); to preach this gospel "throughout the whole world" (Matt. 24:14); to see that "repentance and forgiveness of sin should be preached in his name to all nations, beginning from Jerusalem" (Luke 24:47); and to be "witnesses in Jerusalem and in all Judea and Samaria and to the end of the earth" (Acts 1:8). Out of this, there are critical, consuming, even all-important questions for the Church—for you and me today. Was the Lord earnest when He established the great commission (did He really mean it)? Did He intend the Church to be the instrument for carrying it out?

Did He expect it to be fulfilled literally? Was it conditional or absolute? Let us consider the questions in order.

First, was the Lord earnest when He established the great commission (did He really mean it)? At the last supper, just before His trial and crucifixion, Jesus made an intense statement to His disciples. He said "I have earnestly desired to eat this passover with you before I suffer" (Luke 22:15). Unless we understand the earnestness of communion and corporateness in that meeting, we fail also to understand substitution at Calvary. That was the meaning of the Eucharist—"my body which is given for you" (v. 19) and "the new covenant in my blood" (v. 20). And if we do not grasp the intensity of the life and death and death and life struggle that was Golgotha, then the depth of the river of reconciliation has swept past us without baptizing us. They are part and parcel, bone and sinew, warp and woof of each other. When Revelation speaks of the ransom of men from "every tribe and tongue and people and nation," the purchase price is also clearly stated: "thou wast slain and by thy blood didst ransom" them (Rev. 5:9). But if the seriousness of the ransom is clearly stated, we only have one half of the reconciliation equation. The other half is the commission. Paul not only declares that "in Christ God was reconciling the world to himself," but also clearly states the other half of that equation that He was also "entrusting to us the message of reconciliation" (2 Cor. 5:9). In effect, He set us to work completing in reconciliation what Christ began. This is not simply a fancy notion. Jesus Himself established our carrying forth of the plan and commission on the same high level that His part assumed when He said, "As the Father has sent me, even so I send you" (John 20:21). If He does not return until every segment of the world is reached, that is a spur in our side, since He will not return until we finish His divine commission. This, then, is our responsibility. The last words He left to echo in the hearts and consciences of His people down the corridors of the centuries were: "my witnesses ... to the end of the earth" (Acts 1:8). He was earnest.

Second, did He intend the Church to be the instrument for carrying out the great commission? Ephesians 2:11–3:13 gives an extended treatment of the one new man or body created through reconciliation in the cross. This new man or body is mystery-Church—believing Gentiles fused together with believing Jews. And through mystery-Church God is unfolding or demonstrating His manifold wisdom. So we have "the whole structure ... joined together.... the mystery of Christ ... that ... Gentiles are ... members of the same body ... the mystery ... that through the church the manifold wisdom of God might now be made known" (2:21; 3:4, 6, 9, 10). It is almost inconceivable that the unfolding or demonstrating of that wisdom does not include bearing it to the end of the earth in the completion of the great commission. And the instrument here for the demonstrating of that wisdom is none other than the Church.

But we also have the reconciliation passage in 2 Corinthians 5:16–21. Because God "for our sake ... made him to be sin who knew no sin" (v. 21), He could enter into "reconciling the world to himself" (v. 19). But to us, the Church, He not only "gave ... the ministry of reconciliation," but also "the message of reconciliation" (vv. 18–19). Both the work and the word are ours; the task and the tool. We are the instrument for that job, the only instrument we can find in the word. If there are those to be reconciled "from every tribe and tongue and people and nation," we are the ones chosen to do it (Rev. 5:9). If there are those to be reconciled "who have come out of the great tribulation," who "have washed their robes and made them white in the blood of the Lamb," then we, the Church, the only ones to be entrusted with the ministry and the message of reconciliation, are the instruments to effect that reconciliation (see Rev. 7:9, 14).

In His ministry, Jesus Himself gave examples of sometimes working only through human instruments before unleashing His power. In the resurrection of Lazarus, He called upon human hands (and waited for them) to move the stone before giving His resurrection command: "Lazarus, come out" (see John 11:38–44). When He appeared to the disciples on the seashore following His own resurrection, He provided a school of fish, but called on the disciples to cast their nets to bring them in. And thus He chose the Church as the agent of reconciliation to carry the great commission to its completion. Men cannot hear and believe without a preacher, but He has commanded only the Church to be the heralds of the gospel (Rom. 10:14). And He has said, "If you love me, you will keep my commandments" (John 14:14).

Third, did He expect the great commission literally to be fulfilled? Beyond expecting it, He made it an absolute requirement and pronounced it as an accomplished fact when He said, "And this gospel of the kingdom will be preached throughout the whole world, as a testimony to all nations; and then the end will come" (Matt. 24:14). Furthermore, when the Lamb is declared to be the only one worthy to open the scroll, the four living creatures and twenty-four elders will declare: "thou wast slain and by thy blood didst ransom men for God from every tribe and tongue and people and nation" (Rev. 5:9). There we see it accomplished. And "from every nation, from all tribes and peoples and tongues" there were those who had "come out of the great tribulation" and had "washed their robes and made them white in the blood of the Lamb" (Rev. 7:9, 14). Here, also, we see all reached.

It would be nearly impossible to find a more distributive or all-inclusive combination to show the reaching to the "end of the earth" than the use of these terms: "every tribe and tongue and people and nation." "Nation" (εθνος) means "nation" or "Gentiles" (foreign peoples). "People" (λαος) means "people" in a variety of ways—as a crowd, a populace, people versus leaders or versus the Pharisees, or people as a nation. "Tongues" (γλωσσα) can mean languages in general or unknown languages. "Tribe" (φυλα) refers either to a tribe of Israel or to a tribe of people otherwise. A tribe would probably be about the smallest division of distinguishable people. Thus, with the combination of the four terms, all the bases have been covered. We are talking about nothing less than a worldwide permeation of the gospel. In modern terms we would probable say "all people groups" of the world. In 1999, when this work was first published, the United States Center for World Mission in Pasadena, California claimed that there were twleve thousand of these "people groups" or about 40 percent of the world yet to be reached with the gospel. But the Scriptures say it will be done. The commission will literally be fulfilled.

Finally, was the great commission conditional or absolute? We have already seen the absolute character of Christ's pronouncement that the gospel will indeed "be preached throughout the whole world, as a testimony to all nations" before the end (Matt. 24:14). We have also seen the worldwide reaching of all people groups for Christ (Rev. 5:9; 7:9, 14). But what of the opposition from the adversary, Satan?

Harold Sevener, of The American Board of Missions to the Jews, made an interesting commentary on satanic opposition to Jewish evangelism. He stated:

As incredible as it may seem, I believe Satan and his angels have a special interest in Jewish evangelism which should really concern you and me. If this is true, it could have a profound impact on every child of God who's involved in bringing Jewish people to Christ. Please let me explain.

In Matt. 23:39, Jesus told the Jewish people that He would not come back again until they were ready to acknowledge Him as their Messiah. We read the same thing in Hosea 5:15–6:3.

> Thus, Satan will do everything within his power to keep Jews from turning to Christ. It's one of the ways he can try to delay our Lord's coming back to earth. So everyone who is involved in Jewish evangelism can expect to become a special target of Satan's attacks. (From *The Chosen People*, April, 1983).

This is undoubtedly true. It is also true that he will have special attacks against those trying to complete "all nation" world evangelism to bring in "the full number of the Gentiles." There is a clear indication in Matthew 16:18 that there would be satanic opposition to the Church and to the building of that Church. When Jesus came, Satan sought to defeat Him by temptation and then by death. Satan could not know that the death of Jesus was planned and actually would be the instrument of his own defeat.

But he does know clearly that the goal of the resurrected Christ was to take the good news of reconciliation to the whole world. And Satan fights with might and main against the success of this mission. Therefore, where the gospel is preached, Satan is there to oppose it. Every tactic of Satan against believers is aimed against this endeavor. If he influences them to fall into temptation, if he brings illness and weakness to them, if he causes discouragement, if he makes them look ridiculous or foolish, if he brings bickering and division in their midst, if he drives a wedge of a party spirit between them, if he causes them to doubt, if he entices them with the baubles of materialism, if he causes them to follow "good" and "noble" pursuits that divert them from the best goal, it is all to that greater end of turning them aside from completing the great commission. This is why his agent, the Antichrist, will use the death penalty against Christians so extensively in the tribulation. They will be "beheaded for their testimony to Jesus and for the word of God" (Rev. 20:4). But success for the commission is absolute. The "gates of Hades" or the "powers of death" will not prevail against the Church and the building of that Church (Matt. 16:18). The Church will be planted in every culture and people group.

Thus, if individuals are to be ransomed from every tribe and tongue and people and nation, then it should be obvious that the Lord intended for the Church to accomplish this task and that they indeed do accomplish it. But it also shows us that it is a task that must yet be fulfilled or finished since we have not yet reached all people groups of the world. The goal, however, is absolute and the success is assured, since He who is in us is greater than he who is in the world (see I John 4:4).

In the first century, the gospel was carried to much of the known world. In the great commission, Christ commanded the disciples to to go to the earth's extremities with the good news. Paul was its chief missionary. His aim was to preach "not where Christ has already been named." Peter was the missionary mathematician or logician. He heard Christ say that the gospel message had to be preached everywhere in the world before the end came. So he added his twos and came up with a four. In his second letter he says that the only reason God seems to be slow in bringing in the day of the Lord is because of His patience and His desire to see all men reached, because He doesn't want them to be lost (see 2 Pet. 3:9-12). And there are three things for believers to do before that day, or to prepare for that day. First, we should pursue purity—we ought to live "lives of holiness and godliness" (v. 11). Second, we need to exercise our own patience to match God's by "waiting for ... the coming" of that day (v. 12). Finally, we need to be about the task of "hastening the coming of the day of God" (v. 12). If the gospel must be preached in all the world and if God is patiently holding off His day to allow the reaching of the lost because He doesn't want them to perish, then we can speed up the coming of that day by finishing the job of evangelism in the world. He won't come until we do it.

### Missions: 1000 Versus Missions: 2000

Nine centuries passed and the year 1000 approached. The Holy Roman Empire had disintegrated with the death of Charlemagne's son, Lewis. But a few years later it was restored under Otto the Great. The papacy had reached a peak, but by now had seriously deteriorated into its darkest hour. Though the pope was supposed to be the head of the church, it was actually the emperor who held this power. As Philip Schaff says, "The demoralization began in the state, reached the church and culminated in the papacy ... No church or sect in Christendom ever sank as low as the Latin church in the tenth century" (From History of the Christian Church, vol 4, p. 280).

Actually, Christianity in these Middle Ages was confined mainly to Europe. There were large pagan areas that were unreached, and much of the "missionary" work of the time was done through the educative process rather than through evangelism. Some of the pagans were "reached," but most had their own native religions, and aside from the unreached pagans, there was at least 10 percent of the world of that day (in the Euro-Asian-North African area) that was dominated by the opposing religious force of Mohammedanism. Beyond their unreached world lay another world that was not yet known and, therefore, also unreached. America, for example, would not even be discovered for another five hundred years. Proportionately, more of their world was unreached than of ours today. Also, their "reaching" was not evangelizing. And they lacked the zeal and ability to do so. Thus the commission was far from complete in their day.

In a.d. 1000 there was a Roman Empire of sorts. But the restored Holy Roman Empire was a far cry from both the Roman Empire of old and from the Roman Confederacy described in Scripture for the last days. Israel was not only no nation at the time, but the Holy Land was under the occupation and control of the Mohammedan Arabs as it had been since the seventh century. Nothing suggested a political or religious climate that would fit the picture for the last days. There was no semblance of a fullness of time for the return of Christ.

When Christ came the first time, He came in "the fullness of time." The Pax Romana set the climate for successful missionary endeavors. There was a common (κοινη) Greek language so that the message could be heard and received by nearly all. The Roman highway system and well-arranged sea routes made missionary travel relatively simple. The Jewish law prepared the Jews in a negative way for the gospel message, since they could not be justified by that law. And the philosophical and religious systems of Greece and Rome were pretty well bankrupt at the time, so that every man was practically a law unto himself. This could be seen in the attitude of the Greeks on Mars Hill in Acts 17. One of the Greek philosophers even stood up in a meeting before Christ's advent and set forth the quandary: "Can God forgive sin? It may be, but I don't see how."

Yet, even though the prophetic pieces were not in place on the threshold of the year a.d. 1000—even though the overall climate could not justly be called "the fullness of time" for eschatology—there was a storm cloud over Europe. Everything seemed to be "going to the dogs." Therefore, some who were ordinarily judicious, responsible believers invested the approach of the second millennium with a special magic. As Schaff put it, "The dissolution of the world seemed to be nigh at hand. Serious men looked forward to the terrible day of judgment at the close of the first millennium of the Christian era, neglected their secular business, and inscribed donations of estates and other gifts to the church with the significant phrase "appropinquante mundi termino" ('at the approaching end of the world') (History of the Christian Church, p. 280).

As a.d. 2000 approached we were poised on the brink of a new dawning. We looked in the face of a new millennium. The year a.d. 2000 drew on with an accelerating downhill momentum. Did we make the same mistake as some of our brothers a millennium ago? Was there magic in the number? Couldn't Christ come in a.d. 2169? Indeed. It seemed fitting, however, that His Millennium would forge its beginning at the end of one of our flawed ones. But was there something beyond the number itself? Were there other factors that said, "The Judge is standing at the doors"? Could we pick up echoes of the approaching hoof beats from the four horsemen of the Apocalypse?

In terms of looking for the day of the Lord in the tenth century, perhaps the strongest point to be made besides political and religious disintegration, was the fact that Europe did have a Roman government.

Just coming out of the threefold division of the kingdoms of Charles, Lewis, and Lothair (following the death of Lewis the Pious), it was restored under Otto. But it was not the glory that was Rome and it was not a ten-nation confederacy, so great changes would have needed to take place to prepare for its fragmentation and ultimate lawless leader.

Today we do have the kind of strong/loose confederacy seen in the image of the book of Daniel. In fact, our generation has seen the first iron/clay kind of confederacy in Europe since the Roman Empire ceased to exist as a united world power. It would require some adjustments now for the number of the confederated nations to shrink back to ten again.

Also today we have witnessed what some might have considered a miracle even in the early days of the 20th century. Since a.d. 70 Israel had been, for all practical purposes, a non-entity in the Holy Land. Today Israel is not only a presence in the land, but a bona fide nation that has repeatedly fought off enemies many times superior to her in manpower. It is obvious that for the tribulation to usher in the last stages of the last days, Israel had to be a viable force in the land.

Even a century ago, not only did Israel not exist as such a

force, but only the foolhardy suggested that the armies from the extreme north of the Holy Land could be identified as Russian armies. Such a land of peasants surely could not represent such power and pose such a threat. But in the space of only a few decades she has moved from a land of peasantry to a world power.

Given the world population of even a century ago, it was doubtless felt by many that the hordes mentioned in Revelation 9:16 had to be figurative. After all, how could even a confederacy of nations come up with a force that was numbered "twice ten thousand times ten thousand"? At the time, our entire nation was not even two hundred million. And yet today China itself has the capability of fielding just such an army.

There is a prophecy that when Jesus comes "with the clouds ... every eye will see him" (Rev. 1:7). In the first century, which originally heard these words, and in the tenth century, which prepared for the event, the statement presented no problem. For them, the earth was flat, and anyone, therefore, could look up in the air and see such an event from anywhere, if it happened high up in the sky. As we look back on those two time periods, however, we know that it was actually a tremendous problem, since we know that even as the world is a sphere today, it was also a sphere in their day. They simply didn't know it.

If the Lord had returned a millennium ago, how could people in outlying areas that they knew of then (like Russia, Norway, the British Isles, Spain, and Ethiopia) have seen the Lord returning in the skies above Jerusalem? And how would potential "viewers" in the far corners that they didn't even know about (such as Japan, Alaska, Argentina, South Africa, and Australia) see that event? It would have taken an astounding miracle of physics. The Lord could have caused the light to refract or bend around the curvature of the earth, or He could have made the earth transparent, but in either case He would have to add a dimension of magnification so that those far off could see. Or Jesus could have returned slowly in a polar orbit so that He passed over every part of the world before touching His foot on the earth. But the Lord did not use blatantly miraculous means for establishing the "fullness of time" at the first advent, and it seems unlikely that He would at the second advent (aside from His judgments during the tribulation, and even many of these might be accomplished through the application of physical laws that we now understand). Certainly the modern affairs of state mentioned above (Israel becoming a nation, Europe becoming a confederacy, Russia becoming a power, and China becoming populous) came about by basically natural means.

In today's technology, and particularly with our dramatic breakthroughs in the area of communications, a worldwide viewing of any event anywhere in the world by people over the entire sphere is commonplace. Ever since we first placed three synchronous satellites in their "stationary" orbits around the earth and spaced them apart so that they covered the entire curvature of the globe, we have had worldwide transmission and reception of events happening at any given point. And we have done much refining since that time. Thus, if tomorrow an amazing and unexplainable disturbance began to take place in the skies above Jerusalem, cameras could be trained upon it, it could be transmitted to all the major television networks of the world, and everybody on earth would be able to see it as it happened.

So in our generation we have seen affairs of state and technology combine in what appears to be a new "fullness of time" to prepare for the second advent, just as affairs of state and technology and "religion" combined to prepare for the first advent. What about the "religious" aspect of the world today? Is it also joining together with politics and technology in a conspiracy of readiness? Or, since the completion of the great commission is given as a necessity prior to the end, is there any possibility of the task being finished in our generation? If that could be answered in the affirmative, we could expect to see all the other final events fall into line as well.

The 20th century—particularly the latter half of the century—witnessed a phenomenal "explosion" of interest not only in missions, but in the concept of completing the great commission as well. Furthermore, among evangelicals there was a sweeping zeal to set a.d. 2000 as the target date for seeing the goal reached. Before examining this phenomenon, however, let us take a brief look at missions from Acts to the present generation.

## MISSION THRUST: PENTECOST TO THE TWENTIETH CENTURY

Viewing roughly two millennia of missions in a broad way produces a remarkable pattern that looks something like this: A. 300 years; B. 200 years; C. 1000 years; D. 200 years; E. 300 years. Looking at the periods in terms of matching up similar periods, however, would produce a radar picture: A; B; C; B; A. That is to say, the first period (a.d. 30 to 300) and the last period (a.d. 1700 to 2000) have a remarkable resemblance that produces a mirror effect. This same reflecting pattern appears in the second period (a.d. 300 to 500) and the fourth (a.d. 1500 to 1700). In each case the latter period complements the former; the other bookend is put into place.

### Pentecost to A.D. 300: Original Missions

The first period (the first three centuries) was the beginning of what was basically "pure" missions. The gospel was preached throughout the Roman Empire. Evangelism was the order of the day. People believed and were joined to the universal Church. By the end of this period, approximately 20 percent of the Roman Empire had become Christians. This victory was won in the face of great persecution. It began in Acts 5 and continued throughout much of this period.

### A.D. 300 to 500

The next two centuries saw great change in the relationship between the Church and the State. In the decade between a.d. 311 and 321, many liberties were granted to Christians. Christians and all others were granted the right to follow the religion of their choice. The clergy was not subjected to military duties, and their property was not taxed. Customs offensive to Christians were abolished. Sunday had to be observed by civil entities. For all practical purposes, Constantine had made Christianity the religion of the State.

Since this arrangement set up a practical theocracy, subjects were automatically assumed to be Christians. Over the next two centuries, any external opposition to Christianity was defeated. The Church that had become secular had also become largely pagan. What the Empire could not do by persecution (stop true missionary work) it had accomplished by giving privilege and power to the Church.

### A.D. 500 to 1500

The next one thousand years (a.d. 500 to 1500) are called by some the Middle Ages and by others the Dark Ages. Each term in its own way seems suitable. This period lies between the first five hundred years of church history and our present five hundred year period, which some see as the final five hundred years of church history. It was "dark" in a number of ways, but not in all respects. It was beneficial in terms of the preservation of Scripture. In many monasteries the Scriptures were faithfully copied and studied. But it was otherwise a dark time for investigation and research in general. It was a dark time for the Church overall. The papacy grew strong and then weakened. The concept that the ruler could tell the subjects what they believed continued into this period. For example, right in the midst of that time (a.d. 922) when Russia's King Vladimir was baptized as a Christian, his subjects followed his example—by force. Christians were, in this respect, much like their Mohammedan opponents, who won converts by the sword. Obviously, this was not the evangel the Church was called to spread. Though here and there some true gospel work was done, it was a very dark day for missions.

### A.D. 1500 to 1700

The Europe of 1505 was fallow ground. There were subtle currents in the air bearing seeds of reformation. A young man of peasant stock walked toward Erfurt, Germany, where he had just worked his way to a Master's degree. Storm clouds thickened, and when lightning crashed around him, he fell to the ground like a modern-day Paul and vowed to become a monk. Thus, in a flash of light, the seed was planted that would take Luther to a monastic life of studying the Scriptures at Erfurt and Wittenburg. Ten years later, after receiving his Doctor of Biblicus degree, he was back at the university and the monastery lecturing on books of the Bible. He had just finished the Psalms and was going through Romans. The next year he would lecture on Galatians. Somewhere in these lectures a new light began to shine. It was not a passing flash of lightning, but a sunrise whose increasing brightness would leave Germany and the world in a radiance that would change them forever: THE JUST SHALL LIVE BY FAITH. And the young tree of Reformation saw the light of day.

For the Reformation, however, "missions" would be restricted mainly to their own "Jerusalem" for the next two centuries. There was a church in Europe that needed their attention. Members of this church had moved away from indulgences and works in growing numbers to the liberation of the teachings of grace and justification. The work of missions was for the most part left to the Counter-Reformation in the Catholic Church. Rome had seen its numbers and power and influence eroded by the dynamic of the Reformation. As noble as some of these new missionaries were, however, those efforts need to be contrasted to missions as they were at the beginning—in the first three centuries when the gospel was preached and those who believed belonged to Christ and His worldwide Body. Now there was an Eastern Church and a Western Church. But there was also the new kid on the block—the Reformation Church. When Rome undertook her Counter-Reformation missionary efforts, she had to be certain that all of the new works (hospitals and schools as well as churches) were committed to loyalty to the Mother Church, which was not the same as dedication to Christ. Some efforts were so bent on gaining numbers of loyal followers that the missionaries adopted many of the local pagan customs and simply baptized the customs to make them "Christian." The Jesuits, among other examples, transferred the Chinese ancestor worship to the worship of Catholic saints. In fact, the Dominican and Franciscan missionaries brought so much pressure to bear on the use of these tactics that it resulted in a papal condemnation of those practices.

## A.D. 1700 to the Present: Modern Missions

So, we have seen the original missionary movement in the first three centuries, the Church-State fusion in the next two centuries, the medieval, "dark," millennium brought on through that union, and the two centuries of the break up of that alliance occasioned by the Reformation. With the onset of the eighteenth century, the period that could be called modern missions began. What distinguished it from endeavors between a.d. 300 and 1700 is that it offered its hearers justification by grace and forgiveness through faith. In essence, it picked up the baton of the original missionary work that had been dropped somewhere in the fourth century. Evangelical missions have evolved over the last three centuries, while the goal started by the Counter-Reformation missionary movement has remained basically intact: enlist loyalties for the Mother Church. The three stages of Evangelical mission evolution were: first, the establishment of denominational churches tied to the church group sending out its missionaries; second, the development of interdenominational or nondenominational sending boards and the establishing of New Testamental churches on the field, free from sectarian ties; third, the shifting of responsibility and governing to the foreign churches, making them truly indigenous and independent. Consequently the work of missions has finally come full circle. And we are once again headed for the goal.

A small, tentative beginning was made in modern missions by German Pietists, and in 1705 the Halle-Danish mission was founded. This was followed shortly by Moravian missions, and then Quakers began to reach out to foreign lands. It was not until near the end of the century, however, that modern missions would be launched with a dynamic that has continued growing until the present day. William Carey became captivated by the need of the heathen. He, in turn, convinced twelve Baptist ministers in England to establish the Particular Society for Propaganda of the Gospel among the Heathen in 1792 (they would later become the

Baptist Missionary Society). Three years later the London Missionary Society would be formed. Then in 1799 came the organizing of the Church Missionary Society of the Evangelicals in the Church of England, which, until the middle of our own century, remained the largest of Protestant mission societies. In that same decade and in the first three decades of the next century, mission societies sprang up in other European countries as well. In Scotland there was The Scottish Missionary Society, the Glasgow Missionary Society, and the Church of Scotland Mission Boards; in Switzerland, the Basel Evangelical Missionary Society; in Denmark, the Danish Missionary Society; in Germany, the Berlin Missionary Society; and in France, the Paris Missionary Society. Then in America at that time two were founded—the American Board of Commissioners for Foreign Missions (1810) and the Baptist Missionary Union (1814).

During this period, the adventure of vital missionaries again picking up the baton and passing it on captivated the imagination of those at home who had sent them. Carey would go to India; Robert Morrison, to China; John Williams, to the South Sea Island; Robert Moffat, to South Africa; William Ellis, to Madagascar; Alexander Duff, to India; and, of course, David Livingstone, to Africa. During the same period, and strengthening the impetus for evangelizing through missions, came the revival movement under the likes of John Newton, William Wilberforce, Joseph and Isaac Milner, and John and Charles Wesley in England, and Robert and James Haldane in Scotland. The impetus of these four decades (1790–1830) continued in the nineteenth century, and the majority of today's missionary societies were founded after 1830.

The first dynamic stride in modern missions came at the end of the eighteenth century with William Carey and his fellow missionary warriors. The second came near the end of the nineteenth. D. L. Moody was hosting the annual Northfield Conference in Northfield Massachusetts in August, 1885. A. T. Pierson was speaking on missions and urged "believers everywhere" to join in the task of completing the great commission by 1900. Moody was so challenged that he appointed a committee of six to work out a declarative document that would throw down the gauntlet of global evangelization to the Christians of the world.

The very salutation sounded like the opening of the epistle of James: "To Fellow believers of every name, scattered throughout the world, Greeting." And the burden of the letter carried an earnestness and practicality worthy of James, lamenting the plight of "nearly a thousand million of the human race ... yet without the Gospel; vast districts ... wholly unoccupied." But a mathematically sound equation was offered as a solution: "If but ten millions, out of four hundred millions of nominal Christians, would undertake such systematic labor as that each one of that number would, in the course of the next fifteen years, reach one hundred other souls with the Gospel message, the whole present population of the globe would have heard the good tidings by the year 1900!" After quoting the great commission, reminding the hearers that Christ said the gospel would be preached worldwide before the end, and citing Peter's exhortation that we should "look for and hasten the coming of the day of God," the framers of the document posed a question that, sadly, is not raised today: "and what if our inactivity delays His coming?" They called for "prevailing prayer" and a great council meeting on missions in London or New York. A meeting did take place in London the following year and the needs of the world were considered, but the Church did not accept the challenge, and 1900 came and went with the dream unfulfilled. Calvinists would say that it wasn't God's time; Arminians would claim that men weren't ready for the idea.

Even though the Northfield Convention document of 1885 did not succeed in its goal of world evangelization by 1900, Moody initiated something else two years after the Northfield Conference that was destined to shape America into the largest foreign missionary training pool the modern world had ever known. Moody had done great things for God at home and abroad. But he regretted his lack of training. He envisioned a school where dedicated young men could be trained as pastors, but also as missionaries. And thus began the Moody Bible Institute. Certainly there were other schools for missionary training before this, but this one allowed youth without a college degree to study the Bible and related subjects and carry a knowledge of the Bible and redemption with a missionary zeal to the far corners of the world. Other such schools sprang up in her wake, and soon these institutions became the major suppliers of missionaries from our land or from any land.

Unfortunately, however, two elements at this time worked against the completion of the task of world evangelization. First, by the turn of the century, the fervor that had produced the Northfield Convention document had cooled. Some accepted the challenge. But it was not embraced with enthusiasm by the "disciples everywhere" to whom it had been addressed. And when 1900 came and went, the concept "by the year 1900" was altered to "in this generation." Furthermore, there was a national euphoria in the first decade that spilled over into the thinking of some of the Church. Some theologians even speculated that man was making such strides that we might actually be in the Millennium. After 1914 and WWI such optimism was shattered, however, and never really returned.

The second element that blunted the driving force of the goal of world evangelization was more complex and sadly ironic. The seeds of the irony appeared in the final challenge found in the Northfield document. The concluding sentence before the benediction exhorted: "Obedient to our marching orders, let us 'go into the world, and preach the gospel to every creature,' while from our very hearts we pray, 'Thy kingdom come.' " The Northfield Conference stood in the tradition of Bible Conferences that were held at that time in England and America. Although missions was a theme in these meetings, the topic was generally prophetic. J. N. Darby was a leading force in these conferences and he proclaimed the concepts of Dispensationalism, which he had developed and which featured a pretribulation rapture of the Church.

Even though a number of early supporters of these views parted company with Darby upon further study, two significant groups joined his ranks and guaranteed the success of the movement. One included the editors of the Scofield Reference Bible and the other, the organizers of the Bible school movement. For most of the schools, Scofield was the acknowledged official study Bible. This spawned two generations of students who were to be future pastors and missionaries spreading both the gospel message and Dispensationalism. There was an inherent conflict that did not immediately appear and that is still not recognized by some to this day. It has been suggested that the embryonic problem showed up in the Northfield document in the words "preach the gospel to every creature" and in the following charge to pray "Thy kingdom come."

Dispensational teaching in the Bible schools fostered a zeal for preaching the gospel—particularly for preaching it on the mission fields of the earth and especially on those fields where Christ was not yet known. But a teaching promoted side by side with this was the concept that the return of Christ was very near. In fact, it was used as an incentive to get out into the work quickly, since we did not know how much time was left for us to do the work. There has been an evolution in that particular doctrine from the beginning of this century until now. Just before 1900 in the Northfield document, they were praying from the heart, "Thy kingdom come" from the Lord's Prayer. In the first quarter of the 20th century, signs were seen as being fulfilled and the coming was drawing near. In the second quarter, signs began to take on a new significance. After some notable development in the world, here and there speakers would venture that "Now the Lord can come at any time," and the spotlight focused more intensely on imminence. This was especially true in 1948 (the year of the creation of nation Israel) and following. So keen was the anticipation and so critical was the "any-momentness" that Bible students were dissuaded from more advanced studies in favor of advancing into the ripened fields and harvesting while it was yet called today, for the night was coming when no man could work. Since the middle of that century the urgency has become, if possible, even more acute. What was heard only sporadically before the birth of Israel in 1948 has become nearly a unanimous theme among dispensationalists. One hears it from speaker after speaker and reads it in author after author: "There is no prophetic event that must happen before the rapture."

The logical consequence of such a teaching was a weakening of pioneer resolve. The work of missions certainly did not cease, but it suffered a heart attack. Numbers were more important than penetration and permeation. It was more important to win as many as we could in what little time we might have left than to consider toppling the strongholds of the frontiers. That would take prayer and effort and planning. And we might not have time for that.

Between a.d. 300 and 1700 the enemy had brought missions to an effective inactivity by a wedding of the Church to the State. In our century what better way could he devise for delaying or defeating completion of the missionary task—the great commission to the very end of the earth—than to concede the importance of winning souls, but to soothe the very conscience of missions by suggesting that we do not have to finish this job, because it isn't a requirement for Christ's coming for His Bride? The implications of what could be considered "spiritual" reasoning ran thus: His coming is near; nothing needs to happen before then; He could come today; we may not have much time to work; let us work quickly (let us get some work done) before He comes and the rapture takes us away. And at this point the subtlety that is worthy of a fox (or a serpent) takes over, but at a deep subconscious level. Deep down the question gnaws: WHY? If we do not have THE TASK (worldwide penetration and permeation of every people group with the gospel) to complete before the rapture, then what is the urgency? We have been engaged in a sort of chess game with our foe. He has allowed us the thrill of capturing his pawns in the center of the board, but it has been a strategy of sacrifice on his part to keep us from his end of the field—the uttermost part—and his key pieces. We have needed more Auca gambits, the leaving of the center to gain an advantage at his end, even if we must give up pieces in order to mount a threat there.

### Latter Day Missions

But amazing things happened in the last quarter of the 20th century. Some began before that time but have grown to a quiet crescendo in our present day. Multitudes have turned to the Lord. Billy Graham made note of this in Decision magazine, where he stated that "in the past 15 years there has been the greatest evangelical renaissance that we have known in several centuries. Throughout the world God is at work. Thousands of people daily are coming to know Jesus Christ as their Lord and Savior" (Decision, July-August, 1998). And much of this is in areas formerly considered mission fields: Africa, Indonesia, Korea, Muslim territories, and areas of South America. Amazingly, we have witnessed in our time a great work of the Spirit among Muslims. The Lord has appeared to many of them in dreams and visions to turn their hearts to Jesus Christ. Perhaps the most surprising of all has been the revelation of what had happened behind what was the bamboo curtain in China. It had been generally supposed that when our Western missionaries were forced out of the land, the fledgling church there withered or died. What a wondrous revelation to find that it had not only survived but had also thrived under communist persecution. There existed not only a church, and scores of thousands of house churches, but also literally millions of Chinese Christians. One of the advantages of this development in the third world, beyond the sheer number of new believers, is the vast missionary pool this has created in those lands. But the strategic benefit of this new reservoir is that there are closed or frontier lands that would willingly accept natives of some of those lands, but would steadfastly reject emissaries from the Western world.

One of the most electric manifestations in the 20th century's last quarter was the renewal of the vision of the Northfield document. Completing the great commission "by the end of the century" had again become a battle cry. But then it was also "by the end of this millennium." What is astounding is what has taken place in the thinking of many dispensationalists and many others in the pretribulation rapture school. For those with a posttribulation position, the completing of the task has never been a problem. But even though many in the pretribulation camp still are lifting their eyes heavenward daily and in that gaze removing their eyes from the review of the corners of the harvest field, still many others are making the field their concerted study and display a refreshing openness. Some, while still holding the pretribulation position, act as if it depended on them to complete the task. They are much like the man who believed that salvation came from the Lord, but lived as if it depended on him. It is as if they have either deserted the concept of an "any day" rapture or have pushed the obvious contradiction between that idea and the necessity of completing the commission to a far corner of their minds. Whether for one of these reasons or yet another, the development is a happy one. Given their present dedication, one could only wonder at the zeal that might consume them if they truly believed His coming for us actually depended on us finishing that commission.

## Now!

It seems as if the the fourth quarter of the 20th century brought with it a radical current of resolution. It was as if a breath from above whispered in command: "NOW! It is time." Perhaps the first two men to translate that voice were two Americans in Lausanne, Switzerland in 1974. One of those men was evangelist Billy Graham, who had organized the International Congress on World Evangelization that was taking place right then in Lausanne. The other was a former missionary, Ralph Winter, who was then a professor at the School of World Mission at Fuller Theological Seminary. Winter brought the plenary address on a Saturday morning at that congress. He spoke of language and cultural barriers that separated us from more than half of the world's population. The statistic that startled the hearers was the fact that five out of six of the unsaved people of the world are in that unreached half of the world. He represented this as the challenge of the unfinished task.

Ralph Winter would leave his post at Fuller in considering that challenge. In 1976 he founded the United States Center for World Missions in Pasadena, California. Other such centers would spring up in the Midwest in 1984 and in New England in 1986, as well as overseas. The center was devoted exclusively to new missionary outreach—among people groups not yet reached. This concentration of focus went under varied names. One time it might be the "hidden peoples," another time, the "unreached," and again the "frontiers." In each case, however, they referred to those who have not heard and from whom people have not been won to Christ. Their goal was stated simply: "A Church for Every People by the Year 2000," which was nothing short of seeing the missionary task completed—a viable church in each "people group" by that date. Extraordinary things happened at the center. Dozens of missionary agencies stationed representatives at the center in a pooling of minds bent toward a single goal. Never before had there been a uniting of such groups at one place for the purpose of working out strategy and of planning mobilization to make it happen. Still, the bulk of the iceberg lay beneath the surface. Much was happening in scattered areas, in separate groups and organizations, and in individual minds and hearts, which all tended toward the same goal, as if a mind were marshaling its body parts independently toward a common thrust. But more of that after a look at the Lausanne Congress.

There was a preliminary meeting to Lausanne 1974. Billy Graham organized the World Congress on Evangelism to be held in Berlin in 1966. From one hundred different countries, twelve hundred delegates assembled. To maintain a sense of continuity between that assembly and Lausanne 1974, there were intervening regional conferences—in Singapore, Minneapolis, Bogota, Ottawa, and so on. Then came Lausannc 1974. Time called it "a formidable forum, possibly the widest-ranging meeting of Christians ever held." Probably the key element of that congress was the vision of realizing world evangelization. In practical terms also, strategies for reaching specific people groups were considered. Their basic "mandate" was "to hasten the evangelization of all peoples of the world in obedience to the command of Jesus Christ and in anticipation of his return," and they had as a stated objective "to advance biblical organization as reflected in the Lausanne Covenant among all the peoples including those unreached people groups where the church has not yet taken root indigenously." The vision of Lausanne was so deep and the flame so bright that what began simply as Lausanne '74 developed into The Lausanne Movement.

In 1983 there was the Amsterdam Congress on Evangelism. Leighton Ford stressed the inescapable implications of Matthew 24:14 where Jesus said that this gospel definitely would be preached in the whole world before the end. He stated that "in some way the return of Christ depends on the repentance of man, and evangelism is the link ... If Jesus says it will be done, it will be done." Then in a 1984 bulletin of the Lausanne Committee they saw as their vision: "completing the task of world evangelization." Billy Graham (honorary chairman of the committee) called for a cooperative effort, saying, "It is time to set aside all needless duplication of resources—whether in terms of people, ideas, tools, strategies or finances. The task is enormous; working in isolation or separately will only delay its completion." This kind of dedication to world missions was also pressed by John R. W. Stott, who said, "To do nothing about the Christian mission in areas of the world where he is not acknowledged is to deny his Lordship. And to deny the Lordship of Jesus in any respect is to set ourselves against the purpose for which he died and rose again."

Even as the Northfield document had said that above all else their "immediate and imperative need is a new spirit of earnest and prevailing prayer," so in this generation a counterpart to that burden is seen in a movement called the Great Commission Prayer Crusade. It was set up under Bill Bright and his Campus Crusade for Christ movement and is implemented by Ben Jennings, who travels throughout the world and organizes prayer groups and prayer campaigns whose purpose is to pray earnestly for world evangelism and the completing of the great commission. In addition to the prayer thrust, Campus Crusade's missionary staff grew from nine thousand to eleven thousand from 1980–1981 and serves in over fifty countries. But they also held EXPLO '85 to "accelerate the fulfillment of the great commission" and they expanded this in EXPLO '90. They have a goal of raising a billion dollars and of seeing the salvation of billions of people.

## Mission 2000

The year 2000 became a goal for world evangelization among established denominational groups. In the November 4, 1987 issue of the Evangelical Beacon, the official publication of the Evangelical Free Church, Trinity Evangelical Divinity School's Dr. David Hesselgrave represented a growing conviction of evangelical leaders in stating that the world could indeed be evangelized by a.d. 2000. America's largest evangelical denomination, the Southern Baptists established three clear objectives for itself: (1) To reach every living person in the world with the gospel by the year 2000; (2) To provide every person on earth the opportunity to hear the gospel by the close of the century; and (3) To enable every person in the world to have an opportunity to hear and respond to the gospel of Christ by the year 2000. In July 1987, the largest missions gathering in history (35,000) met in New Orleans. Their announced aim was to be able to give the Lord Jesus a special two thousand year birthday present—believers from every people group on earth. Near the end of 1987 there was a missions conference in Sao Paulo called COMIBAM. They had a goal of being able to reach the world with the gospel of Christ by 2000. The Lausanne Committee's magazine, World Evangelization, took as its theme for 1988 "Unto 2000 A.D." In the January 1988 issue of Moody Monthly they ran a whole page entitled "Mission Groups Push to Reach World by 2000." The same month, Christianity Today featured the article "Completing the Task by 2000 A.D.—Reasonable Goal or Wild-Eyed Dream?" According to estimates, there were more than four hundred different plans proposed by Christian individuals and groups to finish the work of evangelizing the world before that century closed. In January 1989, the Global Consultation on World Evangelization by A.D. 2000 and Beyond met in Singapore. This was considered an extremely important gathering since many of the originators of these plans were at that conference and work was done on coordinating some of their activities.

The phenomenon had become so widespread that it could not escape the notice of the press. On January 2, 1988, the Los Angeles Times ran a half-page article on the subject, "Christian Groups Reset World Evangelization Goal for Year 2000." This is not to say that everything in the article was necessarily supportive. For example, it highlighted many of the obstacles. In fact, not everything was encouraging even in some of the Christian coverage of the goal. Both the Moody Monthly and the Christianity Today articles contained a paragraph that would cast doubt on the endeavor. They each quote the statistic that "If the population of China would stand still, and we could have a 'Pentecost' every day with 3,000 saved, it would take 900 years before all of China would be saved." What the statistic failed to take into account is what actually happened in the growth of the church in China. There, and in other places, many explosions of evangelism occurred that made Pentecost with its three thousand conversions pale in comparison.

This was not to say that the staff of either magazine ascribed to the discouragement that the statistic quoted suggested. But many people did. In fact, one of the things that had to be overcome was the lethargy of the average Christian toward foreign missions. The interest of many believers went no further than their own church. Some saw their local community as the mission field and indeed joined with other churches in concerted efforts to reach that community. But the only ultimate justification for a thriving Jerusalem was outreach to the ends of the earth. Failure to understand this principle was failure to understand the great commission. By more than one calculation, the average church member contributes less than ten cents of each $100 he earns to the cause of foreign missions. That came out to less than one tenth of one percent of his income. But there was much, much more than enough in the hands of Christians to fund very ambitious plans for completing the work. Bill Bright and Campus Crusade for Christ were looking to God for billions of people to come to Christ, and to that end were trying to raise a billion dollars. We had a number of televangelists who were supported by funds that are in excess of $100 million annually—each. Imagine the kinds of financing that would have been available if every evangelical church in America had said, "We will continue to carry on our ministry in our area, but from this point on we are going to place frontier, unreached areas at the top of our priorities. We will give more to that than to anything else." Or (perish the thought—but we are talking about relative values and priorities here) what if every evangelical pastor had successfully challenged each pet owner in his congregation to give up his pet and use the money that had gone for pet food and supplies to the work of missions? The result would have been more money for missions than is now being given. The tragedy is that the pet owners would not even have had to give up their pets. If they kept their pets and yet gave as much to missions as to their pets, missions would have more support than they do now.

In setting goals, we need to beware of negative suggestions like the "Pentecost" in the Chinese evangelism statistic mentioned. Some would have said that we were already losing the battle, that more and more people were being born and we were not keeping pace in evangelism. Actually, as Ralph Winter, an authority in statistics, pointed out in the January 1988 issue of Missions Frontiers, whereas world population has increased threefold since 1900, the evangelical population in the world is nearly forty times as large as it was then. In spite of the opposition of the enemy, we must never lose sight of Him who is on our side—the opener of closed doors. Do we dare to suggest that if the Church had arisen with hearts aflame to work at completing the task that He assigned to us, He would have sat idly by and not opened closed doors? Remember "hopeless" places like China. Do not forget the place that not long ago was the "Dark Continent" is now a lighthouse of the gospel. How can one forget how unapproachable and atheistic Russia became open to the gospel it had rejected? Bear in mind the "impossible" Muslim areas where today thousands are coming to Christ. We certainly have the choice of sitting on our hands and doubting. But BEWARE! When God is ready, those who say "It can't be done" are almost always the ones He leaves behind as He sweeps through the affairs of men.

As we saw in the chapter on prophecy, certain things must take place before this event. The very revealing of the man of sin takes place in the middle of the tribulation when he stands in the temple and proclaims himself to be god. Then the great tribulation (lasting three and a half years) begins. Even though there is a temple institute in Jerusalem with many plans already made for the building of that temple, the temple itself has neither been built or even begun. Therefore, the man of sin cannot stand in the temple until it exists once more.

There is a certain mathematical beauty in God stepping back into history to complete His program two thousand years after Christ's first advent. But it might be wise to build some leeway into such dating. Abraham was given the covenant promise which had the prediction of the Messiah hidden in it. Abraham was born in 1996 B.C. David, through whom the Messiah was to come, was born in 1084 B.C. It was roughly one thousand more years, but it was actually decades off the mark.

But even if we add two thousand years to the advent of Christ to look for His return, perhaps we are looking at the wrong end of the advent. As beautiful as the Christmas story is, there is good reason to consider the week of the passion/death/resurrection (followed quickly by the ascension) as the significant act of Christ on our behalf and, consequently, the date which is of more import for us than His birth. Perhaps we should be reckoning the two thousand years from the crucifixion/resurrection rather than from the birth. This would mean that we might look for the Blessed Hope somewhere between now and the year 2030.

In the meantime, one thing should be our consuming passion—completing His work of world evangelism and hastening His return—doing our part in "bringing back the king."

## THE HIDDEN AND THE UNREACHED

We need to supply the workers and pray the Lord of the harvest to thrust them out into the fields. He is able. This doesn't prohibit our working on strategy and mobilization and utilization, praying for the mind of Christ while our wheels are moving. Even now there are needs to be met that cry out for help and we are not ready. In the July, 1986 issue of Exciting News from the Frontlines, it was reported that for six years some of the Semaidof people in Papua New Guinea went to the New Tribes Mission station with a request, "Please, can you send us a missionary?" Sadly, there had been no one to send. When a worker at the U.S. Center for World Missions heard this report, he prayed, "Lord, inflame us, get us going, make us give up our comforts, our cosmetics, our RVs, whatever. Break our hearts for the Semaidofs, and the 17,000 other unreached groups."

Not only are denominational groups looking at such needs and working to ready themselves for the harvest (the Evangelical Free Church and the Southern Baptists), but missions organizations are also. The Africa Inland Mission (AIM) listed as a stated aim: "In countries or areas where there is no church, we aim to plant one." When Youth With A Mission (YWAM) began in 1960, they advertised as their personnel needs "those interested in ministering cross-culturally among unreached peoples."

Around that time no fewer than four new agencies sprang up whose sole reason for existence was the reaching of those unreached areas of the world. In 1979, Pioneers was founded. In their statement of purpose they said, "The highest priority of PIONEERS is cross-cultural evangelism and church planting among hidden peoples, from the highlands of New Guinea to the high-rises of Bangkok." They "singled" out as their ministry "all of the five major blocks of Unreached People: Muslims, Chinese, Hindus, Buddhists, and Tribals." In 1980, a group of students began (and officially incorporated in 1983) a venture to challenge young people to reach out to the unreached peoples. They call themselves the Caleb Project. Their Declaration reads: "By the grace of God and for His glory, I commit my entire life to obeying His commission of Matthew 28:18–20, wherever and however He leads me, giving priority to the peoples currently beyond the reach of the Gospel (Romans 15:20–21)." They, in turn, started the Joshua Project, which researches "large Third World cities to identify unreached peoples and to discover means for them to respond to the gospel in a culturally relevant way." In 1982, Frontiers, Inc. was formed with a specialized view to reaching Muslims. Their goal was "to penetrate 200 Muslim people groups by the year 2000" and to "work together to break new ground, evangelize, and disciple new converts." Global Opportunities (GO) was organized in 1984. They were one of the new "tentmaker" missions. Rather than "waiting" for a country to become "open," they recruited professionals to go into countries closed to traditional missionaries. This way, teachers, engineers, social workers, could go into these presently unreached areas, work at their jobs and look for openings to share their faith.

There were some remarkable differences between the push to evangelize the world in the two decades before 1900 and in the same thrust toward completing the task in the two decades before 2000. We have already noted differences in contrasting the anticipation of the Lord's return approaching the year 1000 and that same anticipation as we faced the year 2000. And there were also contrasts to be noted in the efforts to complete the great commission when we look at the framework within which that effort took place near the end of the 19th century and compare it with the framework in which our endeavors took place as we moved toward the close of the 20th century. Actually Scripture weds the two concepts—the return of Christ and the completion of the great commission—for Christ said that this gospel would be preached throughout the whole world as a testimony to all nations and then the end would come (Matt. 24:14). Interestingly, near the year 1000 much was said about judgment and the day of the Lord or the return of Christ, but little or nothing was said about world evangelism. Approaching 1900, much was said about completing the task, but relatively little about Christ's return. Near the year 2000, we heard much about both, and that was a healthy balance, since they are related. Actually, the one depends on the other. Otherwise Peter's statement becomes meaningless when he asks that we be involved in "hastening the coming of the day of God" (2 Pet. 3:12).

We have seen that near the year 1000 the stage was not set with the right props. The predicted conditions were not in place. But near the year 2000, we noted condition after condition in place. Now, what about conditions for world evangelism approaching the year 1900? Could that have taken place? The conditions set down in the Northfield document of 1885 for the accomplishing of the task were: "If but ten millions, out of four hundred millions of nominal Christians, would undertake such systematic labor as that each one of that number should, in the course of the next fifteen years, reach one hundred other souls with the Gospel message, the whole present population of the globe would have heard the good tidings by the year 1900!" Certainly there was nothing wrong with the basic mathematical assumptions. There were somewhat over a billion people at that time, and one hundred listeners each times ten million believers would have produced one billion new people exposed to the gospel. But the "such systematic labor" was not defined clearly enough to assume automatically that the "unreached areas" as such were clearly in view. Before the year 2000, we had the kind of research and knowledge that pinpointed who and where these peoples were. Also, we had many other capabilities that they did not even dream of then—tremendous tools to help reach the goal. They had one clear advantage then. There were relatively few closed doors. But the Lord could easily reopen those for us. But even if the world would have been reached a century ago, the prophetic elements still would not have been established. Israel was not a nation, Europe was not an economic power, Russia was not a national and military force, and China was not the population force that she is today.

## New Potentials

Aside from the prophetic ripeness of the time, we had a number of other advantages that made the task more achievable than it had ever been. Whereas world population had increased threefold since that time, there were about forty times more evangelical Christians than there were then. That means the ratio of people to be reached per believer is actually smaller now than it was in that day. Furthermore, we had at our fingertips the information mentioned above. Research had been undertaken that placed at our command the locations of "hidden" or unreached people groups, who they were, what their religious beliefs were and what their cultural patterns were. Financing has already been mentioned. With forty times more evangelical Christians than we had in 1900 and with a number of wealthy believers and organizations, all we needed for funding was the right motivation. When God's people are moved to do His bidding as He gave commission to do, they can have hearts to give that will duplicate the giving of the Israelites for the tabernacle in Exodus 36:2–7. What a joy it would be to say, "It is enough," because "the stuff they had was sufficient to do all the work, and more." There were also a number of advancements that we could use effectively that would come under the heading of technology.

## At the End of the Nineteenth Century

In 1900 the best and fastest transportation was barely faster than the speed of a horse. Moving people and materials from one point on the globe to another could involve days or even weeks to accomplish. In 2000 we could do the same transporting in hours. Not only did this affect the accessibility of problem areas such as jungles for the work of carrying the gospel to them, but if we had workers ready for a closed field and the doors suddenly opened, we could have them into the culture in a day or two.

A century ago if there were necessary problems of logistics or statistics to solve in ministering the gospel effectively, the problem might take months or even a year or two to solve. Now, with the advent of the calculator and computer, the same problems could be handled in weeks or even days.

### Radio

Doubtless the greatest area of advance in technology in respect to getting the work of world evangelization completed is that of communications. When The Appeal to Disciples Everywhere went out in the Northfield document in 1885, there were no radios to broadcast the challenge and there were no radios to carry the gospel message to the world. It would be a decade before the Italian physicist, Marconi, would prove his theory of wireless telegraphy, and radio would even become a possibility. Today, transistor radios can be found in the hands of natives even in areas that were considered backward only a few years ago. This fact has not been lost on evangelical broadcasters. One century after Northfield, in 1985, the leaders of three major Christian broadcasting stations—HCJB (Ron Cline), FEBC (Bob Bowman) and TWR (Paul Freed)—had a meeting many considered to be historical in the area of Christian communications. In the meeting of these three presidents, they signed a dramatic agreement: "We are committed to provide every man, woman and child on earth the opportunity to turn on their radio and hear the gospel of Jesus Christ in a language they can understand, so they can become followers of Christ and responsible members of His church. We plan to complete this task by the year 2000." It was pointed out by Ron Cline that "Our signals can already reach the remote 'hidden peoples.' " He calculates that over 90 percent of the world population was even able to hear the gospel in a language that was either its own or one it could understand.

**Television**

Likewise, television came to represent a tool that was especially versatile and adaptable to gospel presentation for the entire globe. We saw the rise of the phenomenon known as the televangelist. Around the end of 1996 a new broadcast system called Dominion Video Satellite began operation, offering Christian programming directly to subscribers from synchronous satellites owned outright by the company itself. Most believers are undoubtedly aware of the existence of the two large Christian television networks, the Christian Broadcast Network (CBN) and the Trinity Broadcast Network (TBN). But there may be many who did not know of the extent of the outreach of these two networks. Both are vitally concerned with the gospel being spread through the airwaves to reach the areas of need beyond our own shores. TBN presently has transmitters in seven foreign countries with others in the process of development. It has effectively reached into ten countries and has a total of 995 cable stations. CBN now has transmitters in two Middle Eastern lands and is actually reaching into forty countries with their programming of the gospel.

### Internet

A brief word is also in order regarding the recent innovation of the internet and the worldwide web. Since this system is connected by telephone lines, it has the potential of reaching areas which might be closed even to radio and television. Who can even hazard a guess regarding both individuals and even people groups who might be reached for Christ by this ubiquitous tool?

## THE 144,000 AND THE GREAT COMMISSION

We stand at an interesting crossroads. The task is finally seen as achievable. The commission is being taken seriously by more and more Christian leaders. An ever-growing number of believers has been convinced that the whole world will be reached, based on Revelation 5:9 and 7:9, 14. In evangelical Christianity a major impediment to an all-out thrust toward completion of that task, or what some are calling "closure," is the philosophical and theological mind-set of the dispensational, pretribulation school of thought. The specific problem lies in their central eschatological theme of imminence. This theme has led them (logically, if one accepts that theme) to the maxim, "There is no sign or prophetic event that must be fulfilled before the rapture of the Church." This would include not only the great tribulation, but also the completion of the great commission. Though this belief enervates the strength of mission endeavor, they have a place in their system for the final penetration of the gospel. They do not doubt that the whole world will be reached. Some simply state that it will happen during the tribulation period itself—after the Church is gone.

Of course, this presents a logistical and tactical problem. If the Church is gone before the tribulation, how do we begin the tribulation period with a completely Churchless and Christless society and end it with every corner of the earth reached for Christ with believers produced in each people group? These brethren have found in the tribulation itself a group that they feel can and will accomplish that work. They claim that the 144,000 introduced in Revelation 7 and seen again in chapter 14 will reach the ends of the world for Christ. They make various assertions about this group: These people are literal Jews—twelve thousand from each of the twelve tribes of Israel. They are all flaming evangelists. The Spirit of God is going to work in them differently than He did in the Church—more like he worked in Old Testament days. The multitude at the end of Revelation 7, from all people groups, will be converted by this 144,000, which are called God's first fruits in Revelation 14:4. Let us consider each of these claims.

It is said that the 144,000 is a literal number of Jews. Scholars disagree widely about the identification of this group. The order of the list is certainly unlike any of the nineteen different arrangements in the Old Testament (the tribe of Dan is given in all of those lists, with one possible exception), and Joseph is added to the already mentioned half-tribe of Manasseh. In addition, the highly symbolic number of 12 x 12 in a multiple of 1000 has led many to believe that the group described immediately following this (the "great multitude which no man could number") is the same group (verses 9-17) but with the literal description now following the symbolic description of verses 4–8. There are cogent reasons, however, for believing that it is a Jewish group. There is also an ancient belief that Dan was omitted because the Antichrist would come from that tribe.

Next, these 144,000 are continually identified as Jewish evangelists. If the group is Jewish, the only thing that can be said of them positively from chapter 7 is that they are sealed on their foreheads. Although some believe this means they are marked out for martyrdom, the only clear reference we have to "sealing" on the forehead is found in Ezekiel 9 where it is used as a mark of identification to protect its faithful bearers from the approaching destruction. It is never stated, or even hinted, that these Jews are burning evangels for Christ. It is never said that they preach or even witness for Christ. The only excuse we could have to make them such would be because we were searching for some means by which to overcome a monumental problem. We enter a Christless, Churchless world in a spiritual vacuum when the tribulation begins. Suddenly, in seven years or less, the whole world must be evangelized. How? By the sudden appearance or 144,000 Jewish Billy Grahams.

### OLD TESTAMENT OR NEW TESTAMENT PATTERNS?

Also, God is supposed to work more along Old Testament lines with these 144,000 during the tribulation. The pretribulation position has faced problems with the work of the Spirit of God during the tribulation period. Originally their teaching was that the restrainer of 2 Thessalonians 2 was the Holy Spirit—PERIOD. That meant that when the Church was raptured, the Holy Spirit who inhabited the Church would, together with the Church, be taken out of the way. This, however, created tremendous difficulties for their position, since a now Churchless society, without any assistance from the Holy Spirit, would have to convert people from every geographic area. Aware of the implications of such a problem, they retrenched to the position that the removal of the restrainer would mean the withdrawal of the Spirit with respect to His restraining power only.

Since no man could come to the Father unless the Spirit drew him, this drawing power was still needed. Yet, the converts would not be "born-again" people belonging to the Church, since the Church was now gone. Nevertheless, the scenario remains incredible. A Churchless world develops 144,000 Jewish evangelists who then reach every tribe on earth without the Spirit's full power (lacking, at least, His restraining power). The Church, on the other hand, had not been able to accomplish this feat, though millions strong, with great resources and the full power of the Holy Spirit. This they had not accomplished in nineteen and a half centuries. Now this band of Jewish evangelists accomplishes it without the full power of the Spirit in only seven years, and during the last three and a half years of that time they are being hunted from pillar-to-post by the Antichrist and are severely restricted in all their activities.

In terms of the Holy Spirit returning to the kind of operation that characterized His work in the Old Testament, why would God go back to an inferior way of working His purposes in the tribulation? If the 144,000 Jews are believers in Jesus, but of a different quality from the other tribulation believers because of the special Old Testament kind of work in their lives, the whole argument of the book of Hebrews would seem to be overthrown. In Jesus we have been brought to the better, indeed the superior, way. Is God now going to accomplish His purpose by making two classes of believers? And by relating to believers as He did during Old Testament times, is He not going to the lesser, and the poorer way to accomplish the great task of world evangelization? Is the Old Testament way, after all, the better way?

Finally, the 144,000 are touted as the seed believers that produce all the Gentile believers in chapter 7, and their designation as "first fruits" in 14:4 is supposed to verify this. Certainly, there is no warrant at all for making the 144,000 in the first half of chapter 7 the source of the multitude of believers seen in the last half of that chapter. The only connection between the two groups is that both belong to the Lord. Even if they are thus saved early in the tribulation and followed by a multitude of other believers, they were no more the cause or vehicle of the larger number that followed than the first fruits in the Old Testament were the cause or vehicle of the subsequent harvest.

Furthermore, the picture of the first fruits as a promise of the harvest is much more fitting when both first fruits and harvest are "in kind." That is, it seems a bit incongruous to have Jewish first fruits followed by a Gentile harvest. It would be much more fitting to see Jewish first fruits followed by a Jewish harvest. In truth, from Romans 11, we know that the Jews as a people will be saved, and we know that this will occur at the return of Christ to earth (see Zech. 12:10–13:1). What could be more appropriate than to have a first fruits ingathering of this 144,000 during the tribulation in order to show that the full harvest is about to follow?

Clearly taught eschatological truths can be agreed upon. The world will be reached because chapters 5 and 7 of Revelation tell us so. This will happen because the gospel of the kingdom will be preached in all the world before the end.

And this, in turn, is true because Jesus predicted it in Matthew 24:14. Jesus will return and take us to Himself because that is what He promised us in John 14, and that is what other Scriptures also proclaim. So, the desire to see Jesus is a legitimate desire and our reunion with Him is the culmination of the divine/human love story. But the blessed hope only reaches its highest priority when it is ranked below the completion of the great commission.

Over a hundred years ago, A. T. Pierson and D. L. Moody and other men of God had a burning desire to finish the task of world evangelization before their century ended. Even though prophecy was not poised for the return of Christ then, they could have finished the job if the hearts of God's people had caught the flame that glowed in these men. But if the heart of the Church would be consumed today with a zeal for the task, the work that should be done, would be done. We have the power of heaven harnessed within us. The same explosive might that erupted at Pentecost is ours today. The Spirit of God is still in the business of convincing men of sin and of righteousness and of judgment. He is ready. We have the manpower that they lacked in 1885. We have the wealth in our coffers to underwrite the Magnificent Endeavor. And with all this, we have the technology to make it happen. In the TV series The Six Million Dollar Man, the physicians look at the mutilated body of Steve Austin and see him not in the light of what he is, but of what he can become through bionics. They conclude: "We have the technology. We can make him stronger, faster, better." We can look at the harvest field this day in the light of the great commission with a holy confidence and say, "We have the Counselor, we have the people, we have the wealth, we have the technology. We can change things, we can do the work: mightily, quickly, completely."

Dedication or commitment is the essential link that will join earth to heaven in this undertaking. God has always been willing. If we become willing, He will unleash the power that our apathy has blocked. What an awesome sight it is to see a slumbering giant awaken, rouse himself, and roll up his sleeves to move a mountain. In October 1957 a new sound was heard from space. It was produced by the Russian Sputnik, which was the first manmade object to orbit the earth. The United States was challenged. In 1961 John Kennedy stood before Congress and said, "These are extraordinary times." He requested funding to put a man on the moon. Only eight years later, on July 20, 1969, Neil Armstrong left the Apollo 11 and stepped onto the surface of the moon. Imagine what the awakened Church of Christ could do if it established the completion of the great commission as its primary goal. Picture every cell, every body member working together toward one accomplishment—the gospel message in every culture.

God used the glory that was Rome for His own purposes two thousand years ago. Rome spread her power and fame and greatness through her road and waterway systems, through her enforced "peace," and through her Hellenizing. God picked up these vain accomplishments and enlisted them for the use of the Church in starting the work of evangelizing. Today, God can take our proud technology and baptize it for the use of His saints in completing that task and hastening the coming of His day.

After David's son, Absalom, died, the exiled David ruled only his own tribal area until the elders of Israel realized their need of being ruled by David once more and asked the question of their people: "Now therefore why do you say nothing about bringing the king back?" (2 Sam. 19:10). We actually have it within our reach today to hasten the return of the greater Son of David. We need Him back to rule. We need only to finish the harvesting work entrusted to us. Let's start talking about bringing back the King. Let us be about the work to make it happen. Even so come, Lord Jesus.

*Lord, infect us with an incurable passion*
*to finish your work!*

# 13

## THE BLESSED HOPE: THE RESURRECTION-RAPTURE

*Rapture Song*

*Come, Lord Jesus! Come and take your Bride away.*
*Come transform this mortal tent of clay.*
*Let our longing souls soon hear the trumpet call.*
*Lord of lords and kings, become our all!*

The blessed hope of the Christian is "the appearing of the glory of our great God and Savior Jesus Christ" according to the scriptural definition in Titus 2:13. But the child of God is also allowed to step into an aura of mystical magic surrounding that "appearing." There are certain splendors that legitimately accompany it. The apostle John assures us that "when he appears we shall be like him" (1 John 3:2). Our ancient yearning, "O, to be like Jesus!" will be realized. But being like Him demands radical change. This glittering mystery of change is unfolded for us in 1 Corinthians 15. We will have a body like His. It will never perish. It will be glorious. It will be powerful. It will no longer be adapted to all that is physical within us, but to the spirit itself. At the trumpet call, for those who have slept the sleep of death, that body will be immediately reconstituted, but with all of these eternal alterations. That is the resurrection. For those who still live, that body will be instantaneously transformed in a breathtaking metamorphosis. The earthbound cocoons shall vanish and the new life forms shall rise to the skies. And rise they shall, ascending together with their resurrected siblings "to meet the Lord" they have loved and longed for "in the air." That is the burden of the closing words of 1 Thessalonians 4. That "catching up" is the rapture. And rapturous it will be. It is the buoyant joy of the Bride who had been sadly sundered from her Bridegroom, suddenly meeting Him again. Ah, but henceforth—the crest of ecstasy—she "shall always be with the Lord." This is the confirmation of the gracious promise He made to her just before their parting, "I will come again and take you to myself, that where I am you may be also" (John 14:3).

Those are the salient truths of the blessed hope. We will see and take part in His appearing in glory. Those who are dead shall be raised incorruptible and those who are alive at the time will be transformed into incorruptible beings as well. The two groups shall, together, be caught up to meet the Lord in the air and, from that point on, they shall never again be parted from Him. In all of those Scripture passages just noted it is only this wondrous truth that is treated. What we will do afterward is not even remotely referred to. What we were doing beforehand is not mentioned or even hinted at. For those teachings we must go elsewhere in the Scriptures.

So, we have seen what the blessed hope is. It includes the resurrection, or raising up of deceased believers and transformation of living believers. It includes the rapture. And it includes an eternal blessed state of forever being with Jesus and sharing in His glory. There is one term covered here that is not found in the Scriptures. It is the word rapture. But the activity we call the "rapture" and the truth of it do appear in the Bible. Just as the term Trinity is not found there, but can be seen clearly in the relationships among Father, Son, and Holy Spirit, even so the rapture will occur, though the word is not found there. The word is derived from the Latin word rapio. Thus, it is not surprising not to find this word in a Greek text. It is the exact counterpart or translation of the Greek word αρπαζω, which is translated by the English "caught up" (1 Thess. 4:17). One could have transliterated the Greek word and called it the harpazo, but we would have no

English cognate words to express related concepts, as we do with "rapt" and "rapturous." So, the rapture is the catching up of the saints right after the resurrection of the dead and transformation of the living.

There are certain teachings of the pretribulation school that add to or change the meaning of the blessed hope as it has been presented above. One of these teachings is the belief that the blessed hope means being raptured out of the world before the tribulation begins. To make such a claim is, at the very least, begging the question, since there is no Scripture that shows this to be the blessed hope. As we have seen, the blessed hope is the coming of Christ, our resurrection or transformation and our being caught up to be with Him forever. Why is it unthinkable that the Church as a whole should suffer persecution from the Antichrist and the world and then be raptured, when countless saints throughout the ages have suffered incredibly for Christ already? Why is this any more unthinkable than the similar experience of our Master "who for the joy that was set before him endured the cross, despising the shame"? (Hebrews 12:2) If our glorious Head spent three days and three nights in the tomb for us, why can't we, His Body, spend three days and three nights of that 70th week in the shadow of the tomb for Him?

Another contention among pretribulationists is that the rapture itself is the blessed hope not for those who are dead in Christ, but for living believers of the time of His coming. This obviously presents a sharp distinction between their position and that of posttribulationists. In this belief they confuse the mystery of the transformation of living believers in 1 Corinthians 15 with the mystery of the translation (the rapture) of all the saints in 1 Thessalonians 4, where we are told that the living saints "shall be caught up together with" the resurrected dead. Both groups share in being caught up. They are caught up together. It impugns the testimony of Scripture itself to say that the Blessed Hope is only for the living believers. The rapture is a hope presented not only to the living, but also to the dead. The hope of the resurrection of the dead (believers) is intimately tied to the return of Christ.

Jesus told Martha that her brother would rise again and

she replied, "I know that he will rise again in the resurrection at the last day." Then Jesus told her that He Himself was that resurrection (John 11:24). His coming and the resurrection of believers are inseparable. This is the hope of believers who die, even as it is the hope of believers who live at that day when they shall be transformed.

Indeed, the message of the rapture itself is first for dead believers, then for living believers. Paul tells us that the rapture will occur "in a moment, in the twinkling of an eye, at the last trumpet. For the trumpet will sound, and the dead will be raised imperishable, and we shall be changed" (1 Cor. 15:52). Certainly that is a hope for both the dead and the living.

Furthermore, as a hope, the emphasis is put on the dead believers. Their primacy is evident. "But we would not have you ignorant, brethren, concerning those who are asleep, that you may not grieve as others do who have no hope. For since we believe that Jesus died and rose again, even so, through Jesus, God will bring with him those who have fallen asleep. For this we declare to you by the word of the Lord, that we who are alive, who are left until the coming of the Lord, shall not precede those who have fallen asleep. For the Lord himself will descend from heaven with a cry of command, with the archangel's call, and with the sound of the trumpet of God. And the dead in Christ will rise first; then we who are alive, who are left, shall be caught up together with them in the clouds to meet the Lord in the air; and so we shall always be with the Lord. Therefore comfort one another with these words" (1 Thess. 4:13–18). The emphasis is clear—hope and comfort; dead and living believers together, but the dead first.

The very verse that coins the term "blessed hope" calls it "the appearing of the glory of our great God and Savior Jesus Christ" (Titus 2:13). It is not even suggested that the blessed hope is escape from death, but solely the appearing of His glory. It would seem, then, that the posttribulation position is on solid scriptural ground if they hold that hope to be the prospect of seeing and being with the Lord in eternity.

John, the writer of the Revelation, eschews any mention of escape from death when he says, "Beloved, we are God's children now; it does not yet appear what we shall be, but we know that when he appears we shall be like him, for we shall see him as he is. And every one who thus hopes in him purifies himself as he is pure" (1 John 3:2–3). This hope is obviously and purely seeing Him and being like Him.

It would seem that the pretribulation position considers the joy of escaping death as its blessed hope. I say "it would seem" because a closer inspection reveals that it is specifically death during the tribulation that is their joy to escape. In fact, their blessed hope, upon further investigation, turns out to be escape from the tribulation itself—from every aspect of it, from suffering, as well as from death. As bad as the tribulation will be, and certainly we should never minimize its difficulties, the concept of the blessed hope should never be demoted to an escape hatch from the tribulation rather than that which the Scripture claims it to be—imperishable transformation and the presence of Christ.

Certainly we are taught that our expectation in this world is tribulation. Jesus told his disciples, "In the world you have tribulation; but be of good cheer, I have overcome the world" (John 16:33). Paul, after being stoned and left for dead went on preaching and "strengthening the souls of the disciples, exhorting them to continue in the faith, and saying that through many tribulations we must enter the kingdom of God" (Acts 14:22).

The desire to be caught away so that the Church may not have to go through these extreme difficulties found its way into the folk song of the Netherlands, "We Gather Together" (arr. by E. Kremser). In the third stanza we hear the words, "Let Thy congregation escape tribulation."

I suspect that very few who hold the posttribulation position are closet masochists. But they do look at themselves as realists. There is hope and there is hope. There is a false hope and there is a blessed hope. We will go through the tribulation, not because it has been willed upon the Church by wild-eyed posttribulationists, but because that is the indication in the Scriptures. Certainly the hymn writer Isaac Watts touched the cardiac nerve of the servant who is willing and ready to suffer for His Master, the Suffering Servant, when he asked the poignant question:

*Must I be carried to the skies,*
*On flow'ry beds of ease,*
*While others fought to win the prize,*
*And sailed through bloody seas?*
"Am I a Soldier of the Cross?"

This hymn text closely reflects the spirit of the apostles who were beaten for speaking in the name of Jesus and then "left the presence of the council, rejoicing that they were counted worthy to suffer dishonor for the name" (Acts 5:40–42).

Hebrews 11 describes the Old Testament heroes who "were tortured, refusing to accept release, that they might rise again to a better life. Others suffered mocking and scourging, and even chains and imprisonment. They were stoned, they were sawn in two, they were killed with the sword, they went about in skins of sheep and goats, destitute, afflicted, ill-treated—of whom the world was not worthy—wandering over deserts and mountains, and in dens and caves of the earth. And all these, though well attested by their faith, did not receive what was promised" (vv. 35–39). Still, they had a hope, not that they would escape death, but "that they might rise again."

### WHY A RAPTURE?

The charge has been made against posttribulationists that they cannot come up with a good reason for a rapture to take place when Christ returns. Furthermore, they claim that since Christ is coming to earth to set up a kingdom, posttribulationists are left without any reason for a last-minute rapture before the kingdom is set up. One additional complaint that they lodge is that none of the passages dealing with the coming of Christ to earth show a resurrection or rapture. Thus, this is perceived as an argument from silence against the posttribulation position.

When the charge is made that the posttribulationists have not resolved the question of any need for a rapture at the Second Coming, it is assumed that the pretribulationists have resolved it. Indeed, they feel that they do have an answer. In a word, time is their answer. Time is needed to fit in all the things that must take place before Christ sets foot upon earth. First, time is needed to take the Church to heaven. They take the passage in John 14:3 ("I will come again and will take you to myself, that where I am you may be also") to mean that He is taking them to the place He has been preparing and that His coming for His own means that He is taking them to His Father's house. This, they say, would suggest a possible large chunk of time before "touchdown" on earth. Look at the great distance between our sky (the first heaven) and the location of that "prepared place" (the third heaven). How much time would it take to get there? But we are never told that this trip is going to be made or is even necessary. (Even if such a trip were taken, we will see why one human day could more than suffice for it.) We know that wherever He is, we will be with Him (John 3). But when He comes, He will no longer be in heaven—He will be above the earth.

Time is necessary, they say, to complete a lengthy judgment seat of Christ process, which they are convinced will take place in heaven. Imagine. Each individual Christian must be called to account for the deeds done in the body. Millions and millions of Christians and each with hundreds or thousands of deeds. But we are not told when (before or after He touches the earth) or where (in the air or on the earth) this takes place. Even if it does take place in the air before He comes to earth, one very important fact is being overlooked. We would now have left behind the limits of the time/space continuum and would have begun existence in the medium called eternity. Hours would suffice for all of this, and a few days would be an unneeded luxury. Having now begun to partake of eternity in a new and practical way, we will no longer be time-bound creatures. Just as millions of people on earth can look at the same time at their individual home movies on video, so we would be able, individually, to have audiences with the omnipresent Lord at one and the same instant.

But what about the marriage of the Lamb and the marriage supper? Traditionally, the Jewish marriages took place at the bridegroom's home (and our Bridegroom will be in the air at the time). Even if it were in heaven, the trip there and back and the wedding itself could easily fit into mere minutes of earth time. Once again, we will not be restricted by time as we had been on earth in our temporal bodies. In fact, the marriage supper presents a big problem in logic for the pretribulation position. It is apparent that this supper takes place at the end of the tribulation (Rev. 19). If the Bride met the Bridegroom seven years earlier, why has it taken all that earth time to get around to the marriage supper? And when the foolish virgins went out to buy oil why did the bridegroom come immediately, without any delay, and "those who were ready went in with him to the marriage feast"? (Matt. 25:1–13). The marriage supper traditionally took place at the bride's home. Seeing that we came from the earth and are to rule with Him on the earth, the earth would likely be considered our home, and this supper would probably be there. But regardless of a supper in the air or on earth, the same freedom from the strictures of time would apply. When Peter spoke of the coming of the Lord and time relationships he stated "that with the Lord one day is as a thousand years, and a thousand years as one day" (2 Pet. 3:8). Every item imaginable in that meeting and in that togetherness could be accomplished in less than a day of earth's time.

If there is no logical need for time in order to explain why the rapture would take place before the bodily return of Christ to the earth itself, then the pretribulation position would seem to have more of a problem in answering "why the rapture?" than the posttribulation position. Why are seven years of time used before that return when only a few days at the most or a few moments at the least are all that are needed to accomplish the Church events surrounding the rapture?

The other reason given by pretribulationists for the need of a rapture is that a rapture spares the Church from the great tribulation (if the rapture comes before that tribulation). The major difficulty with this claim is that it rests on supposition and wishful thinking rather than on Scripture itself. The rapture is clearly taught in 1 Thessalonians 4. A pretribulation rapture is not found in any scriptural passage. The two passages most often used for support of this idea do not bear up under scrutiny. Both are dealt with in more detail elsewhere, but a passing comment on each can be made here. In Revelation 3:10, God tells the church in Philadelphia, "I will keep you from the hour of trial." The Greek construction does not promise us being kept away from the presence of the trial, but being kept while in its presence. It is the precise language used by Christ in John 17 when He is praying for the believers and asking that God would "keep them from the evil one." The other passage that is perhaps used even more widely in support of the Church being kept out of the tribulation is 1 Thessalonians 5:9, where Paul states that "God has not destined us for wrath." Since God's wrath will be poured out in the tribulation, the argument goes, that we, as a Church, cannot be in the tribulation, because we, as a part of the world, would be feeling or experiencing that wrath. But the wrath of God that is discussed in the 1 Thessalonian passage is not about short-term, physical and temporal punishments. It is about ultimate destinies. "God has not destined us for wrath, but to obtain salvation through our Lord Jesus Christ." Our destiny is salvation. The opposite destiny is wrath or eternal damnation. The passage concludes by affirming that Christ "died for us so that whether we wake or sleep we might live with him." When He does come, whether we have already died in Christ (sleep) or whether we are alive (wake), our ultimate destiny is to "live with him." The ultimate destiny of the unbeliever is wrath. That ultimate horror is not the tribulation, but the opposite of our destiny, that is, eternally not living with Him.

But the question does remain. Why, indeed, a rapture? For many the question is not one of grave importance. Some may not even pose the question. They also may never ask, "Why a millennium?" Such questions may be in the same category as, "Why will we be like the angels?" For them, it is sufficient that the Bible states these things, and they simply accept them, being convinced that God knows what is best. Others of us are nearly consumed by the desire to know if there is an answer to the questions. Even when we can find no definite resolution, we attempt to see whether there might be an answer. For us, it is healthy to recognize the borders between probability and the twilight zone of reason.

Are there sound and logical reasons for the rapture? This

cannot be separated from the reason for the resurrection and transformation, since we will be raptured in changed bodies. We will either experience a dead body being raised, or a living body being transformed. That part has been explained sufficiently for us by Paul in 1 Corinthians 15. We need a spiritual body for life lived completely in the spirit. Such a body will be superior to the physical body in every respect—it will no longer be tired, hungry, sorrowful, perishable, or mortal. At least on that ground, no one should ever raise the question whether it might be just as well to go into the kingdom in our natural bodies.

But why the rapture itself? It is not sufficient simply to answer "Why not?" When the whole redemptive plan of God in Christ is considered, however, it becomes nearly unthinkable not to have the rapture or something like it. God has paid the supreme price to accomplish this redemption. He has promised to redeem both spirit and body. This redeeming has been developed in the context of a love relationship—indeed a relationship of Lover/Beloved or Bridegroom/Bride. Paul reflects the intensity of the longing for the completion of the relationship when he says (though using a different metaphor) that "we who have the first fruits of the Spirit, groan inwardly as we wait for adoption as sons, the redemption of our bodies" (Rom. 8:23). It would seem highly improper if not impossible in light of the intimacy of that meeting and the completion of the promised union (specifically the marriage of the Lamb and His Bride) that Christ would not have a private meeting with the Church. There must, therefore, be a priority of this private meeting first before attending to affairs on the earth. Thus, we meet Him in the air before He brings us with Him back to the earth.

Though some of us find this exciting, others find it strange. Taking the setting up of the kingdom as the sole reason for Christ's coming to earth, the pretribulationists wonder why the posttribulationists would have the saints meet Christ above the earth at the rapture if they are going to come back to the earth immediately after that meeting. First, the establishment of this kingdom is not the purpose of Christ. It is a purpose. But so is His union with His Bride. And that union is even more important. The Church becomes His wife and they will rule this kingdom together. The disciples were told that they would sit "on twelve thrones, judging the twelve tribes of Israel," and we as believers learn that "if we endure, we shall also reign with him" (Matt. 19:28; 2 Tim. 2:12). Also, since we know that He is going to be ruling on the earth and that, once the rapture has taken place, "we shall always be with the Lord," henceforth, it is our joy to be with Him there to help in the administration of that kingdom (1 Thess. 4:17).

The pretribulation position is that tribulation ("non-Church") saints will enter the millennium in their physical or natural bodies. Nowhere does Scripture state that those who are the (ruled over) populace in the millennium are saints in mortal bodies. In fact, there is more reason to believe that these are unbelievers in their mortal bodies.

There is a pretribulation concern about the fact that there is no reference to the rapture of living saints or to the resurrection of the "Church" (see Rev. 20:4). This is seen as a convincing "argument from silence" for a pretribulation rapture. It seems very strange that the teaching of such an important doctrine would not be found in Scriptures that speak in detail about His coming to earth. In another place, we show why all aspects of the Second Coming/resurrection/rapture need not be mentioned every time the subject is brought into a portion of the Scriptures. But this argument from silence is much more telling against the pretribulation position than it is against ours. At least we have a time and a place where something is said about resurrection. We can place resurrection in Revelation 20:4. They cannot show any passage that speaks of rapture or resurrection before the tribulation, and at that point we can use their own argument against their position. How amazing it is that a doctrine of such consequence should be missing from those Scriptures that deal specifically with the time period when these things are supposed to happen.

## Scriptures Relevant to the Resurrection and Rapture: What They Do and Do Not Say

### John 14

The relevant passage here is verses 2 and 3—"In my Father's house are many rooms; if it were not so, would I have told you that I go to prepare a place for you? And when I go and prepare a place for you, I will come again and will take you to myself, that where I am you may be also." Jesus gives a five-fold promise: (1) I am going away; (2) I will be preparing a place for you; (3) I will return; (4) I will take you to myself; and (5) You will be with me. Pretribulationists believe that Jesus is speaking from the vantage point of heaven and that He, therefore, will take believers to the Father's house in heaven, to the place Jesus has prepared for them, at the time of the resurrection-rapture.

It is certain that Jesus said there were many rooms in His Father's house. It is also certain that He said He was going there to prepare a place for His disciples (most likely for all of His followers). Other matters are not certain. One of the most interesting of these is what the Father's house is. Perhaps the strongest case could be made for it being the New Jerusalem itself. That the disciples have a place there is obvious from the description in Revelation 21. The very names of the disciples are written on the twelve foundations. That we will have a place there also seems obvious, since "those whose names are written in the Lamb's book of life" shall "enter it" (v. 27). That it could be the Father's house seems a strong likelihood, since "its temple is the Lord God the Almighty" (v. 22) and "the glory of God is its light" (v. 23).

But John 14:1–3 says nothing about taking His own to the Father's house at that time, even though pretribulationists have been sure that it does. Even if it did, a question would naturally be: what if He were to do so? Why "come" all the way down from heaven only to return there again with His own and then "come" again in order to set foot upon the earth? This would make the Second Coming both a second and third coming, since the next resurrection event involves those who belong to Christ "at his coming" (1 Cor. 15:23). Thus, even as they have split the first resurrection into multiple parts, they have split the Second Coming into two parts.

Actually, there is nothing surprising about a meeting in the air between the Bridegroom and His Bride (lasting for minutes, hours or even a few days of earth time) before His final descent to earth. First, this has been a mutually anticipated meeting, and second, it is natural that the saints should have first claim on His program. What more private place in the midst of His "coming," or in the process of His return than in the air?

What pretribulationists make a certainty is, in fact, no certainty at all, namely when we shall go to that place. Jesus certainly could have said, "I will come again, and receive you to myself; that you also may be in my Father's house," but He didn't. There is not only a lack of warrant for such an interpretation, but the text itself tends to show a different meaning, which is supported elsewhere in Scripture relative to this same time and event.

But let us look at precisely what it is that Jesus Himself did say here. He states, "I will come again and will take you to myself, that where I am you may be also." First, note that He said He would take them to Himself, not to the Father's house. Second, consider that the two most logical interpretations would look at the meaning of that present tense "where I am." When Jesus spoke these words, He was with the disciples. One meaning could be "where I am right now," but that would contradict the announcement that He was going away and would be parted from them. The other meaning would be "where I am when I take you to myself." He was, indeed, going to His Father's house, but when He would "come again," He would not be there (in His Father's house), but in the air above the earth (coming from His Father's house) and from that point He would receive them to Himself. The overriding concern that the disciples had was not the details of the place they would someday see, but the fact that Jesus was leaving and they would not see Him for who knew how long. The only thing He is promising them at this time is that He would be receiving them to Himself "so that where I am" (wherever that might be—at the resurrection, it would be in the air) "there you may be also."

Remember, Jesus had just told them that He was leaving them and they would not be able to follow. Peter practically begged Him to be allowed to follow (he would even lay down his life for Jesus). It was against this backdrop that Jesus gave the promise that they would never be separated from Him again: "I will come again and will take you to myself, that where I am you may be also."

This corresponds perfectly with what is said about that same time and event in 1 Thessalonians 4:17, that all we believers "shall be caught up ... in the clouds to meet the Lord in the air; and so we shall always be with the Lord" never to be parted from Him again. After the Millennium ends and the New Jerusalem comes down to earth, and the Lamb along with the Lord God the Almighty is its temple, and when the Lamb is also its lamp, then, also, we shall be with Him, and then we shall occupy the place He has prepared for us. Any suggestion of a visit there before then is, at best, pure speculation.

**1 Thessalonians 4**

The last six verses (13–18) are those that are concerned with the resurrection-rapture. It is a section that relates certain joyous events that will happen speedily for the believer at Christ's return. Unlike the world, we have a hope regarding the dead. They will rise upon hearing a cry of command, the archangel's call, and the sound of a trumpet. But living believers will be caught up with them when they rise and all of us believers will meet the Lord in the air and never part from Him. We should use this hope for dead and living believers to comfort one another.

The biggest difficulty for the pretribulation position in relationship to this passage is not with what the passage says, but rather with what they assume that it says in addition to, or instead of, its clear meaning. They rightly note that the chapter does not mention the tribulation. They also claim (not necessarily rightly so) that even chapter 5 does not place the rapture after the tribulation. Furthermore, they take a mammoth leap of logic at this point and infer from the lack of the mention of the tribulation in chapter 4 that the Thessalonians had been taught an any-moment return of Christ and that, therefore, the comfort they were given is that they would escape that time. Anyway (the reasoning goes), there could be precious little comfort in the idea that they might go through that terrible suffering before their "hope" could be realized.

There are some serious misconceptions in the treatment of this passage in 1 Thessalonians 4. A supposed Thessalonian doctrine is treated as if it were a fact. They would have us believe that the Thessalonians' hope of the Lord's return for living believers was an imminent hope, that they were waiting for His return any day, at any moment. This is a position that they have no right to assume and one that certainly cannot be demonstrated.

They also believe that the challenge to comfort one another refers to the concept that the rapture spares living believers from the awful time of suffering represented by the period of the tribulation. This is one of the key failings of the pretribulation position—it lowers the blessed hope to mean escape from the tribulation. But Paul's actual words of comfort relate to the fact that we have a resurrection hope for our loved ones in Christ and that we will join them as immortals.

They also strongly suggest that there is precious little comfort to be found in outliving a period of terrible suffering and trial. This stands in sharp contrast to the concept that there is a special hope and joy for those who have experienced the depths of trial. Not only did Jesus say that they who endured that time would be "saved" (whatever the special significance of that was), but James also states that the enduring of trial should be counted "all joy" and that we call such steadfast people "happy" (Matt. 10:22; 24:13; Mark 13:13; James 1:2; 5:11). Lord Byron in his "Sonnet on Chillon" saw Liberty as shining its "brightest in dungeons." And there was for Jesus a special joy that could only be realized after He had "endured the cross" (Heb. 12:2).

Furthermore, their treatment of the passage misses the true significance of the "comfort" that Paul is talking about. Paul reminds the Thessalonians that our prospects regarding the dead are not to be compared with those of grieving worldlings without hope. The Thessalonians knew dead believers would be raised, but they didn't know when that would occur. And they didn't know when the dead would be raised in relation to the time when living believers would see Him. They also didn't know where the resurrected dead would be—they might be in a different place than the living believers (in heaven?). The comfort was threefold. First, the time when dead believers would be raised would be the same time when living believers would see Him—at His coming. Second, they and the dead believers would be "together" in their meeting of the Lord. Finally, this would be an eternal condition—they (living and dead believers) would be together and with the Lord FOREVER. This was comfort indeed.

We all can agree with their contention that chapter 4 does not mention the tribulation as coming before the rapture. If, however, we do not ignore the artificial chapter division between chapters 4 and 5, Paul himself sets forth just such an idea by saying that the Thessalonians themselves should be aware of the "times and seasons" surrounding this event. It is a logical assumption that this theme is intended as a reminder that there is something by which we can gauge or measure the coming of that time, namely the coming of this time of trial. It would come bearing destruction and travail in the world around them. But believers would not be surprised by it as unbelievers would be. It would seem patently absurd for Paul to say, "let us not sleep" and "let us keep awake" if a rapture would take us away before that time. On the other hand, it would make perfect sense for him to tell them these things to prepare them for entering into that very time. Furthermore, in Paul's very next correspondence with the Thessalonians it would appear that they had lost sight of this very fact. In the opening of 2 Thessalonians 2, Paul said that the "coming of our Lord Jesus Christ and our assembling to meet him" would not happen until two things happened first: (1) the rebellion, and (2) the revealing of the man of lawlessness. Then in verse 5 he says, "Do you not remember that when I was still with you I told you this?" indicating that they had been told of tribulation followed by rapture.

## 1 Corinthians 15

This, of course, is the resurrection chapter of the New Testament. It gives us the treatment of the nature of the resurrection itself as well as the nature of the resurrection body. But it is also the chapter of living hope that buoys the heart of the believer in terms of ultimate victory as no other chapter of Scripture.

The first message it brings is: Christ is risen, Christ is risen, CHRIST IS RISEN! On that overwhelming truth hangs all that follows. In fact, our own resurrection is inseparably tied to His, since He is the first fruits of all who have fallen asleep. This is good news and bad news: bad news to those who will be raised to enter into their own eternal judgment at "the end, when he delivers the kingdom to God" at the second resurrection; but good news "at his coming" to "those who belong to Christ" in the first resurrection. The surpassing glory that is theirs is that their resurrection will follow the pattern and goal of Christ the first fruits. No resurrection before had ever been like His. As Paul put it in another place, "Christ being raised from the dead will never die again" (Rom. 6:9). No resurrection but His had been of that sort. But those who belong to Him will share in it exactly, since "we know that when he appears we shall be like him, for we shall see him as he is" (1 John 3:2).

The child of God can revel in the description of the body he will have. As he looks at himself now, he sees a body that is perishing, dying inch by inch and day by day. It is rife with dishonor and has to be pampered cosmetically and propped up medically. It is weak and constantly in need of nutrition, vitamins, minerals, and remedies. It is itself physical and subject to all of the principles and restrictions of physics. It bears the image of the dust from which it came. But the body that shall be in the resurrection will actually be incapable of corruption or death. It will be glorious, and a thing of enduring beauty—a joy forever. It will be the essence of power and self-sufficiency, needing no props or additives. It will be governed only by spiritual principles—beyond the beck and call and the tug of the physical. And, finally, it will bear the image of the Maker to whom it goes. And what is true of the resurrection of what has fallen asleep in Christ will also, mysteriously, be true of that which is alive at His coming. Instantaneously, quicker than a gleam can appear in the eye of a lover, those living will be transformed into the exact kind of glory that the resurrected will know. And all of this will be instantly generated at the last trump. Since this is true, nothing can budge us. Our labor for the Lord will endure.

The passage is one of the key gems in the Christian treasury and it is of special significance to the posttribulation position. It is here where we discover a crucial element of timing. It is not the mention of a year, the naming of a month, or the selection of a date on a calendar. But it is just as sure. The resurrection-transformation will occur at the last trumpet. When all other trumpets that affect God's program and people have sounded, then this one will resound. No mental gymnastics can realistically place seven tribulation plague-trumpets of Revelation after God's last trumpet. But there is a trumpet that sounds at the end of the tribulation and, hence, after those seven trumpets, which would qualify it as the last trump that issues in the gathering of God's elect (Matt. 24:31).

It is assumed by the pretribulation camp that since this passage makes no mention of the tribulation, it automatically means that the tribulation must come after the rapture. Otherwise it would be unkind of Paul not to warn them in this passage that they must first endure that terrible time.

There are two major fallacies in this assumed confirmation. One is the idea that since an extended passage on resurrection is given, then it is logical to mention what happens before that resurrection. If the subject is singularly and totally the nature of the resurrection (which it is), anything else, though perhaps associated with it, would be extraneous. In fact, the passage is not even about the rapture. It is about the resurrection-transformation. If it were about the rapture, wasn't it cruel for the apostle not to tell them about that rapture that would happen after that transformation—that the living saints would be together with the resurrected dead? Wasn't it also cruel not to tell them that they wouldn't walk aimlessly about afterwards, but would be "caught up," that they would meet the Lord and that they would never be separated from Him again? To get the insights both of the "before and after," we need to study the other New Testament passages about the return of the Lord. Then we would get a composite of the full teaching about it, rather than expecting any individual passage to give all the details.

Another fallacy in the assumption of the order of events in this passage is the implication that Paul did not say anything earlier in the letter about the time of trouble they were to go through. But a thorough study of the letter does not support this claim. Paul speaks of a time of distress in light of which believers should not make any radical changes in their life commitments (7:26–31). There is more evidence to suggest that it was something he saw on the horizon (about to happen) than something they found themselves in at that time. Even though the RSV and NASV render the term "the present distress," they both add as a footnote the alternate "or impending." Indeed both the Bauer, Arndt and Gingrich and the Thayer Greek-English Lexicon of the New Testament list this concept as the preferred rendering of this verse (Bauer, Arndt and Gingrich: impend, be imminent, p. 266; Thayer: close at hand, p. 217). In verse 28 there is no grand significance in the fact that the word worldly "troubles" is the same word elsewhere rendered "tribulation." It may be suggestive. But what is significant is the fact that Paul uses the future tense, "will have worldly troubles." If it were a present distress, the married would already be having such troubles, and a more appropriate comment would be "those who are married have worldly troubles, and I would spare you that." Rather, he says he would spare them the troubles they will have if they find themselves in a married state, which they have time now to avoid. He states that "the appointed time has grown very short" (vs. 29) and recommends a radical outlook in the face of this observation. The cumulative effect of these statements is a feeling of portent. If Paul sounded a note of imminence anywhere in this letter, it is here, not in chapter 15. If he felt that at any time they could enter this great distress (whether or not he named it the tribulation), then the Corinthians fully expected to go through that time before the resurrection.

The Lord revealed the idea of transformation to Paul as a mystery, but Paul wrote these words before John wrote his Gospel, and there is something in John's Gospel that indicates that Jesus may also have revealed the idea of resurrection-transformation to Martha at Bethany some twenty-five years earlier. Jesus had just told her that her brother would rise again, and Martha, supposing that He was referring to the raising of the just on the day of resurrection, professed her faith in this teaching by saying, "I know that he will rise again in the resurrection at the last day." Jesus then pronounced that He Himself was the resurrection and the life personified. It would seem the most logical interpretation that Jesus picks up on Martha's reference to the framework of the resurrection on the last day when He says that whoever believed in Him and passed through death would live again, but that the person who was alive at that time of resurrection and believed in Him would never die. We can conclude from the text that Jesus is saying that just as a dead Christian will live again on the day of resurrection, so a Christian who is alive on the day of resurrection will never pass through death. The phrase "whoever lives and believes in me shall never die," should not be interpreted to mean never die "spiritually" (as many do). This would make the dying of the second group a different kind of dying than the dying of the first group. That would be to say "He who believes in me may die physically, but He will live again physically, whereas whoever believes in me and is alive may die physically, but he will never die spiritually." This creates quite a strain on straightforward meaning by shifting the interpretation of what dying means in midstream. Much more to the point and consistent with logic would be to render the meaning, "he who believes in me, though he die physically, yet shall he live physically, and whoever lives and believes in me shall never die physically." And this is precisely the mystery that Paul proclaims in 1 Corinthians 15: "We shall not all sleep, but we shall all be changed ... the dead will be raised imperishable, and we shall be changed" (vv. 51–52).

## 2 Thessalonians 2

Between those who hold the pretribulation position and those who are convinced of the posttribulation view this is the most debated of all passages dealing with the Second Coming. More has possibly been said about what the passage does not say than about what it does say. It would be helpful to establish first what the passage does say clearly before conjecturing whether this better fits one or the other of these positions.

The Thessalonians had a great interest in the coming of the Lord and the assembling of believers to meet Him. Now they were agitated. They had somehow heard that the day of the Lord had already come. This report may have come to them through some spirit or by word (whether by word of mouth—through the grapevine—or by a supposed "word from the Lord") or perhaps from some letter claiming to be from Paul himself. Whatever the source, it was a deception. There was no need for such agitation among the Thessalonians. There were two clear and notable indicators to mark the beginning of that time. Unless one had seen these two signposts, the day of the Lord had not yet begun. There would be a spiritual rebellion (or "apostasy") and the man of sin or lawlessness would be revealed (for all the world to see) when he would take his seat in the temple of God and proclaim that he is God. In fact, Paul had told the Thessalonians this when he had been with them before. They also knew that there was a power restraining this enemy and that the Lord would withdraw the restraint at the proper time, so this lawless one could be revealed. But his evil power would be short-lived, since Jesus would destroy him at His coming with no more than a simple breath.

Beyond this, certain conclusions have been drawn or certain charges have been made. There is a pronounced division within the pretribulation camp itself on the significance of the word apostasia (αποστασια). Some would like for it to mean "departure" (that is the rapture) rather than "rebellion" or "apostasy." It seems that it is a minority hope, however, since most, even in their own camp, appear to distance themselves from this interpretation. Even though the noun form of the word used here is related to the verb that can mean "to depart," this noun form is always used negatively as a departure from a positive and legitimate commitment, such as a commitment to the Lord or to a marriage partner. To try to make something positive out of it would be like an attempt to take the negative word voyeur and make something positive out of it. One might argue that since a related word (clairvoyance) has a non-negative meaning, we could, perhaps, squeeze something positive out of it (like viewer) because it comes from a participle form of the French voir: "to see." But it would be in vain, since voyeur is always negative.

What is more important is the identification in this chapter of just what "day" this rebellion introduces or begins. In speaking of "the coming of our Lord Jesus Christ and our assembling to meet him," Paul begged them not to be upset over the rumor "that the day of the Lord has come." It would appear obvious from placing these two together (His "coming ... and our gathering to meet him" and "the day of the Lord") that they are part and parcel of each other as they were in 1 Thessalonians 4 and 5.

Why would this be upsetting to the Thessalonians? There are two possibilities. First, they were told in 1 Thessalonians 5 not to sleep, but to keep awake. But if this rumor was true, they had not been on their guard, and had missed part or perhaps all of that day. Second, a certain kind of lifestyle and commitment belonged to that day for believers. Paul told the Corinthians that the normal relationships of life would be disrupted (1 Cor. 7:29–31). If the Thessalonians were in that day, what should they be doing differently? They had not been alert. What should they do?

If the pretribulation theory were correct, and if the coming of the Lord and "our assembling to meet him" did not belong to that "day of the Lord," this would have been the perfect place for Paul to calm their fears in a clear and unmistakable way. He should then have said, "Let no one deceive you in any way; for the day of the Lord will not come, unless our assembling to meet him comes first." The fact that the circumstance they should first look for was the rebellion and the revealing of the man of sin before the day of the Lord would actually begin indicates that they would be there to see these things. Knowing that the road sign was there would be an assuring circumstance in terms of where they were in God's program.

The identity of the "restrainer" is another point of contention. Early pretribulationists not only viewed the restrainer as the Holy Spirit, but also had Him completely removed from the earth together with the Church. When this was seen to conflict with His omnipresence, it was basically altered to mean that His restraining influence through the Church is removed. Though the Spirit could draw back His restraining influence even apart from the Church, there are strong reasons for choosing a different interpretation. If the restrainer were the Spirit, there would be no reason for Paul to be cryptic or coy about the matter. There would be nothing to prevent him from saying clearly that the Spirit was now restraining the man of sin and would do so until He was removed.

The traditional view of the Church down through the centuries would seem to fit more evenly. Government has been restraining the revealing of the man of sin. Lest one be tempted to say that Satan would then be a house divided against himself, it should be noted that leadership in world affairs is ultimately under the control of the Lord. Certainly Romans 13 not only tells us to obey rulers but also why we should do so. They are "what God has appointed" and they are God's servants for our good. When the day comes when there is widespread drawing back of the normal power of government, when anarchy begins to set in, then the stage is ready for the entrance of a "law and order" man, even though he turns out to be the man of sin. With this as the meaning of the "restrainer," Paul could logically be cryptic and coy. After all, at that time the power of government was Rome and its emperor, and Rome could seize and punish any who were speaking or writing about her in a seditious manner.

Argument over this section will probably continue. But my own study of the passage years ago led me to the overwhelming conclusion that it was not possible for that "assembling to meet him" to occur before the events mentioned in verses 3–4 took place. This conviction came through a study undertaken while I was still in the camp of the pretribulationists and through accepting what seemed to be a clear meaning of the text. Certainly, from my own personal experience in that study, I would be forced to conclude that there is nothing in it that teaches pretribulationism. A natural reading of the text would probably lead one to believe that the Lord's coming and our meeting Him were part of the "day" that they were told had come, and that they thought they had somehow missed it, in part or wholly. It is reminiscent of the warnings of Christ given in Matthew 24 that believers should not believe the reports that Christ had come and was in the desert or in the inner chambers. That coming would be obvious and marked by events preceding it—particularly, the revealing of the desolating abomination.

**Revelation 3:10**

In His message to the church at Philadelphia the Lord said, "I will keep you from the hour of trial which is coming on the whole world, to try those who dwell upon the earth." When this verse is treated by pretribulationists, they single out this particular church and make it stand for the believing Church in the world in the last days. Then this particular verse is used as a proof text to show that the believing Church will be kept completely out of that hour of trial. They are careful to deny that the members of this church are told that they will be kept in or during the hour of trial. But that is nearly precisely what they are told: that they will be kept in the trial. The verb τηρεω means "to keep watch over, guard ... keep, reserve, preserve" (Bauer, Arndt and Gingrich's Greek-English Lexicon of the New Testament).

There are only two instances in the New Testament where it is used together with the preposition εκ (primarily "from out of")—here and in John 17:15. Not only must the basic flavor of "guarding" be retained when used with this preposition, but also the basic "from out of" must somehow be incorporated into the guarding idea. For example, in John 17:15, Christ's prayer is not that His followers should be "taken from out of" (αιρω plus εκ) the world, but that the Father keep or "guard" (τηρεω) them from (εκ) "the evil one." Obviously the believers here are not to be taken away from Satan's influences and presence, but to be protected in the face of them. It is precisely this construction that we have in Revelation 3:10, where Christ says, "I will keep (the verb τηρεω) you (the Philadelphian church) from (εκ) the hour of trial that is coming on the whole world." That is to say, "I will protect you in the very face of that hour."

If, indeed, the Lord had meant to say that He would take them from that hour without them even entering it, there were two clear ways in which it could have been expressed. In Mark 14:36, Christ prays for the cup to be taken away from Him, if possible. The verb used (παραφερω) generally means "to bring to," but combined with the preposition απο ("from" signifying separation from an object) it actually means to "remove from." In this case Christ had not yet taken the cup and asked for its removal. If this construction had been used, the church could be shown to be removed from the hour without even entering it. The other clear indication would have been the usage of απο preceded by the word αιρω meaning "to take away from." Indeed, to make the matter most convincing, the very word αρπαζω "to snatch away" (whence we get our word "rapture"—from the Latin), could have been used.

Another difficulty exists for pretribulationists when they single out the church at Philadelphia as the believing Church in the last days. Many of them hold that all of the Revelation churches are represented in the world today. Yet belief is found in some of the other churches. Pergamum "did not deny" the Lord's faith. Thyatira had "love and faith." Smyrna was spiritually "rich." Yet she was to have tribulation for ten days. Why do these not also represent the believing Church? And why will they not be spared tribulation?

**Revelation 4**

In this chapter John is summoned to heaven and there witnesses glorious things. Few among present representatives of the pretribulationists still seriously defend the concept that when John hears the words, "Come up hither," he thus represents the Church being raptured just before the beginning of the great tribulation, but one does still run into the idea here and there. It is, obviously, illogical to cast John in such a role. He has heard the Lord's message to the seven churches and is to deliver that message to them. Shall he now, suddenly, be the symbol of those churches or even of some individual "true" Church? There would be as much excuse for a posttribulationist to make the two witnesses of chapter 11 represent the true Church. Then, since there are two of them, they could represent the Jewish believers and the Gentile believers. There is also a voice from heaven calling them to "come up hither!" (v. 12). In fact, this happens after a trumpet (9:13), the voice calling them is a loud voice, there is obvious resurrection involved (they had been dead), they went up in a cloud and there was a great earthquake. But using this to stand for a posttribulation rapture would be a theory as full of holes as is the idea of making John stand for the Church. John can no more stand for the Church in chapter 4 than Paul could when he was caught up to the third heaven in 2 Corinthians 12. These things (including the Bride of chapters 19 and 21) are being shown or represented to John. But if John stood for the Church in chapter 4, and if the Church is the Bride, John would, in a sense, represent the Bride also. He would need to be a split personality looking at himself as he is shown such things. He would be both the reporter and the object being reported.

There are other desires from a pretribulation point of view to see the Church gone as of chapter 4. Because John was to see "what is and what is to take place hereafter" (1:11), they would like to believe that the first part, "what is," refers to the churches of chapters 2 and 3 and, therefore, of the entire Church age, and the second part, "what is to take place hereafter," as all that will happen after the rapture, meaning chapters 4 through 22.

It may well be that "what is" views the Church age up to the point where the end days of the tribulation begin, that is when "what is to take place hereafter" starts to unfold, but there is no scriptural warrant for believing that it is until the rapture, or that the future time includes all those happenings after the rapture. In fact, when the four living creatures sing their song, they speak of the Lord in the same temporal terms (past, present and future) as the events shown to John ("what you see, what is and what is to take place hereafter"). Here the Lord is called the one "who was and is and is to come!" (4:8). In other words, He is classified as the one who still "is to come." There is no basis upon which we are allowed to divide that coming and say that though the one coming (for His own) is not mentioned, that it has already taken place. If chapter 4 is in the future, at the beginning of the last days, or the onset of the tribulation, then the Lord is depicted as one who is yet to come. That is, the tribulation is beginning, and He is yet to come.

There is even the thought that because John sees seven torches before God's throne (v. 5), this proves that the rapture has taken place by this time, since the seven golden lampstands were seen by John on earth in 1:12. That these are not the same lamps is clear from a number of points. First, those mentioned in chapter 1 were called golden, and here no material of composition is mentioned. More important, those in chapter 1 are called "lampstands" (λυχνιας), meaning candlesticks or candelabra—devices that hold lamps or candles, whereas the word in chapter 4 is "lamps" (λαμπαδες), meaning torches or the actual lamp or candle that itself flames (indeed, they are said to be "burning" or "blazing"). Most important, however, is the fact that we are told what the lampstands of chapter 1 are—the seven churches; and we are also told in this chapter what the seven lamps are—the seven spirits of God. These are the same seven spirits mentioned in 1:4 as being "before his throne," where they still are in this passage. It is a graphic object lesson to the Church that we are vessels and the light that we shed is God's light. But we need to distinguish, as does John, the light holder from the light itself.

## MATTHEW 24 AND REVELATION 19 AND 20

Matthew 24 gives us warnings of things that will trouble the earth leading up to the time of the end. It also gives some key elements of that grave time of trouble called the great tribulation. Then it tells us of the appearing of the Son of Man on the clouds and of the gathering of His elect.

Revelation 19 shows rejoicing in heaven over the fall of

Babylon and depicts the unbridled exultation at the marriage of the Lamb. Then we see the King of kings defeating the beast and the false prophet.

Revelation 20 tells about the binding of Satan, the first resurrection and Christ's millennial reign, the loosing and defeat of Satan, and of the second resurrection and the great white throne judgment.

The pretribulation camp sees in these passages a major problem for the posttribulation position. They claim that there is no proof in these first two passages of either the rapture or of the resurrection. Then they say that the resurrection that is mentioned in the third passage is a resurrection only of the tribulation saints and not of the Church, since the term "the dead in Christ" (used of the rapture in 1 Thessalonians 4) is not used here.

If the failure to find any mention of the rapture or the resurrection in the timeframe at the end of the tribulation in Matthew 24 and Revelation 19 proves to be a major problem to the posttribulation position, that same reasoning would lead us to say that the failure to find the rapture and resurrection in the timeframe at the beginning of the tribulation either in Matthew 24 or in Revelation 4 and 5 is more than a major problem for the pretribulation position. It is a monumental problem. If the rapture-resurrection concept is so vitally important (and it is), why is there not even a hint of it in the Scriptures dealing with the period just before the tribulation begins? At least a resurrection is mentioned in Revelation 20 after the tribulation. There are reasons for believing that the Church is in that resurrection. Before considering these reasons, however, let us attend to the passages mentioned and then look at the concept of prophetic detail.

The Revelation 19 passage deals with judgment rather than with resurrection. Revelation 20, however, does deal with resurrection. There are many Scriptures that deal with a particular theme and leave out other related themes without casting doubt on these other themes or denying them. Thus, when Paul states that God's Son was "born of woman," he does not mention the fact that it was a virgin birth (Gal. 4:4). When John in the great prologue to his Gospel speaks of the mystery and majesty of the Incarnation, he also fails to say that it was through a virgin. Only Matthew and Luke speak of the virgin birth, but we know that everywhere else where Christ's humanity is mentioned, this truth is included, even if it is not mentioned specifically.

Regarding the material leading up to Revelation 19 (chapters 4–18) it seems to be an assumption on the part of the pretribulation position that this represents a comprehensive revelation of all the steps that lead up to the Lord's coming in chapter 19. This is assuming too much. Revelation itself makes no such claim. It may be the most extensive treatment of the subject, but it is far from exhaustive—even on important details. We find no reports of false Christs appearing, as we do in the treatment of the tribulation in Matthew 24. We do not even find a passing thought about that astounding event of the man of sin standing in the temple proclaiming himself to be God, as we do in Matthew 24:15 and 2 Thessalonians 2:4. We don't find a word about the judgment of the nations when He comes as we do in Matthew 25:31–46. True prophetic scholarship demands of us that we put the pieces together to form the mosaic. If something is missing from one passage, that means that the passage does not give a complete treatment of the subject, but it doesn't mean that we have license to break the mosaic into parts again and to say that this part happens at one time, and the others at yet another time.

If the posttribulation position on the rapture is accused of resting on an inference, it must be added that the pretribulation position doesn't even have an inference to lean on, which makes even a weightier objection to their position. There is, moreover, a point at the end of the tribulation where the posttribulationist would be able to see a rapture before the marriage supper of the Lamb. In Revelation 18:4 the Lord says to His own in Babylon, "Come out of her, my people." It may be a matter of days before Christ's coming to the earth "with His saints" when this rapture call "for His saints" takes place. In spite of the fact that not everything in Revelation 4–19 is chronological, if much of it is seen as being chronological, why does the marriage supper of the Lamb come at the end of the tribulation rather than at its beginning? If it is felt that the judgment seat activity must take place before the marriage feast (a position difficult to insist on dogmatically), then we do God a disservice by requiring Him to need seven days, let alone seven years to be able to fit in the various segments of the "program" before Christ sets foot upon the earth. If we humans have the technology that would allow millions of people in one hour of time to be sitting at their own TVs, each watching his own "home movie" on videotape, can God's technology be inferior to ours? Let us not limit the Eternal by the bonds of our time boundaries. Then, He will be able to deal with each of us individually in a moment of time even as He now fields, and responds to, millions of our prayers simultaneously. Surely the Lord, with whom a day is as a thousand years, doesn't need seven years to accomplish the judgment seat of Christ and the marriage supper. And we, who will now be part of eternity, do not need that much time either.

It is also claimed that Matthew 24 shows no indication of a rapture or a resurrection. Though those very words may not be employed, their equivalent concepts are. There is a "loud trumpet call." We are told elsewhere in Scripture that these events will occur with a loud trumpet call—indeed, at the last trump (1 Thess. 4; 1 Cor. 15). Here we are told that "they will see the Son of man coming." Paul says that these events will occur when "the Lord himself will descend from heaven" (1 Thess. 4). Here we see angels sent to "gather his elect." Paul also speaks reassuringly to the Thessalonians because they had heard that the day of the Lord had already come. He speaks to them "concerning the coming of our Lord Jesus Christ and our assembling to meet him" (2 Thess. 2:1). The word assembling is precisely the same Greek word used in Matthew 24 (in its verb form) and translated gather. Here the Son is coming "on the clouds." In 1 Thessalonians 4 resurrected and transformed saints are caught up together "in the clouds to meet the Lord." Here (with support from the synoptic account in Mark 13:27) believers are gathered from "heaven" (the souls of the dead in Christ) and from the four winds, or earth (compare the Mark passage: "from the ends of the earth"). These are the living believers. Both 1 Corinthians 15 and 1 Thessalonians 4 tell us that there will be a gathering of saints who have died and of those who are living.

We are told that the Berean "Jews were more noble than those in Thessalonica, for they received the word with all eagerness, examining the scriptures daily to see if these things were so" (Acts 17:11). The spirit of comparing Scripture with Scripture must prevail in our studies. We don't get the full teaching on a given subject by a single verse. If a truth is stated in one section and omitted in another section that discusses the same subject, the section that is lacking that truth must be supplemented by the one that included it. For example, in a small text such as Numbers 14:20–30, we could arrive at three separate conclusions depending on where we stopped in the text. If we stopped at verse 23, we would assume that the entire generation that saw God's signs in Egypt and the wilderness would be excluded from entering the promised land. If we stopped at verse 24 or 25, we would believe that only Caleb would be allowed to enter the land as a representative of that group. If, however, we read through verse 30, we would have the full picture and would see that there would be two from that group who would enter the land—Caleb and Joshua. Thus verses 22 and 23 are not complete without verses 24 and 30, and verses 22, 23 and 24 are not complete without verse 30.

In an even broader broader context, there is much teaching in the Old Testament about the coming of the golden age of the kingdom. Different passages emphasize different aspects of that kingdom. Four examples from the book of Isaiah should suffice. We hear that men will turn from war to peace (2:4). We see peace in the animal kingdom (11:6–9). We find Israel ruling over her former enemies (14:2). We note that Ethiopia is bringing gifts to the Lord in Jerusalem (18:7). We cannot say from looking at any one of the passages that the other three elements don't apply since they aren't mentioned in that one passage. And we cannot take any three of the passages and say that the fourth element doesn't apply since it is found in none of the other three. Thus, for a full picture, we need a mosaic built from all the pieces.

Such is the teaching of the rapture-resurrection in the New Testament also. It consists of various tiles that must be placed in juxtaposition in order to see the whole scene. Let us begin with 1 Thessalonians 4:13–18. This is the only passage where the rapture ("catching up") term is used (in fact verse 17 is the sole verse in the entire New Testament where it is used). Resurrection is treated. We have the themes of the Lord's descent from heaven, the cry of command, the archangel's call, and the sounding of the trumpet of God. Living believers join the resurrected dead in the clouds, they meet the Lord in the air, and they remain forever with the Lord. This represents more detail on the resurrection-rapture concept than is found in any other New Testament passage.

Next, let us examine 1 Corinthians 15:51–53. This passage shares some concepts with 1 Thessalonians 4. The dead are raised in both passages. But even on this theme there are distinct differences. That passage identifies the dead as "the dead in Christ." This one tells us of the nature of the resurrected bodies—they will be "imperishable." The trumpet sounding is mentioned in both, but in this passage we have a refinement on the identification of that trumpet. It is the "last trumpet." There are details that are added here that are absent from the Thessalonian account. The suddenness of the event is stated—it will occur "in a moment, in the twinkling of an eye." Also, only I Corinthians 15 tells us about the transformation of the bodies of living believers: "we shall be changed." It also tells us what kind of a change it will be—we will "put on immortality."

Now, because there are elements in each of these accounts that are not found in the other account, we have no license to discredit the one, or to prefer the other, or to make both of these accounts occur at different times in order to try to reconcile the different approaches they take or the different aspects of the event that each stresses. Accordingly, because "rapturing" occurs in 1 Thessalonians 4, but not in 1 Corinthians 15, we cannot say that it does not occur in the 1 Corinthians 15 event, and because "changing" occurs in 1 Corinthians 15, but not in 1 Thessalonians 4, we cannot say that it does not also occur in the 1 Thessalonians 4 event or that because it is not mentioned there, it must mean that the living saints are caught up in their mortal (unchanged) bodies.

The same principle should also apply to other passages that treat this subject of the coming of the Lord-resurrection-rapture. We need to put the pieces together to get a unified whole. Earlier in 1 Corinthians 15, when Paul describes the differences in bodies, particularly the physical and spiritual bodies, this obviously relates to what happens in the "change" that he says is necessary later in the chapter (vv. 35–50). Still earlier in the same chapter, Paul gives a three-fold order of the resurrection: "Christ the first fruits, then at his coming those who belong to Christ. Then comes the end" (vv. 20–25). For the sake of objectivity and honesty, this too must be added to the schematic. This is the only passage where this is given, and we must use it in other passages where the order is not given. Christ rises first in a glorified body. When He comes, all those who belong to Him will be resurrected (or "changed," if still alive—in the light of other Scriptures). "Then comes the end" when the last enemy (death) is destroyed, and we have the general resurrection of the rest of mankind.

In Matthew 24:29–31 and the synoptic accounts in Mark 13:24–27 and Luke 21:25–28 we see elements that are the same as some already seen in some of the passages above, or we see equivalent expressions. We see the Son coming. He is on the clouds of heaven. Angels are involved in a call. It is a loud trumpet. Believers are gathered from heaven and from earth. But there are also additional details. There are signs in the sky (affecting the sun, moon and stars). And it is "after the tribulation."

Now let us look at the passage in Revelation 20 where pretribulationists would limit that resurrection to the martyred tribulation saints and do not see the Church having part in that resurrection. Certainly God's focus is particularly on the tribulation martyrs at this point. The cry of the martyrs under the fifth seal doubtless still rings in His ears: "how long before thou wilt judge and avenge our blood on those who dwell upon the earth?" (6:10–11). And their temporary white robes and the admonition to "rest a little longer, until the number of their fellow servants and their brethren should be complete, who were to be killed as they themselves had been" was a stopgap measure at best. According to the pretribulation position, the singling out of the tribulation martyrs in this resurrection suggests that the Church has previously been raptured. This could only be true if this were the only passage that dealt with the resurrection. We must bring into play, however, all the other truths we have about this teaching. It was to happen at the coming of the Lord. Here we have the coming of the Lord. It was to be after the tribulation. This is after the tribulation. It was to include all the "dead in Christ." According to Revelation 14:13 (in the midst of the tribulation) those believers who were dying were considered "dead in Christ" (those "who die in the Lord"), but there are many other "dead in Christ" other than the tribulation martyrs. All this was to take place in the resurrection order following that of Christ Himself as the first fruits. This is called the "first resurrection" and no other is mentioned before it. Indeed, the very language of verse 6 should move us rather strongly to that conclusion. It does not say "Blessed are these in the first resurrection," but "Blessed and holy is he who shares in the first resurrection," for sharing involves others in addition to the ones already mentioned.

### The Rapture—Secret Or Obvious?

If the rapture occurs at the end of the tribulation, there is no reason why the universal viewing described in Revelation 1:7 cannot apply to believers as well as unbelievers: "every eye will see him." If it occurs before the tribulation, one can see the need for believing in a secret rapture. If the rapture were to take place then and be seen by the world, it would be so momentous in terms of those remaining on earth and seeing it that one would suspect that some comment must be found in Scripture on its effect on the worldlings who gazed at it. It would be even greater than the event of the resurrection and ascension of the two witnesses: "But after the three and a half days a breath of life from God entered them, and they stood up on their feet, and great fear fell on those who saw them. Then they heard a loud voice from heaven saying to them, 'Come up hither!' And in the sight of their foes they went up to heaven in a cloud" (Rev. 11:11–12). If, however, the rapture occurs before the tribulation and is secret, then there is no visible marvel to strike such terror into the hearts of the unbelievers who are left. Thus, a secret rapture is followed by conjecture rather than terror.

Aside from this logical need to develop a secret rapture if one accepts a pretribulation rapture, one must wonder at the basis and origin of this belief. Where does it come from, and who first suggested it? The Scriptures do not support the idea of a secret rapture. Indeed, when Jesus tells His disciples about the great tribulation, He tells them not to be deceived about His presence and their gathering together to Him. He says, "So, if they say to you. 'Lo, he is in the wilderness,' do not go out; if they say, 'Lo, he is in the inner room,' do not believe it. For as the lightning comes from the east and shines as far as the west, so will be the coming of the Son of man. Wherever the body is, there the eagles will be gathered together" (Matt. 24:15–28 italics mine).

This passage tells us a number of things about the great tribulation period. First, true Christians (members of the Church) will be there: "if they say to you." Second, the appearance for the time of gathering will be obvious to all (not only to believers): "as the lightning comes." Third, the gathering together will not have to be strained for, because it will be automatic: "there the eagles will be gathered together." The Lord likely took the figure of the eagle from Job 39:30: "where the slain are, there is he." In the light of the admonition not to listen to rumors of His appearance and the assurance that it will be visible to all, the figure of the eagle doubtless indicates that our gathering to Him when He comes will be as automatic and instinctive as is the drawing of birds of carrion to a fallen body. We won't have to be told and we won't have to strain.

Some seem to feel that His coming like a thief in the night supports a secret coming. There is, however, no need to see anything beyond unexpectedness and suddenness in the expression. Unless, of course, one must have the idea of secretness to support a pre-established position.

### NOAH AND THE FLOOD—PROPHETIC SYMBOL?

Though those who hold a posttribulation view have not said much about the flood as a symbol of prophecy, the pretribulation school feels they have found a good example of the Church being taken before the inundation of tribulation judgment. The Church is lifted up above those being judged.

But the judgment of the flood of Noah stands as a much better type of a posttribulation rapture than it does of a pretribulation rapture. With a pretribulation rapture, the believers would be taken out of the world and then God's judgment would fall on the world, but not on all the world. Those who hold the pretribulation position agree that the account in Revelation 7 says there will be 144,000 Jews and millions of others (Gentiles) who will believe during the tribulation. God's judgment will not fall on them. In Noah's account, all but those in the ark were judged. With a posttribulation rapture, all believers shall be taken out, and then all those who are left shall be judged—in one way or another. This fits the figure of the flood. The tribulation cannot stand as a figure of God's judgment on the whole world, whereas the end of the tribulation can.

## Resurrection Order

In 1 Corinthians 15:23–24 the order of resurrection is clearly given: "But each in his own order: Christ the first fruits, then at his coming those who belong to Christ. Then comes the end, when he delivers the kingdom to God the Father after destroying every rule and every authority and power."

This sets up a clear three-fold pattern for us:
1. Christ—the first fruits.
2. Those who are His at His coming—the first resurrection.
3. The end, when the kingdom is delivered up to God—the second resurrection.

The first thing that needs to be established in this order is the fact that the first fruits is a category that is distinguishable from the first resurrection. This is not to say that it is not related. In fact, it is vitally related. But even as a father and his son are vitally related and the son cannot exist if the father had not first existed, even so the first resurrection has an intimate relationship to the first fruits, but they are distinguishable from each other.

In the Old Testament offering of first fruits, the first fruits were not the harvest. In a technical sense, they were not part of the harvest, per se. They were a harbinger of the harvest. They were a thank offering for the anticipated harvest. They may even have been considered an earnest of the harvest itself, but they were not the harvest. In modern technological terms, we might use a different figure to understand the relationship. An aircraft manufacturer may build a prototype of a new plane. The prototype does everything that the future models would do and is used to convince the market that it is desirable. When the market is convinced, the manufacturer sets up an assembly line for mass production of the plane. The prototype is not part of the assembly line, but it led to it, and by virtue of the fact that it worked properly, it assured the production that followed. This is the relationship that exists between Christ and the first resurrection. But in the original figure of the harvest, we knew on the basis of the first fruits that the harvest would surely follow. Thus the Scripture says, "as by a man came death, by a man has come also the resurrection of the dead. For as in Adam all die, so also in Christ shall all be made alive." Because He lives, we shall live also.

The Scriptures say that:
1. "We shall not all sleep, but we shall all be changed in a moment, in the twinkling of an eye, at the last trumpet" (1 Cor. 15:51–52).
2. "The Lord himself will descend from heaven with a cry of command, with the archangel's call, and with the sound of the trumpet of God. And the dead in Christ will rise first; then we who are alive who are left, shall be caught up together with them in the clouds to meet the Lord in the air" (1 Thess. 4:16–17).
3. "After the tribulation of those days ... he will send out his angels with a loud trumpet call, and they will gather his elect from the four winds, from one end of heaven to the other" (Matt. 24:29–31).
4. The souls were seen "of those who had been beheaded for their testimony to Jesus and for the

word of God, and who had not worshipped the beast or its image and had not received its mark on their foreheads or their hands." They came to life, and reigned with Christ a thousand years.... This is the first resurrection." (Rev. 20:4-5).

Based on these statements the only logical conclusion is that all believers—Old Testament and New Testament alike (including the last mentioned tribulation saints)—are resurrected or changed together at the end of the tribulation, at the last trumpet, in the first resurrection.

Following this comes the millennium and following the millennium "comes the end, when he delivers the kingdom to God the Father after destroying every rule and every authority and power," which is to say, then comes the second resurrection and the white throne judgment.

A passage that has come under question from the pretribulation camp regarding the resurrection is Daniel 12:1-2: "At that time shall arise Michael, the great prince who has charge of your people. And there shall be a time of trouble, such as never has been since there was a nation till that time; but at that time your people shall be delivered, every one whose name shall be found written in the book. And many of those who sleep in the dust of the earth shall awake, some to everlasting life, and some to shame and everlasting contempt." Some believe that this refers to Old Testament saints and does not include the Church since the Church is not identified here at all.

It is curious that the subject of the Church should be applied to this passage in Daniel. The passage itself is a rarity in that it refers to the resurrection at all. The theme can hardly be found in the Old Testament. But the concept of "your people" can certainly be expanded to include a "spiritual" Israel, since we are here talking about deliverance to those who are "found written in the book," rather than to those who are merely Israel according to the flesh. Indeed, the Church can be included in this spiritual people on a number of grounds. We must go, however, to the New Testament for the revelation of such a mystery, since the Church, as such, is not depicted in the Old Testament.

Not only does Paul call all believers Abraham's offspring

in Galatians 3:29, but his picture of the olive tree in Romans 11 leaves no doubt that this group consists of all the faithful or believing, both in the Old and New Testaments. When pretribulationists believe that the resurrected group in Daniel 12 would include the Old Testament saints, they doubtless include them with the martyred saints of the tribulation. However, a clear rendering of the Daniel passage shows two, and only two, resurrection groups: (1) believers who awake "to everlasting life," and (2) unbelievers who awake "to shame and everlasting contempt." This fits together beautifully with the New Testament order of the resurrections. Revelation 20 speaks of a first resurrection at the end of the tribulation followed by a subsequent resurrection after the millennium. In like fashion, Paul depicts the order of those resurrections as comprising "at his coming those who belong to Christ" followed by the rest at "the end, when he delivers the kingdom to God the Father after destroying every rule and every authority and power" (1 Cor. 23–24).

Even in the Old Testament, however, God had indicated that the day was coming when He would say to "Not my people" that "You are my people" (Hos. 2:23). Thus, the fact that pretribulationists see no identification that includes the Church in the resurrection of Daniel 12:2 could lead us to apply the same logic to other passages that are the clear birthright of the Church. We could just as reasonably assert that when Isaiah 53:5 states that "he was wounded for our transgressions," the Church is not identified and, therefore, that this substitutionary and redemptive truth does not apply to the Church.

## THE SECOND COMING OR THE SECOND COMINGS?

There are in the Old Testament conflicting prophecies concerning the coming of the Messiah. There were many predictions of the coming of a glorious one who would reign in power and peace and prosperity. Moreover, this reign would be an eternal reign. In contrast to these prophecies, however, were statements about the suffering and death of this servant of the Lord—especially typified by Isaiah 53.

The pretribulationists have seized upon this as a pattern

to help them in separating the rapture from the coming of Christ to earth. While they must admit that the same terms are used in the New Testament both for that rapture and that coming of Christ to earth, they say that the use of the same terms for both does not make them the same event any more than the "coming of Christ" the first time was the same event as His coming the second time. That is, the argument runs, the rapture and the coming to earth are different events and, therefore, likewise happen at different times.

But there is a stronger argument for both happening together on the basis of the fact that the same terms are used for both than there is for separating the rapture from the second coming to earth because these are two operations. The great objection to both happening together—His coming for His saints and to the earth; His appearing to His saints and to the world; and His revealing Himself to His saints and to the world—is the predisposition that they must happen separately. When terms are used elsewhere in Scripture to refer to a common place or entity, even though the terms are different, we accept them as synonyms. Thus, in the Old Testament "Mt. Zion" and "the city of our God" meant Jerusalem, even though Jerusalem was not named. In the New Testament many terms are used to mean "a member of the Church." When we put the passages together, we know that sheep = elect one = servant = son = heir = body member = saint, which in turn = "member of the Church." So here, when we see the same term used for two operations, we can logically assume that the two operations belong to the one event.

There is a vast difference between conflicting prophecies concerning the coming Messiah on the one hand and differing activities involved in a single event—the return of the Messiah—on the other. In the first instance, prophets wrote about the fact that the Christ would suffer and also that He would come in glory. But according to 1 Peter 1:10–11, the prophets themselves recognized the conflict. They simply didn't know how to solve it. It was solved for us by the revelation of these truths in the advent of Christ and in the unveiling of these truths in the New Testament. Having received by God's revelation the resolution of a real conflict in the two advents of the Messiah is one matter, but to suppose a conflict in the second advent is an assumption to begin with. Then to take an assumed conflict and attempt to solve it exegetically goes beyond the original assumption and becomes presumption. Whereas Old Testament prophets saw a conflict in the advents of the Christ, there is no indication whatever that New Testament authors see any difficulty or conflict when writing about the rapture and coming to earth by Christ at the second advent.

It is true that the two activities of that advent—the rapture and the return to earth to set up the kingdom—are presented with contrasting details, but this is a matter of their being different activities and because they are seen from extremely opposite points of view. One would not expect, for example, similar details regarding the marriage of the Lamb, on the one hand, and the defeat of the beast, on the other. It is like a triumphal procession of Caesar. Details and viewpoints would be very different to a prisoner following in his train and to a loyal citizen watching the procession. Even in the old-time Westerns, one event might produce the rescue of the fair maiden and the meting out of justice against the villain. In the second advent, the rescue of the Bride comes before the defeat of the villain, but no more than hours (or, at the outside, days) are in any way needed for all the conflicting details to be completed.

So, there was in the Old Testament a distinction in advents—one in suffering (typified by Isaiah 53) and one in glory, which the prophets themselves did not always understand (see 1 Pet. 1:10–11). There was, however, a clear necessity for the one to come first and the other to follow. Jesus Himself charged two of His apostles on the Emmaus road with being "slow of heart to believe all that the prophets have spoken," and told them that it was "necessary that the Christ should suffer these things and enter into his glory" (Luke 24:25-26)

They had likely fallen into the same trap as the religious rulers of their day. They withdrew from the concept of suffering and glory existing in the same person. They developed a Messiah of glory and divorced themselves from the suffering servant idea.

There are two similar mistakes made by dispensational

theology concerning His coming. First, there are two operations happening in that one coming. These two operations are His meeting with His saints and His return to earth in judgment. Just as the scribes made a separation of personalities for the suffering servant and the glorified Messiah, so dispensational theology makes separate events of the two operations of Christ's meeting with His saints and returning with them to earth.

This whole line of argument is that if two aspects of a situation contrast sharply, they cannot occur together or in extremely close proximity to each other as part of the same action or event. In other words, because the rapture aspect and the "touchdown" aspect of Christ's Second Coming are so distinctly different from each other, then they could not conceivably happen within hours or days of each other. There must be years of time separating them.

Many illustrations could be marshaled to show that such contrasting occurrences happening in a short timeframe are fairly common in life. A housewife battles car pool problems, shops, cleans house, and settles three problems among the children, but that night she is a vision of beauty being wined and dined by her husband. A general returns triumphantly from battle. He first spends an intimate day with his beloved wife. On the following day, he fires one aide, promotes another, and gives a report to a joint session of Congress. But why look at typical (though hypothetical) cases. Let us look at the New Testament. What could be more contrasting than the triumphal entry of Christ into Jerusalem and the authoritative cleansing of the temple on the one hand, and Gethsemane, the betrayal, His desertion by the disciples, and Calvary on the other. And yet these things all happened within days of each other. Why should there not be as significant contrasts on the week of His return as there were during the last week of His ministry before Good Friday/Easter?

*"Surely I am coming soon." Amen. Come, Lord Jesus!*

# Afterword

I began the writing of this work with a specific audience in view. I wanted to engage those believers who had a keen interest in the return of King Jesus to earth. After all, even in my early years as a Christian, it was a spiritual passion for me. I looked with longing to the skies. But something happened on the way to the forum. Something in the word of God itself gave me pause to ask the question, "Can this be right?" And it was just a beginning. But, as I proceeded in my study of the Scriptures, doubts grew. At that point, I began to cast my lot with the Bereans of Acts 17 who "were more noble than those in Thessalonica since they received the word with all eagerness, examining the Scriptures daily to see if these things were so."

I moved gradually from a point of saying, "This is what I believe" to admitting, "but it is wrong," I felt no joy in migrating to a new position. All of my friends were in the camp I had left. I am thankful that by and large they did not disown me. And I did not disown them. We were looking for the same event. Thus, if you do not agree with me, simply accept the reasons which led me to where I am now. May the passion of both our camps be the completion of His grand commission!

Then I thought, "Perhaps there are others in my audience whom I am neglecting." Before I ever heard of a second coming, I didn't even consider that there had been a first coming. I knew about Santa Claus and had even heard about baby Jesus and Christmas. But I never even dreamed that God came to earth when Jesus was born.

There will be some in my audience who find themselves where I was when I was in my early teens. I knew there was a God. I knew that I didn't want to die because I wasn't "good" enough to pass muster. I even began praying the Lord's prayer to amass some Brownie points, "Our father who art in heaven...." A new young pastor came to our area and came to see us. He played football with my brother and me and we began attending his church. I enjoyed the youth meetings but still did not know this Being, God. Then a visiting pastor preached a sermon and in the delivery at one juncture pointed out into the audience and said, "There are some of you out there who are calling God 'father' and you have no right to do so because you are not in His family."

I couldn't believe that he "knew" about me. People were invited to come for counseling and I responded. In a quiet room, a man asked if I knew I was a sinner. I knew all too well. Then I prayed for forgiveness and believed by putting my trust in Jesus. I entered a new dimension that I never knew existed. That was my first genuine prayer and I entered God's family. If this sounds simplistic to some, it is nevertheless true. God is real. His Son's love for you is real. His payment on the cross for your sins is real. His invitation is real, "Come unto me you who are weary and heavy laden and I will give you rest." Give Him a chance to prove Himself real to you.

## ABOUT THE AUTHOR

Louis Moesta, an ordained minister and graduate of the Pastor's course at Moody Bible Institute, Holds a BA in English from Wheaton College, an MA in English from California State University at Los Angeles, and an MDiv from Fuller Theological Seminary.

After pastoring a church in Colorado, Moesta served with Greater Europe Mission for six years in Germany as an instructor at the German Bible Institute, became a research assistant at Fuller Theological Seminary (where he taught Hebrew, Greek, and theological German), taught English and Bible as Literature in the California public school system for 25 years, and taught Bible at a Christian high school.

Moesta lives in Colorado with his wife of 62 years.

www.ingramcontent.com/pod-product-compliance
Lightning Source LLC
Chambersburg PA
CBHW071145070526
44584CB00019B/2664